FOUNDATIONS OF ACCOUNTING

Edited by
RICHARD P. BRIEF
New York University

A GARLAND SERIES

Financial Reporting to Employees

From Past to Present

Edited with an Introduction by
LEE D. PARKER

GARLAND PUBLISHING, INC.

NEW YORK & LONDON 1988

For a list of Garland's publications in accounting, see the final pages of this volume.

Library of Congress Cataloging-in-Publication Data

Financial reporting to employees.

(Foundations of accounting)
Bibliography: p.
1. Financial statements. 2. Corporation reports. 3. Communication in personnel management. I. Parker, Lee D. (Lee David) II. Series.
HF5681.B2F4633 1988 658.1'512 88-25662
ISBN 0-8240-6129-2 (alk. paper)

Design by Renata Gomes

The volumes in this series are printed on acid-free, 250-year-life paper.

Printed in the United States of America

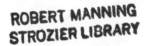

To Edward J.J. Parker for his contributions to employee health and safety

Contents

INTRODUCTION

■ N.R. Lewis, L.D. Parker, and P. Sutcliffe, "Financial Reporting to Employees: The Pattern of Development 1919 to 1979," *Accounting, Organizations and Society* (No. 3/4, 1984), pp.275–289. 1

EARLY STIRRINGS 17

■ Harry Botsford, "How a Plant Publication Helps," *Trained Men* (April 3, 1923), pp.84–86. 19

■ Britton I. Budd, "The Use of Company Publications," *Proceedings of 1922 Conference of the American Electrical Railway Association* (1923), pp.156–161. 22

■ Franzy Eakin, "Business Resorting to Issuance of Special Reports to Employees," *The Controller* (July 1938), pp. 184–190. 28

■ "Telling Your Story to Your Employe[e]s," *Illinois Manufacturers' Costs Association, Monthly Bulletin* (February 1939), pp.1–2. 35

■ L.W. Bennett, "Annual Report to Employees," *Cost and Management* (October 1939), p.308. 37

■ James W. Irwin, "Periodical Reports to Employees", *Executives Service Bulletin* (January 1939), pp. 7–8. 38

REPORTING RATIONALES 41

■ Keith R.Yorston, "Reporting Financial Information to Employees," *The Australian Accountant* (February 1960), pp.80–88. 42

■ W.R. Anderson, "Should a Company Tell?: Disclosure of Information to Employees," *The Accountant* (April 8, 1961), pp.403–407. 51

■ J.R. Dyson, "Audits for Employees: The Right to Know," *The Accountant* (March 8, 1973), pp.309–310. 56

REPORTING METHODS 58

■ Marvin J. Barloon, "Financial Reports to Employees," *Harvard Business Review* (Autumn 1941), pp.124–131. 60

■ Frank Wallace, "Getting Down to Earth in Explaining Profits to Employees," *Controller* (February 1946), pp.75–77. 68

■ J.A. Fuller, "Presentation of Company Information to Shareholders and Employees," *Cost and Management* (September 1948), pp. 280–286. 71

■ Stephen Arthur Derry, "How to Communicate Financial Information to Employees, and What to Say," *Journal of Accountancy* (April 1949), pp.307–311. 78

■ Walter C. Burnham, "A Simplified Income Statement for Employee Use," *National Association of Cost Accountants Bulletin*, (July 15, 1949), pp.1325–1335. 82

■ J.B. Heckert and J.D. Wilson, "Reports to Employees and the General Public," *Controllership* (Ronald Press, New York, 1952), pp.445–462. 93

REPORTING PRACTICES: CASE STUDIES AND SURVEYS 111

■ B.C. Heacock, "Making the Annual Report Speak," *Executives Service Bulletin* (April 1940), pp. 3–4, 6. 113

■ Dickson Hartwell, "Telling the Employees," *Public Opinion Quarterly* (March 1941), pp. 93–101. 115

▪Stephen Arthur Derry, "Presenting the Facts on Company Operations to the Employees," *Proceedings of the Ohio State University Tenth Annual Institute on Accounting* (May 21, 1948), pp.41–53. 124

▪John H. Myers, "Annual Reports to Employees," *New York Certified Public Accountant*, (February 1956), pp. 100–102, 122.. 137

▪L.D. Parker, "Financial Reporting to Employees: A Growing Practice in Australia," *The Chartered Accountant in Australia* (March 1977), pp.5–9. 141

▪Geoffrey Holmes, "How UK Companies Report to Their Employees," *Accountancy* (November 1977), pp.64–66, 68. 146

ASSESSING EMPLOYEE INTEREST 149A

▪George E. Bennett, "Corporate Financial Report Content of Interest to Employees," *New York Certified Public Accountant* (October 1941), pp.63–68. 150

▪Daniel J. Hennessy, "Survey Reveals Financial Information People Want to Know About a Corporation," *Journal of Accountancy* (September 1948), pp.224–227. 156

▪J. Charles Libby, "Employee Interest in the Financial Report," *Illinois Certified Public Accountant* (September 1952), pp.43-46. 160

▪Sterling H. Schoen, and Maurice P. Lux, "The Annual Report: How Much Do Employees Care?," *Personnel* (July-August 1957), pp.40–45. 164

▪David Flint, "Employees' Interest in the Business: Financial and Other Information," *The Accountant's Magazine* (November 1958), pp, 778–790.

▪R. Hussey and R.J. Craig, "Employee Reports—What Employees Think" *The Chartered Accountant in Australia*, (May 1979), pp.39–40, 42–44. 170

REPORTING IN AN INDUSTRIAL RELATIONS CONTEXT 187A

▪ Otis Brubaker, Lane Kirkland, William Gomberg, Nat, Weinberg, and Solomon Barkin, "What Kind of Information Do Labor Unions Want in Financial Statements?," *Journal of Accountancy* (May 1949), pp.368–377. 188

▪ Ernest Dale, "The Accountant's Part in Labor-Management Relations," *Journal of Accountancy* (July 1950), pp.12–25. 198

▪ Tom Climo, "The Role of the Accountant in Industrial Relations," *The Accountant* (December 16, 1976), pp.701–703. 211

▪ David Cooper and Simon Essex, "Accounting Information and Employee Decision Making," *Accounting, Organizations and Society*, (No. 3, 1977) pp.201–217. 214

BIBLIOGRAPHY 233

FURTHER READING

Selected Texts and Monographs 237
Selected Articles and Papers 239

Acknowledgments

Financial Reporting to Employees: The Pattern of Development 1919–1979.
Reprinted with permission from *Accounting, Organizations and Society,* Volume 9, Lewis, N.R., Parker, L.D. and Sutcliffe, P., Financial Reporting to Employees: The Pattern of Development 1919–1979, Copyright 1984, Permagon Journals Ltd.

Business Resorting to Issuance of Special Reports to Employees.
Used by permission from *The Controller,* July 1938, copyright 1938 by Financial Executives Institute.

Telling Your Story to Your Employees.
Reprinted with permission from *Illinois Manufacturers' Costs Association, Monthly Bulletin,* February 1939, copyright 1939, Illinois Manufacturers' Association.

Annual Report to Employees.
Reprinted from an article appearing in *Cost and Management,* by L.W. Bennett, October 1939, by permission of The Society of Management Accountants of Canada.

Reporting Financial Information to Employees.
Reprinted with the permission of Lady Yorston from *The Australian Accountant,* February 1960.

Should a Company Tell?: Disclosure of Information to Employees.
Reprinted with permission from *The Accountant,* April 8, 1961, copyright 1961, Lafferty Publications Ltd.

Audits for Employees: The Right to Know.
Reprinted with permission from *The Accountant,* March 8, 1973, copyright 1973, Lafferty Publications Ltd.

Financial Reports to Employees.
Reprinted by permission of the *Harvard Business Review.* "Financial Reports to Employees" by Marvin J. Barloon, Autumn 1941. Copyright © 1941 by the President and Fellows of Harvard College; all rights reserved.

Getting Down to Earth in Explaining Profits to Employees.
Used by permission from *The Controller,* February 1946, copyright 1946 by Financial Executives Institute.

Presentation of Company Information to Shareholders and Employees.
Reprinted from an article appearing in *Cost and Management* by J.A. Fuller, September 1948, by permission of the Society of Management Accountants of Canada.

How to Communicate Financial Information to Employees, and What to Say. Copyright © 1949 by the American Institute of Certified Public Accountants, Inc.

A Simplified Income Statement for Employee Use.
Copyright July 1949. Reproduced with the authorization of *Management Accounting* (U.S.A.) magazine.

Reports to Employees and to the General Public.
Reprinted with permission from *Controllership,* Heckert, J.B. and Wilson, J.D., "Reports to Employees and to the General Public." Copyright ©1952, John Wiley and Sons, Inc.

Telling the Employees.
Reprinted with permission from *Public Opinion Quarterly,* March 1941, copyright 1941, University of Chicago Press.

Presenting the Facts on Company Operatives to the Employees.
Reprinted with permission from *Proceedings of Ohio State University Tenth Annual Institute of Accounting,* May 21, 1948, copyright 1948, Ohio State University.

Annual Reports to Employees.
Reprinted with permission of *The CPA Journal,* February 1956, Copyright 1956.

Financial Reporting to Employees: A Growing Practice in Australia.
Reprinted with permission of L.D. Parker from *The Chartered Accountant in Australia,* March 1977.

How UK Companies Report to Their Employees.
Reprinted with the permission of G. Holmes from *Accountancy,* November 1977.

Corporate Financial Report Content of Interest to Employees.
Reprinted with permission of *The CPA Journal*, October 1941, copyright 1941.

Survey Reveals Financial Information People Want to Know About a Corporation.
Copyright © 1948 by the American Institute of Certified Public Accountants.

Employee Interest in the Financial Report.
Reprinted with permission from *Illinois Certified Public Accountant*, September 1952, copyright 1952, Illinois CPA Society.

The Annual Report: How Much Do Employees Care?
Reprinted by permission of the publisher, from *Personnel*, July-August 1957, © 1957, American Management Association, New York. All rights reserved.

Employee's Interest in the Business: Financial and Other Information.
Reprinted with the permission of Emeritus Professor David Flint from *Accountant's Magazine,* November 1958.

Employee Reports—What Employees Think.
Reprinted with the permission of R. Hussey and R.J. Craig from *The Chartered Accountant in Australia*, May 1979.

What Kind of Information Do Labor Unions Want in Financial Statements"
Copyright © 1949 by the American Institute of Certified Public Accountants, Inc.

Preface

The seeds for this volume were discovered in the early 1980s when Neil Lewis, Paul Sutcliffe, and I were setting out to study employee responses to corporate financial reports especially designed for them. In constructing a suitable contemporary literature base, Neil Lewis discovered that the subject had a far longer history than any of us had imagined. His discovery led us to a major change in immediate research direction, reflected in our paper that is reprinted at the beginning of this text. That paper was based upon 216 collected publications spanning the years 1919 to 1979. While the paper analyzed trends, patterns of interest, and possible influences, it alone could not do justice to the rich history of this accounting and reporting tradition.

This text offers a sample from that sizable collection of data and provides a first-hand glimpse into employee reporting practices and issues since the 1920s. While in the U.K. and Australia many contemporary writer on the subject assumed it to be a recent phenomenon, this collection demonstrates all too clearly how much of the groundwork had already been laid decades before. The material presented in this volume reflects contributions from the U.S.A., U.K. and Australia.

I would like to express my gratitude to Susanne Parker and James Atkinson for their research and editorial assistance in bringing this project to fruition.

L.D. Parker

Introduction

This book of readings is designed to introduce accountants and managers to an historical perspective of corporate financial reporting to employees. It presents a resource for research and practice based upon a literature that for its pre-1970 decades has been largely unfamiliar to contemporary educators, researchers, and practitioners alike. In addition the readings not only provide an historical view of issues and arguments, but of actual reporting practice and audience responses. Here then is an example of historical data's potential to provide direct input into contemporary application. For the student and researcher, these readings offer a first-hand glimpse into the intentions of employee report producers, the critiques of observers at the time, and the requirements of employees in some instances. For report producers, managers, and accountants it reveals some of the reporting traditions that we have inherited today as well as reporting practices that have already been recommended, tried, and tested in the past.

The readings selected cover a sixty year period from the 1920s through to the close of the 1970s, with the exception of the first reading by Lewis, Parker, and Sutcliffe (1984) that serves as the historical overview and analysis for the whole text. The limitations of space have of course necessitated the omission of publications worthy of note and, by way of partial remedy, these are referenced in Further Reading at the end of this text. Similarly a number of valuable texts dealing with reporting financial information to employees are listed in that section.

The text is divided into a number of sections. *Early Stirrings* provides some examples of the type of papers appearing in the 1920s and 1930s. It represents the more substantial of the early papers on this subject and it will become evident that even 1930s papers represented a significant advance upon what was published in the 1920s. Thereafter, each section is devoted to a particular aspect of the literature on reporting to employees. *Reporting Rationales* includes examples of papers discussing reasons for report producers embarking on this form of reporting and rights that employees may have to receiving such information. *Reporting Methods* encompasses discussions of employee report content, simplification, presentation, and explanation. *Reporting Practices: Case Studies and Surveys* presents descriptions of particular companies' actual reporting efforts as well as general surveys of actual reporting practices. *Assessing Employee Interest* includes both discussion of report content felt likely to be of interest and concern to employees as well as surveys revealing their stated information and presentation preferences. *Reporting in an Industrial Relations Context* considers the wider issue of providing financial information to trade unions for general decision-making purposes and for collective bargaining. The text concludes with a complete bibliography of all papers reprinted and a comprehensive listing of texts, monographs, articles, and papers in this field for further reading.

Each section of the text includes papers drawn from a number of different time periods. Papers are presented from earliest published to latest published. While *Reporting Rationales* only incorporates papers from 1960 onwards, subsequent sections all include papers drawn from the 1940s onwards. Also notable is the fact that quite a number of these papers were authored by executives and accountants actually involved in the production of reports to employees in their own organizations.

The first paper in this text, written by Lewis, Parker, and Sutcliffe (1984) introduces the reader to the historical development of corporate financial reporting to employees. It traces variations in interest (as measured by publishing frequency) in this form of reporting over time, considers the range of issues that have been raised and discussed in the past, and examines the nature of sources (accounting and non-accounting journals and authors). In addition the paper develops evidence for four major factors that appear to have generated peaks of interest in reporting to employees. These were application of new technology in the workplace, increased corporate merger activity, groundswells of anti-union sentiment, and economic recession or fears of recession. Two inferences may be drawn from this research. First it is clear that issues of reporting aims, report content, report presentation, and dissemination of information were repeatedly discussed over the period studied to the extent that very few new issues were raised in the literature of the 1970s. Second it might be argued that a common theme linked those factors found to be associated with peaks of literature interest in the subject. They all reflected corporate management's interest in telling its own story or version of events that had overtaken, or were about to overtake their employees. This may suggest a legitimizing or propagandist role for such reports, at least in the perception of some report producers.

Accounting, Organizations and Society, Vol. 9, No. 3/4, pp. 275–289, 1984.
Printed in Great Britain.

0361–3683/84 $3.00+.00

FINANCIAL REPORTING TO EMPLOYEES: THE PATTERN OF DEVELOPMENT 1919 TO 1979*

N.R. LEWIS, L.D. PARKER and P. SUTCLIFFE
Department of Accounting and Finance,
Monash University, Melbourne, Australia

Abstract

This paper examines the literature on financial reporting to employees between 1919 and 1979. It finds that the level of publication interest has varied widely during the period as has the relative interest of accountant and non-accountant groups. Periods of heightened publication activity appear to repeatedly coexist with four major socioeconomic factors, and arguments that this coexistence is not coincidental are considered. Finally it is noted that the same reporting to employee issues are frequently recalled and re-examined; possible reasons for this are considered. 1

Most accounting literature published in the 1970s treated reporting to employees as a new or emerging issue. However, a great body of literature on the topic had been published prior to the 1970s. For example, the generalised conceptual problem of how "best" to impart knowledge to employees (plant magazines) was discussed in 1921 (Department of Labour, Canada, 1921, pp. 7–12), and the need for special reports was discussed as early as 1923 (Botsford 1923). The earliest special financial report to employees, called "Report to Employees" appears to be an International Harvester Co. (U.S.A.) report in 1936 (National Association of Manufacturers of the U.S.A. 1938, p. 84)[1] and research indicates that there were at least 20 companies in the U.S.A. issuing special annual reports to employees in 1937.[2] This paper is based on an analysis of a sample of the literature published between 1919 and 1979. The objectives of the research project are:

(a) to document the interest in reporting to employees in the 1900s as evidenced by publication activity;
(b) to identify the specific reporting to employee issues that were considered most important during that period, and
(c) to isolate any socio-economic factors that may have influenced the general pattern of interest in reporting financial information to employees.

* The authors would like to thank Coopers and Lybrand (Chartered Accountants, Australia) for their financial support. The authors would also like to thank the following for helpful comments: Professors R.R. Officer and C.G. Peirson of the Department of Accounting and Finance, Monash University; Mr. D. Merrett of the Department of Economic History, Monash University; Louis Goldberg, Emeritus Professor, Melbourne University. The paper has benefited from comments of participants in the Department of Accounting and Finance, Monash University Staff Seminar Series.

[1] Derry (1948, p. 44) argues that the greatest change in preparing (financial) reports came in 1937 when Johns–Manville (U.S.A.) became one of the first companies to issue a special annual report to employees.

[2] Included in these companies were Kodak, Monsanto Chemical Co., Cluett, Peabody & Co., Kroger Grocery & Baking Company and Piggly Wiggly Corporation, Mergonthaler Linotype, Thermoid Company, Westinghouse, Worthington Pump & Machinery Corp. and the Union Bag and Paper Boys.

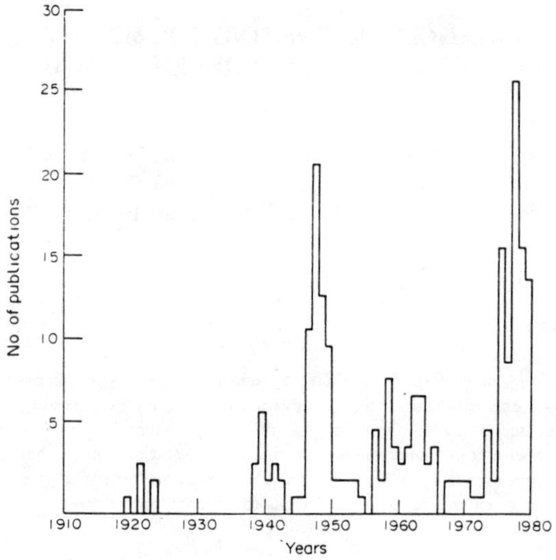

2

Fig. 1. Total annual publications 1918–1979. Observations for the years 1938–43 and 1950–55 are omitted due to high proportions of uncertain identity (1938–43, 50% uncertain; 1950–55, 38%). Observations for 1956–65 were retained, even though 38% of the sample was of uncertain identity, as the sample size was significantly greater than for the two omitted periods.

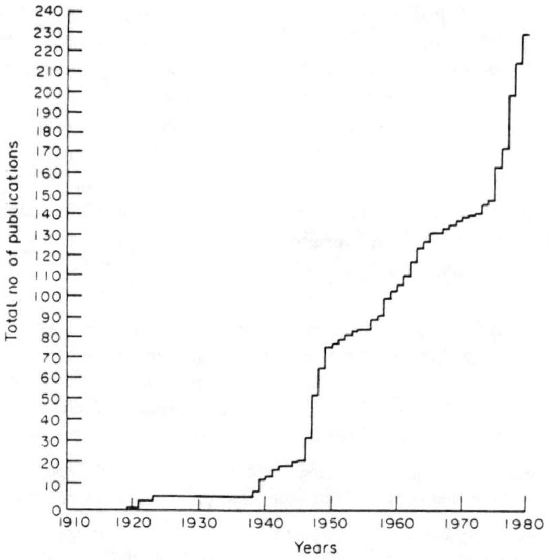

Fig. 2. Cumulative publications 1918–1979.

THE LITERATURE SAMPLE AND ITS SOURCES

The literature base was identified by a search of business indexes which referenced English language periodicals of the 20th Century. Available indexes included the Business Periodicals Index, the Accountants Index, Public Affairs Information Service Index and the subject indexes of the Monash University Library (Australia) and the Australian Society of Accountants Library (Australia) plus other miscellaneous sources. As a result, a major portion of the "English language periodicals" and published monographs were included.[3] The literature identified from these sources covered 232 publications between 1912 and 1979 inclusive. The subject areas covered in the search were diverse and included accounting, advertising, public relations, banking, communications, economics, finance and investment, industrial relations, marketing, occupational health and safety, and business, industry and trade fields in general.

Of the 232 publications concerning financial reporting to employees identified, 216 (93%) were obtained for analysis. These 216 publications were referenced from 109 different periodicals and covered the period from 1919 to 1979.

FEATURES OF DEVELOPMENT: INTEREST AND ISSUES

Interest in reporting to employees, as measured by publication activity, fluctuated widely between 1919 and 1979; a period of high interest being followed by a period of little or no interest before the pattern was repeated. In addition, little progress appears to have been made in the identification of new issues from period to period.

Variations in interest

The publications were ordered by publication date, and both a histogram of annual publications (Fig. 1) and a cumulative publications graph (Fig. 2) were constructed. These revealed wide variations of interest in financial reporting to employees. There were five distinct periods of high publication activity (see Fig. 1):

Period 1 1919–1923
Period 2 1938–1943
Period 3 1944–1955
Period 4 1956–1965
Period 5 1966–1979.

An analysis of rates of change in publishing frequency resulted in the following subperiods being identified (see Fig. 2): 3

Period 3(a) 1944–49
3(b) 1950–55
Period 5(a) 1966–72
5(b) 1973–79.

These periods are subject to further analysis in subsequent sections of this paper.

The repetition of issues

Having identified variations of interest in financial reporting to employees, further analysis of the sample was undertaken to trace the development of specific issues. To this end, the publications were analysed in terms of the number of times an issue was raised per period. Individual issues were grouped into four major categories:

---

[3] Business Periodicals Index is published by H.W. Wilson & Company, New York, U.S.A. and covers the period January 1958 to July 1979. It referenced 119 periodicals in 1958 and 270 periodicals in 1979. The Accountants Index is published by the American Institute of Certified Public Accountants, New York, U.S.A. It was originally published by the American Institute of Accountants, New York, U.S.A. in 1920. The Index was referencing 236 periodicals in 1979. The first edition of the Index was published in 1920. It claimed to have referenced known English accounting literature since 1912. The P.A.I.S. Index published by the Public Affairs Information Service, New York, U.S.A. references periodicals, proceedings, conferences, monographs and governmental reports. The Index claims indexing of 20th Century Publications in Economics, Political Science, Social Welfare, International Relations and related subjects. All materials indexed are in the English language.

TABLE 1. Recurrence of key issues in financial reporting to employees

	1919–23	1938–43	1944–49	1950–55	1956–65	1966–72	1973–79
1. Aims and reasons for reporting to employees							
Heralding changes	2					1	5
Vehicle for management propaganda	4	1	10		4	8	9
Promoting interest in understanding of company affairs and performance	3	2	12	1	4		6
Explaining management decision			6		6		8
Explaining the relationship between employees, management and shareholders	1	2	7	2	2		6
Explaining the objectives of the company			3				
Facilitating greater employee participation	1		1		1	1	10
In response to legislative or union pressure		1	1				8
Company image building	1	1		2		5	
Meeting information requirements peculiar to employees		1	9	1	5		17
Fear of wage demands, strikes and competitive disadvantages	4	4	11	3	12		16
Degree of employee interest		3	8	1	9		6
2. Report content							
Employee relationships	1	7	23	1	3		7
Future prospects (firm and employee)	1	5	9		9		25
Statement of value added		1	3		1		8
Corporate–government relations		1	2		1		1
Corporate objectives	1				1		4
Cash flow			2			1	4
Where money came from – where it went	1	1	4		3		6
Profit and loss			2				1
Balance sheet			2				1
Social balance sheet							11
Breakeven chart					1	1	3
Role of profits		2	3	1	1	2	
Personnel related information	1		4		2		4
Chairman's address		2	2		2		4
Competitions to encourage readership			5		1		2

Table 1 contd.

	1919–23	1938–43	1944–49	1950–55	1956–65	1966–72	1973–79
Highlights statement			1				2
3. Presentation							
Report length	1	2	7			1	5
Degree of simplification	1	8	17	2		3	24
Relevance to employee	2	4	17	2	10		12
Clarity and readability	3	7	31	1	7		19
Question and answer style		2	9	1	2	1	1
Who should produce	2		3		1		6
Cartoons and illustrations	4	4	26	1	15	2	34
Graphs and charts	1	10	30	4	11	1	48
Shareholder report plus supplementary information		5	10	2	7		9
Report credibility			12	2	7		9
Identical to shareholder report	1	2	6		2		2
4. Dissemination of information							
Mailed direct to employee		1	3	1	1		9
Report issued plus a management meeting		3	7	2	6		10
Letter format		2	7				1
Newspapers		1	3				
Slides and films			1	1	5	1	2
Employees' family involvement			3				
Frequency			2		4		4
Need for employee feedback					4	1	3
Radio		2	3		1		
Notice boards			1				1
Video tapes					2	1	4
Pay packets					1		1
On request			1	1	2		3
Through supervisors							1
Financial training					1		5
Integration with total communication network							3
Timeliness			1		3		5
No. of issues 56 — No. of publications examined	5	16	53	8	47	9	78

1. Aims and reasons for reporting to employees.
2. Report content.
3. Presentation.
4. Dissemination of information.

The frequencies obtained for each issue are displayed in Table 1. Further analysis was then undertaken to determine the comparative degree of repetition between issues. Table 2 shows that 55% of identified issues (31 of 56) appeared in four or more periods of the seven classified periods studied.

The most frequently discussed category was "presentation", with eleven different issues being considered on a total of 483 occasions between 1919 and 1979. The least frequently discussed category was that of "dissemination", with seventeen issues being considered on a total of 129
6 occasions between 1919 and 1979 (see Table 1). Of the other categories, "aims and reasons for reporting to employees" included 12 issues considered on a total of 268 occasions and "report content" included 16 issues considered on a total of 196 occasions.

Only three issues raised in the 1973–79 period had been raised on two or less occasions before 1972. There were:

Category 1 "In response to legislative or union pressure", considered only once in 1938–43 and once in 1944–49.

Category 2 "Social balance sheet", not previously considered.

Category 3 "Financial training", considered only once in 1956–65.

All other issues had been considered in at least three separate periods. In fact only eight issues (14% of 56) appearing in the post 1950 literature had *not* been raised in publications before 1950. This analysis suggests that rather than new issues being raised over time, the same issues were repeatedly recalled and reconsidered.

VARIATION OF INTEREST IN FINANCIAL REPORTING TO EMPLOYEES

Since the literature of financial reporting to employees prior to 1972 was found to be published almost exclusively in the U.S.A. (90% of publications (125 of 138) see Table 5), an analysis period was conducted. Independent socio-economic factors which may have affected employer–employee relations and which appear to have recurred simultaneously with periods of rising interest in reporting to employees were then identified. Arguments to support the contention that such simultaneous recurrence of socio-economic factors and increased interest in reporting to employees was not purely coincidental were considered. Subsequently the sample of literature

TABLE 2. Frequency of issue repetition (56 specific issues were identified during the period)

Number of periods in which the issue was repeated	Number of issues repeated in these periods	Column 2 as a % of total issues (56)	Cumulative % of total issues (56)
7	2	4	4
6	9	16	20
5	12	21	41
4	8	14	55
3	13	24	79
2	7	12	91
1	5	9	100

TABLE 3. The frequency with which the four socio-economic factors are referred to in the reporting to employee literature

Period		References to:				
No.	Years	Technology	Merger activity	Union power	Economic recession	Number of publications per period
1	1919–23	1	0	1	2	5
2	1938–43	2	4	5	2	16
3(a)	1944–49	9	5	29	6	53
3(b)	1950–55	1	1	3	0	8
4	1956–65	4	5	14	6	47
5(a)	1966–72	0	0	4	1	9
5(b)	1973–79	10	19	46	9	78
Number of times the issue is referred to		27	34	103	26	

7

on reporting to employees was re-examined to determine which of these socio-economic factors were reflected in that literature.

The analysis of possible socio-economic influences on the level of interest in reporting to employees revealed the repeated co-existence of the following four factors with periods of high interest in reporting to employees:

1. Application of new technology in the workplace.
2. Increased merger activity in the corporate sector.
3. Groundswells of anti-union sentiment.
4. Economic recession and/or fears of recession.

While these may not have been the only factors to coexist with the heightened interest in reporting to employees, a number of arguments support the contention that the simultaneous appearance of these factors with a rise in interest was not coincidental. Indeed it is possible that increased interest in reporting to employees may have been prompted by these influences in some combination. Through such reports, management might well have hoped to:

(1) allay fears of lost rank, skill or employment through technological advances;
(2) counter fears of "bigness", monopoly power, employee relocation and loss of identity through corporate mergers;
(3) take advantage of community anti-union sentiments by bypassing union communication channels (reporting directly to employees), emphasising management prerogatives and the need to control wages and associated costs and generally weakening the unions' potential to disrupt operations, and
(4) prepare employees for hard times, confirm or dispell rumours of imminent company failure, allay fears of unemployment and urge employees to greater efforts in difficult economic times.

Since arguments that these four factors were influential in promoting and supporting interest in reporting to employees are persuasive, they merit more detailed examination.

Application of new technology

The end of World War 1 witnessed significant advances in industrial mechanisation: the electrification of factories, new techniques of mass production and the mechanisation of many productive operations proceeded at a greatly accelerated rate (Robertson, 1964, p. 545; Brownlee, 1974, p. 268; Tuttle & Perry, 1970, p. 568). Similarly, the emergency demands of World War 2 accelerated industrial mechanisation and automation, the trend continuing into the immediate post war period in response to strong consumer demand (Robertson, 1964, p. 545; Handlin & Handlin, 1975, pp. 220–231; Tuttle & Perry, 1970, p. 705; Flamant & Singer-Kevel, 1970, pp. 76–83). Both of these periods of intense mechanisation coincided with increased interest in reporting to employees.

During the 1950s and 1960s the modernisation of plant and equipment with modifications and improvements of existing technology continued.
8 The late 1960s and early 1970s again experienced a period of accelerated automation with advances in computer and support technology being applied to both production and administration in industry and commerce (Gappert, 1979, pp. 30–40; Albin, 1978, pp. 34–36, 52–56). In the late 1960s and early 1970s another resurgence of interest in reporting financial information to employees coexisted with these innovations in the work place.

Corporate merger activity

The 1920–24 period witnessed a marked increase in the numbers of mergers of U.S. corporations. This merger activity gained momentum in the late 1920s and continued into the 1930s before slackening. A similar resurgence in merger activity was experienced between 1945–49 and, after a minor waning in 1950–54, built up to renewed heights in the years 1955–64.[4] There were, however, major differences in the types of businesses merging. Until the end of the 1940s mergers had predominantly been between firms in the same industry seeking either vertical integration or monopoly power. The wave of mergers that took place from the mid-1950s onwards differed, in that they mostly took the form of mergers of firms often having quite unrelated product lines (Brownlee, 1974, p. 325; Peterson & Gray, 1969, pp. 426–431; Robertson, 1964, pp. 560–561). Indicative of the public concern about the number of the post-World War 2 mergers was the apparent alarm amongst journalists, academics and the courts. Indeed, between 1937 and 1948 more antitrust procecutions were begun in the U.S. than in the entire history of the Sherman Act (1890) before 1937 (Robertson, 1964, p. 567). The mergers which occurred after 1955 resulted in oligopolies appearing in some 50 branches of industry. There was evidence of pricefixing and collusion which renewed and maintained public interest in the maintenance of competition and antitrust legislation (Russel, 1964, p. 497). These periods of heightened merger activity coincided quite closely with increased interest in reporting to employees.[5]

[4] Mergers in manufacturing and mining industries (U.S.A.)

(Five year totals)

1895–99	1,649	1020–24	2,235	1945–49	1,505
1900–04	1,363	1925–29	4,583	1950–54	1,424
1905–09	440	1930–34	1,687	1955–59	3,365
1910–14	451	1935–39	577	1960–64	4,366
1915–19	625	1940–44	906		

(Peterson & Gray, 1969, p. 431).

[5] The sudden and rapid increase of interest in financial reporting to employees in Australia in the 1970s is consistent with the U.S. experience in that it co-existed with increased merger activity (see below).

Corporate take overs in Australia 1960–1979 (10 yr totals)

1960–69	238
1970–79	353

Source: The Stock Exchange of Melbourne Annual Reports 1960–1979. The above data recast in periods used in this study:

1966–1979 (Periods 5a and 5b) – (7 yr totals)

1966–72	189
1970–79	252

Anti-union sentiments

The years 1914–1920 saw trade union bargaining power increase as a result of wartime labour shortages. Post-war depression, an unsuccessful series of post-war strikes and a renewed wave of employer antagonism saw that power decline after 1920 and paved the way for enticement of employees into corporate profit-sharing and welfare programmes.[6] In the U.S.A., union membership fell from greater than five million in 1920 to 3.5 million in 1923, a membership which was fairly stable through the early 1930s (Robertson, 1964, pp. 618–619; Handlin & Handlin, 1975, p. 220; Bagwell & Mingay, 1970, pp. 208–209).

The Wagner Act[7] of 1937 established union rights (Robertson, 1964, p. 622; Handlin, 1975, p. 220). At the end of World War 2 labour made strong drives for improved wages and fringe benefits,[8] the average duration of strikes increasing markedly in 1945. The public reacted to this growing union militancy, fearing that unions had become too powerful. After 1945, the tide of public and legislative opinion turned against the unions, particularly in the form of the Taft–Hartley Act of 1947[9] (Robertson, 1964, pp. 605, 623–625; Bagwell & Mingay, 1970, p. 211). Public antagonism towards union power in both post war periods was repeated and reinforced by legislature in the mid-1950s. The AFL and CIO[10] reunited in 1955, partly as a reaction to punitive American labour legislation and hostile public opinion (Robertson, 1964, p. 619). Both post-war periods of public antagonism towards union power, and the mid-1950s period of public and legislative antagonism co-existed with a rapid increase in the literature and interest in reporting to employees.

Economic recession

Recession, or fears of recession, also appear to recur almost simultaneously with heightened interest in reporting to employees, however co-existence of these phenomena is not as consistent as with the other factors identified. Any relationship between reporting to employees and economic recession must therefore be treated with caution.

The post-World War 1 recession occurred at the same time as increased interest in reporting to employees. Despite the fact that management of the post-World War 2 economy was superior to that of post-World War 1, an atmosphere of 9
pessimism and fear of depression existed in the U.S.A. Indeed by 1949, economic activity had begun to slacken with production falling and unemployment rising (Link, 1967, p.634; Flamant & Singer-Kevel, 1970, pp. 78–79). During the 1956–64 period of increased interest in reporting to employees, there were recurring periods of recession in the U.S. The years 1957–58, 1960–61 and 1962 all saw varying degrees of economic setback. From the mid-1950s onwards there was general concern about the "stickiness" of the unemployment rate, even during periods of economic expansion (Flamant & Singer-Kevel, 1970, pp. 92–97, 104–107, 115–117; Robertson, 1964,

---

[6] Supreme Court judgements in the 1920s also hampered trade union activities (Bagwell & Mingay, 1970, pp. 208–209; Peterson & Gray, 1969, p. 431).

[7] The Wagner Act established the principle of collective bargaining, required employers to recognise bona-fide labour organizations and to deal with them in good faith (Robertson, 1964, p. 622).

[8] This was particularly so in mass production industries. Hard bargains were struck in the steel, meat packing, coal and automobile industries (Tuttle & Perry, 1970, p. 704). Indeed it was observed that around the close of World War 2, union leaders no longer argued for improved wages on the basis of labour's productivity but on the basis of the income statements of corporate employers (Tuttle & Perry, 1970, pp. 704–707).

[9] The Taft–Hartley Act protected the rights of the individual worker and preserved his or her right to join a union, thus outlawing the closed shop. The legislation effectively counterbalanced the earlier Wagner Act.

[10] The mid-1930s had seen a conflict within the Americal Federation of Labour (A.F.L.) concerning proper structure of the organization. In 1935 eight industrial unions formed the Committee for Industrial Organization (C.I.O.) within the A.F.L., but in 1936 were suspended from membership of the A.F.L. In 1939, the suspended group became a formal separate organization, the Congress of Industrial Organization (C.I.O.). In 1955 however, they were driven to unity by public antagonism and in a merger, formed the AFL–CIO (Robertson, 1964, p. 619; Tuttle & Perry, 1970, p. 571).

p. 617). The 1970s experienced significant economic difficulties in the U.S.A. at the same time as interest in corporate financial reporting to employees grew again[11] (Albin, 1978, pp. 10–12).

A qualification to the above arguments is that there appears to be no interest in financial reporting to employees during the period of the great depression (1929–1932).[12]

Corroborative evidence

Table 3 documents the frequency with which the four socio-economic factors identified above were discussed in the reporting to employee literature sample. This table provides some support for the contention that these four factors influenced interest in financial reporting to employees.

10 ISSUE DEVELOPMENT: CONTRIBUTING FACTORS

An iterative pattern in the development of specific issues in financial reporting to employee can be identified from the literature. The following factors may have contributed to this pattern:

1. Lack of recognition of prior research;
2. Variable interest of different professional groups;
3. Different countries of publication.

Each of these will be examined in some detail.

Recognition of prior research

Analysis of the 216 publications in the sample was undertaken to determine the extent to which authors referred via footnote, bibliography or reference within the literature to publications on financial reporting to employees in prior periods. The results of this analysis appear in Table 4. Throughout the period studied only 5% of total publications (10 out of 216) referred to literature in the immediate preceding time period and only 6% of publications referred to literature published in any prior time period. It appears that lack of recognition of the work of authors of previous periods contributed to a repetitive rather than a progressive process of issue development.

Interest of different professional groups

An analysis of the mix of publication type and author category was undertaken to isolate the relative interest shown by the accounting and non-accounting groups. Publications were classified by type (accounting or non-accounting), author category (accountant or non-accountant) and country of publication. Where there was considerable doubt as to the identity of author or journal, it was classified as "unidentified" (see Table 5).

Before drawing any inferences from the results of this analysis one qualification is required viz: a sizeable proportion of books and papers are classified in the "unidentified" category with respect to author type. In the period 1938–1943 the percentage in that category was 50% and in two other periods (1950–55, 1956–65) the percentage was 35%. However for the sample as a whole, author category was identified for 76% of the publications and hence inferences about the population can justifiably be made.

In Fig. 3, a graphical representation of the percentage of accounting and non-accounting publications contributing to the literature in the years 1919–1979[13] clearly shows the two categories of publications in opposing relationship to each other. When the percentage of accounting publications was falling, non-accounting publications, as a percentage of the total, appeared to be rising (and vice versa). This pattern took the form of oscillations of sizeable magnitude over time. Similarly, in

[11] In the 1970s the U.K. also experienced significant economic difficulties (Stewart, 1977, pp. 188–232; Black, 1979, pp. 256–259; Wright, 1979, pp. 161–191) at the same time as interest grew in financial reporting to employees.

[12] Reasons for this anomoly can be proposed. For example, the crash may well have occurred so unexpectedly, and so completely, that any attempt to communicate information to employees was precluded. In the light of such a major crash it is unlikely that a report could provide employees with news not already public.

[13] Referring to Table 1, the percentage is related to total sample size for each of the following periods: 1919–23; 1924–38, no observations; 1939–43; 1944–49; 1950–55; 1956–65; 1966–72; 1973–79.

Fig. 4, a graphical representation of the percentage of accountant and non-accountant authors contributing to the literature shows a countercyclical relationship between these two groups. Again the variation between peaks and troughs over time was quite wide. When Figs 3 and 4 are compared with Fig. 1, it becomes clear that the cyclical movement of accountant authors and accounting publications, as percentages of total contribution, moved in approximate phase with the cycle of the total number of books and papers published per year. The cyclical movement of non-accountant authors and non-accountant journals on the other hand were distinctly out of phase with the cycle of total publications.

The results indicate a countercyclical pattern of relative interest and sizeable amplitudes between the two groups over the 1919–79 period. Each group had less chance of recapping on its own literature because a previous period of its own high relative interest was usually about 20 yr previous to its current high level of relative interest. Such conditions are likely to produce a high incidence of repetition of issues in the literature of the period.

Country of publication

From 1919–1972, the major proportion of publications on financial reporting to employees appeared in the U.S.A.[14] with an occasional contribution being published in the U.K. or Canada. (See Table 5) In the period 1973–1979 the absolute number of U.S. publications in the sample declined. At the same time the U.K., and to a lesser extent Australia, emerged as publishing locations of equivalent importance to the U.S.A.

SUMMARY AND CONCLUSION

This study set out to investigate the history of the literature on financial reporting to employees with the intention of documenting developments during the 20th century. The period 1912–79 was selected for examination and the population was identified. The sample collected covered the period 1919–79. The results of investigations indicated the existence of fluctuating total publishing frequency over the sample period as well as a repetitive development of issues.

An analysis of the American business environment during the periods of increased interest in
financial reporting to employees was undertaken. 11
Arguments that for socio-economic factors influenced interest in financial reporting to employees were advanced. Further, it was argued that lack of prior-period bibliographic referencing and inconsistent interdisciplinary interest over time appeared to encourage repetitive issue development.

Further research is required to determine whether accounting writers adopted significantly different approaches to the subject compared with management writers, whether the literature is capable of revealing any pattern of change in corporate reporting practices over the decades, whether there are any major industry differences in reporting to employees, and what factors have influenced the sudden increase in interest in the U.K. and Australia after 1972.

---

[14] While the indexes used covered publications in all countries, they were of U.S.A. origin, therefore bias in the sample is possible and observations are accordingly qualified.

12

TABLE 4. Frequency of publication referral to prior period literature on financial reporting to employees

	1919–23		1938–43		1944–49		1950–55		1956–65		1966–72		1973–79		1919–79 Total	
	No.	% of row 3	No.	% of row 3	No.	% of row 3	No.	% of row 3	No.	% of row 3	No.	% of row 3	No.	% of row 3	No.	% of row 3
1. Number of publications in a period which referred to the immediately previous period	0	0	0	0	0	0	2	25	2	4	0	0	6	8	10	5
2. Number of publications in a period which referred to any previous period	0	0	0	0	0	0	3	38	2	4	1	11	8	10	14	6
3. Number of publications per period in the sample	5	–	16	–	53	–	8	–	47	–	9	–	78	–	216	–
4. Cumulative number of publications	5	–	21	–	74	–	82	–	129	–	138	–	216	–	–	–

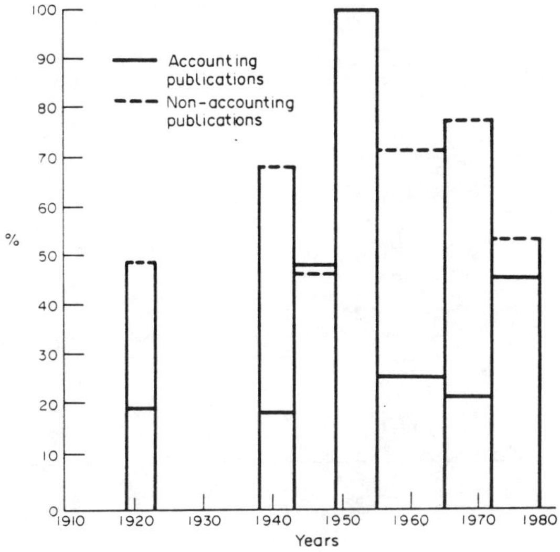

Fig. 3. Accounting and non-accounting publications as a percentage of total publications.

13

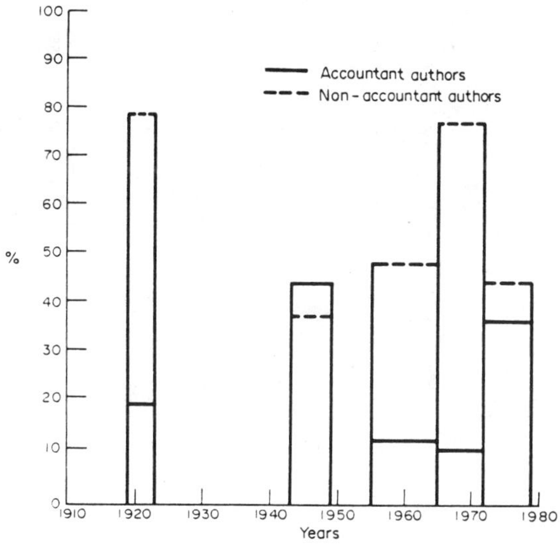

Fig. 4. Accountant and non-accountant authors as a percentage of total publications.

TABLE 5. A cross-sectional analysis of publications over time

Period	1	2	3	Publication 4	5	6	7	Author 8	9	10	11	Country of publication 12	13	14	15	16	17
1919 to 1923	6	5	83	1 (20%)	4 (80%)	—	5 (100%)	1 (20%)	4 (80%)	—	5 (100%)	1 (20%)	3 (60%)	—	1 (20%)	—	5 (100%)
1924 to 1937																	
1938 to 1943	16	16	100	3 (19%)	11 (69%)	2 (12%)	16 (100%)	5 (31%)	3 (19%)	8 (50%)	16 (100%)	—	15 (94%)	—	1 (6%)	—	16 (100%)
1944 to 1949	56	53	95	26 (49%)	25 (47%)	2 (4%)	53 (100%)	24 (45%)	20 (38%)	9 (17%)	53 (100%)	—	52 (98%)	—	1 (2%)	—	53 (100%)
1950 to 1955	9	8	89	8 (100%)	—	—	8 (100%)	3 (38%)	2 (24%)	3 (38%)	8 (100%)	—	7 (87%)	—	1 (13%)	—	8 (100%)
1956 to 1965	47	47	100	12 (26%)	34 (72%)	1 (2%)	47 (100%)	6 (13%)	23 (49%)	18 (38%)	47 (100%)	3 (6%)	40 (85%)	1 (3%)	—	3 (6%)	47 (100%)
1966 to 1972	10	9	90	2 (22%)	7 (78%)	—	9 (100%)	1 (11%)	7 (78%)	1 (11%)	9 (100%)	—	8 (89%)	—	1 (11%)	—	9 (100%)
1973 to 1979	88	78	89	36 (46%)	42 (54%)	—	78 (100%)	35 (45%)	29 (37%)	14 (18%)	78 (100%)	48 (62%)	16 (21%)	12 (15%)	2 (2%)	—	78 (100%)
Total	232	216	93	88 (41%)	123 (57%)	5 (2%)	216 (100%)	75 (35%)	88 (41%)	53 (24%)	216 (100%)	52 (34%)	141 (65%)	13 (6%)	6 (3%)	4 (2%)	216 (100%)

Legend:

Period
1. Population
2. Sample
3. Sample size as percentage of population

Publication
4. Accounting
5. Non-accounting
6. Unidentified
7. Total

Author
8. Accountant
9. Non-accounting
10. Unidentified
11. Total

Country of publication
12. U.K.
13. U.S.A.
14. Australia
15. Canada
16. Other
17. Total

BIBLIOGRAPHY

Albin, P. S., *Progress Without Poverty: Socially Responsible Economic Growth* (New York: Basic Books, 1978).

Black, J., *The Economics of Modern Britain* (Oxford: Martin Robertson, 1979).

Botsford, H., How a plant publication helps, *Trained Men* (3 April, 1923), pp. 84–86.

Brownlee, W. E., *Dynamics of Ascent: A History of the American Economy* (New York: Alfred A. Knopf, 1974).

Department of Labour, Canada, *Employees' Magazines in Canada*, Bulletin No. 4, Industrial Relations Service (Canada: Department of Labor, 1921).

Derry, S. A., Presenting the facts on company operations to the employees, *Ohio State University Proceedings Institute on Accounting* (1948), pp. 41–53.

Flamant, M. & Singer-Kevel, J., *Modern Economic Crises* (London: Barrie and Jenkins, 1970).

Gappert, G., *Post-Affluent America: the Social Economy of the Future* (New York: New Viewpoints, 1979).

Handlin, O. & Handlin, M. F., *The Wealth of the American People: A History of American Affluence* (New York: McGraw-Hill, 1975).

Link, A. S., Catton, W. B. & Leary, W. M., Jr., *American Epoch: A History of the United States since the 1890s, Volume I, 1897–1920*, 3rd ed. (New York: Alfred A. Knopf, 1967).

Link, A. S., Catton, W. B. & Leary, W. M., Jr., *American Epoch: A History of the United States since the 1890s, Volume III, 1938–1966*, 3rd ed. (New York: Alfred A. Knopf, 1967).

National Association of Manufacturers of the U.S.A., *Making the Annual Report speak for Industry* (1938), pp. 73–168. 15

Peterson, J. M. & Gray, R., *Economic Development of the United States* (Homewood, IL.: Richard D. Irwin, 1969).

Robertson, R. M., *History of the American Economy*, 2nd ed. (New York: Harcourt Brace, 1964).

Russel, R. R., *A History of the American Economic System* (New York: Appleton-Century-Crofts, 1964).

Stewart, M., *The Jekyll and Hyde Years: Politics and Economic Policy Since 1964* (London: J. M. Dent, 1977).

Tuttle, F. W. & Perry, J. M., *An Economic History of the United States* (Cincinnati: South Western, 1970).

Wright, J. F., *Britain in the Age of Economic Management* (Oxford: Oxford University Press, 1979).

EARLY STIRRINGS

This section presents a number of papers concerned with the communication of information to employees and published in the 1920s and 1930s. Budd's (1923) paper on the use of company publications was initially presented at the 1922 conference of the American Electric Railway Association and deals with communications to both customers and employees. He advocates both educating and informing employees on financial matters. Readability and interest are stressed. Botsford (1923) argues for the production of a plant publication as an investment in employees' morale and pride in their work—explaining corporate financial condition, demonstrating employee contributions to corporate performance, and promoting attention to organizational efficiency.

Franzy Eakin (1938), controller of A.E. Staley Manufacturing Company of Decatur, Illinois, presented this paper at a regional meeting of controllers in Indianapolis. He discusses a whole range of reports produced by such companies as United States Steel Company, International Harvester Company, Swift and Company, The Detroit Edison Company, Allied Chemical and Die Corporation, Bethlehem Steel Corporation, Illinois Central System, A.E. Staley Manufacturing Company, The Caterpillar Tractor Company, the Johns-Manville Company, and the Monsanto Chemical Company.

James Irwin (1939), assistant to the President of Monsanto Chemical Company in St. Louis, explains his company's experience in issuing a special edition of a financial report designed for employees. He details preparation procedures, employee reactions, and the subsequent issuance of interim reports to employees. *Telling Your Story to Employees* (1939) puts forward the report to employees as management's means of reacting to attacks on business in the community. As an example, the report of the Laclede Steel Company of St. Louis is discussed in detail. Bennett (1939) provides some introductory comments on possible contents for such reports.

While ideas were clearly developing in the 1920s, the papers from the 1930s strongly evidence a rapid pace of adoption in terms of corporate experiments with reporting to employees. It is of interest however to note that a number of these papers reveal an underlying motivation of writers—the desire to defend the honor of business and to reinforce employee loyalty to their employing organization.

How a Plant Publication Helps

"Shirt-sleeve" days of healthy intimacy between workmen and boss are gone. The employes' publication has been devised to offset that lost intimacy

By Harry Botsford

Mr. Botsford writes on this subject after two years or more study of it. Part of that time he was editor of *The Dodge Idea* published by the Dodge Manufacturing Company, from which position he recently retired to take up special free-lance business writing. His articles have appeared in such magazines as *Factory, The Nation's Business,* and *Collier's.*

PLANT PUBLICATIONS, or employe publications, are a logical outgrowth of modern economic and personnel conditions. Time was when almost every industrial organization was small; back in those days the head of the concern was an individual whose time was more or less equally divided between his office and the plant. These "shirt-sleeve" days had a tendency to breed a healthy intimacy between the head of the business and individual workmen. It was a two-track comradeship which made it possible for the "boss" to come out to the bench and talk things over with the workman; or it made it possible for the workman to come to the office of the boss and talk over matters of mutual or individual interest. Such a condition was more or less ideal, but as each business grows, such intimacy is broken up by a force of circumstances which demands that the head of the business spend more time in his isolated office and traveling. It is a regrettable but incontrovertible fact that the end of this intimacy usually marks the beginning of labor trouble.

To offset this situation the employe publication was devised. In theory the plant publication has only *one* function—and that is to sell the job to the worker. To fulfil this function, however, the plant publication must do a number of things—and it must do them extraordinarily well. In reality a plant publication is a publication, issued at stated periods, at no cost to employes. Its size may range from one sheet of mimeographed paper to a beautiful publication of 150 pages with a handsome cover. Physically, a plant publication is merely a combination of ink, paper, cuts, and type, judiciously proportioned as to quantity and quality. Essentially the ability and pull of the internal house organ is measured by its *soul* and its *sincerity.*

Many plant publications do not have these essentials and the lack of them is responsible for a mortality rate of around 30 per cent. Industry is spending around $3,000,000 a year in printing alone for plant publications; this sum would approximately double if salaries and engraving bills were taken into consideration. In the aggregate this constitutes a sizable sum for industry to spend in "good-will" missionary work. The question naturally arises: Is the expenditure justified by results? A two years' study of the matter, which has been as intimate and as analytical as possible, forces me to the inevitable conclusion that money spent for plant publications should not be considered as an *expense* but should be considered as an *investment.* I can back this conclusion with some facts upon which the conclusion is based.

In one of the larger Southern cities there is a large fertilizer plant. For years this plant had a very heavy labor turnover. Things really came to a head when it was

Typical employes' publications issued by The Curtis Publishing Company, the New York Central Railroad, the National Cash Register Co.

discovered that this heavy turnover was the one item which stood between red ink and dividends. This plant paid high wages and the hours were within reason. But workers came and went; the average length of employment was less than 60 days. The situation finally resolved itself down to the fact that pride counted for the heavy turnover. Working conditions, at the very best, are far from pleasant in a fertilizer factory. There is an odor in such places which can only be described as being a rank smell. There is no known method of eliminating it.

After considering the seriousness of the situation, the management decided that the only way to keep men on the job would be to increase their pride in the work they were doing to a point where pride would keep them at their work. A plant publication resulted from the conference which discussed the matter. The publication was placed under the direction of the advertising manager with the
20 assistance of the employment manager. That house organ is not a pretentious appearing publication, but it has accomplished a big job. To increase morale, and to stimulate pride in the work at hand, the plant publication each week published two pages of photographs of farms, gardens, and green houses which used the brand of fertilizer manufactured. The healthy growths made possible by their product, the beauty of the flowers grown, and the size and quality of vegetables and grain produced by virtue of the fertilizer gave the workers a new insight into their industry. Pride was stimulated and fostered further by a monthly prize given some employe who used the fertilizer in his own garden.

This propaganda was pleasantly interspersed by the usual plant publication features: the news and notes pertaining to the personnel of the workers in various departments and other items of interest to workers only. The plan slowly but surely proved its soundness. Today labor turnover in that plant is normal and the company is earning the normal profits to which it is entitled. The cost of the plant publication in this particular organization is considered as an investment.

PRIDE! Every man and woman in this world—especially in the industrial and business world—wants to be proud of his or her job. All of us are anxious to justify to any one that our work is essential, that we are helping to mould a unit or to build something which the world needs and uses.

Often the pull of the plant publication is greater than the management believes. A textile mill in the New England states employs around four thousand men and women. During the war this concern established a plant publication in charge of a keen young chap who had been exempted from military service by reason of a crippled foot. The management used to smile tolerantly when outsiders complimented them on the quality of the company's plant publication. As a matter of fact, they never believed in its efficiency until their attention was called to it in a rather dramatic manner.

Trouble developed with labor—it was not a question of hours or wages—but simply one of these annoying situations which employers run up against too often. The problem seemed unsolvable; the situation went from bad to worse. Came a day when labor was about to pick up and walk out. Management knew that if they acceded outright to the demands that profits would be threatened seriously. If the workers went on a strike or a walk-out, profits were again thrown in the balance.

In desperation the management asked the labor leaders if there wasn't some way in which the matter could be settled or arbitrated. The spokesman of the workmen stated emphatically that there was only *one* man in the entire office with whom they would arbitrate. That man was the editor of the plant publication! To say that management was surprised is to put the matter mildly. They had considered the editor simply as a normal employe—one who had about as much importance in the organization as the assistant employment manager. Here he was: the one man with whom the workmen would deal!

They sent for the editor and told him the ultimatum delivered by the labor leaders. They explained frankly the situation they were in—that is, the situation from the standpoint of finance. Needless to say, the editor already knew the worker's side of the matter. He had already devised a plan of mutual fairness. He outlined it to the management, and they were so well pleased that they offered a big bonus if he could put it across. He conferred with the labor leaders, and in less than an hour an agreement was reached. Every one was well pleased.

A great variety of groups are represented by these personnel publications—American Rolling Mills, Abram & Strauss, and National City Bank

The management of this textile mill now values their plant publication highly. They realize they would have faced a heavy loss, if the house organ had not been edited in such a way as to win the complete confidence of the workers. The editor is still with them, but today he heads a new department of personnel. This organization has—as the ancient revivalist used to say—seen the light. It knows that there is more to a plant paper than merely selling faith, loyalty, and a job to the worker with some incidental editorial matter about thrift and safety first. These things are known to be essential; they constitute the every-day job of the plant publication. But that management knows now what every organization should know: that a properly conducted plant paper represents an emergency shock absorber with almost unlimited possibilities.

PRESENT-day business conditions may bring up almost any kind of an industrial emergency which the house organ can help to solve. Investigation in an automobile plant disclosed the fact that fire insurance rates were too high. Heads of departments did everything they could to reduce hazards, and this lowered the rates somewhat. The plant publication put the matter squarely up to the workers and asked them what they could do. Within three months, additional hazards were eliminated to such an extent that insurance rates were lowered 22 per cent. The saving effected paid for the printing of the plant paper for over a year!

During the industrial depression more than one plant paper justified a wage cut to such an extent that the workers accepted that cut without a whimper, believing that the economic situation demanded it. This, in itself, is a tremendous achievement. Such plants had a high morale; the workers were gratified and flattered that the "front office" had taken them into their confidence. That touch of intimacy brought to light the old-time spirit of loyalty that made a workman stick to the boss through bad times.

It is, of course, axiomatic that a plant paper cannot benefit the worker without, in turn, working some measure of benefit on management. Such was the experience of a certain watch company, which two years ago was having considerable difficulty because of the steady and unusual return of its product from dealers. Many of these returns, which cut heavily into profits and prestige, were due to minor defects, caused by careless or unthinking workmen who slighted some small angle of their operation. Aware of this condition, the editor of the plant paper began an educational campaign. "Why Our Watches Are Returned" was soon closely watched by all the workers. Exact causes for all defects were given and the blame definitely placed on the department where it belonged. Of course, that was unpleasant publicity. Other departments waxed sarcastic, but soon pride of craftsmanship saved the day. Better work became the standard, until at present the return of watches from dealers is so small that it never causes comment.

> PLANT PUBLICATIONS represent a tremendous influence in our industrial life," says Mr. Botsford. "The limit of that influence is unknown. But plant publications have sold thrift to workers and made them save sums which cannot be estimated. They have kept workers on the job of being sane and sensible citizens. They have brought to the worker a realization of the importance he bears to all industry, sowing the seeds of pride of craft. They have increased production and increased efficiency. Better homes and better working conditions have developed."

In an automobile organization, the editor of the plant paper cooperated with officials who faced a necessary wage cut. Under the heading, "Your Dollar — What Makes It?", these officials took their turn in writing a series of articles in which they put the matter up to employes in a direct and dramatic manner. A large drawing, representing a dollar divided in exact proportions, showed what percentage of the dollar of wages was represented by each operation, and gave the worker an insight into the importance of his individual job.

THEN the comparison went further and showed the employe what share of wages was charged to the finished product. It made the worker think. In one case that thinking led to a manufacturing change in a department that speeded up production 45 per cent. and helped lower the price of the finished product. Prices of competitive cars were shown with the labor charges against them as compared with a higher wage charge of this organization. The sales manager came out with a statement that if wages could be cut a certain amount, the price of the product could be lowered until it would be on an equal basis with that asked for other cars of the same class, and he would guarantee to sell enough cars to keep the plant busy for the year. When the wage cut came, it was accepted without dissenting. Workers and management profited greatly, for the former were kept busy during the year when the automotive trade was seriously hit.

Management in a machinery manufacturing business came out in its plant paper each month with a prize contest for suggestions. Ideas poured in. Many were impractical, of course, but on the other hand many were very much worth while. One plan put in operation in the foundry saved hundreds of tons of iron each year. Prizes were small but worth working for, and the men who showed initiative in this work were given the preference in promotion. Furthermore, this prize contest put the workers into the habit of thinking along constructive, helpful lines. Today the prizes are still offered and awarded each month. This plant is an example of efficiency—there is little lost motion, and no antiquated methods are in use. Best of all, the workmen are keen and alert, and eternally look for ways to improve conditions and manufacture methods.

PLANT PUBLICATIONS represent a tremendous influence in our industrial life. The limit of that influence is unknown. Plant papers have sold thrift to workers and made them save sums which cannot be estimated. Plant publications have discouraged radicalism to a large extent and have kept workers on the job of being sane and sensible citizens. Plant publications have brought to the worker a realization of the importance he bears to all industry, and in doing this have sown the seeds of pride of craft. Plant publications have increased production and efficiency. Short-cuts in manufacturing methods have been developed by workmen stimulated by plant publications. Better homes and better working conditions have resulted.

The plant publication has done much to retain the old spirit of loyalty that was common when the plant was small and the boss knew every worker by name. The old and much-to-be-desired intimacy will never return—modern economic conditions will not permit it. But if the plant publication fulfils its job, it will sell the worker on the company which employs him; it will sell him on the relationship which exists between his work and the finished product. With this accomplished, management will have a satisfied and loyal worker on whom cannot be put a monetary value approximating his real worth.

THE USE OF COMPANY PUBLICATIONS

By Britton I. Budd, *President,*
Metropolitan West Side Elevated Railway Company,
Chicago, Illinois

The importance of the company publication, as a medium through which a company, its customers and its employes, can be brought closer together in the interest of better service, is becoming more and more appreciated by electric railway companies. Much remains to be done in this field, however, for it is a subject which, in my opinion, deserves more serious consideration on the part of executives than it has received in the past.

No public utility company can give the best service of which it is capable without the co-operation of its customers and of its employes.
22 This co-operation necessarily is three-sided and a company publication, so-called, can be used to cement and hold together the three sides of the triangle.

There are two kinds of periodicals which go under the name of "company publications," each having separate and distinct functions, yet closely connected. The first is issued for general circulation, intended primarily for the customers of a company and secondarily for the employes. It carries a message from the company as one factor in the equation to the other two factors, with the result that all three are drawn closer together and brought to a better mutual understanding.

The second kind of company publication is intended for employes only, its function being to inform and interest them in affairs that are closely related to themselves and the company for which they work. In this paper I shall treat the two kinds of publications separately, pointing out some of the things which may be accomplished by each in its own field, although I realize that there is some over-lapping in their respective functions.

The company publication which goes to customers as well as employes may be used to advantage in a variety of ways. It may be used both as a business and as a goodwill getter, by setting forth the advantages of the service which the company has to sell. It can be used to establish and maintain a spirit of goodwill between the customers and the employes and promote courtesy and safety. It offers the passenger a medium through which he can express appreciation of an act of courtesy shown him by an employe.

That passengers will take advantage of such opportunity to express appreciation, has been amply demonstrated in my own experience. When we first began to issue a little publication of this kind on the Chicago elevated lines some six years ago, the first issue contained no commendations of employes. At the present time hardly a day passes without one or more letters being received from grateful passengers commending some employe for recovering a lost package, for finding a seat for a standing passenger, for being attentive to a woman with a baby in arms, for calling stations distinctly, for lending a woman carefare or for one or other of the hundreds of little things which an employe can do to please and accommodate customers. Each issue of this publication now carries regularly from twenty to forty such commendations, the particular employe being identified by name and badge number.

That may appear a trifling matter, but the effects are far-reaching and much more important than appears at first glance. Such commendations stimulate employes with a desire to please. They encourage them to do better work. They bring them into closer relationship with their customers and at the same time create a friendly feeling on the part of the passenger toward the company.

If you consider for a moment how reluctant most of us are to write letters which we are not required to write, you will realize that a passenger who takes the trouble to write a long letter commending 23
some employe must feel rather friendly toward the company. It is a word from a pleased customer, which is the most valuable form of advertising a company can get and is a valuable asset in public relations.

But that is only one of the ways in which such a publication is valuable. On every large property there are always details of operation which the average passenger does not understand and which frequently create irritation and cause complaint. The passenger wishes to know why certain things are done the way they are and why they are not done in the way he thinks they ought to be. He wishes to know why certain trains pass certain stations some days and not on others and many other things similar in character.

When such inquiries are received care is taken to explain them fully in the next issue. We have found by experience that some of these operating details are read with more interest than any other items in the publication. Passengers after reading some explanation of that kind will write letters saying they had often wondered what the reason was, but now it was perfectly clear to them and they were satisfied. Frequently they will end such letters by asking for an explanation of some other detail in a future issue.

Now the effect of all that is that it gets the customer interested in the company and the character of the service it gives. His interest is of a friendly character. He looks forward to the appearance of the next issue to see the explanation of the detail about which he asked. If you can get your customers interested in your company you get their goodwill at the same time.

There are many other ways in which a publication of this kind can be made helpful in maintaining good public relations. In recent years many changes in rates of fare have come about and the company publication is a good medium through which to explain the necessity for the changes. This can be done by a plain statement of the facts, avoiding all appearance of complaining or making pleas of poverty. Matter written on this subject should point out the high quality of the service being given and the advantage to the public in having it maintained, rather than to show that a company is not making any money.

The company publication can be used to inform its customers of improvements being made or contemplated. If a new station is being built, tell your customers about it. If new rails are being laid, tell about it, giving briefly in some detail the benefit the public will derive from the improvement and incidentally the cost to the company. If a new class of service is to be installed explain how it will benefit passengers.

Such items are "news" and are read with interest. The benefit to the company in printing such items is that the customers talk about it and get the impression that the company is constantly doing something in the way of improving the service. Care should be used in the
24 preparation of such items to avoid all semblance of propaganda. Treat them solely for their news value and let the customers draw their own inferences.

The second kind of publication to which I have referred, the one which is intended mainly for the employes, must be a little different in character from the one intended for public consumption. There are differences of opinion as to the nature of the material to be used and the manner in which it should be presented.

In the case of the Chicago elevated lines we have the two kinds, and as both are mailed to the home addresses of employes each month, naturally we seek to avoid duplication of news matter. None of the same material is used in both publications, except the commendations of employes. The reason for the exception is that in the employes' magazine we use commendations coming from superintendents and foremen as well as those coming from passengers, while in the other only letters coming from the public are used.

While, as I have said, there are differences of opinion about the kind of material that should be used in employes' magazines, my own opinion is that first of all such publications should be educational and informative in character. They should have a definite purpose in view and that purpose should be to acquaint the employes with the business of the company by which they are employed.

In every large corporation the great majority of the employes are totally ignorant of the financial and business side of the enterprise. I do not believe that this ignorance on the part of the employes is due to lack of interest in the business of the company, but rather to lack of information. They do not know because the company has not given them an opportunity to learn. The main purpose of the employes' magazine, therefore, should be to supply such information in a readable way which can easily be understood.

That is the kind of information which the employes ought to have and which a company ought to supply. The real problem, however, is how best to put it "across" so that it will register.

I need hardly say that an employes' magazine must be made interesting to the employes if it is to be read. If it contains too much company business it will not be read, so the effort is entirely wasted. If it contains only long, heavy articles, no matter how well they may be written, or how important the subjects dealt with may be both to the company and the employes, it will not be read by the majority.

To make it interesting the greater part of each issue must be devoted ot items that are of peculiar interest to the employes themselves. The employes must be made to feel, as far as possible, that it is their own publication and to accomplish that the company must be kept largely in the background. For one item dealing with purely company affairs there should be three dealing with the activities of the employes themseives. The employes' magazine should chronicle all the activities in which 25
the employes are interested. In the summer time they will have their ball games, field sports, picnics and other social and athletic events. In the winter they have bowling contests, indoor athletic meets, dances and other entertainments.

These events should be featured in the employes' magazine and if such stories are illustrated with plenty of pictures it will add to the interest. Publication of such activities may not appear of any direct benefit to a company, but they are. They are there for a definite purpose, which is to get the employes interested in the publication and insure its being read.

Some company publications seem to rely on their attractive appearance to arouse interest, rather than on the matter they contain. I believe that is a mistake. Fine paper and beautiful colored pictures will not take the place of interesting reading matter, for the employes know little and care less about the printer's art. They are interested in the little every day affairs in their daily lives and if such things are written in a sympathetic, human interest way they will be read and appreciated without respect to the quality of the paper on which they are printed. I do not mean by that, that a company publication should be cheap looking, my point is that more attention should be paid to the quality of the reading matter than to the dress in which it appears.

That an employes' magazine which is read all the way through, is an important factor in building up the morale of the working forces and creating a friendly feeling between a company and its employes, there is no doubt in my mind. If it is the right kind of a publication it is well worth what it costs the company.

Although the two kinds of company publications I have described are somewhat different in purpose, the scope of the first being much broader than that of the second, there is one important characteristic which applies with equal force to both. They must both be well edited if they are to arouse and sustain interest. Too little attention is given many times to that important part of the work. Preparation of the material should be done by a skilled writer, who not only knows how to write, but who understands and appreciates news values.

An engineer, for instance, may know everything about a machine and be able to describe every part in exact detail, but it does not follow that he is able to write about it in a way that will interest the reader. Some incident of daily occurrence may seem of no importance to the technical man who is accustomed to such happenings, but in the hands of a skilled writer, who knows the value of news, that incident may be made into a story worthy of space on the front page of any newspaper.

A thing that is worth doing, is worth doing well and that applies to the editing of a company publication. If the publication is left to some department head who has his own work to do and who has had no special training in writing, the result is bound to show in the quality of the work. It is a waste of time and money to issue a publication
26 that has every indication of being edited by the office boy. It will fail to interest those for whom it is intended.

If the company publication is the asset which I believe it is to the company, it is important that it should not be merely a piece of printed matter. It should show character and originality if it is to compete with other periodicals making a bid for attention. The worth while company publication is not produced with scissors and paste-pot. It must have an individuality of its own and that can be given it only by one who has special qualifications, training and experience in that line and who devotes time and attention to the work.

Chairman Brush:—The next speaker is Barron Collier, President of Barron G. Collier, Inc.: Mr. Collier is the Treasurer of the American Electric Railway Association, and the largest purchaser of car advertising space in the street cars in the United States. Mr. Collier and his associates carry on a highly organized and intelligent business at 42d street, from gold mines to Luna Park, Coney Island, and from an Island Golf Course and a hotel on the west coast of Florida to steam yachts and a prominent position in New York City in the business world. Mr. Collier has put his organization at the disposal of the Association when the need arose, and his intelligent development of car advertising has brought a large increase in returns from this source to the street railways, who have turned over their business to him. One of his interesting diversions is that of co-church member and fellow-worker with John D. Rockefeller at Pocantico Hills, N. Y.

Mr. Collier cannot be present as he is being sworn in as Deputy Police Commissioner in New York City. He would need no introduction if he were here, and his associate, Mr. E. C. Faber, has kindly consented to read his remarks for him. Mr. Faber is President of the Chicago, Aurora and Elgin Electric Railway Company.

27

Business Resorting to Issuance of Special Reports to Employees

Large Companies Take Workers into Confidence, Give Them Detailed Information About Operations, Income, Outgo—Fundamental Costs Set Forth in Simple Statements—Have Profound Effect on Employees and Public—Paper by MR. FRANZY EAKIN.

THIS *magazine is happy to publish the paper that follows, the substance of which was presented by* MR. FRANZY EAKIN, *vice-president and controller (it is spelled "comptroller" by his company) of the A. E. Staley Manufacturing Company of Decatur, Illinois, at a regional meeting of controllers in Indianapolis, on May 23, under the title, "Financial Reports to Employees." The paper describes what is believed to be a constructive movement to inform workers on a number of points concerning which much confusion has been created by recent economic and political developments.*

In this field MR. EAKIN *is a pioneer. He has been advocating wide use of the plan which is described here, and the fact that many large companies have thought well enough of it to try it indicates that it has much merit. It is a work that devolves largely upon the controller.*

—THE EDITOR.

During the last few months several large companies have issued a new type of accounting report. Several of these reports have been prepared especially for distribution to employees, some of them have been prepared for distribution to stockholders and employees, and in some cases the regular stockholders' report was sent to employees together with a special report or with a letter commenting upon various features of the annual report to stockholders.

A few years ago had the chief executive of any of these companies suggested to his board of directors that he desired to issue such a report to employees, he would probably have been subjected to severe criticism. Many of the top executives of our business enterprises have felt that it was inadvisable, if not dangerous, to publish such vital information concerning the operations of our companies. Many of them have felt that if such information were given to the employees it would be used as a basis for developing demands for increased wages, improved working conditions, and possibly for demanding a larger share in the management of the business.

From the position of maintaining that secrecy was desirable, to that of publishing full, complete, and intimate information, represents a substantial and radical change. The reasons for this change are of interest. During the past few years business has been subjected to many bitter attacks. In these attacks such information as was available has been misinterpreted and presented as proof that business was an enemy of employees, consumers, and government. These attacks have been so violent and in many cases so convincing that governments have sought to force upon business many regulations which business managements have known would operate against the public interests. Being under such pressure managers have sought means whereby they might make a counter attack. This counter attack has in part taken the form of "Financial Reports to Employees."

BUSINESS REPLIES TO CRITICISMS

In these reports the fundamental facts of businesses have been set forth in simplified balance sheets and profit and loss statements. In the process of simplification these statements have been made more complete and understandable than those which heretofore have been issued to stockholders. This has been accomplished in part by the use of the common language of every man, and in part by use of elementary but basic accounts to record the fundamental facts and relationships of business. In addition to these balance sheets and receipts and costs statements several of the reports have included discussions of such questions as "How do we earn our living?", "Who is the real boss?", "What distribution is made of funds received?", "Is competition wasteful?", and other questions of like nature.

In the June, 1937, issue of THE CONTROLLER I discussed a method of reporting profits in such a way as to set forth the economic significance of our business operations. In this article I wrote as follows:

> "Such accounting also reveals that business enterprises are but processes or facilities by which persons possessed of savings invest them in tools and other equipment and loan them to a group known as employes, who use them, together with their skill and knowledge, in the production of goods and services which are sold to customers. Or, stated in other words, the mutual dependency of customers, employes, and owners stands revealed for all to see."

And again:

> "The foregoing statement clearly reveals that profits are cost or wages, that they are paid by customers as a return to the owners, and it also reveals that if wages to employes or taxes to government are to be increased, the customers must pay more, or owners must be paid less. When put in this form all of the interested parties—customers, public, government, employes, and owners—are fully informed, that they may deal justly one with another and in such dealings find a method by which individual and national well-being may be advanced."

Through reports of the kind which **should** be made to employees, we can **establish** throughout our economy **knowledge** that only as people labor **and** produce does an economy prosper. **Further**, we can reveal so that all may **understand** that there is no conflict be**tween** capital and managers on one **hand** and employees on the other. As **we establish** an understanding of these **facts** we lay the groundwork for the **removal** of fear and establish a desire **which** will make itself felt that the un**sound** practices of our present govern**ment** be discontinued and that govern**ment** and business join in a coopera**tive** program whereby prosperity shall **be** created and maintained.

Unquestionably these reports are **having** a profound effect upon the **employees** and the public. Many re**ports** are being received which indi**cate** that employee relations have been **improved** and that the public under**standing** of business has tended to be**come** more favorable.

I shall now turn to an examination **of a** number of the financial reports **which** have been presented by several **companies** to their employees.

United States Steel Company

In early December of last year the United States Steel Company in its house organ, *U. S. Steel News*, published a nine-year statement of its operations.

This publication was heralded as an unprecedented one. It was news, commented upon by the press throughout our country. Together with this statement there was published a discussion entitled, "How We Earn Our Living." In the January, 1938, issue of the same house organ, this statement was republished together with another discussion entitled, "Who Pays Wages?"

The statement published by the United States Steel Company was in very simple form. Because it was probably the first statement published widely in this form, and because of the impression which it made upon executives of other companies, I am going to read you the form in full.

(See Form at Botton of Page)

FOUR POINTS EMPHASIZED

There are a few points which should be emphasized with respect to this statement. (1) That it states that all of the income was received from the public in exchange for goods and services. (2) That a considerable portion of this income was paid to other persons in exchange for goods and services purchased from him. (3) That of the balance remaining 85% was paid to employees in wages and salaries. (4) That the remaining portion together with a small amount of the capital was paid in interest and dividends as wages for the tools which were used by the employees in the production of goods and services that were sold to the public.

With these facts in mind it is quite easy to understand the conclusions which the United States Steel made:

> **"There is nothing mysterious about what United States Steel Companies do to earn a living. They are bound by exactly the same rules as those who work for them. They live on the money they get from the public in exchange for goods and services. That is their pay check."** 29

And again they state:

> **"All of us are dependent, one on the other. Only together can we earn a living."**

Further, in answer to the question which they posed, "Who Pays Wages?", they conclude:

> **"United States Steel does not actually pay any wages or salaries. It seems to pay them because it fills the pay envelops and writes the checks. But really it is only a paymaster. It can pay only out of the money paid to it. . . . . When a man is working for himself, he knows exactly where his wages come from—what he does and what he gets for doing it are tied together. . . . . United States Steel, as a paymaster, can distribute as wages only the money that comes to it from production. . . . . Wages cannot for long be paid at the expense of anyone. They can be—and have been—increased only by all producing more goods to share. Wages are paid by the public in the products which it uses and the public uses the products only when they are of a satisfactory quality and at a price which it wishes to pay. The public pays the wages."**

International Harvester Company

The 1937 annual report of the International Harvester Company makes a few statements that are of interest to employees. It reveals the total amount

January 1, 1928, to December 31, 1936
(000,000 omitted)

U. S. Steel received from the public in exchange for goods and services....		$5,921
This was disposed of as follows:		
Items over which U. S. Steel had no control:		
Goods and services purchased from others........................	$2,142	
Taxes	379	
Depreciation and depletion	457	2,978
(of which $87,000,000 was wages paid directly by U. S. Steel and not included in "Wages" below)		
Balance remaining (being 49.7% of the Gross Receipts)................		$2,943
Disposed of as follows:		
Wages and salaries (being 85% of "balance remaining").........		2,502
Leaving a balance of		$ 441
Disposed of as follows:		
Interest paid for the use of assets representing savings, the ownership of which is evidenced by bonds and mortgages	$ 77	
Dividends paid for the use of assets representing savings, the ownership of which is evidenced by preferred and common stock, being 13.7% of "balance remaining"	405	482
Leaving a deficit of		$ 41

provided from savings made on behalf of the owners by U. S. Steel during prior periods.

(The sum of $482,000,000 paid for the use of assets by U. S. Steel reduced to an average annual return on the average amount of assets used during the period amounts to 2.829% per year. Since $41,000,000 was withdrawn from prior earnings, the earned return was 2.497% per year.)

that was paid in salaries and wages and the total amount that was paid in taxes. It also discusses wage increases and certain other items that are of interest to employees as well as to stockholders. This report was issued under date of February 17, 1938.

Swift & Company

Another report which should be mentioned in this connection is the Year Book of Swift & Company issued December 20, 1937. This report contains in addition to the usual financial statements, information of great interest to the public and to employees. Among the subjects discussed there are three which are of great importance: (1) Is competition wasteful? (2) Consumers have the last word, and (3) The Swift & Company sales dol-
30 lar. In this last article the company states the distribution which was made of every dollar received by it from the sale of its products. The figures in the 1937 Year Book are for the year 1936. They are as follows:

		Cents
Paid to Producers (For Cattle, Calves, Hogs, Sheep, Lambs, Dairy and Poultry Products, etc.)		76.0
Paid to Employes		10.6
Paid to Manufacturers of Supplies		4.1
Paid to Railroad and Trucking Companies		3.4
Paid to Various Other Agencies:		
Banks and Bondholders	.2	
Federal, State, and Local Governments (Taxes)	.9	
Miscellaneous—Rent, Telegraph, Telephone, Advertising, Pensions, Insurance, and other small items	2.5	
		3.6
Depreciation (to be paid to manufacturers of new equipment		.8
		98.5
Balance remaining with Swift & Company as earnings		1.5
Total		100.0

The Detroit Edison Company

The Detroit Edison Company in its report for the year 1937 issued January 17, 1938, also made a new departure in giving information that is helpful to the public and to the employees in understanding the operations of a business enterprise. I quote in full one section of this report:

Income—Outgo

"Conforming to a recent fashion we itemize in brief our disbursement of gross earnings:

Payrolls	$14,329,714.31
Fuel for Power Houses and Heating Plants	6,648,013.72
Other Expense Items, Including Maintenance Materials	6,878,738.61
Taxes	7,703,986.77
Appropriated to Retirement Reserve, to replace working assets as they are worn out or become obsolete	7,730,800.00
Interest (What we have to pay during the year for the use of money invested in)	6,016,555.08
Dividends (our plant and equipment, about 4.2% of total invested)	7,612,529.13
Appropriation to Casualty and Contingency Reserve	44,741.25
Total	$56,965,078.87
Balance carried to Earned Surplus	2,293,666.34
Gross Earnings	$59,258,745.21

"In addition there was expended $15,-690,127.09 for the construction of new plant, paid for with funds retained in the business by appropriation to Retirement Reserve and the increase in Earned Surplus, and by drawing down cash balances and borrowing from banks."

Allied Chemical & Dye Corporation

The Eighteenth Annual Report of the Allied Chemical & Dye Corporation was issued March 17, 1938. In one paragraph the president of the company states a fundamental truth so concisely yet so clearly that all of us at least should remember it if not memorize it.

"Net income for the year was $24,770,-845. This is the amount which remained out of the company's gross receipts after providing for taxes, depreciation, materials consumed, salaries and wages and all other expenses, but without providing for any compensation for the use of the company's assets which represent the savings of the stockholders and are the necessary tools of the business. ***Net income thus represents compensation to the stockholders for the use of the tools just as salaries and wages represent compensation to employes for their labor, both of which are required for the production of goods for customers."***

(Italics by the writer)

Bethlehem Steel Corporation

The Bethlehem Steel Corporation in its house organ, *Bethlehem Review* dated March 5, 1938, gave a statement of its operations for the twelve-year period 1926-1937. The statement as presented was as follows:

		%
Received from the public in exchange for goods and services	$2,942,235,550	100.0
This was disposed of as follows:		
Wages and salaries	1,176,353,933	40.0
Materials, Supplies and Expense	953,731,861	32.4
(Other than wages, salaries and inbound R. R. Freight)		
Inbound Railroad Freight	320,710,475	10.9
Depreciation and Depletion	168,646,382	5.8
Interest Paid (Less other income)	68,403,856	2.3
Taxes paid	107,909,537	3.7
Paid to Stockholders	124,657,120	4.2
Balance (Retained in the Business)	21,822,386	.7

Illinois Central System

On April 14, 1938, the Illinois Central System wrote a new page into history of the relationships of our railroads to the public and to their employees. The Illinois Central System issued a special report to the "Employee Members of the Illinois Central System." Mr. Downs, president, introduced this statement in a way which I think worthy of quotation:

"It might have seemed strange a dozen or more years ago for the management of a railroad to offer a financial report to its employes in addition to that customarily given its stockholders; but events within recent memory have shown how deep a concern employes must have in the success or failure of the business enterprises which their jobs make possible and upon which their jobs depend. I therefore make no apology for taking you all into full business confidence regarding the operations and results of the Illinois Central System for 1937. This report supplements and interprets the report I must make to our stockholders at their annual meeting."

The statement which was presented by the Ilinois Central System was composed of twelve items and was a comparative statement for the years 1937 and 1936. The first five items in this statement pertain to the sources from which their revenues were received, which sources are: (1) Transporting freight, (2) Transporting customers, (3) Transporting baggage, mail, express, milk, (4) Switching, storage and related services, (5) Rents, interest and similar income.

The expenses were given in six items. They are: (1) Pay rolls (current operations), (2) Materials and charges related thereto, (3) Taxes, (4) Rent of equipment, joint track, and the like, (5) Rent of leased lines and related charges, (6) Interest on indebtedness.

The last item in the statement is net income, the difference between grand total of receipts and grand total of expenses. Each of the items was discussed in the special report to the employees in such everyday language that any person could understand it. All the technicalities of financial terms and of accounting procedures were eliminated. The facts of the operation were told in a straight-forward manner and in words that are commonly understood.

A. E. Staley Manufacturing Company

The company with which I am associated, the A. E. Staley Manufacturing Company, at Decatur, Illinois, has used two methods of presenting information to its employees. First, we use letters signed by the president of the company and directed to the employees. In the letters we attempt to state the facts as they are. In addition to these letters we use also a house organ for circulation only to our employees at Decatur. In this house organ we present statements and discussions of our affairs.

In both the letters and in the house organ we attempt to use words that are generally understood. The statement of operations which we give to the employees consists of the following items: (1) Receipts from customers, (2) Purchases of goods and services, (3) Salaries and Wages, (4) Interest and bond expense, (5) Taxes, (16) Rentals, (7) Depreciation, (8) Dividends on preferred stock, (9) Dividends on common stock, (10) Corporate savings or losses. In certain of our letters to employees we have explained the nature of the items that are included under each of these captions.

In a letter dated February 14, 1938, we gave to our employees a statement such as I have outlined, and with this letter we sent the employees a copy of the annual report which we made to our stockholders.

In our house organ we presented the balance sheet as contained in the annual report to the stockholders broken down so as to reveal the amount of investment per employee in the various assets used in the business and to show the source from which the funds invested in these assets were derived.

In our presentation of the balance sheet we describe plant account and capital account in the following manner:

Total original investment in lands, buildings, and equipment used in our operations	xxxx
Less the amount that has been deducted for depreciation and reinvested in various assets	xxxx
Present investment in tools	xxxx
Stockholders' original investment in the company	xxxx
Add: Investment of funds which could have been withdrawn as profits were earned	xxxx
Total investment of stockholders	xxxx

The Caterpillar Tractor Company

The Caterpillar Tractor Company under date of February 3, 1938, also made history in that it issued an annual report to stockholders and employees. The opening paragraphs of this report are worthy of quotation:

> **"This year we vary the form of previous annual reports by addressing this year's report to employes as well as to stockholders. Not only have employes many interests in common with stockholders, but it would seem that perhaps much good might come if the employes, as well as stockholders, were possessed of information regarding operations of the company, the better to weigh the various economic, social and political theories now being so generally discussed.**
>
> **"It is upon the men and women who make up factory, office and management staffs—all employes of the company—that the customer-appeal of our products depends. The employment of all of us, in turn, depends upon customer-satisfaction. The customer must be satisfied with the competitive quality and price of our products and must experience an economy in their use; otherwise, he will patronize someone else. In the final analysis it is from him that we get the money for materials, for wages, for taxes, and, last but not least, for profit, without which the enterprise cannot endure and employ."**

In this report the company discusses the balance sheet and income accounts and also gives considerable information with respect to engineering, products, labor relations, employment, and other subjects of interest to the employees. A number of illustrations and charts were used to assist both the stockholders and the employees in understanding the statements being made. In addition to the balance sheet in the regular accounting terms, a special balance sheet and income statement were included. These were entitled respectively, (1) Explanatory Statement of Assets, Liabilities and Net Worth, (2) Explanatory Statement of Income, Expenses, Profits, and Dividends.

31

In the explanatory statement of assets, each item of the balance sheet is described at some length. To illustrate, the item cash is described as:

> **"Cash in banks in the principal financial centers of the United States and in cities and towns in which the company has a factory or parts distributing depot. The amount is normally equivalent to the cash required for about two or three weeks of operations."**

The explanatory statement of income, expenses, profits and dividends is very simple and is also written in descriptive language. The statement consists of two items of income, four items of expense, one item of dividends, and the balance is described as:

> **"A balance which was retained in the business and used for expansion of employment during the year."**

The Johns-Manville Company

The Johns-Manville Company issued a special report to its employees. Mr. Brown, president of the company, in his letter to the employees which precedes the statement makes these statements:

> **"Our stockholders put their money into the company. In return, when business is good, they are paid 'dividends.' When**

business is bad the stockholders are 'laid off' in that they receive reduced dividends or sometimes no dividends at all.

"The jobholders put their work into the company. When business is good they receive regular pay and the opportunity to earn more in wages or salary. If business conditions force the company to slow down production, some jobholders have to be 'laid off,' in that hours may be reduced, pay may be cut or actual lay-offs may be necessary.

"It is the chief concern of the managers to try to plan for the best possible, uninterrupted annual wage or salary for both jobholder and stockholder. Then neither of them will have to be 'laid off.' Your company managers know that both stockholders and jobholders are dependent upon each other, and that neither could profit without the support and cooperation of the other."

This report of the Johns-Manville Company contains a rather complete analysis of its purchases, a statement of
32 its total income and how it was distributed, a balance sheet in descriptive language, a brief history of the company, and a discussion of several other items which were of special interest to the employees. The report has a number of illustrations which makes it very readable and increases its interest. After deducting from the total amount received from customers, the amount which was paid for materials and services related thereto, the balance in addition to being set forth in amounts is given in cents of each dollar. To quote from the report we have the following:

"Summing up then, each of the $39,-861,579 we added to the value of the raw materials and products bought for resale was divided in this way:

Wages and salaries	51	cents
Dividends	11½	cents
Depreciation and depletion	6	cents
Research	1½	cents
Addition to surplus	2	cents
Taxes	5	cents
All other expenses	23	cents
Total	$1.00	

This report of Johns-Manville Company makes one statement which is not contained in any of the reports which I have mentioned. It is stated in these words: "Here is what happened to the $39,861,579 which we added to the value of the raw materials and products bought for resale after they reached our plants . . . ."

The point to be emphasized here is that they speak of the value added to the raw materials and products after they reached the plants.

Monsanto Chemical Company

The last report which I shall discuss is that issued by the Monsanto Chemical Company, St. Louis, Missouri, under date of March 15, 1938. This report is entitled, "Employees' Edition of the Annual Report for the year 1937." Probably the opening sentence will tell you more of its subject matter and attitude than can be told in any other way. On the first page of the report there is a very fine picture of Mr. Edward M. Queeny, president of the company. The first sentence under this picture is: "Let us sit down together and talk for a little while about our business." The balance of the report is just that—a discussion with the employees, of their joint business. A number of illustrations are used. The report is printed in two colors which increases its interest and readability. In the course of the discussion, Mr. Queeny develops in a very fine manner the answer to two questions, (1) Who is our real boss?, and (2) What is back of my job?

In answer to the first question he reveals that it is the customer who in the final analysis provides employment for the employees and stockholders. In answer to the second question he shows that each employee has on the average approximately $10,000 worth of assets provided by the stockholders, for use in earning his salary or wage and paying a return to the owners of the tools used. This report is deficient in only one respect. It does not contain a statement of income and expense. However, it does contain an explanatory balance sheet in which the various assets and liabilities are described in terms easily understood.

SUMMARY OF REPORTS

Review of several of the financial reports which have been issued to employees discloses at least five points worthy of consideration. These are:

(1) That these reports are written in simple language. The technicalities of the financial men and the jargon of accountants are not used. It is the language of one common man talking with another common man.

(2) That the financial statements, that is, balance sheets and income and expense statements, are complete, yet brief and concise. They are reduced to the fundamental elements.

These fundamental elements of the income and expense or profit and loss statement are:

Receipts		
Receipts from goods and services sold to customers		$ x
Costs		
Purchases of goods and services to be used in production.....	$ x	
Payments to employees—Salaries and wages	x	
Taxes paid to local, state, and Federal Government	x	
Depreciation to be used to replace the plant as worn out and obsoleted	x	
Rents and Royalties	x	
Interest and related expenses....	x	
Dividends paid to stockholders as rental for the assets or tools which their investment has provided for use of the business..	x	
Total cost		x
Savings retained in the business to provide for expansion and to assure the permanency of the business		$ x

These fundamental elements have been recognized in the best of the statements which have been issued to employees. However, unfortunately, certain accountants in preparing these statements have not analyzed carefully their costs to determine the fundamentals and have therefore included other items and sometimes have grouped a number of items together under one caption, "Other Costs and Expenses." This failure to reduce to the fundamentals serves to confuse and detracts from the value of these statements.

These receipts and cost statements are a consolidation of the accountants' profit and loss and surplus accounts. In our regular financial reports these two accounts are reported in separate statements, but in these reports they are consolidated into one statement and the remarkable thing about it is that the consolidated statement, i.e., the statement of receipts and costs reveals a greater number of fundamental facts and reveals them more clearly than does the traditional financial statement.

(3) An endeavor is made to remove the mystery which generally surrounds corporate activites and to reveal that the operations of a company are in their fundamental aspects similar to the operations of an individual.

(4) An attempt is made to show that the assets are tools used by the employees, that these tools are furnished by stockholders, and that any return in the form of interest or dividends is but a rental or wage paid for the use of such tools. Furthermore, it is emphasized throughout these reports that the income of the company, which income provides the salaries and wages of the employees, results from labor on the part of the managers and the employees using the tools provided by the stockholders.

(5) There is no propaganda in these statements; there is no attempt to deceive. An earnest endeavor is made that all may understand the facts, and in such understanding may not be deceived by those outside business who would gain political and economic advantages.

In nearly, if not all of the financial reports to employees that I have seen, there has been a frank acknowledgment by the management that the employees have an interest in the business. A number of the reports speak of stockholders, managers, and employees as being dependent one on another.

Source of National Income

A few minutes ago I referred to the statement made in the Johns-Manville report concerning value added. While all of the reports which I have discussed and probably a great many others which have been issued during the past few months have made a substantial contribution to our understanding, I recommend that one further statement be incorporated into these reports. This is a statement which would reveal quite simply and quite clearly that the income and distribution of our business enterprises is produced by this added value, and that income produced by each business enterprise is a part of the national income.

In speaking at the annual meeting of the Controller's Institute of America in New York last October I presented a form of statement which accomplishes that which I have just recommended. The statement consists of only eight items. These items are the items that are used by statisticians and economists in measuring national income paid out and national income produced.

The statement follows:

National Income Paid Out and National Income Produced

Payments to Employees—	
Salaries, wages, pensions, and other compensation	xxxx
Payments to government—	
Federal, state, and local taxes	xxxx
Payments for use of assets—	
Rents and royalties	xxxx
Interest and related expenses	xxxx
Dividends	xxxx
Total National Income Paid out	xxxx
Corporate Savings	xxxx
Total National Income Produced	xxxx

In discussing this statement I said:

"National income, in all its aspects, is merely the sum of the income produced and paid out by private businesses. This statement for a single business enterprise reveals all the elements of national income. Of greater importance than this is that it reveals the source of income. The source of national income exists in private businesses producing goods and services used by the people."

Need and Benefits

I know of no better way to emphasize the need for, and to disclose the advantages of financial reports to employees than to quote a part of Mr. Merryle S. Rukeyser's column printed last Wednesday, May 18, 1938. These statements were made by Mr. Rukeyser in discussing the report of the Standard Oil Company of Indiana, just issued to its employees. Mr. Rukeyser said:

"Political business baiting and labor union agitation are rapidly changing the attitude of corporation executives toward their employes.

"With their backs to the walls, executives are no longer eager to gild the lily. But they are eager to rest their case before the bar of public opinion on the unvarnished truth.

"Accordingly, they are using new and greatly simplified accounting tools to tell employes and the public about the authentic nature of their operations.

"The old attitude of corporate secrecy and mystery is rapidly going out of the window. Accordingly, a significant new fashion of issuing financial reports to employes as well as to stockholders is currently developing.

"Corporate executives are coming to see that the best way to discredit demagogic lies about them is to give the low-down in the form of elementary arithmetic.

"The United States Steel Corporation 33
got the new vogue well underway last December, and since that time others have rapidly fallen into line.

"Sometimes executives do not seem fully aware of the power behind the new tool. Some think of it merely as a means for making old accounting technique more intelligible to the laymen. But there is more than that behind it. It is also a device for answering the whole Marxian credo against private enterprise, making it clear that what is commonly termed profit is in reality a wage payment for the iron man, consisting of machines and other tools.

"Every time a business executive thus takes employes into his confidence he not only provides an intelligent basis for collective bargaining, but also helps to eradicate misconceptions which are detrimental to national progress."

In Conclusion

It appears not out of place to quote from the introduction to Adam Smith's famous work, "Wealth of Nations":

"The annual labour of every nation is the fund which originally supplies it with all the necessaries and conveniences of life which it annually consumes, and which consist always either in the immediate produce of that labour, or in what is purchased with that produce from other nations."

That which he said and that which is true is this: The only source from which the goods and services necessary to maintain life and desirable to make life enjoyable can be secured, is found in the work of the people of an economy. Money, prices, are secondary factors. They are important, but they can have no being and no importance unless preceded by products, the result of labor.

Adam Smith stated a fundamental truth. Labor, the work of man, is the only source of individual and national well-being. When we fail, as we now are, to recognize this, and attempt by price manipulation, by creation of debts, by shortening of working hours, and by restriction of production to provide plenty, we deceive ourselves. The end of such actions is universal and abject poverty.

In about 1845 Thomas Carlyle, investigating the reasons for a depression then prevailing in England, made an analysis of business operations. Included in his analysis was an examina-
34 tion of the relationship of owners, managers, and employees. He appeared to have concluded that if the problems of this relationship could be solved, depressions, with their attendant unemployment and poverty, could be avoided or at least greatly minimized. Towards the end of his writings on this subject he asks a question and indicates an answer which unquestionably, in the light of our present knowledge, is the right answer. I quote:

> **"A question arises here: Whether,—, your Master-Worker may not find it possible, and needful, to grant his workers permanent *interest* in his enterprise and theirs? So that it become, in practical result, what in essential fact and justice it ever is, a joint enterprise; all men, from the Chief Master down to the lowest Overseer and Operative, economically as well as loyally concerned for it?—The answer,—, is perhaps, Yes;—."**

Thomas Carlyle suggested the correct answer to the question, "Who has interest in business?" The interest of the lowest ranking worker and of the manager and of the owner is mutual. Each is dependent upon the other. Their enterprise is a joint business venture.

This does not mean that all of the interests and rights of the owners, managers, and employees are identical. It merely means that if either is to secure the benefits and returns which he desires all of them must work together harmoniously and cooperatively.

Labor—work, is the only solution to our problems. Therefore, let us do our reporting so that all may understand, and in understanding, produce plenty that we may live abundantly!

A Partial List of Companies Which Have Published Financial Information to Their Employees:

United States Steel Corporation
International Harvester Company
Swift & Company
The Detroit Edison Company
Allied Chemical & Dye Corporation
Bethlehem Steel Corporation
Illinois Central System
A. E. Staley Manufacturing Company
Caterpillar Tractor Company
Johns-Manville Company
Monsanto Chemical Company
Standard Oil Company of Indiana
Western Electric Company
Union Bag & Paper Corporation
Armstrong Cork Company
Westinghouse Electric and Manufacturing Company
Yale and Towne Manufacturing Company
Jewel Tea Company
McGrath Sand and Gravel Company

MONTHLY BULLETIN

Illinois Manufacturers' Costs Association

No. 142 | 120 S. LA SALLE ST., CHICAGO, ILL. | February, 1939

TELLING YOUR STORY TO YOUR EMPLOYES

Many Far-sighted Manufacturers Are Giving Intimate Details in Annual Statements

EMPLOYES are being taken into the confidence of their employers to an increasing extent. Effort is being made by many companies to present data to employes in clear and intelligible language.

The reasons are obvious.

For several years business management has been the subject of bitter attack.

Its policies have been misinterpreted and maligned.

An attempt has been made to create the impression that huge profits were being made at the expense of the wage earner and that a small group of stockholders were becoming wealthy at the expense of a large group of employes and that restrictive and punitive legislation was needed in order to more equitably distribute the wealth.

Government Control Threatened

The purpose of such attacks has obviously been to lay the foundation for governmental control and ultimately governmental ownership of productive enterprise. So the imperative need of informing employes has strongly appealed to many industries.

How can a statement be prepared by industrial managers that will present a true and intelligent picture to employes as well as stockholders?

One type which has attracted much attention is a special analysis of the preceding year's operations of the company that is not too technical. It gives something of the company's history, its sources of material, the markets for its products, and when there is more than one manufacturing plant—photographs of the various plants and descriptions of their particular products.

Laclede Steel Company's Model Report

A report of the Laclede Steel Company of St. Louis, Missouri, is typical of such statements. It consists of a 16-page brochure with some of the products at the various plants illustrated, including ingots, hot rolled strip, wire rods, reinforcing bars and bar mats.

It also has a map of the United States showing the states in which the products are distributed, including all but four states in the Union, also Mexico, Canal Zone, Puerto Rico, Greece, Alaska, China and Hawaii.

The report shows that the products are used in many fields, including railroads, buildings, highways, agriculture, oil and gas, containers, machinery, export and automotive.

The explanatory balance sheet of the company lists under Assets—Cash, Customers Owe Us for Products We Sold Them, Inventories, Other Assets, Real Estate, Buildings, Machinery and Equipment, Bills Paid in Advance, and Total Assets.

The Liabilities include such items as: To Pay for Raw Materials and Wages, To Pay Federal, State, and Local Taxes, Notes Due, Reserve for Maintenance, Operations and Other Contingencies, Capital Stock — Investment of Stockholders in Common Stock, and Savings from Past Earnings Reinvested in the Business.

Where a Manufacturer's Money Goes

There is a significant diagram showing "Where the Money Goes." It is divided as follows:

Retained in Business	0.4%
Salaries of Officers	1.2%
Taxes	2.3%
Dividends	4.1%
Miscellaneous Expense	7.1%
Fuel and Power	7.5%
Wages and Salaries	28.2%
Raw Materials	49.2%
	100.0%

From Company Policies which occupies one page of the report, the following is extracted:

"1. THE CUSTOMER:

A. We must give him the kind of steel he wants.

B. And deliver it to him when he wants it.

C. Obtaining for the steel a price that is fair both to him and us.

"2. THE EMPLOYES:

A. We expect to pay our employes the best wages possible consistent with the Company's competitive situation. This has always been and will continue to be a definite Company policy.

B. We must endeavor to keep the continuity of employment at the highest level possible.

"3. THE STOCKHOLDERS AND NOTE-HOLDERS:

The people whose money is invested in our plants and our steel-making operations are entitled to a steady return or 'interest' on their money, since it is to them we must look for further funds when needed. Our earnings must be adequate to pay promptly our obligations when they are due.

"4. THE GOVERNMENT:

Little has been said in this booklet concerning taxes. We all know, however, that the Federal, State and Local Governments are paid taxes in various ways during the year. We must earn enough to help support our government in carrying on its work in education, relief, national defense, and many other activities. This, as a financial obligation, is important and necessary*."

Similar reports prepared by other companies which have been mentioned by the National Industrial Conference Board include:

- Armstrong Cork Company
- Caterpillar Tractor Company
- Illinois Central Railroad
- International Harvester Company
- Johns-Manville Corporation
- Monsanto Chemical Company
- Westinghouse Electric & Mfg. Company
- Yale & Towne Mfg. Company

The National Industrial Conference Board has undertaken to go still further. It has endeavored to construct a report of all industrial concerns in this country . . . a report of industrial management to stockholders and wage earners, and the entire American public . . . based upon official sources. Such a report is contained in the following table:

COMBINED REPORT OF AMERICAN INDUSTRIAL MANAGEMENT TO EMPLOYEES AND STOCKHOLDERS, ALL MANUFACTURING CORPORATIONS, OPERATING STATEMENT FOR 1935

Income:				
1.	We billed our customers for products purchased from us	$46,055,311,000		
2.	From which we had to deduct for bad debts	197,460,000		
3.	Leaving us a net return from sales of	$45,857,851,000		
4.	We received dividends from other corporations amounting to	613,164,000		
5.	And interest, rents, and income from other sources amounting to	1,258,776,000		
6.	Which gave us a total income to work with of	$47,729,791,000	= 100.0%	
Disbursements:				
7.	We paid others for materials, fuel, transportation supplies and other expenses	$33,398,041,000	70.0%	
8.	We set aside to replace wearing out plant and equipment	1,416,415,000	3.0%	
9.	And paid interest for borrowed money and rent for leased property	624,853,000	1.3%	
10.	While government tax collectors required	1,315,190,000	2.8%	
11.	This left for employees, management and stockholders	$10,975,292,000	23.0%	= 100.0%
12.	Our employees received in salaries and wages	8,041,706,000		73.3%
13.	The management of the Corporations received for services	812,046,000		7.4%
14.	Leaving for stockholders net earnings of	2,121,540,000		19.3%
15.	Cash dividends paid to stockholders amounted to	2,193,481,000		
16.	Leaving a deficit draft on capital of	$ 71,941,000		

After deducting for bad debts, American industry in 1935 had $47,729,791,000 income with which to carry on its business, comments the National Industrial Conference Board. Of this amount, 70 per cent, or about 33⅓ billion dollars, was spent for materials, fuel, advertising, transportation, and other such goods and services. A large portion of this amount constituted wage payments by the companies furnishing these goods and services, but this wage disbursement is not included as wages in this statement because these amounts were not paid as wages by the reporting companies.

There remained about 14⅓ billion dollars for all other demands of industrial operation. Some of this, 3 per cent of total income, was set aside to replace plant, machinery and equipment when it should become necessary to replace it—what is generally called depreciation. Interest on borrowed funds and return for leased property claimed another 1.3 per cent. Taxes required by Government took 2.8 per cent.

Employes Received 73.3 Per Cent

This left 23.0 per cent, or nearly 11 billion dollars, for payment to employes, management and stockholders. Considering this 11 billion dollars as 100 per cent, employes earning wages and salaries, not including officers of the companies, received 73.3 per cent or nearly three-quarters of the total. This amounted to over 8 billion dollars. Company officers received 812 million dollars, or 7.4 per cent, almost exactly one-tenth of the amount paid out for other wages and salaries. Stockholders in all the corporations, which include many groups such as insurance companies, employe pension and investment funds, individual employe investors, those dependent on small incomes from investments, as well as banks and wealthy individuals, received 19.3 per cent, or a little over 2 billion dollars.

Here a significant fact becomes evident. If the amounts paid in wages and salaries to employes, in salaries to company officers, and in dividends to stockholders, are totaled, this total exceeds the amount left for division among these groups by $71,941,000. Wages and salaries are paid first, and dividends become available only after wages and salaries have been paid. This makes it appear that nearly 72 million dollars were paid in dividends that were not earned during the year. Since this is a combined report for 91,676 corporations, what actually occurred was that while some companies made profits—and these were the companies that paid most of the dividends—others suffered losses, and when the total profits and total losses are set off against each other there is an excess of losses of nearly 72 million dollars. It was primarily the companies that made profits that declared dividends.

*Taxes, however, are increasing at an alarming rate. One hundred and fifty typical concerns paid taxes in 1937 of $631,000,000, or twice that of 1932 and 19% more than in 1936.

37

Annual Report to Employees

By

L. W. BENNETT.

A few big Companies are now placing Company facts and figures before their employees. If more would do this there would be a greater appreciation of the rights of Shareholders, Bondholders and investors in general.

The employee will have greater pride in his job when he realizes the amount of money invested to make his job possible. The annual Report as given to Shareholders is of no value for this purpose; but it can be used as the base from which the employees' statement is prepared.

There are many ways in which the information can be presented and will depend in part upon the business in question. The Balance Sheet, however, can always be used and on the Asset side should be a separate column showing the amount of each item and total which is invested in each employee's job. The Balance Sheet should, however, be written in a language which the employee can understand. That is, do not say "Accounts Receivable", but say "Owing Us For Goods Shipped". A statement showing how each Dollar of Income was distributed is also of value and in many cases will surprise the Executive as well as the employees.

One United States Company—The Container Corporation—recently gave a 32-page booklet to every employee. There was a chart that classified the time of the average week. This showed that in a week the company worked:—

Two days to pay for raw materials.
One day for expenses.
One day for wages.
Half day for selling and management.
Quarter day for depreciation.
One and a quarter days for taxation.
One hour and forty minutes for dividends.

The Consolidated Paper Corporation Limited sent a report this year to each of their 3,860 employees, showing that it required a total of $22,851.00 to provide a job for each employee. Information such as this gives the employees an appreciation of the problems of Management and of the rights of Shareholders.

Periodical Reports to Employees

By JAMES W. IRWIN, *Assistant to the President, Monsanto Chemical Company, St. Louis, Mo.*

JAMES W. IRWIN

To make the special employee edition of the annual financial report really informative and understandable, Monsanto has given considerable thought and care to its preparation. Even the advertising agency is called in for counsel on art and typography. To sustain interest, this annual version is supplemented by interim reports published in the employees' magazine. The way employees have reacted, Mr. Irwin believes, has been most gratifying.

AT THIS time of the year it is likely that major executives of hundreds of companies are turning their attention to the preparation of annual reports to stockholders, and perhaps to specially written and illustrated interpretive reports for employees.

It will be recalled that last spring, spreading with the speed of the miniature golf fad of 1929, employee financial reports became epidemic. Many companies published excellent interpretations. Some did a halfway job. Others put out mediocre reports.

Such a variation in quality and content was no doubt due to lack of experience, and it is also quite true that there is no pattern to be followed for certain success with such statements. And there is no assurance that success will be attained with the best report, because, like advertising, the effect is intangible and there is no sure way by which reaction can be gauged.

Monsanto was in a rather fortunate position when it was decided to rewrite the annual financial statement and the president's report to shareholders and, in that rewritten version, to attempt answers to many of the questions on Monsanto policy and status for the enlightment of the men in our 12 plants here and abroad, the chemists in our research and analytical laboratories, and the secretaries, stenographers, file clerks, and others in our offices.

The report, which had an original press run ample to take care of all our employees, wherever located, and a few extra copies for their friends, was considered only as an item in a program that Edgar Monsanto Queeny, president of the company, had been following for 10 years in endeavoring to throw more light on Monsanto policies and balance sheets. The purpose was to take shareholders, employees, and customers alike back of the scenes and let them see in detail the reason behind certain policies decided upon by management, as well as to acquaint them with the dollars-and-cents status of the company in sales volume, taxes, reserves, physical assets, and all the other routine classifications of a company, large or small.

This disposition to lift the curtain was first evidenced in 1928 immediately after Mr. Queeny had become president. A study of financial statements and annual reports to shareholders from that time on shows a steady evolution of improvement, each year's report giving a more understandable statement of the company's status, accomplishments, and problems than that of the year before.

Personnel Not "Bowled Over"

In addition, *Monsanto Magazine*, the company publication sent regularly to employees, shareholders, and customers, had carried signed statements by the president of the company. In those statements were discussed current problems having an effect upon the company or upon its employees, shareholders, or customers, as individual groups or collectively.

With this background, such departure from routine as a special edition of the financial report did not bowl over the personnel of the company because they had been accustomed for years to receive authentic information from the head of the organization.

As to the routine of the report, the preparation was simple. Mr. Queeny, with the assistance of Charles Belknap, executive vice-president; John W. Livingston, vice-president [in] charge of manufacture; Fre[d] A. Ulmer, treasurer; Dani[el] M. Sheehan, comptroller; ar[d] managers of some of o[ur] larger plants, analyzed th[e] regular financial report [to] shareholders and asked them selves those questions whic[h] they would like answered [if] they were plant, laborator[y] or office employees.

On this premise, they se[t] about finding the answe[rs] and stating them in such [a] way that those employees who wer[e] not financially minded could obta[in] facts from the cold figures and un familiar statistics.

After this advance work, Mr. Queen[y] wrote the report, circulated it for crit cism, called in artists from the adve tising agency, and with them decide[d] what illustrations should be used ar[d] what typographical style and forma[t] should be followed. It was then sent [to] press, for a total of 30,000 copies aft[er] the second and third printings had bee[n] made.

It is probable that most readers [of] the EXECUTIVES SERVICE BULLETI[N] have seen the report. While the ide[a] was by no means original with Mon santo, reports of a similar nature b[y] other companies having preceded it b[y] weeks, requests came in from shar[e] holders, customers, and competitor[s] and from other companies for from on[e] to 100 copies.

Employees reacted in various ways, these reactions being learned throug[h] the daily contacts of our plant an[d] office supervisory personnel with th[e] men and women in their departments. Monsanto is fortunate in having [a] policy of management under whic[h] operating executives are seldom shifte[d] from one city to another, the resu[lt] being that they have an unusually wid[e] acquaintanceship with their men. Th[is] means that their men regard them a[s] friends and not as bosses and therefor[e] speak freely in their presence.

It is rather difficult to gauge the[ir] reactions precisely, but we believ[e] bout 25 percent read the report thor-ughly and got something from it, 25 ercent read it and obtained nothing, 5 percent scanned it, and 25 percent id not read it at all.

But that is not disheartening. If nly 10 percent had actually read it, hat 10 percent now has a clearer pic-ure of the company and its policies, nd understands a little bit better the nterdependence of the company with heir daily activities and future, and ow all gain when industry is success-ul and all lose when industry is nsuccessful.

There is no question in our minds ut that the report was read by and as informative to a large percentage f the members of families of our em-loyees, and in many instances passed n to and discussed with neighbors and iends employed in other industries or n other businesses.

Issued Interim Reports

Following through in 1938, em-loyees were given a six-month report n the September issue of *Monsanto Magazine*, and a nine-month report in he November issue, both over Mr. ueeny's signature.

The reasoning that sponsored these eriodical or interim reports is self-pparent. Naturally, it is not to be xpected that an employee—or, for hat matter, anyone else—will feel sus-ained interest or acquire an under-tanding of financial statements and perating results if the report should e given to him only once a year. This bound to be the case, no matter how ell set up and informative the annual tatement may be made. The employee as other things to think about, too. o it is only good sense to restate the acts, to repeat information in different ords and ways, and to report develop-ents, making sure that the method of resentation is such as to receive favor-ble attention from all the people.

The two periodical reports were writ-en in an easy and simple style. The rst was introduced by Mr. Queeny ith the statement that "We are past he middle of the year, and, as is ustomary, I have reported our present usiness conditions to Monsanto stock-olders and so will report them to you." brief description of business condi-ons was followed by the profit and loss statements, after which there was given information relating to activities and developments in several of the Monsanto plants. The statement closed with the hope for still better business in the fall. The entire presentation covered only one printed page.

The message at the end of the third quarter was practically the same in content and in length, carried an opti-mistic note, and closed with the hope that "through understanding and co-operation, general unemployment will be reduced and our spirit of optimism will become a reality."

THE articles published in the BULLETIN *reflect the opinions of the authors and not necessarily the viewpoint of the Policyholders Service Bureau.*

Our plans for 1939 call for a report along the same lines as the one for 1938 —a separate brochure. Quarterly re-ports will be published in *Monsanto Magazine* in April, July, and October. In addition, we plan, at this writing, to have a sound motion picture version of the employee report for showing to employee groups and to clubs in our operating communities. This project now is in the idea stage, and our think-ing has not reached the actual out-lining of approach or technique.

Summing up the results after nine months of detached observation since the publication of the report, the man-agement believes most definitely that it is advantageous to any company to make a special report to employees. The management feels that a stock-holders report is used mainly by market analysts in assembling their advice to investors. Market analysts want cold figures and statistics. What they must have to reach conclusions has not the value to either the employee or the stockholder that the employee version offers.

But Monsanto experience shows that one policy must be followed very care-fully. The employee version must give all if not more facts than does the regu-lar report, and the employee must be given the opportunity to receive the regular stockholder report if he so de-sires. Only through such a policy can frankness and understanding between employee and employer be furthered.

. L. I. CO. PRESS—10769—PRINTED IN U.S.A.

REPORTING RATIONALES

In the following three papers (one Australian and two British) we find, amongst other subjects, discussions of rationales for reporting to employees drawn from the 1950s, 1960s, and 1970s. Keith Yorston (1959), President of the New South Wales Division of the Australian Society of Accountants, argues for the provision of maximum information to interested parties, including employees. He considers reporting rationales based upon management's moral obligation to inform, employees' decision-making needs, employees' commitment of time and skill to the organization, and the need to foster better understanding between employees and management. Yorston goes on to consider report producer and recipient reactions and methods of reporting.

Anderson (1961) argues for the provision of financial information to employees as suppliers of labor, just as information is provided to investors as suppliers of capital. Such provision is said to be influenced by trade unions, legislation, and public opinion. Anderson considers particular merits and demerits of reporting to employees and then considers some approaches.

Dyson (1973) argues that corporate reporting is biased in favor of the shareholder. He argues for employee entitlements to such information on the basis of their larger personal commitment of time and effort to the organization. As a result he proposes the "employee audit."

These papers are noteworthy for the substantial range of rationales which they identify in support of this form of reporting. Their arguments predate virtually all subsequent rationales advanced by authors who followed them from the mid-1970s onwards.

Reporting Financial Information to Employees

The twentieth annual research lecture in the University of Melbourne, endowed by the Australian Society of Accountants, delivered by R. KEITH YORSTON, O.B.E., B.COM., F.A.S.A. *(President of the N.S.W. Division of the Society), on* 30 *September,* 1959.

ONE result of the industrial revolution in England in the eighteenth century was that aggregations of capital to provide factories and machinery became more common. A further and natural result was a general increase in the number of employees in the typical industrial unit. Both the aggregations of capital and the increase in the number
42 of employees in a single business entity have been intensified in this century, and in many industries appear to be a natural development.

The former of the "effects" of the industrial revolution mentioned led to the invention of the limited liability company, from which arose the concept of "accountability" to shareholders by the directorate and management of companies. This sense of "accountability" gave impetus to the growth of the accountancy profession. Both the provisions of the company statute and the activities of our profession recognise this "accountability" to members of companies. The members of companies, as the owners of the corporate enterprise, are entitled legally and morally to an account of stewardship.

This paper is an enquiry as to whether any such "accountability" exists, or should exist, by the directorate and managements of companies, to those comprising the work force of a company.

Legally no such "accountability" exists. Employees of a company, unless they also be shareholders, are not entitled by the provisions of the company statute to information as to the result of operations or financial health of the company. Is it in the interests of the company as a whole that there should emerge some measure of "accountability" to employees? Is it in the interests of an individual company itself that employees should be regularly apprised of the progress and financial condition of a company? If the answer to this question is in the affirmative — it then follows, how is such information to be supplied and what should it comprise?

One of the greatest obligations that rests upon accountants, both as individuals and as members of an organised profession, is that of acting in the interests of those who as shareholders, employees or vendors entrust their savings, their time, their products to the care of others. Such an obligation exists whether we be in the public or commercial practice branch of our profession. Employees, and others, may be unable to measure the quality of our stewardship. This does not obviate or vary our obligation — if such an obligation does in fact exist.

One of the hallmarks of members of a profession, and we seek to have accountancy recognised as a profession, is the unwillingness of its members to seek reward at the expense of others due to ignorance. Confidence is being placed increasingly in the members of the accountancy profession. Ours is a profession of trust and privilege. The basis of our work is integrity. Has our profession any "accountability" to employees of companies, even to those unable to "appreciate" the results of such "accountability"? Acceptance of an obligation, if such exists, is the duty of members of a profession.

Before considering the problem expressed, it is obvious that the term "employees" is one of wide variation and of quite different requirements as to financial information about the corporation which employs them. Female operatives in, say, a textile mill, who require a "job" for a few years until marriage "couldn't care less" as we say, about the progress of the company which supplies their wages week after week. At the other end of the scale, we could put the financial executives of large enterprises who are personally, as well as from the company angle, interested in the company's progress and stability.

I consider it beyond the scope of this paper to determine which employees or which class of employees should be supplied with financial information. The employees of each organisation will be either interested or not interested in the company's financial affairs. It is my view that those interested should be given the maximum of information. This observation particularly applies to "key" personnel. No harm can result from supplying information to those in the "not interested" class. The fact that they are even "remembered" by the "management" may do good even if the financial information supplied is not understood.

Admittedly a majority of employees may be disinterested in the financial operations of their employing company, but it is possible that if they were encouraged to be interested, such interest would react to the benefit of both the company and themselves. Might not the supplying of information make employees feel that they are one section of a team? The only objections I can see to giving financial information to employees are: the information may be misunderstood; it may be misrepresented; the information may provide knowledge to competitors of the company.

As employees comprise such a large segment of the population, one purpose which will be achieved by supplying financial information to employees will be to educate a considerable proportion of the population about the private enterprise system. On the grounds alone that the misconception existing regarding the earnings of corporate ventures will be decreased, the supplying of information to employees can be supported. If the private enterprise system is to persist, it requires explanation and employees present an excellent medium for such explanation. Proper explanation should encourage enthusiasm for the system. It would seem natural that employees should evidence more interest in an organisation which employs them if they know something about its operations and results, than if they do not. As there are always more employees than there are managements, and often more employees than there are shareholders, it seems that if we are to succeed as an industrial nation we are at present neglecting to give en- 43
lightenment to the greatest number of people whose very security and standard of living depends upon the success of their companies.

Some years ago, with the assistance of three companies, a questionnaire was sent by me to employees seeking their views on the financial statements issued by their company. Asked what information they would like, as employees, to be included in the financial statements, they brought forth answers of which the following are typical:—

> "How much each share is worth."
> "Further information in profit and loss account."
> "Information regarding waste of materials, etc."
> "A straight-out statement of how much the firm's profits are and how much it owes the bank."

The request to suggest how the company's financial statement might be made more intelligible elicited the following replies:—

> "Comparisons should be made of the results of firms of a similar nature."
> "Too much detail—state plain facts."
> "Such statements as 'authorised capital,' etc., could be indexed inside the cover and their meanings briefly stated."
> "Break down of the big words."
> "One page in simple language about how much profit was made would be sufficient for the ordinary worker."

But most answers to this section of the questionnaire asked for explanations of the financial statements in a simpler form.

As this paper is of a research nature it is concerned with a critical examination of basic assumptions and it is my view that we as accountants, acting as part of the management team, should assume a moral obligation to see that financial information is supplied to employees. I would suggest that an individual who gives of his time and talents to an organisation is entitled to more than his weekly or monthly pay cheque. I suggest he is entitled, at least, to the same financial information that a holder of shares is awarded by the company statute. Admittedly the degree and probably the quantum of financial information supplied
44 will depend upon the status of the employee in the organisation. All should, I suggest, have available to them enough information to be able to gauge for themselves, or to have a person skilled in accounting interpret for them, the financial progress and financial condition of the company which employs them. Should a shareholder be in a better position to change his investment than an employee to change his employment? Is it not good employee relations to supply information to employees to make them feel they are a part of a team? Surely on moral grounds the holder of one hundred 5/- shares in a company is not of more consideration to the management of the company than an employee who may give years of his labour, even in some cases his whole working existence, to the company.

The moral obligation of an employing organisation to supply financial information to employees may also be substantiated on the grounds of the notion of "permanent" employment which both the employer and employee tend to create. Both the employer and the employee desire to avoid "labour turnover" and this desire leads towards permanency of employment. In the larger organisations the provision of amenities, provident and superannuation funds, is made for the express purpose of avoiding labour turnover. The notion of permanent employment is engendered by the organisation and adopted by the employee. This notion of permanency of employment carries with it, I suggest, the obligation to supply employees with financial information as to the operations and conditions of the employing organisation.

Loyalty to the organisation and long association with it leads to recruitment of employees from families already employed. This, I suggest, adds to the moral obligation.

I have referred to the moral obligation to keep employees informed about the financial condition of the employer. An employee's livelihood is affected favourably or adversely by the progress or retrogression of the organisation employing him. In theory, an employee is at liberty to change his employment but in practice his ability to do so is restricted. The demand for his particular professional or technical skill may not be great; changes of locality may be involved with attendant costs and the severing of valued associations; the accumulation of sick leave and long service leave and similar matters may be lost by a change.

The employee's job is the centre of his existence; his hopes, fears and, in an increasing segment, his pride hover around his job. A worthwhile employee is interested in hearing about the progress and stability of the company which employs him — lack of such knowledge must tend toward uncertainty.

Generally it is in the best interests of both the employer and employee that labour turnover be reduced. It is my view that in the years ahead the company statute will recognise the claims of employees in the manner I have indicated. This may be a move in the direction of greater co-operation between capital and labour.

The main difficulty in conveying financial information to employees is that there is no uniformly understood objective as to what employees' reports are to achieve, what the employees want to know, or how to get the message across to them.

In other words it is difficult to arrive at a standard by which to judge the effectiveness of reporting financial information to employees. What is to be achieved? Is it

(a) to show employees how well off they are compared to those in other companies;

(b) to stimulate employees to greater efforts by showing them that wages have increased greater than production;

(c) to create employee pride in the company;

(d) to recognise the part played by employees in achieving the results for the year;

(e) to supply employees with information recognising that an employee well supplied with facts is less likely to be led astray by rumours and unsubstantiated information about the company's financial condition;

(f) to encourage others to join the work force of the company;

(g) to reduce, as suggested above, the turnover of labour?

The main reason prompting the supplying of financial information to employees is, I suggest, the establishment of better understanding between employees and management.

In order to ascertain whether or not financial information was being supplied by Australian companies to employees a questionnaire was sent by me to 155 companies. The companies were a random selection from Jobson's *Investment Year Book*. Replies were received from 90 companies (three of whom advised that it was not the policy of the company to supply such information) this being a phenomenal response of 58% (a 10% reply would have been considered a good one). The high percentage of replies indicates the considerable interest in the problem of this paper and the fact that most companies do not appear to know the answer to the problem. Many appear anxious to find a solution. The results of the questionnaire are as follow:

In reply to the question as to whether the company supplied financial information to *all* employees only 20 out of the 87 companies replying said that they did so.

As a reply to whether the company supplied information to a section only of employees 43 out of 87 companies said they did this.

Asked what class or section of employees this information was supplied to brought the following answers:—Management and senior employees, 25; executives, 7; employees who are shareholders, 6; selected employees, 1; two years and more of service, 1.

It would appear from these replies to be rare for employees other than senior executive staff to be supplied with any 45
financial data about the company employing them.

In reply to the question as to whether the information given to employees was the same as that supplied to shareholders the answers were: same as given to shareholders, 41; more detail, 19; simplified form, 1.

The manner in which the information was supplied by the company indicated that the annual printed report as supplied to shareholders was the medium used (37 companies). Other methods were: monthly reports, 6 companies; verbal reports, 5 companies; staff newsletter, 3 companies.

It would seem that most companies are making little effort to keep employees informed and that possibly less than one in four companies even supply the members' annual report to employees.

The question "Is your company satisfied that it has achieved its object by the practice adopted?" brought the following interesting replies:—

"We consider it would be unethical to supply information to members of the staff which is not supplied to shareholders."

"Yes. We think our employees are better informed than most about the state of the business on which their livelihood depends."

"No. But we have gone some of the way."

"Yes. At this stage the objective is limited to executives having a sound knowledge on which to manage the company."

Some interesting replies were received to the question, "Any general comment you wish to make on the subject of this questionnaire?"

"It is our aim to make each department (and sections within departments) function as a separate business, having regard to an overall plan. Statistical information probably more important than detailed financial information."

"Daily costs and efficiency figures are supplied to factory foremen, but 'financial'
46 accounts are confined to executives and the board."

"As secretary of the company I think it is important to give employees an understanding of the financial affairs of the company. However, this is not board policy."

"We have given balance sheets, etc., to all employees but have discontinued the practice because we could not see any good result coming from the practice."

"Not considered in the best interests of the company to supply financial information about the company to employees."

The above statements confirm my view that the problem of giving information to employees is one which is realised by company managements and that most of them do not know the answer to the problem. The results of my brief survey indicate, I suggest, the desirability of a much more detailed survey and discussion of the whole matter. It must be remembered that the conventional financial statements are as unintelligible to the average employee as they are to the average shareholder.

In addition to the questionnaire, I have made other enquiries in Australia and overseas, and I would summarise the generally accepted methods of communicating information to employees as comprising the following:

(1) By the issue of an annual report:—
  (a) A report specially prepared for employees.
  (b) A section of the shareholders' annual report directed to the employees.
  (c) The issue of the normal shareholders' report to employees.

(2) By means of information contained in a house organ or company magazine issued —
  (a) monthly;
  (b) every other month;
  (c) quarterly.

(3) By the issuing to employees of a copy of any important statement made on behalf of the board.

(4) By the holding of staff meetings at which one of the chief executives explains the company's health to the employees. This may be, depending upon the circumstances, a meeting of
  (a) the whole staff;
  (b) a consultative committee, which reports back to employees;
  (c) those above the level of supervisors who report to those 'supervised'.

(5) By means of wall charts or notice boards.

(6) By means of pay envelope inserts.

(7) By the use of films and film strips.

(8) By information in the press.

The method to be adopted depends upon many factors. The Ruberoid Company of New York says: "There is no doubt in our minds that bringing the financial facts about our company to the attention of employees is important in those cases where the employee grasps the meaning of our performance. We feel that keeping him fully informed makes him more aware, and consequently, a better employee. However, like most corporations, we are very much uncertain about the best way in which to do this."

Before discussing the advantages and disadvantages of each of the above methods it should be stressed that it is quite wrong to "talk down" to employees. Any report to employees, written or spoken, should endeavour to arouse their sense of pride in the company by informing them of the "wonders" of the company. If productivity is to be increased, should not employees be given greater information about production, prices and similar matters?

As a means of obtaining independent views on the methods suggested, I communicated with some dozens of business friends overseas and in the next few paragraphs views of overseas experts will be given concerning the different methods of giving information to employees.

The first method mentioned concerned *the issuing of a special report for employees.*

The development of thought on this special-purpose statement is best explained in the following extract, with which I agree:

"For some years we did prepare a special annual report for employees. The last such special report was for the fiscal year ended 31 August, 1945. Up to this time, numerous companies in the United States prepared separate reports for employees. Our employee reports included more charts, pictures and color, and displayed the source and disposition of funds in graphic form and included a simplified balance sheet. During these years, our annual report to stockholders was very conservative and there was very little use of graphic presentation and color. At about this time, the trend in annual reporting began to change. It was felt by a great many companies who had formerly issued separate reports that there was some resentment on the part of employees in that the company might be attempting to talk down to them. We feel that our employees' general intelligence is equal to that of the average stockholder and now address our annual report to our stockholders and employees. Much thought and effort goes into the preparation of the report so that it tells a story of interest to stockholders, employees, security analysts and others in the financial community. Much greater use is being made of color, art work, pictures, charts, and comparative operating statistics covering a period of at least ten years." (*Oklahoma Natural Gas Company* of Tulsa, Oklahoma, U.S.A.)

The dangers of the issuing of a separate report to employees are summarised thus:—

"However, two years ago we concluded that we were creating suspicion in the minds of employees by giving them a report different from that prepared for stockholders—that is, a suspicion we were withholding some information from them, and so ever since then we have been distributing the full stockholders' report to employees." (*Armstrong Cork Company of Lancaster,* Pennsylvania, U.S.A.)

On the other hand there are views that a separate report is desirable —

"You ask for the benefit of our experience regarding the annual report specially prepared for distribution to our employees. Our experience in this conection has been good, with no particular set of statistics to prove the point but, from general comments written to the editor of *Republic Reports,* we know that the annual report issue is read and is more easily understood by the average employee than the more technical formal annual report sent to all stockholders. *Republic Reports* is sent to each employee's home and, as a consequence, reaches into the family better than if it were merely a 'pick-up' brochure at the plant gate." (*Republic Steel Corporation* of 47
Cleveland, Ohio.)

The greatest danger is that separate reports, by endeavouring to concentrate exclusively on matters of interest to employees, may foster and increase the sense of class consciousness and separate class interest, whereas every business executive must desire to develop more community feeling and interest among all the groups with whom he has to deal.

Having a section of the shareholders' annual report devoted to the employees. This is the method adopted by some Australian companies and is really only a variation of the method of sending the shareholders' annual report to employees. Instead of just a brief word of thanks being included in the report, either a page or a few pages is devoted specifically to employee interests.

The issue of the normal shareholders' report to employees. This is the method adopted by most companies in Australia which supply information to employees. This method is commented on later in this paper.

By means of information contained in a house organ or company magazine. There are various methods of achieving this and the following views expressed will supply them.

"For a number of years we did issue a specially prepared annual report for employees. We have recently begun to have some doubts as to the value of the employee annual report. These were prepared in a simplified manner and we have been occasionally criticised for talking down to our employees and under-estimating their ability to understand the regular annual report. My experience indicates that this is a rather prevalent criticism of specially simplified reports for employees. In order to halt this criticism, we changed our procedure this year and merely supplied the employees with a summary of the annual report information through the regular divisional newsletter. These newsletters are issued by each of our operating divisions approximately once a month and contain overall corporate news as well as divisional news.

"This year we attached a questionnaire to the newsletters containing the annual report information and asked the employees which method they preferred. The vote was almost unanimously in favour of the newsletter procedure. We also made copies of the annual report available at each division. We mentioned in the newsletters that these could be picked up by any employee at the personnel
48 office, but found that practically no employee was sufficiently interested in the annual report to pick up copies." (*Worthington Corporation* of New Jersey, U.S.A.)

Charts and graphs are to be preferred to actual figures, which latter are not usually remembered. If the information is to be supplied in the house organ or magazine, too much information should not be given in the one issue. It is considered wise to spread the report over a few issues.

An alternative method:—

"We have been following this policy for many years and have found it very worthwhile. We prepare a special annual report for our employees and publish it in our employee magazine, *News Pictorial,* which is mailed to the homes of all J-M employees. We also publish a mid-year report in the same manner and run brief items covering our quarterly sales and earnings figures." (*Johns-Manville Corporation* of New York.)

"The regular report is supplemented by a thumbnail sketch in our weekly house organ." (*Jewel Tea Co. Inc.* of Illinois.)

The issuing of important statements made by the board of directors. This is explained as under:—

"Our President, Mr. James N. Symes, devotes a great deal of time and effort towards the improvement of conditions affecting our company and the railroad industry and whenever these issues are of a significant nature, his remarks are usually distributed to employees in a printed form. This, of course, keeps them currently aware of our problems and their needed solutions. In our opinion the distribution of information plays an important part in management-labour relations." (*The Pennsylyvania Railroad Company* of Philadelphia.)

The staff meetings may be in addition to other means of dissemination of information. Thus:—

"It is certainly characteristic of the Jersey organisation to keep its employees well informed regarding company operations. We feel that the approach to effective communications embraces varied programs, including the publication of unit newspapers, group meetings, notices on bulletin boards and internally circulated reports of special newsworthy events." (*Standard Oil Company* of New York, U.S.A.)

I have elsewhere suggested that the normal type of annual report may be simplified. This report should be sent to employees, as to shareholders, at quarterly or half-yearly intervals, accompanied by a statement of source and disposition of funds in a condensed form. The report and statement must be devoid of accounting jargon. I see no reason why the funds statement should not commence with the turnover of the company and comparative figures be given. I consider it is virtually useless sending a revenue statement and balance sheet to all employees, again as to all shareholders, but employees who desire a copy should be able to obtain one upon request. Those sufficiently interested, either financially or otherwise, would then obtain them, some to submit to their financial advisers. As the financial statements are historical "documentaries" based on a cost which may have materially altered by the time the member receives the information, the directorate's quarterly or half-yearly resume, it is suggested, is the employees' best guide as to the financial progress and stability of the company which employs them.

It is my view that employees, like shareholders, should be informed of —

(1) the total turnover. (Probably of interest to employees, but not so much to members, would be details of the turnover by different States or branches);

(2) the cost of goods or services produced — this is usually only given in diagram form and employees will be interested in the

information normally given in the members' annual report;

(3) thanks and tribute to employees, mention of special achievements;

(4) length of service of employees and photos in large organisation;

(5) total payments to employees. Show employees what share of revenue they are getting compared with shareholders, taxation, and other interests;

(6) information about profits, the return to members, the number of members, average return. There is not much point in stressing to employees that shareholders are risking their capital—employees may risk all. Employees desire to know how the profits are "spent";

(7) amount left in the business in the form of profits retained;

(8) employees may be interested in profits, for a different reason to members: incentive schemes may be based on profits;

(9) employment statistics—here again for a reason different from members' interest;

(10) the future prospects are equally as important to the employee as to the member.

(11) employees are interested in knowing who owns the company, where do the members live—in the community or in some other State—what are their occupations—are they bankers, stockbrokers, investors or just ordinary people like themselves;

(12) the employee is interested in the product or service he has helped produce—its value and importance and the part it plays in the life of the community or State.

One of the main objects of supplying financial information to the employee is to make him feel that he is part of the company, and to help him identify his interests with the company's continuing success.

I would like to reiterate that an employee, because of his employment possesses a moral right to information concerning the financial progress and position of his company.

Having decided to issue an annual report to employees, there are three main methods of doing so:—

1. The whole of the report may be prepared by the management and then be printed as a normal printing job. A few companies can handle the printing themselves.
2. The matter is prepared by the management and given to a printer who has someone on his staff with special knowledge of preparing annual reports, who actually prepares the report.
3. To have the whole report prepared by a public relations consultant possessing expert knowledge in the preparation of annual reports.

If there is little difficulty with employee relations and the staff is adequately skilled, the first method is used. The second method is often used by small- and medium-sized companies, whilst a few of our large companies use the services of a public relations consultant in the preparation of their annual report.

I would suggest that at intervals — something between every five and ten years — a special annual report should be issued and directed specifically to the employees. I think that, for such special types of annual reports, financial executives should strive towards evolving some generally accepted standards of what
should be communicated to employees. 49

The economic revolution in which our profession was born is still in process. The forces which brought the accountant into prominence are still gathering strength. If our profession is to take advantage of the tremendous opportunities ahead, we must be clear as to the degree of our "accountability", especially to employees.

In the early years of this century, the chief end of accounting was held to be the ascertainment of the worth of the business undertaking and the balance sheet was deemed the most important financial statement for it was held to show the financial position of the business enterprise. Later the going concern concept with its emphasis on the return on the capital employed in an undertaking became the chief end of accounting, with the profit and loss statement the most important financial statement, for it showed the profit made, but often this profit was not able to be distributed to the owners. To members, and it is suggested to employees also, there is coming a change in that the most important financial document is one which highlights the significance of the cash flow in and out of a business enterprise.

A statement of source and disposition of funds becomes of prime importance. The working capital position and the cash funds available are often of more importance than the "financial position" as disclosed in the balance sheet or the "profit" disclosed in the profit and loss statement.

Employees should be encouraged to be interested in the financial health of the company employing them and to increase the size of the "cake" and therefore their own share of the "cake".

Before the interest of employees can be obtained in financial information about the company there must exist a genuine desire on behalf of the board of directors and the management to deal justly with employees. This is, of course, evidenced
50 by a sound personnel policy, provision of amenities and the taking of an interest in the general welfare of the staff.

A business conducted by a management which shows consideration to its employees, and I suggest the supplying of financial information to employees is giving consideration to employees, will tend to make for more loyal employees and the giving of better service by them.

In the same way that the accounting profession has become greatly interested in taxation, so in the future it must, I suggest, become similarly interested in supplying information to employees and the representatives of employees. Organised labour should be sufficiently apprised of the activities of companies in an industry so that the demands it makes are made with a knowledge of all the pertinent facts. There is one thing that is very prevalent in the minds of employees and that is the thought that the shareholders get all the money and the employee is grudgingly given the least amount that management can get away with. This, of course, is very far from the truth, but how can this thinking be changed, or can we blame our workers throughout Australia for having this thought if we withhold from them the facts of business. All that is happening by withholding such information about his company, is the confirmation in his own mind that he might be right, because if this situation were not true management would not be afraid to make the facts available to him. I suggest that where there is ignorance there is also fear, suspicion, insecurity and unintelligent selfishness.

Should a Company Tell?

DISCLOSURE OF INFORMATION TO EMPLOYEES

by W. R. ANDERSON, F.A.C.C.A., A.C.I.S.

DURING the past fifteen years there has been a growing tendency for the more enlightened of managements to attempt to bridge the gulf between employer and employed by encouraging employees to take a more personal interest in the fortunes of the enterprise for which they work. To this end greater cognizance is taken of the contribution made by employees and less conservatism is shown in the disclosure of information. Industrial relationships are invariably improved when the employer goes beyond the limit of giving his employees the minimum information necessary for the performance of their duties, and instead adopts a policy of filling in the background to management decisions. Some enterprises go further than this, and provide details of their financial position.

Public Disclosure

Before the merits and demerits of disclosing financial information to employees are examined, it is necessary to bear in mind the statutory requirements concerning disclosure to the public and other interested parties.

Nationalized undertakings, that is, those responsible to a Minister of the Crown, are obliged under their respective statutes to submit annual reports and annual accounts to the appropriate Minister. These accounts and the accompanying reports are subsequently presented to Parliament, where their contents are made available to members of both Houses. These documents are in considerable detail and the wealth of information provided greatly exceeds that which must be disclosed by registered public companies. Copies are offered for sale through Her Majesty's Stationery Office.

Before a joint stock company, registered under the Companies Acts, may invite members of the general public to become shareholders or debenture-holders, it must first publish details of its present and past financial position. Thereafter the company must provide each shareholder and each debenture-holder with a copy of its annual accounts and directors' report. Copies of these documents must also be filed with the Registrar of Joint Stock Companies, where they are available for inspection by the public on payment of a small fee.

Because a private company may not invite members of the general public to subscribe for its shares and debentures, there is no requirement to disclose publicly any information relating to its finances. However, in common with public companies, it must provide each of its members and debenture-holders with a copy of its annual accounts and directors' report. Copies must also be filed with the Registrar of Companies. Although exempt private companies are relieved of the obligation to file annual accounts they must provide each of their members and debenture-holders with a copy of the annual accounts and directors' report.

The accounts of friendly, industrial and provident societies are prepared in the form of returns, which have to be submitted to the appropriate Registrar annually as part of an overall return providing information on all aspects of the society's activities. Copies of this return must be supplied on request to each member or person interested in the funds. In addition, a copy of the last audited balance sheet must be hung in a conspicuous place at a society's registered office. A building society must provide a member on application with a copy of its annual return, but in addition it must send to each shareholder who has a minimum shareholding of £25, a copy of the annual accounts and directors' report. Members who are not entitled to receive these documents must be provided with copies on application. Annual returns and, where appropriate, accounts and reports filed with the Registrars are open to inspection by the public on payment of a small fee.

Unlike nationalized undertakings, joint stock companies and registered societies, there is no statutory requirement for partnerships and sole traders to prepare an annual account of their finances (other than for tax purposes) and in consequence there is no legal obligation to circulate the contents or to lodge copies with a public official where they may be examined by the public.

From the foregoing, it is evident that disclosure of financial information is primarily intended for those who provide the capital. This fact is confirmed by the statutory regulations which are especially applicable to registered companies.

Contributors to Production

The production of goods and the provision of services result from the combined efforts of management, providers of capital, suppliers of material, and labour. Each group makes its contribution in the expectation that it will be rewarded, and although some groups may have priority over others in this respect, the total reward is eventually dependent upon the sale of the end-product, and ultimately therefore on the fortunes of the enterprise.

Management is in possession of all information, as indeed it must be if it is to fulfil its function effectively. It is aware at all times of the financial position and the prospects for the future. Providers of capital (shareholders and debenture-holders) are required generally by statute to be informed annually of the financial position for the past financial year. When capital is provided in the form of loans or advances, the lender may insist on being given details of the borrower's financial state; if the sum involved is large, he may require as a condition of the arrangement some representation at director level.

Suppliers of materials and services normally satisfy themselves of the standing of their prospective customers before conducting business with them. For day-to-day transactions which represent individually a relatively small part of their business, suppliers will rely initially on trade references and subsequently on their own experience. If, however, the transaction is an exceptional one, or a long-term arrangement is envisaged, the supplier will have to evaluate the risk, and for this purpose he will usually obtain details of his prospective customer's financial standing direct; or if the customer is a body which files accounts, he may refer to this record. Thus, although a supplier has no statutory right to receive information concerning a customer's financial affairs, his position is such that normal commercial practice and procedure will enable him to obtain the information required.

So far management, providers of capital and suppliers receive or are able to obtain information concerning the enterprise in which they are interested. But what of the fourth group – labour? It can be said that current commercial practice and law affords some protection to the supplier of labour; this is true as far as payment for services rendered is concerned, and as far as there are provisions for notice on termination of service. But is this enough? In this modern age the continuous effort of industry and commerce to operate with greater efficacy results in an increasing division of labour, and a corresponding rise in the ratio of skilled and specialized employees to other employees. Because of this, movement from one employer to another is not easy and tends to become more difficult as the employee grows older and his skill and experience becomes more contained. Further, the provision of superannuation schemes, social amenities and the problem of accommodation all contribute to deter movement. In consequence, employees have a greater interest in the fortunes of an enterprise because their prospects are now allied more closely to them.

Labour as an Investment

The supplier of labour is in fact rather like the provider of capital, in that he also invests something in the business, namely, his labour and personal skill. The return on this investment comes in the form of wages or salary. In common with the supplier of capital, the supplier of labour can also withdraw his investment and find an alternative use for it. It may be argued that this comparison is unrealistic, because if the enterprise is not successful the capital invested may not remain intact, whilst in the event of failure the total capital may be lost and nothing left for further investment. Labour, on the other hand, can find alternative employment although it may be less remunerative. Against this, it must be remembered that capital has an indefinite life and can appreciate, whilst labour ceases to exist on the death, incapacity or retirement of the supplier; it also depreciates with age.

If it is accepted that the supplier of labour and the provider of capital make a comparable contribution to production, should not the supplier of labour also be advised periodically of the financial progress of his employer, so that he too may have an opportunity of assessing the worth and prospect of his investment? At the present time, with comparatively few exceptions, the supplier of labour is the under-privileged contributor to production in this respect. His group alone is left in ignorance of the position and prospects of the enterprise in which he has a vital stake.

Nature of Information

The progress of a business and its current state can be assessed only if trading results and the resultant financial position are given regularly in sufficient detail to disclose the efficacy of the enterprise, and if some indication is given of plans for the future. Such information can be provided by financial statements accompanied by vital statistics, valuations and the order book position. As the value of financial statements and other facts deteriorate with the passing of time, it is essential that they should be made available as soon as possible after the close of the period to which they relate. It is also desirable that the period covered should be as short as practicable.

Factors Affecting Disclosure

The financial results of activities carried on by an individual, group of individuals or by a legal entity, are basically matters of a confidential nature for the information of those responsible for the enterprise. There still exists a certain reticence on their part to disclose details of their incomes, although the growth of the trade union movement has to some extent breached this attitude. The publication of basic wage rates both within and outside an industry, and the practice of some concerns to disclose not only basic wages and salaries, but also average earnings and fringe benefits help to remove the confidential nature of an individual's income.

Sole traders and partnerships have been affected little by this current trend, and details of their financial state remain a confidential matter revealed only to the select few.

The growth of the joint stock company has resulted in the periodic review of the legislation applicable to these companies, and subsequent Acts of Parliament have called for the disclosure of more and more information for the providers of capital, so that the interests of this group may be given some protection. This legislation still respects the basic confidential aspect of the finances of certain companies, notably exempt private companies and those who avail themselves of the provisions of Section 149 of the Companies Act, 1948. The finances of the nationalized industries, by the very nature of their State ownership, are treated with the minimum of secrecy.

It is apparent, therefore, that size, and presumably strength, of an enterprise has an important bearing on disclosure; a fact borne out by the increasing number of large public companies which tend to give more information than the legal minimum. The strength of an enterprise is determined by its ability to face competition, deal with wage demands, withstand adverse trading conditions and accept public criticism.

Competition is undoubtedly the biggest single factor to be taken into consideration, and it is obvious that the smaller concern is more vulnerable to challenging influences which could be re-enforced by disclosure of its financial position. Adverse trading conditions will also have a greater impact on the smaller organization which has neither the resources nor diversity of interests spread over a wide field as has the larger counterpart.

Wage demands and public criticism operate in the opposite direction. The larger enterprises suffer most from industrial discontent; labour in these instances is well organized under strong leadership. Because of their size and their impact on the nation's economy, these enterprises are well known, and in consequence they are more liable to public criticism than the smaller concerns whose activities are of local interest only.

When considering disclosure of information to employees, care must be taken to ensure that they do not become more informed than the suppliers of capital. If the inference is accepted that capital and labour make a common contribution to production, no distinction should be drawn between them when revealing details of progress made, and results achieved, by the enterprise in which they have a joint interest.

Merits and Demerits of Providing Information

Because the prime duty of management is to manage an undertaking efficiently, it is necessary to examine the effects of disclosure on efficiency. To a considerable degree efficiency will depend upon the nature of the relationship between employer and employee. Good industrial relations can be based only on the elimination of distrust by employees and frank disclosure by employers. Such relations are enhanced further by the removal of any feeling of insecurity, and by encouragement to employees to identify their future with that of their employer. With this in mind, it is fair to assume that any information which will improve industrial relations will also improve efficiency; and for this reason alone there is considerable merit in taking employees into the confidence of the management.

On the other hand, it would be disastrous to provide information which could be used advantageously by a competitor or by employees or any section of them. Further, under no condition should employees be provided with information which could be used to interfere with the management of the concern. Any information given must be for information and not for the endorsement or otherwise by labour of any particular policy.

Publication of information during boom periods could create a feeling of apathy, whilst disclosure during lean times might result in an unsettled atmosphere. As both conditions directly affect efficiency, the greatest care must be taken in the presentation of the information. All information must be given honestly; it must never be used as a rostrum by management to propagate partisan views.

Discrimination Between Employees

Most undertakings have a pyramidal organization with management at the apex and the bulk of the labour force at the base. Between these two extremes there are all groups of employees; whilst somewhere nearer the apex than the base there are the transitional grades between supervisory and executive staff. In general, it is reasonable to assume that labour in the lower grades will be less equipped to understand
54 financial and statistical statements than the higher grades. Further, it is also reasonable to assume that senior staff, by virtue of their appointments, are well able to follow and comprehend such statements and reports. The provision of the same information to both senior and other grades raises a problem, because any information given must be intelligible to the lowest grades. If this is not so, the main purpose of disclosure cannot be achieved. On the other hand, to restrict the degree of disclosure to the level understandable by the lower grades, is unfair to the intelligence of the senior staff. Experience has shown that the lower grades are more interested in the overall result and broad prospects for the future; this latter point is extremely important when losses have been incurred. The middle grades show a wider and deeper interest; the senior staff, as we might expect, shows the greatest interest of all.

There is another aspect of disclosure within a concern to be taken into consideration. If senior staff are supplied with regular progress reports of the undertaking's progress (that is, information additional to that essential for their duties), they will be encouraged to examine their own particular participation in the organization in the full light of the overall position. As a result, they will have a greater appreciation of what is going on, and they will be in a position to make a greater contribution to production.

Information should be supplied to employees in a form understandable by each grade, but as job grading is not necessarily synonymous with comprehension, such distinction would be unwise. Nevertheless, there are grounds for discriminating between senior and other staff, particularly as the senior staff will undoubtedly already be entrusted with certain information of a confidential nature.

Personal Approach

The provision of information to individual employees on a personal basis is effective only if there exists a real personal relationship between employee and employer. For this reason the personal approach should be restricted to senior staff. An attempt to assume a personal relationship with each of hundreds of employees in the lower grades can easily be misinterpreted, and quite rightly so, as a condescending attitude and one calculated to sow the seed of suspicion in the employer's motive.

Dissemination of information can be achieved by a circular, setting out the salient results and facts. This is a useful means of advising staff of interim progress and of calling their attention to the final achievement, details of which are published separately. Such a circular can be easily designed; it can be brief and to the point, and so provide the basic information of greatest interest to the majority of employees. The content of interim progress reports must be watched, so that employees are not placed in a more privileged position than shareholders and debenture-holders.

The point has already been made that employees should be in no worse position than shareholders, and therefore if this is accepted, all employees should receive a copy of the annual accounts, directors' report and chairman's speech. These documents, particularly if they are well presented, can provide the employee with all the information he requires. Although a distinction has been drawn between the capacity of different grades of staff to understand financial information, this should not detract from the principle of treating shareholder and employee alike, particularly as no distinction is made between shareholders, either according to their degree of comprehension or the size of their shareholdings.

There is a lot to be said for getting away from the present minimum statutory requirement in published accounts and for presenting them in a more attractive and imaginative manner. Distribution to employees would no doubt tend to accelerate this process. Although the cost of providing each employee with a copy of the annual accounts and associated documents would amount to a small fraction only of the annual cost of each employee, it may be desirable to restrict issues to those members of the staff who have a minimum period of continuous service, because it is these employees who are most likely to continue to invest their labour. Copies should, however, be available to the shorter service employees on application by them.

Impersonal Approach

The local and national Press can also be used as a means of disseminating information to the staff. Although this has value also as an advertising medium, it is a poor substitute for a copy of the accounts and other documents, because there is no guarantee that staff will see the papers in which the information is published, and even less will read the actual display because of the competition from the other contents. A house magazine is a far better vehicle for broadcasting information, particularly if it is a magazine designed primarily for employees. It provides an excellent means for the disclosure of progress reports, which incidentally can be absorbed much more effectively if they are built into or accompanied by a brief digest of the position by the managing director or chairman.

It is an accepted fact that publication of detailed information on notice-boards is the least effective method of advising staff. Notice-boards must, of necessity, be few in number, and although they may be well sited at strategic positions for maximum availability, they do not attract employees. Strategic locations usually mean transit areas which are busy, and where movement is impeded if people halt to study the information displayed. Notice-boards should be restricted to the publication of information which can be read quickly and which has a personal interest.

The Spoken Word

Financial information can be given by word of mouth, either over an internal broadcasting system or by talks. Broadcasting is unsuitable for any information which requires thought and appreciation, and its use should therefore be restricted to announcements of immediate interest only. Any lengthy use of an internal system would in any event be impracticable. Talks by the supervisory staff to employees are an excellent method of disseminating information. They can be pitched to the general level of comprehension, and the speaker has the opportunity, when answering questions, of clarifying points and removing any misconceptions that may arise. The success of this method depends on the ability of the supervisors to understand their subject and to put it across in a manner which is both interesting and informative. Talks by senior staff, particularly from those who are normally far removed from the bulk of employees, can be particularly effective. The personal touch can link the various departments together and underline the inter-dependence of units within an enterprise. Talks by these top staff and by specialists are normally possible only in the large organizations which operate internal training schemes. The great disadvantage of the spoken word is that of lack of time on the part of the speakers and the difficulty of addressing all staff.

Conclusion

Although there is a strong case for providing employees with copies of financial statements when such statements are available to the general public, it is difficult to justify the disclosure of similar information to employees of other enterprises, particularly exempt private companies and those firms which have no statutory obligation to prepare and publish an annual account and report. Yet if an employee is in a comparable position to that of the provider of capital, no distinction should be drawn between types of companies or firms other than that dictated by competitive influences or circumstances in which disclosure would be harmful. If this contention is accepted, all employers should therefore supply the supplier of labour with the same information as he supplies to the provider of capital. As this usually takes the form of an annual statement of account and a report, this information should be given unless the disclosure is harmful. If this is the case, a statement to this effect should be made. The value of the employer's reports can be enhanced if they include comment on future prospects and refer to matters in which the employee has a vital interest.

In the past fifty years the working population has taken an increasing interest in international and home affairs, and through their trade unions they have shown a desire for an improvement in the relationships which exist between labour and the other contributors to production. Today the working population is better educated and more widely read than ever before. Some employers have recognized this fact, and in conjunction with the trade unions concerned are attempting to create a real partnership in industry and commerce.

Audits for Employee.

The Right to Knov

by J. R. DYSON, B.A., A.C.A., Senior Lecturer in Accountancy, Liverpool Polytech

COMPANY reporting is highly biased in favour of the shareholder. The Companies Act 1948 is largely responsible for this state of affairs; under that Act, for example, members of a company have the right to receive a copy of every balance sheet and a copy of the auditors' report. Debenture-holders must also be provided with a copy of the accounts, but creditors and employees (who have a very special relationship with the company) do not have this right.

56 This is no different from the position in the early 1850s, a date from which we can trace many of our present reporting obligations. As Professor Edey has written: 'The time . . . was one in which great weight was laid on freedom of private enterprise from control. There were many who thought that the disclosure of company accounting information was a matter to be left to be decided between shareholders and directors.' He goes on to say: 'As for creditors, they were, after all, free to choose whether or not they entered into contractual relations with a company.'[1] This applies equally well to shareholders and debenture-holders, as well as to employees. Why then, should there be so much emphasis placed on reporting to the owners of the company and not to other interested parties?

Limited disclosure

Even the owners have not had established rights to the disclosure of information for very long; after all, it was only as recently as 1929 (in the new Companies Act of that year) that an annual profit and loss account (as well as a balance sheet) had to be laid before members at a general meeting. And of course, forty years later, members need only be supplied with a minimum amount of information; there is no statutory right to full disclosure. It has taken a very long time for shareholders to develop their present rights, so to argue that other contractees should enjoy similar benefits still appears breathtakingly radical. Certainly, it is by no means general for accountants to accept that there is any need, or indeed any right for employees to be informed of their company's progress.

The argument in favour of employee reporting is a simple one: shareholders, debenture-holders and creditors usually invest only a part of their available funds in a particular company. Employees, however, usually invest all of their labour in one enterprise; their standard of living and their basic security is often bound up in it, particularly if they have worked there for a very long time or it happens to be a monopoly. This is often the case in small towns and of large companies employing only a f men of very specialized skills. Consequently, the wh way of life of themselves, their families and possiby ev the community, revolves around the success or otherw of one company. They have an interest and a need know about the security and possible return of their o very real investment.

Annual statement to employees

This is not a new argument, but it is one which h been given greater force through one of the provisions the Industrial Relations Act 1971. Employers employi more than 350 persons (subject to certain exceptio are required to issue to their employees an annual stateme A detailed specification has not yet been issued, but c can expect it to be a watered-down copy of the sha holders' annual accounts. This would not be very help for even a simplified version of such accounts is qu meaningless to people who have no basic accountar training.

Then, too, as the accounts will be prepared by the e ployer, it would be difficult to assess just how far they wou be accepted as 'fair'. It is easy to imagine that self-respecting employee would dream of accepti 'management' reports without some means of independe assessment. How can he satisfy himself on this point?

A statutory outside audit would be one answer; t auditors would be appointed by, and report directly to t employees. Their role would be as independent as that the shareholders' auditors, but their report would ne to be quite different. Employees are basically interest in the wage they are getting, the wage increase they c reasonably expect to get in the near future, and the unde lying security of their job and of the company. The a counts presented to them, and the accompanying audito report, would need to reflect these basic individu requirements.

Two main problems arise: who would appoint t auditors, and what should the accounts and the audito report contain? Until we were certain that the syste was working satisfactorily, a statutory employees' au would only be necessary in establishments employing mc than, say, 350 people, and where the employees themselv (or the unions acting for them) had requested it. Concer of such a size would probably have a recognized trade uni structure. The auditors would be appointed by the unions who had bargaining rights; an annual gene meeting of all employees would be needed to which t auditors would report. Their fee (approved by the meetir would be paid for out of union funds.

This is all very similar to shareholder audits; it is

[1] 'Company Accounting in the Nineteenth and Twentieth Centuries', an article originally printed in the *Certified Accountants Journal*, April and May, 1956.

nature of the accounts that a marked difference would ›ly for they would have to reflect the employees' own cialized interest in the company's present and future sperity. At this stage, it is only necessary to give a ıeral idea of what the accounts might contain. Before ng this, however, it would be helpful to establish some ding principles.

'irstly, it would be necessary to keep them very simple l clear of all jargon and professional terminology. ondly, they must be as brief as possible – they should tainly not be more than three or four pages in length. irdly, whilst absolute figures should be given, they must related to some sort of ratio; most people are comtely bewitched by figures with a lot of noughts after them.

ssible presentation

e type of information might be presented under two in heads: 'Financial Results' and 'Prospects'.

'inancial results

) Operating profit, non-operating profit, tax, preference and ordinary share dividends, undistributed profits for the year, undistributed profits brought forward.
2) Details of return on capital employed, how it is calculated and what it means.
3) Total number of employees split into divisions and works: numbers by job grades. Wages and salaries in total and by divisions and works. The cost to the company of a £1 per week increase in basic rates to all employees as well as by grades, divisions and works.
4) An explanation of non-operational and exceptional profits.
5) The corporation tax rate and the actual rate as it applies to the company.
6) Preference and ordinary share dividend rates, the market price for each share and the yield to a prospective purchaser.

'rospects

) An explanation of the company's liquidity and whether this is likely or not likely to prove satisfactory (various types of liquidity ratios could be used).
2) Details of expected capital expenditure.
3) Trade prospects for existing products.
4) Prospects for new and recently launched products.
5) A statement of already announced closures, shut-downs and run-downs of divisions, works or products; whether any more are likely and where.
6) Using all available evidence, a statement to the effect that a merger or take-over in whole or in part is/is not likely during the ensuing year.

t is very important that anything which is disclosed is ily understood by all employees. For the most part, ventional accounting terminology would not be parılarly helpful; even pictorial diagrams using £1 worth ales or £1 worth of profits are likely to lead to confusion.[2] viously, much thought needs to be given to what should disclosed, and what it would then mean to the average ployee.

Many difficulties arise, of course, from this proposed eme. As far as the company is concerned, its officers ıld have to get used to the idea of another firm of litors examining their results, from a completely different nt of view. There certainly would be more people who l access to confidential information; in these situations there is an opportunity for some unscrupulous individuals to make personal gains out of information obtained in confidence. But the main irritant for the company would be the time taken in dealing with yet another report. However, a statement will shortly be required anyway (even if it will not have to be scrutinized by outside auditors) so this is not an objection peculiar to this particular scheme.

The main difficulty would come from the employees themselves; would they be prepared to accept the independence of outside auditors? This is a most important question, for there is a great deal of empirical evidence to suggest that many trade unionists believe that a union official, once trained either as an accountant or as a lawyer, is *ipso facto* incapable of working for the benefit of the ordinary working man. It may be that Tweedledee & Co might do the audit for the shareholders, whilst Tweedledum & Co act for the employees, but would the average union member understand the reasoning behind Tweedledum's report? Does he realize that profit and loss accounts are only an estimate of profit or loss over a particular period and that balance sheets are a mere snapshot? We know – but does he – that weeks or even hours after the period end the picture can change quite substantially?

Reputations at risk

In May 1972, *The Guardian* reported that 'three-quarters of the companies going bankrupt showed a profit in their last accounts'; thus if the employees receive a satisfactory report and then only a short time afterwards the company goes into liquidation, the independence and the integrity of firms like Tweedledum will certainly be subject to a great deal of heated questioning by aggrieved employees. It follows that the benefit of a statutory employee audit would be destroyed, for in these circumstances it would be contemptuously dismissed as yet another anti-union plot introduced largely to fool a subservient proletariat.

Employee audits would not be necessary if all employers were enlightened in attempting to take workers into their confidence. From evidence available, we know that those companies with good industrial relations tend to disclose a great deal about their activities; for them, a statutory audit is probably not necessary. For others, though, whilst more disclosure would not automatically improve their industrial relations, one can guess that it might help.

The Companies Acts are supposed to protect the shareholder, the debenture-holder and, to a lesser extent, the creditor. The Industrial Relations Act is supposed to protect the employee and it certainly takes a step in that direction; unfortunately, as far as disclosure is concerned, the Act does not go far enough. The employee's right to know is recognized, but until he has the opportunity of verifying what he knows, his right turns out to be toothless.

A statutory employees' audit would therefore be a very effective way of giving him more bite; it would emphasize that employees have rights similar to those of shareholders. But much more than this, it would, in effect, introduce into our industrial life a statutory management audit. This is something that many academics have been calling for for a long time – and, as members of the EEC, it is something we are likely to hear a great deal more about in 1973.

esenting Financial Information to Employees (BIM, 1957).

REPORTING METHODS

There have been a great many papers published on the subject of appropriate content and presentation of financial reports to employees. This section is comprised of papers mostly drawn from the 1940s, during which a significant upsurge in interest occurred.

In the *Harvard Business Review*, Barloon (1941) considers appropriate terminology, content and format, narrative explanations, and graphics. Barloon's contribution is notable in several respects. He argues against the inclusion of a balance sheet, warns of the potential dysfunctional employee response to a president's statement of personal economic philosophy, and calls for an auditor's certificate to counteract managerial bias.

Wallace's (1946) paper is based on a number of proposed normative standards for employee report effectiveness. These are making it understandable to readers, giving confidence in the validity of figures, appealing to the employees' viewpoint, being factual and accurate, and being short in length.

A broader-brush approach to the subject is represented by the text of a presentation by J.A. Fuller (1948), Vice-President of Shawinigan Water and Power Company. Clearly influenced by the Scientific Management school of thought, he conceives employee reporting as being part of a "human engineering" strategy. His discussion includes employee magazines and handbooks, company information programs, meetings and conferences of supervisors, simplified financial reports, and timing of such reporting.

Of further interest is the abridged version of a paper presented at the Ohio State University Tenth Annual Institute on Accounting by a civil engineer named Stephen Derry (1949). Published by *Journal of Accountancy*, it provides a neat summary of types of information that can be provided to employees and a comprehensive listing of methods for disseminating that information.

An academic's contribution to this literature is provided by Walter Burnham, Associate Professor of Accounting at Ohio State University (1949). He examines the format of simplified income statements as well as items of significance to employees and then presents a proposed income statement for employees.

A comprehensive treatment of the subject is provided by Heckert and Willson (1952). They cover objectives, information presented, financial statements, simplified and "per employee" statements, format, media, and dangers in reports to employees.

This collection of papers provides an example of the quite advanced stage of development that thinking and practice on employee report content, presentation, and dissemination had reached during the 1940s in particular. The majority of issues still being discussed and employed in the 1970s and 1980s had to all intents and purposes been fairly thoroughly canvassed decades earlier.

FINANCIAL REPORTS TO EMPLOYEES

BY MARVIN J. BARLOON

IN recent years a number of companies have been issuing financial reports to their employees. In general, these reports are modified versions of the Report to Stockholders, though they tend toward greater brevity and toward placing slightly more emphasis on points of especial employee interest. In addition, some of them attempt to explain the accounting terms appearing in the statements and to stress certain financial
60 points by means of pie-charts and pictorial graphics. For the most part, however, the reports do not appear to have been thoroughly worked out to meet the peculiar needs of employees for information.

A financial report to employees, very carefully devised as to content and form, might prove an implement of industrial relations policy reaching to the very heart of some of the most serious labor problems. This is not to imply, of course, that an employee report is indispensable to successful labor relations or that such a report should constitute the major portion of a labor relations program. But the report to employees may be adapted to the performance of a very fundamental educational function.

There are some things about company finance which it is vitally important that employees know. The first of these is the limit to the company's wage-paying capacity. Over-estimation of an employer's ability to increase wages and employ men probably causes more dissatisfaction among workmen than any other misunderstanding of company finance. Union leaders, in negotiating the renewal of agreements, sometimes press wage and hour demands which, if granted, would reduce profits to the vanishing point or even precipitate insolvency. Excesses of this kind are often contrary to the long-run interests of the employees themselves, especially in the tendency to reduce the wage-paying potentialities of the business. To ascribe these difficulties to the character of unionism or to the personal shortcomings of union leadership is to view only the surface of the problem. In most instances the union program is necessarily designed to appeal to the attitudes and understanding of the rank and file. Any permanent modification of union demands, therefore, must begin by dispelling employee illusions as to the size of the business income.

The same problem partially underlies the industrial relations outlook in non-union areas. Men are prepared for organization and its accompanying disturbances, in part, by the belief that their employer is withholding from them substantial sums which might be wrung from him by collective action. The labor organizer places his main emphasis on the prodigious size of company profits and on the inadequacy of wages. The employer who has long familiarized his employees with the basic facts is in less danger of having the case against him overstated.

Employers may feel some hesitancy in taking up with their workers the question of conflict between wages and profits. If the workers were unaware of this aspect of the wage question, such hesitancy would be fully warranted. In fact, however, the workers are often more inclined to view their interests as being in opposition to those of the employer than the latter suspects. The hardships of the depression and the trend of public discussion and government policy have habituated employees to the conflict view. The employer is not in a position to eliminate prevailing issues from the thinking of his workmen. He is, however, in a position to assure that their thinking will be in terms of the financial facts in so far as his business is concerned.

The second important need which might be served by the employee report has to do with the bearing of worker productivity—in quantity, quality, and waste control—on wages. This aspect of employee education is so widely recognized by employers as hardly to require elaboration here. Financial information can be utilized to increase the worker's awareness of this source of his welfare.

The requirements of a good employee report become evident from these considerations. The report has a specific message to convey. It should state this message as clearly and as pointedly as possible. To do this the following principles should be applied:

1. The information should be stated in terms and on a scale with which the employee is familiar.
2. The report should be organized around the financial interest of the employee in the business.
3. The wording and contents should be such as to impress the employee with the fundamental sincerity and honesty of the report.

The Terms of the Statement

1. Difficult accounting concepts should be omitted.

Some companies include the balance sheet in the employee report, showing, among other things, the Reserves for Depreciation, Capital Surplus, and Earned Surplus. In some reports a parenthetical explanation of each of these items accompanies its listing. It might be better to omit such subjects entirely.

The employee does not understand and often cannot be made to understand the meaning of many of the financial data. In addition, their listing endows the report with a forbiddingly technical appearance and discourages careful reading. Any effort really to explain these items to the worker would constitute an educational program much more extended than the report can encompass. Such terms as "Reserves" and "Surplus" are almost certain to be misconstrued, and the misconstruction is of a particularly unfortunate character in that the employee, in spite of all explanations 61
to the contrary, will insist on regarding these items as sums of cash in excess of the company's needs.

2. A technical accounting term which refers to a lay concept should be replaced with a nontechnical expression.

"Net Worth" might well be called "Stockholders' Investment" and "Liabilities" be called "Debts." However, such terms as "Cash," "Machinery," "Raw Materials," and "Wages" need not be altered.

In general, while the report should be highly simplified and stated in lay terms, the terminology, itself, should not be explained. One company undertakes to clarify the term, "Sales," by pointing out that intersubsidiary shipments have been eliminated. This should be taken for granted. To explain simple things only makes them appear complicated.

3. Financial information may well be reduced to a per-employee, per-week basis.

~~A large rubber company reported to its employees that its net profit for the year was $9,838,797.~~ It is very difficult for the employee to think clearly in ~~sums as large as this.~~ Unlike the com-

Large sums.

pany executives and some of the stockholders, the typical manual worker has had no background in the administration of large investments and is therefore not habituated to thinking in large figures. To most employees, even to some men with a high degree of manual skill, any sum over a million dollars means simply a great quantity of money. In discussing large-scale finance, some employees become confused as between millions and billions and use these terms somewhat interchangeably. There is, therefore, little point in reporting to them in annual aggregate sums.

A second and more serious difficulty
62 is that the employee may relate unfavorably this vast revenue to his own wage income. To appreciate the likelihood of this reaction, it is necessary to remember two things. First, the financial report represents to the workman a matter of great personal and emotional concern, in that it pictures the source of his sole and sometimes precarious livelihood. As a consequence his judgments are impulsive and often highly colored. Second, unlike executives and investors, the workman makes no administrative or investment decisions on the basis of the report and hence is not personally accountable for the conclusions he reaches. He is therefore undisciplined by any need for a considered appraisal of the figures. His initial reaction is thus probably final.

The specific form taken by these tendencies is very undesirable. As with most consumers, the workman is continuously conscious of his need for more income (regardless of its present size). He considers that a possible addition to his wage of, say, three dollars a week would provide a vital improvement in the welfare of his family. Out of a reported profit of millions of dollars, he reasons, his employer could easily spare this paltry sum without real sacrifice. The only apparent obstacle to the coveted advance in wages is the disinclination of the management to loosen the purse strings. Any pressure in which the worker can join toward getting a share of these huge profits is, therefore, an obvious course of action. Where this interpretation does not occur spontaneously, dissatisfied fellow-employees will often draw it sharply to a workman's attention.

The number of employees to whom a wage advance would have to be extended, if it were granted at all, is, of course, not known to the individual man. Even if it were, he would almost never have the inclination and often not even the ability to perform the computation necessary to relate the putative increase in payroll to the profit figure. The whole troublesome question can be very easily avoided and at the same time the employee's understanding more honestly served by dividing the income and profit figures by the average number of employees on the payroll during the year and reporting only the result. In the case of the rubber manufacturer, the net profit was only $215.36 per employee.

Annual income per employee figures remain subject, however, to the same criticism: that, in the employee's understanding, they overstate the wage-paying potential of the business. Employees, in general, are not habituated to thinking in terms of annual incomes. They have usually never, in a lifetime of employment, been paid an annual salary and often not even a monthly salary. Their entire habit of thought is built on the concept of the weekly pay envelope. In discussing annual incomes with workers, the question is commonly voiced: "How much is that a week?" The sum $215.36 is an average of $4.14 a week, net profit per employee of the rubber manufacturer. It should be stated clearly, of course, that figures such as this are averages.

There is one danger in the omission of annual aggregate sums from the employee report. The workers may feel that significant information is being concealed from them. This result may be avoided by posting regular financial statements on the plant bulletin boards or by placing copies of the Report to Stockholders in the personnel office. The availability of the statements should be pointed out in a footnote in the report to employees.

Organization of the Report

1. Materials not bearing directly on the wage-paying and employment potentialities of the business should be omitted.

Some employee reports issued in the past have given considerable space to miscellaneous subject matter, such as illustrations of the line of products and product uses, reports on the progress of accident prevention, photographs of the annual picnic, and tabulations of plant locations, output values, and other assorted facts. The employee cannot possibly remember all these things, and the few things he might and should remember are hopelessly scattered and obscured in the mass of unrelated details. It is extremely difficult, at best, to clarify to the employee the basic financial facts of the company's operations even when these facts are reduced to their simplest terms and coherently organized. To confuse them by the intrusion of even a modicum of diverting materials not essential to the underlying development is to destroy any possibility of promoting the employee's financial insight. While the worker should be informed on other matters than the company finances, such other information should be provided by media outside of the annual report to employees.

2. It is probably better not to include a balance sheet in the report.

In a financial sense, the source of the employee's income and the explanation of the factors affecting it are to be found in the income statement, not in the balance sheet. Concretely, it would be undesirable to give the workman the impression that his wage is normally to be provided by drawing down the assets of the business. Furthermore, the balance sheet contains accounting concepts, such as discussed above, too elusive to be understood by the employee or explained to him satisfactorily. The consequences 63
of including the balance sheet, therefore, might be to mislead and confuse the employee rather than to inform him.

3. The income statement should be organized so as to indicate the bearing of operating and financial factors on the employee's earnings.

In its customary form the income statement is not built around the worker's view and understanding of the business. It is designed rather to inform the investor. For example, costs are classified on the basis of the income-yielding function for which they were respectively incurred so as to submit management policy to the investor's judgment. Analysis of the personal distribution of the business income is exclusively as between different classes of investors. The investor's analytical faculties and financial insight are assumed.

To command the employee's interest, the statement should be redesigned as an explanation of wages. The worker's present understanding does not typically connect his own welfare with successful management. He is therefore not interested in cost and sales control. At the present stage of his insight, what the employee wants and needs to know is why the company does not pay him more ~~wages~~. Before he can be interested in operating problems he must first see their bearing on his own income. This need defines the task of the report.

In this illustration the statement points out, among other things, the ratio of dividends to wages. The accompanying discussion might note that if the owners were to have surrendered a full 50% of their personal income to increase wages in 1939, the employee would have received an advance of only $1.12 per week.

EXHIBIT I. BLANK RUBBER COMPANY
(Average weekly sales and costs per employee*)

	Calendar Year		
	1939	*1938*	*Increase*
Sales	$91.13	$77.33	$13.80
Expenses of Manufacturing and Selling Our Products (Excepting Wages[1])	61.89	52.08	9.81
For Creditors, Employees, and Owners	$29.24	$25.25	$ 3.99
To Creditors (Interest)	1.00	1.54	−0.54
Balance for Employees and Owners	$28.24	$23.71	$ 4.53
To Employees (*Wages*[1])	24.10	21.10	3.00
Balance for Owners' Income and Reinvestment	$ 4.14	$ 2.61	$ 1.53
64 Used to Purchase New Equipment, Materials, and Other Productive Facilities	1.91	0.98	0.93
Owners' Personal Income	$ 2.23	$ 1.63	$ 0.60

* The figures in this statement were obtained by dividing the annual sums by 52 to get the weekly averages. The weekly averages were then divided by the average number of employees on the payroll during the year, 45,686 for 1939 and 44,570 for 1938.

A possible organization of the income statement of the rubber company mentioned previously is given in EXHIBIT I.

4. The significance of each item to the employee should be discussed in terms of the computations in the statement.

The employee's attention, of course, will center on the wage figure of $24.10. The way in which the other items in the statement influence this sum is the key to the employee's interest in operating and financial problems. Each point the management desires to make should be represented by an item in the statement and discussed in terms of the bearing of this item on the employee's wage. The form of the statement thus may vary with the particular message the company wishes to convey.

The meaning of investor income to the worker could be clarified by likening it to rent. In the case of this company, the investment per employee amounted to $4,022. This is the average value of the machinery, materials, building, tools, and supplies necessary to provide a man with a job. The compensation to investors (creditors' and owners' income) amounted to only $3.23[2] per employee each week, about $14.50 per month. This is a rather low rental on a property valued at $4,022. As profits vary widely from year to year, a more sound figure might be the average weekly interest

[1] The term, "wages," as used here includes executive salaries as well as non-executive payroll. Actually, however, a statement for employees should show executive salaries as a separate item to avert suspicion that the wage figure is grossly inflated and to demonstrate the usually inconsequential size of executive salaries relative to total payrolls. The two figures are combined here solely because of limitations in the data available to the writer.

[2] The reinvestment of $1.91 might be added to this and the comment based on the sum, $5.14, corporate profit plus interest. Corporate profits in excess of dividend declarations, however, do not clearly constitute stockholder income.

and dividend amount over the past ten years.

Another matter of demonstrable importance to the workman is that of sales. It will be seen from the statement that an advance in weekly sales of $13.80 per employee was accompanied by an increase in costs of only $9.81. This is because some of the costs are fixed and do not go up with an increase in volume of business.

Increase in Sales	$13.80
Increase in Costs	9.81
Saving	$ 3.99

Of this saving the employee received $3.00, or 75%, advancing his average weekly wage from $21.10 to $24.10. Under circumstances such as those prevailing this year, every increase in sales is obviously very much in the employee's interest.

It is true, of course, that most production and clerical employees are not in a position to increase the company's sales. Workers in all departments, however, can increase sales *per employee* by improving production so that future advances in sales achieved by the sales department can increase the wage-paying capacity of the enterprise for the benefit of present employees. To follow through without antagonizing the workman, it might be stated that the management believes that most of the employees are now putting forth as much physical exertion as can reasonably be expected, but that many of them could work more productively by following job instructions as carefully as possible and by studying their own jobs to eliminate wasted effort.

It should be noted, of course, that such factors as product prices and raw material quotations are beyond the control of either management or workers. Otherwise, in the event of future adverse market developments, resentment may arise from the mistaken belief that a decline in worker incomes necessarily reflects a managerial blunder.

In a manner similar to the treatment of sales, the other data in the statement should be related to the wage figure in order to show the effect on the worker's potential earnings of quality improvement and waste reduction. For this purpose it might be desirable to break down the manufacturing expense figure of $61.89 to present individually the cost factors subject to some control by the workers and to place emphasis on particular cost problems with which the company is currently having difficulty 65
or seeking worker cooperation through other media. Illustrations of economies recently realized in specific departments of the plant should be briefly introduced to demonstrate the workability of the ideas and to make every point as concrete as possible.

If the company has facilities for employee meetings in small groups, the report should be discussed orally. The effectiveness of discussions declines sharply in large gatherings because the men become too self-conscious to express themselves freely and because time does not permit everyone to talk. The leader of each discussion should preferably be someone who understands the report well and who has the personal confidence of the men. Union stewards and business agents should be present if the shop is organized. Considerable tact and self control will be required of the leader, or chairman, to prevent the discussion from becoming too polemic. The chairmen should be thoroughly coached in advance by the executive who prepared the printed report so that their interpretation will be correct and their statements consistent as between the groups.

The discussions will serve to dispose of questions which cannot be appropriately treated in the employee report. An individual worker may wonder why his own weekly wage differs from the average in the statement. This question would furnish an opportunity to clarify the effect of part-time employment on the average weekly earnings and to explain the company's job-rating system and the principle of wage differentials. As these points are not represented by the computations of the operating statement, their treatment in oral discussion will relieve the printed report of material irrelevant to its financial message.

66 *Contents and Presentation*

1. It is better to understate than to overstate the present harmony prevailing in the plant.

Employers often mistake employee quiet for contentment and impute their own good spirit to employees in whom it is lacking. Platitudes relative to employee goodwill or company generosity only intensify hidden resentments. Such expressions as "big, happy family," "fine spirit of loyalty," and "the partnership of management and men" should be avoided. For workers who do not share the management's enthusiasm for the present terms and conditions of employment, fine phrases in the report undermine confidence in the truth of its factual message.

2. Statements of the personal economic philosophy of the president should be omitted.

The report should be phrased in simple, direct, and businesslike language. The workers cannot possibly be induced to embrace an economic doctrine of cooperation by its mere statement in general terms. On the contrary, if they disagree with it, their minds will resist every valid and concrete point offered by the report in which such a philosophy is asserted. It is better, therefore, merely to allow the general economic views of the management to be presented implicitly in the arrangement and discussion of the specific facts.

3. The use of pie-charts and pictorial graphics is subject to some question.

Picturesque graphics may impair the effectiveness of the report because of their close resemblance to advertising technique. Many employees, as consumers, have a deeply ingrained habit of discounting advertising claims, so that any message bearing the tone or color of advertising meets an immediate and spontaneous skepticism. An advertiser can allow for this, knowing that the consumer may be more entertained than antagonized by colorful presentation. But in the employee report picturesque technique may introduce too flippant and unreal an atmosphere, in view of the workman's very serious and mercenary concern in the facts treated, so that he may feel the management is trying to jolly him into believing something which is not quite true. Pictorial graphics should therefore be considered critically before inclusion.

4. The employee report should be certified.

The report to stockholders is usually supported by an auditor's certificate. The employee, however, is almost never provided with a corresponding verification. Such discrimination can be explained only on the premise that the employee has a greater confidence in the management's veracity than has the stockholder. With respect to the employees of many companies this premise is false. Employees often have a predisposition to disbelieve almost any assertion emanating from the management which happens to run counter to their own habitual views.

Certification may best be provided by some agency which the employee knows to be free from any managerial bias. In many cases a firm of public accountants engaged by the management will be the only available solution. Where employees are working under a collective agreement, however, men who are competent to check an income statement may sometimes be obtained from the international headquarters of the union. Acting on the authorization of such men, the local union leader enjoying the greatest employee confidence, usually the business agent, can certify as to the correctness of the report. His signature under the certification will remove the barriers of skepticism more effectively than almost any other device.

Conclusion

Industrial democracy necessarily implies that the workmen will exercise some control over company policies. If the men are to exercise constructively the power which they hold by reason of collective action through their unions, it is essential in their own long-run interests, as well as those of the industry, that they act on an understanding of facts. In nonunion plants the worker's satisfaction with his terms of employment may be materially increased if he appreciates the financial limitations under which his company operates. In either case, the partial provision of this understanding is the function of the financial report to employees.

Because of its vital importance, therefore, the report should be meticulously prepared and presented. While the recommendations herein are to be understood as tentative, they are meant to represent basic principles. These might be summarized as clarity, relevance, and sincerity.

Getting Down to Earth in Explaining Profits to Employees

By Frank Wallace

Current wage demands have become the nation's most critical economic problem. It appears that large masses of people have come to believe that the corporation profit barrel has no bottom, and that the only thing that prevents substantial wage increase is the "greediness" of management.

Employee Understanding Imperative

This mass misconception of profits has developed over a long period of years and has many contributing causes. It is doubtful that industrial harmony can be established soundly until there is a better understanding of industry's profit position among the rank and file in offices and plants. National public opinion polls have shown that a majority of the population believes that "big business" is making net profits of 30 per cent. or more on sales. Probably the actual percentage profits on sales would be nearer two or three per cent.

This shows that industry has much to gain by a better popular understanding of the true profit position. One of the most important starting points for enlightenment of the public is in the rank and file of office and plant employees. This is a place where an individual company can go to work on the problem.

The situation demands reexamination of financial reports to employees, because many managements who feel that they are doing a good job on their financial reports to employees are mistaken. A recent example highlights what can happen even in a company which has done an outstanding job in employee relations.

Case Example of Fruitless Effort

The top management of this company was considerably crestfallen recently by the results of their employee opinion poll.

The President was proud of the generous amount of information given to their employees in the company's weekly paper, monthly magazine and special reports—particularly the annual financial report to employees. This financial report gave a wealth of data—sales trends, analyses of current and past wages, various cost data, profits, the tax situation and balance sheet analyses.

The report was attractive and colorful. Pie charts, bar graphs and clever illustrations dramatized the figures.

The President said, *"I'll bet we have the best informed employees of any company in the country."*

Then came the blow of the poll results! The employee opinion poll had been conducted five weeks after the financial report was given to employees. One question was: "How many cents of net profit do you think the company makes on each dollar of sales?" Each employee checked one of five alternative answers. The employee opinions were:

2 cents— 6 per cent. of employees
6 cents—11 per cent. of employees
10 cents—20 per cent. of employees
15 cents—39 per cent. of employees
25 cents—24 per cent. of employees

The correct answer was 2 cents net profit on each sales dollar. In spite of the progressive reports of this company, its employees shared the public's misconception of profits.

Requirements for Effective Employee Reports

Because of the widespread misconception of profits, the prime objective of the employee report should be to explain the basic facts about officers' salaries and profits as they relate to wages and salaries *of the employees themselves.*

An effective employee report should meet the following standards:

1. *Make it understandable to the employee.*
2. *Give confidence in the validity of the figures.*
3. *Appeal to the employee's viewpoint.*
4. *Be factual and accurate.*
5. *Make it short.*

An employee report meeting these standards is presented in the J. Jay Company illustration on the following page. Except for slight changes in totals to conceal identity, the figures in this statement are actual operating results of a corporation. The weekly averages per employee are *exact.*

Make It Understandable

The proposed employee report probably will appear to be *over-simplified* to many controllers who review it. However, in testing this statement for readability, it was found that many had to study the statements intently and reread them to get a full understanding of them. It must be pointed out that this report contains 24 interrelated figures in the statements which is a large number of variables for persons not accustomed to using figures.

Many controllers will be tempted to add more figures to the statements such as a "percentage to sales" column. It is likely that this would add a complication without actually contributing to the employee's understanding of salaries and profits.

The language of the report should conform as nearly as possible to the vocabulary of typical employees.

Give Confidence in the Validity of the Figures

When the statements of the proposed employee report were tested on plant and office personnel, several employees raised this question: *"How do we know these figures are right? For all we know, they might have been dreamed up in the front office just to make the Company look good."*

Therefore, provision was made for an Auditor's Report in the proposed employee statement and reference was made in the President's letter that the figures conformed to those submitted to the Securities and Exchange Commission. (The independent public accountants should be urged to write their report in simple, straightforward language.)

Appeal to the Employee's Viewpoint

The natural fiscal unit of time for most plant employees is a week. When they hear wages or salaries stated on a monthly or annual basis they usually want to know: *"How much is that per week?"* This is natural since they receive their wages weekly, and their personal budgets are built around expenses per week.

Therefore, the proposed employee re-

TOP MANAGEMENT'S RESPONSIBILITY

The starting point for a workable answer to the problem of current wage demands is the development of understanding by employees of the true nature and volume of corporate profits. And "it is top management's responsibility to see that they set the facts accurately and understandably," says Mr. Wallace, Principal of McKinsey and Company, in this timely and terse manuscript.

—THE EDITOR

port shows all financial data in terms of the average per employee per week. This reduces the figures to a digestible size that conforms to the employee's own viewpoint in financial thinking. To most people $4,000,000 (millions) appears to be about the same as $4,000,000,000 (billions). When the profit figure in the proposed report stands alone, it obviously seems to many employees that the stockholders are becoming unreasonably wealthy at the employees' expense.

The employee report illustrated uses no percentages. It is doubtful that "per cent. of sales" has any meaning to the typical employee. It is a vague concept to many, and it is difficult to get the salary and profit story across in terms not habitually used by the employee in his own thinking.

The explanation of return on investment compares the stockholders' return to the yield on War Bonds. This relates profits to the employee's own experience.

Be Factual and Accurate

It goes without saying that the figures must be honest and accurate. Tricky uses of figures will boomerang.

Arguments or labored justifications of the company's position will antagonize employees. It also is important to avoid a tone of "see how good we have been to you." State the facts simply and clearly with enough interpretation to facilitate understanding. Then leave the rest to the common sense and native intelligence of the employee.

Make It Short

If an employee reads the report he will do it voluntarily, probably in his home or on the bus. There will be many distractions, and if the report is too long he will lose interest.

Information on the company's products, pictures of sales branches, and recreation program plans are interesing, and should be presented to employee.

Consider giving this information in the company magazine or paper. If it is in the annual financial report, it will divert attention from the prime objective.

Balance sheet information is omitted in the proposed report, because it does not help explain salaries or profits.

* * * *

The present anxiety over labor chaos which has moved Congress and the people to think of fact-finding boards and restrictive legislation is evidence enough of the urgency of our number one problem.

But the only valid solution is to be found in the reactions and thought patterns of employees in every plant and office across the country. That is the starting point for a workable answer to the problem.

Industry must educate its rank and file workers so that they have a real understanding of what they contribute to a going concern, how it functions and to what extent they absorb its profits.

Employees have a vital interest in this information. It is top management's responsibility to see that they get the facts accurately and understandably.

* * *

Wage Increase Demands Are Analyzed by Col. Ayres

When the government took the first Census of Manufacturing nearly a century ago, in 1849, the average factory employee worked sixty-nine hours a week and was paid $4.74 for his efforts, Colonel Leonard P. Ayres, pointed out in a recent issue of "The Business Bulletin" of the Cleveland Trust Company. Now the average factory worker, in peace time, works about half as many hours and gets close to ten times as much weekly pay. Because of the numerous present strikes for still higher wages, it is worth while to ask how the wage increases of the past century came into being, and what was their source. The answers are not hard to find, Colonel Ayres says. They are hidden in the figures of the past Censuses of Manufacturing which used to be taken each ten years, then each five years, and then on alternative years, but not during the war years.

Past wage advances came from increases in the production per worker, he states. The increases were made possible by progressive improvements in the machines and tools used by the workers. In 1849 the factory investment per factory worker amounted to $557. When we get a new Census of Manufacturing it will probably show that the present capital investment per worker is as much as $7,000.

There is just one way to continue to pay increasing wages to industrial workers, and that is to make it possible for them to keep on increasing their per capita production. The way to do that is to keep on increasing the investment per worker so that he can keep on using better and better tools. That can be done only if the government does not tax away the savings of the investors, and does not prevent them from earning fair returns.

Probably the present attempts of the administration and the strikers to get wage increases which will be absorbed by the managements, and so not operate to raise prices, will prove to be ineffective. The whole record of the Census figures indicates that the share of the customer's dollar that the factory worker can get is a nearly constant 40 per cent. Professor Willford I. King of New York University discussing this relationship wrote recently that the factory worker's share of the customer's dollar remains almost constant year after year, decade after decade, in good times and bad, in Republican and Democratic administrations, under Old Deal and the New, and whether labor is unorganized or welded into powerful unions.

It seems wholly likely that when the present contests between managements and labor over wages have been settled, and production has been resumed on a reasonably normal basis, it will be found that the century-old rule still holds good. The workers will be receiving higher wages, but these wages will still constitute about 40 per cent. of the value added by the processes of manufacturing. The prices of manufactured goods will increase by amounts sufficiently great to restore the old percentage relationship. There have been 20 Censuses of Manufacturing, and the averages computed from all 20 sets of volumes show that the earnings of the factory wage workers have been just a little less than 41 per cent. of the value added to the raw materials by the processes of manufacturing.

In 1946, concludes Col. Ayres, we shall have much unemployment, much new employment, and more widespread discussions of wages than in any previous year in our history. Out of the experiences of 1946 there will come many disillusionments about the possibility of making wage increases without affecting costs of production, costs of goods produced, or profits from production.

* * *

Hidden Assets

"Excess depreciation charged off in prior years," the American Appraisal Company recently pointed out, is an expression with which most taxpayers are familiar since the United States Supreme Court decided in the Virginian Hotel case (63 Supt. Ct. 1260) that the excess could not be resorted to the depreciation base to be recovered in future years.

While high taxes have developed "tax consciousness," and it is chiefly in relation to taxes and profit and loss that depreciation procedure is considered, there is an important counterpart in the picture of the organization as portrayed in the balance sheet, says the company. Corresponding excess credits to the Depreciation Reserve unduly reduce the Net Fixed Assets to the extent that many complications may arise including the impairment of credit, a surplus deficit prohibiting the payment of dividends, and situations similar to the following:

A Manufacturer's assets were largely acquired during the "Certificate of Necessity" period and have been almost wholly written down through amortization allowances.

During negotiations for the sale of its product, the purchaser requested information covering the company's stability and, upon reviewing the balance sheet, immediately took the position that the company was not equipped to handle an order of the size under negotiation. For some time the prospective contract was in jeopardy, and it was only by a detailed explanation of the facts that it was finally consummated.

It is, perhaps, needless to add that as a result of this experience the manufacturer has decided to establish his corporate balance sheets on the basis of appraisal figures, reflecting the facts relative to the extent of the property.

* * *

Industrial Standard on Injury Rates Set

Providing a practical basis for recording and measuring industrial injury experience, a new American standard on the method of compiling industrial injury rates has been completed by the American Standards Association, it was announced recently.

So that the resulting records may have a uniform experience basis covering the entire country, the association said, the provisions are independent of State and Federal requirements for reporting injuries for workmen's compensation and of rulings as to disability by workmen's compensation agencies.

Injury rates compiled in accordance with this code, it was pointed out, may be used to evaluate: the relative need for accident prevention activities in different departments of an establishment; seriousness of the accident problem in an establishment or industry effectiveness of safety activities in establishments with comparable hazards, and progress made in accident prevention within an establishment or industry.

* * *

Of the six million farms in the United States in 1940, half had no mechanical power —not even a horse.

REPORT TO EMPLOYEES ON OUR 1945 OPERATIONS & PROFITS

To Employees of the J. Jay Company:

This report gives you an over-all picture of our 1945 operations and profits. It shows the total results in dollars as well as the weekly average result per employee.

The figures used in this report are the same as the figures filed with the Government's Securities and Exchange Commission in Washington, except for the way they are arranged.

These financial figures are given in more detail and more complicated form in our Annual Report to Stockholders. If you would like a copy of this report, please drop in at the Personnel Office. They will be glad to give you one.

We want each of our 20,700 employees to understand our income, our costs and our profits. Only in this way can we work together to further our joint and individual welfares.

Yours very truly,

J. Jay, *President*

REPORT TO EMPLOYEES ON OUR 1945 OPERATIONS & PROFITS

J. JAY COMPANY

		Weekly Average for Each Employee	*Grand Total for the Year*
Table A Sales and Costs for 1945			
Sales of our products to customers, plus various other income		$129.91	$139,835,559
Subtract—			
Costs of manufacturing and selling our products (wages and salaries *not* included)	$72.72		78,277,826
Taxes (including income taxes)	6.87		7,397,141
Total subtraction		79.59	85,674,967
Amount left for employees, officers and stockholders after all of the costs are subtracted, an average of $50.32 per week is left for employees, officers and stockholders. Table B shows how the $50.32 was divided		$ 50.32	$ 54,160,592
Table B How the $50.32 Was Divided			
Table A shows that an average per employee of $50.32 per week was left for employees, officers and stockholders. It was divided as follows:			
Employees		$ 46.06	$ 49,576,809
The average employee received $46.06 per week. All employees received a total of $49,576,809 for the year.			
Officers		.45	484,200
Twenty-three officers received salaries totaling $484,200 or an average of $405 per week for each officer. If all officers had worked without any salary and the amount had been used to increase salaries and wages of employees, the average increase would have been 45 cents per week.			
Stockholders		3.81	4,099,583
This is the amount set aside for stockholders. It belongs to them because they have invested their money in the Company. This money was not withdrawn from the Company's funds and Table C shows what they did with their share.			
Total		$ 50.32	$ 54,160,592
Table C What the Stockholders Did with Their Share			
Amount left in the Company to buy new equipment to provide new jobs and to use as a reserve for losses for a rainy day		$ 1.58	$ 1,695,879
Cash taken out of the Company as dividends		2.23	2,403,704
This is a kind of "rent" or "interest" stockholders receive on their investment. The money that stockholders invest provides the buildings in which we work, the tools we use and the money to absorb any losses we may have. The stockholders' investment in the Company (per employee) is $2,957. The dividends they received gave them a profit of $3.9 per cent. on their investment. The reasonableness of this return might be compared with the 2.9 per cent. annual interest on War Bonds, except the interest on War Bonds is guaranteed by the government, while the stockholder's dividends are *not* guaranteed and their investment may be reduced through losses.			
Total		$ 3.81	$ 4,099,583

AUDITOR'S REPORT

We have checked the figures in the "Grand Total for the Year" columns of Tables A, B, and C and have found that they conform with the basic figures filed with the Securities and Exchange Commission in Washington and also with the basic figures in the Report to Stockholders.

We also have test-checked the pay roll records and have been satisfied that the average number of employees during the year was approximately 20,700. The computations in the columns "Weekly Average for Each Employee" were checked and found to be correct.

D. Dee & Company

Independent Public Accountants
and Auditors

Presentation of Company Information to Shareholders and Employees

By J. A. FULLER, R.I.A.
Vice-President Shawinigan Water and Power Co. 71

When your Chairman asked me some time ago to make a few remarks on the subject of company information for the various classes of people who have reason to be interested in a company's affairs I rather hesitated to accept because I cannot claim any qualifications as an expert in this field. However, not long thereafter, I heard an address in which the speaker opened his remarks by saying that an expert is any man away from home and, with that in mind, I decided I would try my best to give you my general thoughts on this subject. I might add that perhaps I do have one qualification and that is an intense belief that employees, shareholders and customers are entitled to know everything there is to know about their company except matters which would be harmful to the company's business or competitive position.

I think your Chairman had in mind originally that I should speak primarily on the subject of company annual reports and, while they offer perhaps the best single opportunity to inform the employee and shareholder about company affairs, I feel that the matter is a much broader one and that no company can write up its annual report, dust off its hands and say there, that job is done for the year and we don't have to do anything more until the next year rolls around. The kind of information in which the employee is interested differs from that wanted by the shareholder and customers again have other interests. The whole job therefore, becomes one of continuous and unflagging effort throughout the year and over an indefinite period of years.

On your program this talk is entitled "Presentation of Company Information to Shareholders and Employees." If it hadn't been such a mouthful I think the proper title should have been 'Preparation and Dissemination of Company Information to Shareholders, Employees, Customers and the Public at large.' Preparation is one job—dissemination another requiring various departments within a company to carry them out. Depending on the kind of information and at whom it is being aimed, you will find that the preparation will involve many departments such as industrial relations, accounting, sales and operating, singly or in combination; the dissemination usually falls to the lot of the public relations and advertising departments. The subject as a whole forms part of a job which perhaps for want of a better name has broadly been given the title of 'human engineering' and which is now considered as important as any other phase of company activities.

Now, if any company is going to do a proper job of 'human engineering' I can say to you unequivocally that the one basic fundamental requirement essential for success is that top management look upon their employees, shareholders and customers as human beings and that they have a sincere belief that these groups want and are entitled to all the facts about a company's affairs. Company managements in the large corporations of to-day are in a rather unusual position. Except in a very few cases they are not the owners of the business—they are really just employees like everybody else. But beyond the usual management responsibilities they occupy a
72 trusteeship position—they must see that justice is done both to employees and shareholders and at the same time keep the customers happy. It is therefore essential that management realize the necessity of good relations with its employees, its shareholders and its public and this in turn requires a tolerant and understanding point of view.

At this point you may well ask why management to-day finds this job of 'human engineering' one of its major preoccupations. The explanation is really rather simple. Back in the early days of industrial development companies were usually small, the boss was very often the sole owner, knew all his employees by their first names and probably knew most of his customers personally. If he had other shareholders they were probably his personal friends and he could tell them how things were going by personal contact. Where such a situation prevails to-day you will rarely find strikes, and the shareholder is usually well satisfied with his investment.

With the development of large corporations and mass production methods bringing in their wake the installation of complicated and expensive machinery, the human element was relegated to a back seat. Labour was considered a commodity to be purchased at the cheapest price possible. The emphasis was entirely on technical and engineering improvements to reduce production costs, and the building up of adequate and highly skilled sales staff to increase sales volume. Specialized service departments became necessary to serve manufacturing and selling departments and in the end few employees in any company had much idea of what the fellows in other departments had to do except perhaps an idea that they sat with their feet on their desks. The man at the machine in particular came to feel that he was a robot and that no one took any interest in his work or in him as a human being. Management was slow to understand the harmful effects of this situation but the awakening has now come. Management now realizes that employees, shareholders and the public generally have very little idea of the purposes and accomplishments of industry and that many of the ideas they have are wrong. For example, the public has had a very decided misconception as to industrial profits. Opinion polls have shown that the public believes industry makes about 25% or more profit and considers that 10 to 15% would be fair whereas actually the profit of most companies runs considerably less than 10% on the sales dollar. The average figure in 1947 in the U.S. was 5½%. Misunderstanding has been responsible for bad employee relations and bad public relations. With the realization that misunderstanding exists, management is faced with the question of what to do about it. The answer is there for progressive management—do away with misunderstanding by telling the facts. This, Gentlemen, is the heart of the whole problem. Without information there can be no understanding.

While this fundamental answer to the problem is relatively simple, the doing of it is another story. It takes money, time, thought and effort and this effort cannot be spasmodic; it must be a continuing one, not only on the part of special departments delegated to handle the job, but also on the part of management.

I am afraid that I have taken rather a long time merely to give you reasons why a company must tell its story. I thought however, that it was worth while to do so because once management is convinced the job must 73
be done and I am speaking to you Gentlemen,—as part of management—the preparation and presentation can be delegated at least in part to those trained in this work. Methods will differ widely from company to company depending on size, location and number of plants and the nature of the business.

Company information may well be separated into three categories corresponding to the interests which the company serves, namely, its employees, its shareholders and its customers, including in this last category the public in general. For the sake of good order I will discuss these three categories separately although there is a considerable amount of overlapping between them, particularly in the case of the annual report with which I would like to deal in some detail later on.

I will pass rather briefly over the category concerned with information for customers and the public because it is of a type which has been carried on by most companies for a considerable number of years. It would include the usual advertising of products and also institutional advertising designed to improve public relations. Perhaps the most important new development in this field is so-called 'plant city' advertising by which a company promotes goodwill in the community in which it has a plant by advertising the benefits which it brings to the community. Included in this field also are exhibits of company products and services at trade fairs, and special publications which may be produced from time to time for circulation to special groups. These publications are for the purpose of promoting good public relations or for example, in the case of a public utility industry, of presenting the advantages and benefits to be derived from the location by industry in its territory. While not exactly part of any program to disseminate information, I would like to make the comment that encouragement of employee participation in community activities is of great benefit in fostering good public relations.

Employee information is a difficult subject and one which only recently has become of serious concern to management. In this category the more usual media of information are the employee magazine or house organ; the employee handbook or as it is sometimes called 'indoctrination book' in cases where it is aimed primarily at new employees; company information programmes; and the annual report designed in such fashion as to be understandable to the employee either as a special report or one which is suitable for employees and shareholders alike. There are of course, many matters which arise from time to time about which the employees should be informed, and management must be on its toes to take advantage of opportunities to keep employees advised of various situations which help them know more about their company. Doing so will benefit employee relations generally.

The employee magazine is perhaps the single most important medium for disseminating information to employees although in my opinion it has not been sufficiently utilized for this purpose. Most magazines have used the greater part of their space for news of employee activities although it is fairly common to include a leading article regarding some phase of the
74 company's affairs in particular articles descriptive of manufacturing plants and processes. While I do not advocate the use of the magazine for company propaganda purposes, I do think that simple explanation of the functions of the various company departments can be made interesting and informative to the general body of employees.

A carefully designed and attractively set up employee handbook has become essential for larger corporations. It is practically impossible for an employment manager or a supervisor to tell a new employee what he ought to know about his company before he starts work, and it is also practically impossible for the employee himself to get any broad understanding of the company's affairs from experience in the job to which he has been assigned. Naturally, most employees want to know about the company's policy on wages, its hours of work and the many benefit plans which the larger companies usually have in effect for employee welfare such as group insurance, pension plans, recreational clubs, etc. Beyond these matters of fact, however, I think it is very desirable for any company to take this opportunity of promoting general understanding of company organization and business and this is being done to an increasing extent. For example, in a recent analysis made of 130 company information manuals, 93 had a section dealing with the company's history and 68 a section on the company's products and services. Production of such information manuals is a long hard task but the effort is well worth while.

A more recent development aimed at improving general employee understanding is what has been called a company information program. As a result of surveys made over the past few years it has been found that senior managerial employees have very sketchy ideas of over all company policy and also of the work of departments other than their own. This is especially true if they are located at some distance from head office. Sometimes right at home it is difficult to fathom the whys and wherefores of certain decisions and to understand why there is so much red tape often about minor matters. Supervisory employees at least should know why—

otherwise a dissatisfied attitude on their part may result and this will naturally affect those who come under their supervision. It has therefore been found necessary to start these company information programmes very near the top. The basic idea is that the senior employees in each department will not only gain a much better understanding of the company's affairs themselves, but will be better able to interpret company policy to those under them. There are of course, many methods of handling such a program. One method for example is to bring supervisory employees in various departments together at head office in groups of about 15, and never more than 20, for a period of about one week. During this time they have an opportunity to meet not only each other but also top management and department heads. Meetings and conferences are held during the entire week at which company policy and affairs are fully explained. To boil it all down, the idea is to give junior executives a pretty good idea of what makes the clock tick.

Now we come to our poor shareholders. They own the business yet from some reports made to them one would think they were strangers in
their own house. It is their money which makes the business possible. They 75
have delegated management to conduct the business for them and they have every right to demand a complete accounting from management as to what it has done and plans to do. The annual report is of course, the principal medium used to advise the owners of the results of management's stewardship. I believe however, that more frequent financial reports should be made and this is being done by many companies in the form of quarterly reports. Beyond just giving financial figures in these reports I think management should in addition give a brief story of the outstanding events and progress made during the past quarter.

As I have already mentioned, the annual report provides the company with its best opportunity of telling its story, not only to its owners but to its employees and the public. It is now generally recognized that it should be written simply and straightforwardly, avoiding the use of $10 words where four letter words will do. I have said that this can be done by preparing a separate and distinct report for employees or by utilizing a combined document. Present day thinking is leaning decidedly towards a combined document because it has been found that the employee can understand the financial figures presented therein just as well as the average shareholder —in fact, perhaps better and some special reports for employees have been over-simplified and cartooned to the extent that they are an insult to the employees' intelligence. As management has come to realize the necessity of informing employees and shareholders alike about company affairs, more and more annual reports have been modernized and streamlined. By this I mean a departure from a dry and dusty recapitulation of the financial results for the year in technical accounting terms. The idea now is to tell a simple story of the company's accomplishments in the previous year, and of its prospects for the future. In order to put this story over it is always helpful to include a certain number of graphs and charts to bring out the important points made in the text and also to make a judicious use of pictures. The job of producing an annual report of this sort is one that must be commenced long before the end of the year to which it relates, because a lot of careful thought and planning is always necessary. It is always hard to get people to read anything. The average employee and shareholder have neither the time nor the inclination to read purely financial comment. The only people who will are brokers, bankers and financial analysts whose job makes it necessary for them to do so.

What then does the average employee and shareholder want to hear about his Company? As a result of very complete analysis of this question, it has been found that the most important items are a brief story giving in highlight just what happened in the previous year; a condensed and simplified statement of what the company took in and what it paid out; a statement in brief terms of how much the company spent on new plant during the past year with some description of the various kinds of plants; and also a story from the management as to future plans. These subjects of course, have to be dealt with in each annual report, but in addition the annual report gives great scope and opportunity for explaining all phases of company activities until over a period of years practically all
76 subjects of interest are covered. Among the subjects which should be dealt with at one time or another are a description of benefit plans for employees; a story on company managment; on the growth and development of the business over a period of years; and the new products which have been developed or are in process of development. In fact, I think it is impossible to run out of interesting subjects which will give both employees and shareholders a better understanding of what the company has done, is doing, and plans to do.

I have mentioned that the annual report should include a simplified and condensed statement of the company's income and outgo. I do not mean by this that the usual form of financial statements should be omitted but I do say that these statements need to be simplified so that they may be understood by those not versed in technical accounting terms, and in this group are shareholders as well as employees. Accounting is your profession Gentlemen,—I also have had a good deal to do with accounting —and I don't believe any of us fully realize how incomprehensible a Balance Sheet and Profit and Loss Account are to the average man. Many of you have no doubt, read a most amusing address by Knowlton which was reproduced in the February issue of the Canadian Chartered Accountant and in which he describes his struggles to ascertain the real meaning of certain accounting terminology. I would also commend to your reading Financial Management Series No. 88 of the American Management Association which covers a seminar on "Reporting to Employees and the Public on Profits and Productivity." Some examples of terms which we consider second nature but which confuse the layman are Profit and Loss Account—why shouldn't it be called a Profit Account or at least, just a Loss Account if there is a loss. It can't be both at the same time. And, why are there so many different kinds of Profit—First, we see an Operating Profit—and then down the line a Net Profit, but that isn't the end—we go a little further along and there is an item called Net Income. Most people think a Profit, by whatever name, is what is left after all expenses have been paid. In between we have a little item calle Sales. This turns out to be not the cost of selling the goods as th implies, but also the cost of making them. And, as for Depreciati what is that all about—and where does the money set aside for that purp go—Why don't we say—"Cost of providing for replacement of plant an equipment?"

And then we come to Surplus. Mr. Webster defines Surplus as 'Being or constituting a surplus; more than sufficient; as surplus revenues or words.' But are any of us willing to admit that the Surplus shown in Financial Statements is an excess which can be paid to the owners. How about that part of it which must be retained in the business for plant expansion or for working capital purposes. And how much of the Balance Sheet Surplus could be paid out? We well know that hardly any of it could—it is all tied up in plant or inventories or both.

And now how about the Balance Sheet? Why does it always balance on both sides and why are Surplus and certain other reserves liabilities?

Well, one could go on with this sort of thing at considerable length. The point is that if we are going to explain financial results and financial
position in understandable terms, some new words have got to be used. 77
The P. and L. account must be viewed as a statement reporting "what we took in and where did it go." Some terms which might be used to review the year's financial record are "Results of Operations," "Revenues and Their Distribution" or "Income and Expenses."

The Balance Sheet rather than being shown as a statement of Assets and Liabilities should be called for example, a statement of Financial Position. If set up to arrive at a net asset figure which would consist of capital subscribed and balance employed in the business, it would be a much more understandable exhibit.

Please do not think from all this that I am criticizing or calling for changes in present accounting terminology. Just as in the case of the legal and medical professions certain technical terms in the accounting profession have over the years attained the status of precise meaning and radical change might result in great confusion. What I want to convey to you is that simplified statements and terms must be used if management wants to get its financial story over to its employees and shareholders.

May I finish my remarks by saying Gentlemen, that the day of presenting annual reports, which contain only the information required by law is over, and that those companies which have not yet done so should make haste to tell their story to their employees, shareholders and public, not only because it is a duty, but because of the benefits which they will derive from doing so.

unicate Financial Information
ees, and What to Say

by Stephen Arthur Derry, Civil Engineer
Louisville, Kentucky

78

• Too many reports to employees have failed in their missions. More than simple words is needed. This author lists five categories of information in which workers are interested, and 12 media for getting it to them. He describes two cases where successful techniques were worked out.

COMPANY OPERATION reports, like companies, have changed with the times. Perhaps the greatest change is the simplification of reports intended for employees. In preparing such reports, some companies make the mistake of thinking that anything in very simple terms will do. They forget that today labor analyzes company reports more keenly than capital. Unions have highly paid analysts on their staffs to do this for their members, and management should consider very carefully the labor reaction to reports it issues to its employees, its stockholders, or the public. In all dealing with labor and management, I have found that almost every time that there is a difference of opinion, the source of difference is a report the company had issued.

However, there is no doubt that a report to employees must be in everyday language. The conventional financial statements are as unintelligible to the average employee as the text of a doctor's prescription is to accountants.

The difficulty of getting employees interested in the company's story is illustrated by the experiment of a company which published its first statement to its employees in 1939, its sixty-second year of operations. The statement, a leaflet entitled, "Looking Ahead," in addition to announcing a change in top management, stressed customer relations, supplier relations, organization, employee relations, wages, recognition for long service, and a resumé of the company's financial obligations to its stockholders and employees in a report entitled "Review of 1939 Operations for Employees," containing a balance-sheet and a statement of operations.

With the 1944 report, there was enclosed a card asking the employees and stockholders to express their views about the report. Management was shocked when less than two per cent of the employees responded. The president, who had risen to the top from his start as a 17-year-old office boy, was so disappointed that he wrote a special message to the employees. The theme of the leaflet was the principles that guided the company in employee relations, stressing wages, rates of pay, mechanical process, credit union, and retirement plan.

As a result of the 1944 experience, the 1945 annual report was modernized, and made "hard to get." The only way a worker could get a copy was by asking for it, either in person or in writing. The company was again shocked when employees made little or no attempt to get copies. In 1946 the report was again revised and this time the management stood at the gate and handed out the reports to workers as they left the plant. The amount of employee interest was still disappointing. The 1947 report was greatly improved and filled with unusual charts, graphs, photographs, and detailed information on company operations. One of the features of this report was the breakdown of expenses. The breakdown showed the distribution in this order.

Distribution:		Per Income Dollar
WAGES AND SALARIES		00¢
Factory employees	$ 00,000,000	
Salesmen and supervisors	0,000,000	
Officers and directors	000,000	
Benefits	000,000	
Total	$ 00,000,000	
RAW MATERIALS		00¢
Supplies and services	$ 00,000,000	
DEPRECIATION		00¢
For use of equipment	$ 000,000	
TAXES		00¢
Federal, state, and local	$ 0,000,000	
DIVIDENDS		00¢
Stockholders for use of their money	$ 000,000	
REMAINED IN THE BUSINESS		00¢
Improvement and emergency uses	$ 0,000,000	

This report was mailed; the employee interest in this annual report was the best the company had obtained.

Another company, a manufacturer of farm equipment, capitalized on the fact that many of its employees were also owners of small farms. This company was founded in 1825 and the theme of its first modern annual report (in 1944) was the farmer and his implements. The report was well received by farmers, because the content was pictorially displayed in such a fashion that the farmer felt proud of his own business. Incidentally, this report revealed for the first time to many local farmers that the company manufactured modern power-driven farm machinery and could no longer be considered a small manufacturer of horse-drawn farm equipment.

The 1945 and 1946 reports followed the same theme as 1944, with more emphasis on products and problems. The theme of the 1947 report was new manufacturing facilities and new products. The pages, including the cover, were well balanced with photographs of tractors, plows, harrows, planters, cultivators, rotary hoes, and several other farm implements in action. Each of these photographs was an action picture demonstrating practical application of farm equipment. The three middle pages conveyed the financial story. Presentation was conservative but very 79
forceful.

I consider the text of these reports excellent because the contents were designed to appeal to the farmer. Since many of its employees owned small farms, the company got across to them the importance and uses of the product they help to make.

Information that Appeals to Employees

The daily job represents the worker's life center; his hopes, fears, and pride cluster around that life center. When he reads a report these emotions are uppermost in his mind. He looks for his part in the manufacturing process. He is interested in knowing the company's progress and stability. He is interested in financial figures which he can relate to his own job and his own prospects. He wants to know how the profit is spent. He is interested in knowing the use, importance, and value of the product he helped to make. He is desirous of knowing who owns the company for which he works. He is interested in knowing the history of the company and what prospects the company has. He wants to know if the stockholders live in his community or several thousand miles away from the plant. He wants to know who they are: bankers, investors, women, radio stars, etc. He would like to know if the stock is available to him. I could list a dozen more subjects that interest the worker, such as how wage rates for his job compare with those paid by other companies in the community, what benefits that are offered by other companies he also receives, etc.

When a worker reads management's report on company operations and fails to find the answers to these items, it is only natural for him to react unfavorably, if at all, to surveys of employee reaction.

Presenting Operation Facts to Employees

Before a company can give its employees an understanding of the financial facts of the business it must have earned their confidence and respect for the truth of its statements.

Prerequisite to employee interest in
80 company reports are

(a) A sound personnel philosophy
(b) Progressive labor policies
(c) A genuine desire to deal justly with all employees.

When these policies have been inaugurated by the company, then management is ready to formulate a program which will dispel misunderstanding about the facts of the company's operations.

The basic principle of this program should be employee education. The company must explain

1. *Financial*

(a) The importance of stockholders
(b) Why reserves are needed
(c) Facts on taxes
(d) Why a profit must be maintained
(e) What is a break-even point?
(f) Why the break-even point is important
(g) Effect of wages on stability of company
(h) Effect of other matters on financial standing of the company

2. *Operation*

(a) The reason why control of expenses is important
(b) The effect of wages and raw material costs on profits
(c) The need for maintaining high productivity per worker
(d) The relation between inventories and costs
(e) The importance of waste and rejected products
(f) How volume affects prices, wages, and waste

3. *Public Relations*

(a) The importance of holding customers' goodwill and general public patronage
(b) Community interest and activity, and its effect on employees

4. *Human Relations*

(a) The importance of harmony with fellow workers
(b) Its effect on the employee himself, management, production, fellow workers, customers, quality and quantity of product

5. *Economics*

(a) Wage trends in competitive industries
(b) Importance of advertising
(c) The relation of company operations to the industrial economy as a whole
(d) The importance of balanced economy within the plant, the community, and the nation

Putting Education Program into Effect

The next step in making this type of program effective is to start training top management. Employees at this level fully understand the policies of the company, but are not usually familiar with details, or able to present operating facts in a manner interesting to the workers.

Getting Operating Facts Across to Employees

First: Information that is to be given to the workers must originate at the top—perhaps in the form of memoranda at regular intervals. All company operations, product data, sales, and other current facts of news value involving the company as a whole should be covered.

Second: From outside sources information must be obtained pertaining to industry-wide trends in products, prices. The opinion of the general public, of the supervisors, and of workers must be discovered. These opinion surveys should be obtained because they give the employee a feeling that he is a part of the management.

Stephen Arthur Derry, a civil engineer, practices his profession in Louisville, Kentucky. For about 30 years he has been engaged in major civil and industrial engineering projects. Mr. Derry is a teacher and lecturer on engineering and business subjects; author of numerous technical and non-technical articles; member of the principal engineering societies and the American Accounting Association.

Once the desires of top management are known and the feeling and thinking of the workers are analyzed, the company's director of industrial and public relations is ready to start the third step in getting facts across to employees.

Disseminating Company Information to Employees

The usual channels in conveying information to employees may be grouped as follows:

1. House Organ: This medium should discuss the worker and his problems in *his language.* The information released through the house organ must be consistent in its character, always personal, always with employee flavor, and by all means newsy and spontaneous. The goal of the house organ at all times should be to build a feeling of belonging.

2. Letters or Memoranda: When legal matters affecting both company and employees come up, the letter or memorandum is probably the best medium to use. The communication should be sent to the employee's home and under no circumstances distributed at the plant. In this way the employee's family is more likely to be brought into the discussion; the employee's family usually has a stake in the matter, and it is desirable to encourage the employee to consider the matter in the atmosphere of his home, instead of the surroundings of the work area.

3. Leaflets: The primary use of this means of communication is to get messages across to customers and consumers. The theme of these leaflets should be the company's viewpoint on some misunderstood or misinterpreted facts about the company, or its product, perhaps some popular subject matter of interest to all workers in the community. Many utility companies insert leaflets with their monthly bills to consumers and some manufacturing companies give leaflets to their salesmen.

4. Annual Reports: This medium has been adequately discussed above. I should like to add that annual reports should be addressed to both stockholders and employees. This helps to make the employee feel that he is given the same information as the stockholder, and the feeling of being excluded from guarded facts is dispelled. It is a mistake, however, for companies to depend wholly on annual reports to get the operating facts to employees. The annual report should serve as a summary of what actually took place.

5. Publicity: It is a good idea to let the employees in on new products before releasing the information to the press. Nothing makes an employee more distrustful toward his employer than to pick up a trade journal or a newspaper and read about a new product his company has released for sale, or developed, of which he knew nothing. Publicity should be given to all worthy achievements of employees. It makes the employee feel that he is appreciated. It strikes deeply into his emotion of pride.

6. Advertising: Perhaps this medium can be best explained by referring to the advertising philosophies used by utility and insurance companies. Many of these organizations use advertising space in current magazines to discuss the interests of their employees.

7. Payroll Inserts: This medium should be limited to those facts pertaining to the employee's pay or conditions affecting his pay. The dissemination of unrelated information in the pay envelope is a gross psychological error. For example, it is a serious mistake to explain here, as some companies have, that the president did not receive the $100,000 salary reported in the newspaper, as take-home pay, because he had to give $60,000 of it for taxes.

8. Biographies of Brass Hats: Explaining to the employee how top-management personnel was elevated to "Mahogany Row" goes a long way in bringing about a friendly and closer feeling toward top management personnel. A thumbnail sketch of one or more executives is an intriguing human interest story and kills the popular myth that top management men are inhuman.

9. Handbook: This medium is primarily used for acquainting a new employee with his duties and responsibilities to himself, the company and his fellow workers. The handbook also serves old employees as a reference and guide to general operating policies.

10. Personal Contact: Direct contact with workers at all levels, up and down, brings about an *esprit de corps* that cannot be created in any other way. Personal contact is one of the best ways to control the oldest communication system known to man—the grapevine. Nobody likes a whispering campaign. When the personal-contact medium is allowed to drop into the background, the grapevine method of passing information can do more harm than written words can undo. Personal contact up and down is very important, not only in the plant or while at work, but at all times.

11. Film: This medium combines all the means of communication previously discussed. Excellent sound films have been produced by the International Harvester Company and a number of other organizations.

This article was suggested by a paper read by the author at The Ohio State University Tenth Annual Institute on Accounting, May 21, 1948.

A SIMPLIFIED INCOME STATEMENT FOR EMPLOYEE USE

by WALTER C. BURNHAM,
Associate Professor of Accounting, Ohio State University,
Columbus, Ohio.

Whether simplified income statements, appearing in varying versions in many company reports, relate to the future of the income statement as such or to one or more of its special purposes is an open question. The present article comments on characteristics of simplified statements regarded as information media for employees, before presenting a form of statement intended to combine features most serviceable for this purpose.

82 MANAGEMENT has a vital story to tell its employees about profits, and it must tell it in such a way that it can be read, believed, and remembered. Misconceptions of the amount of profit and its distribution can be reduced to a minimum by the use of simplified statements. But they must bear the marks of unmistakable sincerity and simplicity. Unrealistic wage demands should be answered by showing the employees that the profits reinvested in the business are only a small per cent of the total wages paid and—what is more—that they are necessary for the preservation of jobs. The feeling among employees that productivity is no matter of importance because management reaps the benefits should be answered by showing the amounts which are paid to management and intelligently indicating their relationship to other amounts.

The practical questions in this area are: (1) what type of income statement should be used for presentation to employees and (2) what type of report should be prepared for employees to show what happened to the funds that were reinvested in the business. It will be the endeavor of this article, first, to consider some examples of simplified statements, whether or not prepared primarily for employees, and, second, to present a proposed basic form of employee statement.

Of course it can well be doubted that separate reporting to employees is appropriate. I believe that, ordinarily, it is. However, care must be used to see that the reports are not too elementary in form. It must be remembered that most of the employees are men and women of average intelligence and should not be treated as juveniles. Some companies, after giving to their shareholders long,

Chain Belt Company
Simplified Statement of Income and Expense
For the Fiscal Year 1947

	Amount	Per Dollar of Sales	
The Company Received			
From customers for the goods and services purchased by them	$24,336,967	$1.00	
The Company's Expenses Were			
For materials, supplies, and services purchased from others. This included such things as iron and steel, insurance, social security taxes, advertising, upkeep of equipment, etc.	10,817,805	.44	
For wear and tear on machinery, tools, and buildings. This is generally known as depreciation ...	266,682	.01	
For income taxes owing to State and Federal Governments	1,900,000	.08	
Making a total of	$12,984,487	$ .53	83
Which left for wages, salaries, dividends, and for reinvestment in the business	$11,352,480	$ .47	
THIS WAS DIVIDED AS FOLLOWS:			
Paid to employees as wages and salaries	$ 8,748,657	$ .36	
Paid to stockholders as dividends for the use of the buildings, machinery, equipment, and working capital provided by their investments	730,163	.03	
Reinvested in the business, to take care of the growing needs of the company	1,873,660	.08	

Exhibit 1.

detailed, statistical statements, give to their employee pie and bar charts and picture graphs. Any hint of "talking down" to the employees should be avoided. In most cases it will be advisable to give both the shareholders and the employees at least some simplified information in the same or approximately the same form, which they may read and interpret simply as individuals. Every effort should be made to show the common interest of shareholders, management, and employees.

Present Style In Simplified Income Statements

Simplified income statements have become frequent in the last year or two, and indeed have achieved a certain degree of standing. They feature nontechnical captions and are generally cast in either of two forms. One of these deducts from revenue as "first costs" the cost of materials, supplies, and services purchased outside, as well as depreciation and sometimes, but not always, taxes.

The form then itemizes the disposition of the balance, indicating the amounts paid to employees and to stockholders, and the amount retained in the business. The other form is the so-called single step form and contains the same general type of itemization but does not draw down a balance after "first costs."

The statements which have been selected for illustration include both sorts. The Chain Belt Company statement, Exhibit 1, and that of Wheeling Steel Corporation, Exhibit 2, show balances after outside payments. The Vanadium Steel Company statement, Exhibit 3, is a single step statement and, incidentally, slights the disposition of profit angle. The principal reason, however, for display and discussion of these statements as a preliminary to presentation of a proposed form of simplified statement for employees,
84 is the attempt which each makes—not only to describe revenue, the elements of cost, and the disposition of profit in everyday language—but also to provide "reduced" figures which may serve to assist employees to interpret the statements. This effect is sought in each statement through the use of a column of figures paralleling the dollar aggregates. In the Chain Belt statement, the column is headed "per dollar of sales." It appears as "grand total reduced to weekly average per employee" in the Wheeling Steel statement. The "per worker" column of the Vanadium Alloys statement offers the corresponding information. This statement also carries, as interpretative data, a percentage to revenue figure beside each cost (or distributive) dollar amount.

Featuring Items of Significance to Employees

Undoubtedly, the one item on the income statement which causes more suspicion and conjecture than any other is executive salaries. None of the statements shown separate this item. In most instances the amount of these salaries has been included in such headings as salaries, wages, direct benefits for employees, and cost of human energy. It is suggested that this is pertinent information for employee readers and should be disclosed. The amount of the salaries may be large but, in juxtaposition to the total payroll, it may be much less significant. Also the mere fact that the executive salaries are disclosed will have a good psychological effect upon employees. Of statements of some fifty companies reviewed, the International Harvester Company, Crown Zellerback Corporation, and National Biscuit Company were the only ones observed to show executive salaries as a separate item.

Wheeling Steel Corporation and Subsidiary Companies

Profit and Loss Statement for the Year 1947

	Grand total for year	*Weekly average per employee**
Amount of money we received from sale of products	$131,721,128	$177.92
Add—Other income including interest and rent received	877,161	1.18
Total income for 1947	$132,598,289	$179.10
Subtract the following two costs:		
1. Cost of raw materials, supplies, electricity, freight, and other expenses including local and state taxes, wear and tear on equipment, interest, etc., but exclusive of wages and salaries	$ 58,713,582	$ 79.30
2. Income taxes paid to the United States Government	8,290,000	11.20
Total costs to be subtracted	$ 67,003,582	$ 90.50
Amount left for employees wages, salaries, employee benefits, and for stockholders ($179.10 minus $90.50)	$ 65,594,707	$ 88.60

HERE IS HOW THE $88 60 WAS DIVIDED

Employees received in wages and salaries:		
For current year	$ 49,173,316	$ 66.42
For prior years (Retroactive Wages)	3,243,166	4.38
Employee benefits cost (represents the cost of social security payments, pension, insurance, workman's compensation, welfare work, and other items for the benefit of the employees	2,733,064	3.69
Total	$ 55,149,546	$ 74.49
The total above shows that for each week the average employee received $74.49 in wages, salaries, and other benefits paid by the corporation or a total of $55,149,546, leaving		
Profit for the year	10,445,161	14.11
Total	$ 65,594,707	$ 88.60

THE ABOVE PROFIT ($14.11) WAS DIVIDED AS FOLLOWS:

Stockholders—received as dividends on		
Preferred stock—$5.00 per share	$ 1,815,830	$ 2.45
Common stock—$1.75 per share	996,728	1.35
(Explanatory text omitted)		
Amount left in the business	7,632,603	10.31
This amount was left in the corporation to buy new equipment, to pay on indebtedness, and as a reserve against losses on a rainy day.		

* Wording condensed.

Exhibit 2

Vanadium-Alloys Steel Company
Simplified Operating Statement
July 1, 1946 to June 30, 1947

		Total	Per worker
We received from customers for goods and services		$8,895,516.31 (100%)	$8,678.55
These receipts were expended for:			
The cost of goods and services bought from others	$3,872,205.18 (43.5%)		3,777.76
The cost of human energy (wages and salaries)	3,522,140.97 (39.6%)		3,436.24
The cost of tools wearing out (depreciation and depletion)	140,144.20 (1.6%)		136.73
86 The cost of payments ordered by Government (taxes)	596,398.81 (6.7%)		581.85
The cost of using the tools (profit)	764,627.15 (8.6%)		754.98
Total expended		$8,895,516.31 (100%)	$8,678.55
Tools in use by company workers		$8,670,128.51	$8,458.66
Ratio of profit to tools		8.82%	

The Vanadium-Alloys Steel Company received also $58,183.87 that was not related to the manufacture or sale of its products.

As of June 30, 1947, the Vanadium-Alloys Steel Company had 1,193 stockholders and 1,025 employees.

Exhibit 3

It is probably also desirable to display, as in the Wheeling Steel statement, the amount of employee benefit expenditures over and above salaries and wages, and to subtotal this amount with salaries and wages. Again the information is pertinent to employee readers of statements and, in this case, directly affects each.

Another relationship frequently developed in income statements for employee use is the dollar amount of company investment (whether in fixed capital or fixed and working capital) per worker. This is set forth in the Vanadium Alloys statement. It was found also in income statements issued by E. I. du Pont de Nemours & Company, Union Oil Company of California, Algoma Steel Corporation, Ltd., and American Rolling Mills Company.

Perhaps even more important in respect of income statements to inform employees, is the manner in which the item of retained profit is handled. The Chain Belt and Wheeling statements show

Illustrative Company
Simplified Statement of Income and Expense
for Fiscal Year 1947

The Company Received	*Amount*	*Amount per employee*	*Per cent dollar sales*
From customers for goods and services purchased	$185,313,000	$8,681	.9899
Dividends from subsidiaries	1,785,750	84	.0095
Interest on receivables, securities, etc...	114,500	5	.0006
Total company received	$187,213,250	$8,770	1.0000
The Company's Expenses Were			
For materials, supplies, and other expenses	$ 96,423,750	$4,517	.5150
For wear and tear on machinery, tools, and buildings. This is generally known as depreciation	2,043,500	96	.0109
For taxes—Federal, state, and local (not including social security)	8,892,750	417	.0475
Making a total of	$107,360,000	$5,030	.5734
Which left for wages, salaries, dividends, and reinvestment in business	$ 79,853,250	$3,740	.4266
THIS WAS DIVIDED AS FOLLOWS:			
Paid to employees as wages and salaries..	$ 66,076,750	$3,095	.3530
For social security taxes, contributions to pension fund, group life insurance, etc...	1,311,500	61	.0070
Total	$ 67,388,250	$3,156	.3600
Paid to officers as compensation	347,750	16	.0019
Paid to stockholders as dividends for use of buildings, machinery, equipment, and working capital provided by their investment	6,735,750	316	.0360
Reinvested in the business to take care of the growing needs of the company......	5,381,500	252	.0287
Total division	$ 79,853,250	$3,740	.4266

Exhibit 4

a consciousness of this importance and related wording is included intended, although brief, to make a reasonable impression on readers. As this article progresses into the presentation of a proposed statement to incorporate the best features of experience to date in reporting to employees, it will be noted that the matter of amounts reinvested in the business is considered of sufficient importance to warrant special treatment.

Proposed Form of Employee Statement

Some fifty company reports were reviewed in a search for the record of experience which might give the major clues to the most effective type of operating or income statement for a company to submit to its employees. Of these statements the three which accompany this paper have already been commented upon. Three others are to be cited later, on the specific matter of explaining the uses made of profits retained in the business. The present paragraphs are devoted to an illustrative employee statement, Exhibit 4, proposed as suitable for general adoption in the form shown or as modified for the circumstances of each company.

88 It will be observed that the "first cost" approach has been selected, in contrast to the single step form. This choice has been made because statements of the "first cost" type have as their final effect the focussing of attention on the division of the balance of revenue left after such costs have been cared for, and it is this distribution in which the employee's interest is perhaps greatest. As to terminology employed in the descriptive captions, the illustrative form leans to a certain extent heavily on the Chain Belt statement. However, changes in wording will be noted, principally in the direction of brevity. The tax caption, included in the "first cost" section, will be observed to be a more inclusive one. Variations from the Chain Belt statement in the distribution section consist of the disclosure of employee benefit payment, a subtotal of these with wages and salaries, and the separate display of executive salaries—all features advocated in comments made earlier in this paper.

On the question of interpretative columns in income statements intended for employees, the presence of two columns of this sort will be noted. It is felt that these are not too many and that they invite a real scrutiny of results from the employee viewpoint. Next to the conventional amount column appears "amount per employee." This is perhaps almost as useful and more simply provided than the investment per employee figures sometimes developed in company reports. It is a ready tracer to the revenue needed per employee if material for each to work on is to be purchased and wages paid. It also shows the relative size of the cost of management (executive salaries), dividends, and reinvestment.

The second column, percentage of sales dollars, is very often found in income statements. The decimals can equally well be thought of as cents per dollar. It is, in fact, a simple index of relationship of the amounts in the dollar columns and, as such, represents the results of arithmetical processes which the normal mind would attempt without it but would not perform accurately or completely.

Explanation of Amounts Reinvested in the Business

A final and important point remains to be given due emphasis. Care should be taken to clearly explain what use has been made of the amount reinvested in the business and this can be done initially on the employee income statement. The statement should show that this reinvested portion of the profits has gone to purchase new tools and equipment, to liquidate long-term debts, and to provide working capital to keep the business virile. All of these 89
ends, when business is well managed, serve in the long run to create new jobs, to improve working conditions in existing jobs, and to increase the earnings of labor. The illustrative statement given as Exhibit 4 adopts the rather brief phraseology of the Chain Belt statement because we are looking to a type of change in working capital statement to further clarify the use of retained amounts.

However, here also, it may be well to see what has been done. In the report of the Barnsdall Oil Company a breakdown of reinvested profits is appended to the simplified income statement in the following form:

	1947	*1946*
The balance retained in the business for future needs, adding to the value of Barnsdall's assets, was.............	$5,679,689	$3,117,644
Of the amount added to assets, there was invested in fixed assets in excess of amounts charged to operations......	$4,174,381	$1,639,227
and the balance was retained in the form of increased working capital and other assets	$1,505,308	$1,478,417

Union Oil Company of California used a two dimension chart (not reproduced here) with its income statement to indicate the division of profits and the ultimate disposition of retained income. A shortcoming of this type of analysis is that it fails to give any recognition to the noncash items, such as depreciation, in respect

UNITED STATES STEEL CORPORATION
Summary of 1947 Financial Operations

Additions to Working Capital		
Income		$127,098,148
Add—Non-cash costs in current year		
Wear and exhaustion of facilities		114,045,483
Other		1,118,833
Proceeds from sales and salvage of plant and equipment		4,084,565
Miscellaneous additions		778,051
Total additions		$247,125,080
Deductions from Working Capital		
Expended for plant and equipment	$206,561,876	
Added to costs applicable to future periods	25,109,687	
Set aside for property additions and replacements	15,000,000	
Deposit with trustee to cover bonds maturing in 1951	5,404,000	
90 Reduction in total long-term debt	4,568,607	
Dividends declared on preferred and common stocks	70,911,750	
Total deductions		327,555,920
Reduction in working capital		$ 80,430,840
Working Capital Per Consolidated Statement of Financial Position		
December 31, 1947	$548,648,098	
December 31, 1946	629,078,938	
Reduction		$ 80,430,840

EXHIBIT 5

of application of proceeds from income, and does not reflect applications during the year of funds on hand at the start. In the report of the United States Steel Corporation, a Summary of 1947 Financial Operations—supplementary to the other financial statements—shows in a very readable manner what disposition was made of the income and noncash cost items (depreciation) for the year. This statement is displayed in Exhibit 5. It clearly shows that even though the net income for the year was only $127,098,148, the company spent $206,561,876 for expanded plant and equipment facilities. It makes it apparent that, after taking into consideration other investments and payment of long-term debts, the company reduced its working capital by $80,430,840, and gives a pretty good idea of where the sums went.

However, even this statement poses a difficulty. The layman is unable to understand quickly why the noncash items are added

Illustrative Company
Summary of 1947 Financial Operations

Additions to Working Capital		
Total Company received		$187,213,250
Less: Cash costs and expenses, and dividends		179,788,250
Excess reinvested in the business		$ 7,425,000
Proceeds from sale and salvage of property		1,028,500
Total additions		$ 8,453,500
Deductions from Working Capital		
Expended for plant and equipment	$15,477,000	
Increase in investment of subsidiaries	1,613,750	
Increase in other assets	311,250	
Total deductions		17,402,000
Reduction in working capital		$ 8,948,500

Exhibit 6

back. This may be overcome by presenting the information in the form suggested in Exhibit 6, which uses the figures in the illustrative income statement, Exhibit 4.

The total of all expenditures was $179,788,250, made up of cash costs and expenses during the year of $173,052,500 and dividends amounting to $6,735,750. The difference between the income of $187,213,250 and the total expenditures of $179,788,250 leaves a remainder of $7,425,000. This was the excess reinvested in the business. It represents the same figure which the accountant would determine by taking the amount reinvested in the business, as shown in the income statement, or $5,381,500, and adding to it the noncash costs for the current year which in this illustration are represented by depreciation of $2,043,500. To the amount to be reinvested from the profits would be added other increases in working capital such as from sale of property, sale of investments, and long-term borrowing. The deductions would include only such items as plant expansion, increase in investments, contributions to sinking funds, and actual reduction of long term obligations.

Summary

It seems to the author rather more than likely that the presentation of annual financial statements, in separate form, to employees of the company, will increase in frequency. If this is so, any attempt to draw together in a basic form the more useful features of the statements of this character which have been issued in individual instances, cannot but prove helpful, however far from final or even definitive the results may be. Such has been the viewpoint of this paper. Readability of captions and a certain "tangibility" of amounts are key objectives. Nevertheless no statement directed to employees will yield beneficial results if it does not stem from a sincere desire to inform.

CHAPTER 23

REPORTS TO EMPLOYEES AND THE GENERAL PUBLIC

Reports to Employees

The Employee and Business.—In reviewing the subject of reports to stockholders, the problem centered, first of all, around the basic attitude of management toward the owners. Does management really want informed stockholders? So, also, in considering reports to employees, it is a matter of understanding the true interest of employees in the business 93
and of deciding whether information should be shared with employees.

On the surface, the major attention of the average employee seems to be on higher wages, shorter hours, and better working conditions. Yet, whether he realizes it or not—and perhaps it is partly management's fault if he does not—the employee has a much greater concern in the business than these day-to-day objectives. For example, consider him in relation to the stockholder or bondholder. The latter makes investments of money; but the investments can be sold and the money recovered. However, the employee also has made an investment—the fifteen, or twenty-five, or forty years of his life. At the age of fifty he is not the same man as he was at twenty-five. During those years the business wanted his skill, his talents, his help in expanding and developing a profitable venture. Now, with his gray hair and stooped shoulders, the employee has lost youth, flexibility, and salability; they may have gone largely into the business. Does he have an interest in the company? To induce employees to contribute wholeheartedly to the success of the enterprise, the day-to-day wage, even including certain pension benefits, is not enough. The need is beyond any mere contractual limitations. For the highest degree of success, there are two other indispensable ingredients: (1) a recognition by management of its obligation to those who spend many years of life as wage-earners in the business, including the obligation to manage wisely, and (2) the encouraging of the wage-earners to demand or recognize a competent management as the best form of social security. The sharing of information with the employees can assist in this understanding and in creating a mutuality of interests.

Objectives of Reports to Employees.—By and large it is recognized that the employee is entitled to information about the company's operations. His job and his wages ultimately depend upon earnings, just as much as do the stockholders' dividends. The fact that an employee has not been interested in the operations may be due in part to his failure to recognize his stake in the progress of the company. Such understanding can be enhanced by providing the necessary facts.

The problem with which management is faced appears to have three aspects:

1. To convey to the employees and the general public an appreciation of the relationship between the stockholder, employee, management, and the customer.
2. To bring about a clear understanding of the company's progress during the year, including its income and its expenses, and its outlook for the coming year or years.
3. To outline some of the economic problems that stockholders, em-
94 ployees, and management must face together in the future.

Giving information to employees in order to meet these objectives does not mean giving them a mass of figures which would confuse; but it does mean giving facts that their natural interests would comprehend. It does imply giving facts which will take them beyond the machines and daily routine to a better understanding of the business. Moreover, business management should be realistic in recognizing that the very existence of the free enterprise system is doomed unless the employees understand the relationship and interdependence between their own work, those who furnish the tools of production, and those who manage them. The employee must be given the facts which will enable him to judge for himself whether the American system offers ultimately more and better living for the individual than does any other economic order.

Special Reports for Employees?—Reports to employees may be of an infinite variety. However, this discussion is concerned principally with whether or not an annual report or other reports on operations should be prepared especially for the employees. It was pointed out in the preceding chapter that logic would favor a special report, but that the circumstances of each case must govern. In defense of a special report to employees, it can be said that employees are usually interested in subjects that are of little or no interest to stockholders. Moreover, even as to items of mutual interest, the viewpoint is different. The wage-earner looks at wages, job security, and other employee benefits quite differently from the stockholder. Whenever the feeling might be prevalent among the employees that facts are distorted or withheld, a compromise solution is the preparation of special reports which emphasize the interests of each group, and the making of both reports available to stockholders and employees.

Information Presented to Employees.—Generally speaking, the job of a daily wage-earner is an important influence in his life. When he reads about company operations, he relates the facts and figures to his own job. And he is interested in a great many things. He is interested in how much income the company received and what happened to it, the past history of the company and its prospects for the future, the use and importance of the products manufactured, the wage rate for his job as compared with the wage rate for like jobs in other companies, and the benefits the employees of other companies receive. There are any number of questions of this nature which the employee raises. If management's reports are to be useful to the employee, if he is to read them, then they must provide many of the answers.

No single list of topics will serve all companies in terms of what in- 95
formation should be given to employees. What one company may find desirable, another will consider inadvisable. Furthermore, the more detailed the listing, the greater the area of disagreement. For example, many will agree that the employee should be provided with financial information about the operations. Yet, one firm would include information on executive salaries while another would not. Some classes on which there is general agreement, however, include:[1]

Company finances	Company products and their uses
Company personnel and organization	Expansion plans
Company history	Sales and order prospects
Labor policies	Research activities
Company position in its own industry	Industry outlook
	Taxation

Many of these are proper subjects for discussion in the annual report.

The emphasis here relates more particularly to the financial aspects of the reports. On this phase there are a great many topics which can be used to bring about a better understanding of the company and the economy. Basically, the employee is interested in his share of the total reward, and the financial statements should set this out in clearly understandable language. If every corporation would make certain that its employees have a full knowledge of the earnings and the disposition of these earnings, employee relations would be greatly improved. As has been mentioned, the employee should understand the relationship between those who provide the tools and those who use them. What the Standard Oil Company (N. J.) said in one issue of the company magazine, *The*

[1] From Alexander R. Heron, *Sharing Information with Employees* (Stanford, Calif.: Stanford University Press, 1942), p. 38.

Lamp, is illustrative of a point which should be understood: "The management has stated that the company's chief asset is its personnel. But the employees, unaided by capital, could not produce a barrel of crude nor deliver a gallon of gasoline. Back of them must be money, i.e. stockholders, management and goodwill. How much capital is required, and what do labor and the management cost?"

A more specific indication of financial subjects which may be covered in employee reports is suggested in the following outline:

A. INVESTMENT
   1. Explanation of statement of financial condition
   2. Nature of properties
   3. Source of capital
   4. Need for stockholders
   5. Investment per employee

96 B. OPERATIONS
   1. Total income (gross) and disposition
      a) Relative share for wages, material, etc.
   2. Comparative or analytical profit information
      a) With other years
      b) Profit per employee
      c) Profit per dollar invested
      d) Profit per dollar of sales
      e) Profit per unit of product sold
   3. Salaries and wages
      a) Total
      b) Salaries of executives
      c) Average weekly or hourly wage
      d) Comparisons with other industries, cost of living, etc.
   4. Taxes
      a) Per employee
      b) In relation to wages
      c) Per share of stock
      d) In relation to dividends
      e) In relation to net profit
   5. Dividends
      a) Total amount
      b) In relation to wages
      c) Per stockholder and per employee
      d) As a per cent of investment
   6. Depreciation
      a) Total amount
      b) Nature and value to employee

7. General
   a) Nature and importance of the break-even point
   b) Trends in industry
   c) Effect of expansion on job opportunities, etc.
   d) Appraisal of future outlook
   e) Discussion of achievements in production, sales, or safety
   f) Explanation of how company benefits the community and the nation
   g) Explanation of changes in pension, welfare, or other such plans or policies

Financial Statements for Employees.—There is no consistent pattern as to the practice of giving financial statements to employees. Some managements give the same statements to both employees and stockholders, while others restate the data in what is considered to be a more understandable form. Other managements do not make financial statements 97
generally available to employees, but rather present extracts from statements, together with explanatory comments. Still other companies feel it desirable to avoid statements in any form and use other devices to get the picture of company operations across to the employees. The authors are of the opinion that it is generally preferable to place understandable statements in the hands of employees.

If statements are to be made available, there is general agreement that such statements should be in simple, nontechnical language. The same general principles applicable to simplified statements for stockholders, as discussed in the preceding chapter, can be applied to employee statements. Such an approach may develop along any one of three lines, or a combination. Employees may be given:

1. The modified or "single-step" earnings statement, and modified statement of owner capital given to stockholders, as discussed in Chapter 22. There is, of course, a certain value in presenting the same type of statement to employees as to stockholders, or
2. A simplified type of statement, which is characterized by departures from conventional accounting form and terminology, or
3. A "per employee" statement or statements which translate the financial data into terms of a single employee.

Modified Stockholder-Employee Statements.—The modified statements, as typified by those issued by the Caterpillar Tractor Co.,[2] are believed to be one form quite suitable for employees as well as stockholders. A somewhat similar form used by Jewel Tea Co., Inc. is illustrated in Figure 144. They are understandable by the ordinary citizen, and

[2] See pages 434 and 440.

98

FINANCIAL STATEMENTS

INCOME ACCOUNT

	52 Weeks Ended Dec. 30, 1950	52 Weeks Ended Dec. 31, 1949
Sales and Revenues:		
Retail sales	$188,688,928	$168,787,620
Wholesale and other sales	175,315	213,405
Interest and miscellaneous income	308,779	169,324
Total sales and revenues	189,173,022	169,170,349
Costs of Doing Business:		
Paid to or for the benefit of employees:		
Payrolls	26,261,485	24,264,017
Social security taxes	471,040	376,437
Contribution to Jewel Retirement Estates	1,366,733	1,056,348
Total	28,099,258	25,696,802
Products, materials, services and rents	146,282,475	130,861,188
Depreciation	1,663,401	1,517,918
Maintenance and repairs	586,394	507,545
Doubtful accounts charged to operations	364,262	358,764
Federal income taxes	3,469,000	2,549,063
Federal excess profits tax	383,000	—
State, local and all other federal taxes	4,007,143	3,507,140
Total costs of doing business	184,859,933	164,998,420
Earnings for the Year	4,313,089	4,171,929
Percent of earnings to sales and revenues	2.3%	2.5%
Dividends on preferred stock	275,400	277,453
Earnings applicable to common stock	$ 4,037,689	$ 3,894,476
Earnings per share of common stock	$ 7.16	$ 6.93

BALANCE SHEET

Assets	Dec. 30, 1950	Dec. 31, 1949
Current Assets:		
Cash	$ 5,252,286	$ 5,256,327
U. S. Government securities	4,123,780	3,547,713
Accounts receivable	4,096,588	3,056,782
Inventories	16,209,707	11,707,434
Prepaid expenses and supplies	692,370	403,369
Total current assets	30,374,731	23,971,625
Claims for Refund of Excess Profits Taxes	—	281,600
Deferred Charge—Premiums Advanced to Customers	1,353,670	1,200,499
Property, Plant and Equipment	9,727,494	9,456,800
Goodwill	1	1
	$41,455,896	$34,910,525
Liabilities		
Current Liabilities:		
Accounts payable and accrued expenses	$ 7,091,200	$ 4,339,550
Dividends payable	68,850	631,066
Accrued federal, state and local taxes	4,759,022	3,318,133
Accrued payrolls and profit sharing	2,996,413	2,355,417
Total current liabilities	14,915,485	10,644,166
Reserves:		
Obsolescence, and inventory valuation	750,000	750,000
Automobile accident and other self-insured losses	250,000	250,000
	1,000,000	1,000,000
Capital Stock and Accumulated Earnings:		
Preferred stock	7,500,000	7,500,000
Common stock	6,171,808	6,095,480
Accumulated earnings	12,024,839	9,789,539
	25,696,647	23,385,019
Less preferred stock in treasury	156,236	118,660
	25,540,411	23,266,359
	$41,455,896	$34,910,525

FIGURE 144. Simplified Form for Financial Statements for Stockholders and Employees

THE PARENT COMPANY
STATEMENT OF INCOME AND EXPENSE
For the Year Ended December 31, 1951

	Total Amount	Amount per Employee	Cents per Dollar of Receipts	
The Company Received:				
From customers for goods and services purchased	$12,490,500	$11,783	97.8	
Dividends from subsidiaries	265,000	250	2.1	
Interest on receivables, miscellaneous income, etc.	12,300	12	.1	
Total Company Received	$12,767,800	$12,045	100.0	
The Company's Expenses Were:				
For materials, supplies, and other expenses	$ 7,392,450	$ 6,974	57.9	
For wear and tear on buildings, machinery, and equipment (depreciation)	267,800	253	2.1	99
For taxes—federal, state, and local, but excluding social security	248,900	235	1.9	
Making a total of	$ 7,909,150	$ 7,462	61.9	
Which left for wages, salaries, dividends, and reinvestment in the business	$ 4,858,650	$ 4,583	38.1	
This Was Divided as Follows:				
Paid to employees (excluding officers) as wages and salaries	$ 3,621,430	$ 3,416	28.4	
Paid for employee benefits, including social security taxes, contributions to pension fund, group life insurance, etc.	365,400	345	2.9	
Total	$ 3,986,830	$ 3,761	31.3	
Paid to officers as compensation	119,800	113	.9	
Paid to stockholders as dividends for the use of buildings, machinery, and equipment and working capital provided by their investment	405,300	382	3.2	
Reinvested in the business to cover the growing needs of the company	346,720	327	2.7	
Total division	$ 4,858,650	$ 4,583	38.1	

FIGURE 145. Illustrative Statement of Income and Expense for Employees

give no indication of "writing down." By and large the average employee is no less intelligent than the average stockholder. What is suitable for one is generally the type suitable for the other. As to operating results, however, such a form does not have an advantage of a "first-cost" statement described in the next section.

1950 Annual Report

HERE'S HOW TP'S ANNUAL

FROM OUR CUSTOMERS, FOR GOODS AND SERVICES, WE RECEIVED

$123,766,265

For goods produced and services rendered in 1950, we billed customers $123,766,265. This was an increase of more than $16 million over 1949.

Sales to manufacturers of automotive, marine and industrial products increased sharply, reflecting the record 1950 output of cars and trucks and continuing emphasis on development of new markets in commercial and industrial fields. Sales of automotive replacement parts also were higher, while shipments to aircraft companies, consisting largely of jet engine components, remained about the same as in 1949.

How this total income was used to pay bills, and to provide for employees, stockholders and the future of the business, is explained in the panels below . . .

100 *FIRST*- WE HAD THESE BILLS TO PAY:

❶

MORE AND MORE TAXES TOOK THE SUM OF

$11,106,369

Sharply higher taxes had to be paid first. More than $11 million of the company's 1950 income went to help pay for the constantly mounting cost of government. This bill was more than 77% greater than in 1949. This large sum, equal to more than $828 per employee, was spread over more than 150 types of federal, state and local levies, including Income, Payroll, Manufacturers' Federal Excise, Real Estate and Personal Property taxes.

Taxes were almost six times greater than the total amount paid to the owners of the business in dividends.

❷

WE BOUGHT MATERIALS AND SUPPLIES AMOUNTING TO

$52,901,503

Largest single item of expense was the nearly $53 million spent for materials and supplies with which we worked in 1950. For each employee, on the average, we bought approximately $4000 worth of steel, aluminum, cast iron, tools, drills, oil, office supplies, etc.

Note this: A saving of as little as 10% in the use of materials during the year would have made available more than $5¼ million additional for constructive job-making purposes.

❸

TO REPLACE WORN-OUT EQUIPMENT WE SET ASIDE

$1,689,998

Out of each year's income we set aside an amount of money to provide for the replacement of worn-out and obsolete machinery and equipment. This depreciation allowance, calculated by careful formula based on the estimated life of each machine and its original cost, is no longer sufficient because of inflated prices. Federal tax regulations do not permit deductions for the additional cost of replacing old machines. **Thus the difference must be taken out of profit money which might otherwise be spent on new job-making projects.**

❹

OTHER NECESSARY EXPENSES CAME TO

$2,076,928

Essential expenses of running the business, exclusive of taxes, materials, and depreciation allowances, were substantially lower in 1950, reflecting economies effected. These include the necessary "housekeeping" expenses of heat, light, power, telephone, telegraph, postage, catalogs, advertising, and legal and engineering services not covered by payrolls.

FIGURE 146. Illustrative Use of Cartoon Technique

to Employees

INCOME WAS DIVIDED

HERE'S WHAT WE HAD LEFT TO BE DIVIDED

$55,991,467

Up to this point necessary expenses have taken $67,774,798 of the company's 1950 income. Now we come to the nearly $56 million that was left to be divided between those who did the work and those who invested in the business, and the amount plowed back into the company to protect its future. This is known as **income available for distribution.**

The division was made as follows . . .

HERE'S HOW THE "SPLIT" WAS MADE: 101

85.3%

1

TO THE WORKERS WENT

$47,739,008

More than 85% of income available for distribution was paid in wages and salaries to employees in 1950. Included in the total payroll figure of nearly $47¾ million are salaries paid to the company's officers. The cost of having this management team to direct operations and plan the future of the business amounted to approximately 3 cents per hour per employee.

11.3%

2

WE REINVESTED IN THE BUSINESS A TOTAL OF

$6,348,811

Second largest portion of the "split" more than 11% was the $6,348,811 that was plowed back into the business to expand plant facilities, pay the higher cost of machinery and tools that had to be replaced, and to strengthen the company's financial position to insure a healthy future. This was more than three times the amount paid out in dividends in 1950.

3.4%

3

FOR THEIR INVESTMENT, THE STOCKHOLDERS RECEIVED

$1,903,648

For the use of their savings in 1950, the company's 4284 stockholders were paid dividends totaling $1,903,648, or 3.4% of the available income, as compared with the more than 85% paid to employees. These modest dividends are the return we pay to investors for risking their money in providing the plants and equipment we use in earning our livelihood. **Note that employees were paid more than 25 times as much from the business as stockholders received in dividends.**

4

Every dollar the company received from customers in 1950 is accounted for in these pages.

Now, what about profit? To find the net profit for 1950, add the $1,903,648 paid out in dividends to the $6,348,811 plowed back into the business. This was a profit of $8,252,459, equal to 6.7% on total income of $123,766,265. This was a modest improvement over 1949, but still relatively low in comparison with the earnings of other companies of like size and status in the industry.

in Annual Report to Employees (Thompson Products, Inc.)

Simplified Statements.—Another possibility for employee statement presentation is the simplified statement. Perhaps the only difference between this classification and the modified stockholder-employee statements is the degree to which conventional accounting terminology has been abandoned. Sometimes these very simplified statements are known as "Mother Goose" statements. In any event, some very capable managements are of the opinion that such a practice is essential to telling the business story—and that is the prime objective.

The extent of the change is varied. Since the emphasis in an employees' report is directed more toward the salaries and wages, the stockholder-employee operating statement may be rearranged to a "first-cost" statement. Basically, this merely involves deducting all costs and expenses from income to arrive at the balance distributed to employees, to stockholders, or retained in the business. An example of such a presentation, together with the inclusion of "per employee" data, is illustrated
102 in Figure 145. No particular additional comments are necessary regarding this attack on the problem except to point out the desirability of showing all other employee benefit expenditures in addition to salaries and wages; and to suggest that there may be good reason for setting out executive compensation to reveal the relative cost as compared to the payments to other employees. Such information is usually available to stockholders, so why not give it to the employees?

An informal presentation of operating results can be achieved by means of comic-strip or cartoon technique. Figure 146 is illustrative of this type of presentation, and Figure 147 is the accompanying summary in "first-cost" style. These statements were accompanied by an explanatory letter from the president of Thompson Products, Inc. Another example of informal presentation is that of Johns-Manville, as in Figure 148, where a graphic statement combination is effective. This graph, which appeared in the company magazine, was supplemented by detailed explanations and illustrations as to the income and expenses for the year.

The "Per Employee" Statement.—"Per employee" figures are determined by dividing the dollar value of each item in the statement by the number of employees in an effort to indicate the relationship of each such item to the individual employee. It is an attempt to convey to the employee what the investment of the stockholder, as well as the items of expense, means to each one individually. There are at least three general methods of presenting the "per employee" statements:

1. *Use of the modified statement.* Accounting terminology is discarded, and ordinary language is used to itemize the elements. See Figure 145. While total figures as well as per employee figures are usually included, some companies present only individualized data.

HOW TOTAL COMPANY INCOME WAS DIVIDED IN 1950

Showing total income of Thompson Products, Inc.

All Plants and Subsidiaries

1	WE RECEIVED FROM THE SALE OF PARTS AND SERVICES A TOTAL OF . . .		$123,766,265
2	OUT OF THE $123,766,265 WE HAD THESE BILLS TO PAY, NOT INCLUDING WAGES OR SALARIES.	Taxes . . . . $ 11,106,369	
		Materials . . . $ 52,901,503	
		Depreciation . $ 1,689,998	
		Other Expenses . $ 2,076,928	
			$ 67,774,798
3	AFTER PAYMENT OF THESE BILLS THERE WAS LEFT TO BE DIVIDED BETWEEN EMPLOYEES AND STOCKHOLDERS →		$ 55,991,467 103
4	HERE'S HOW THE DIVISION WAS MADE...	1—Paid Out in Payrolls (85.3%)* . . . $ 47,739,008	
		2—Paid Out in Dividends (3.4%) . . . $ 1,903,648	
		3—Plowed Back into the Business (11.3%) . . . . $ 6,348,811	$ 55,991,467
		BALANCE	-0-

★ It will be noted that payrolls took 85.3% of all the money that was left to be divided! Stockholders were paid only 3.4%, while 11.3% was plowed back into the business to help make future jobs.

Net profit for the year equals Item 2 plus Item 3. This is $8,252,459, equal to 6.7% profit on total sales for 1950.

FIGURE 147. Another Illustrative Statement of Income for Inclusion in an Annual Report

2. *Use of parallel columns.* In one column appear the data employed in the statement to stockholders, usually with a detailed explanation of the item. In the other column is presented the "per employee" information with further explanation.
3. *Use of conventional statements.* This method presents both the total amount and "per employee" amount in usual accounting form. The description, however, is followed by an explanation of each item in everyday language.

A different treatment of the "per employee" statement is the data per man-hour shown in the Monsanto Chemical Co. summary for the year 1950, illustrated on page 433.

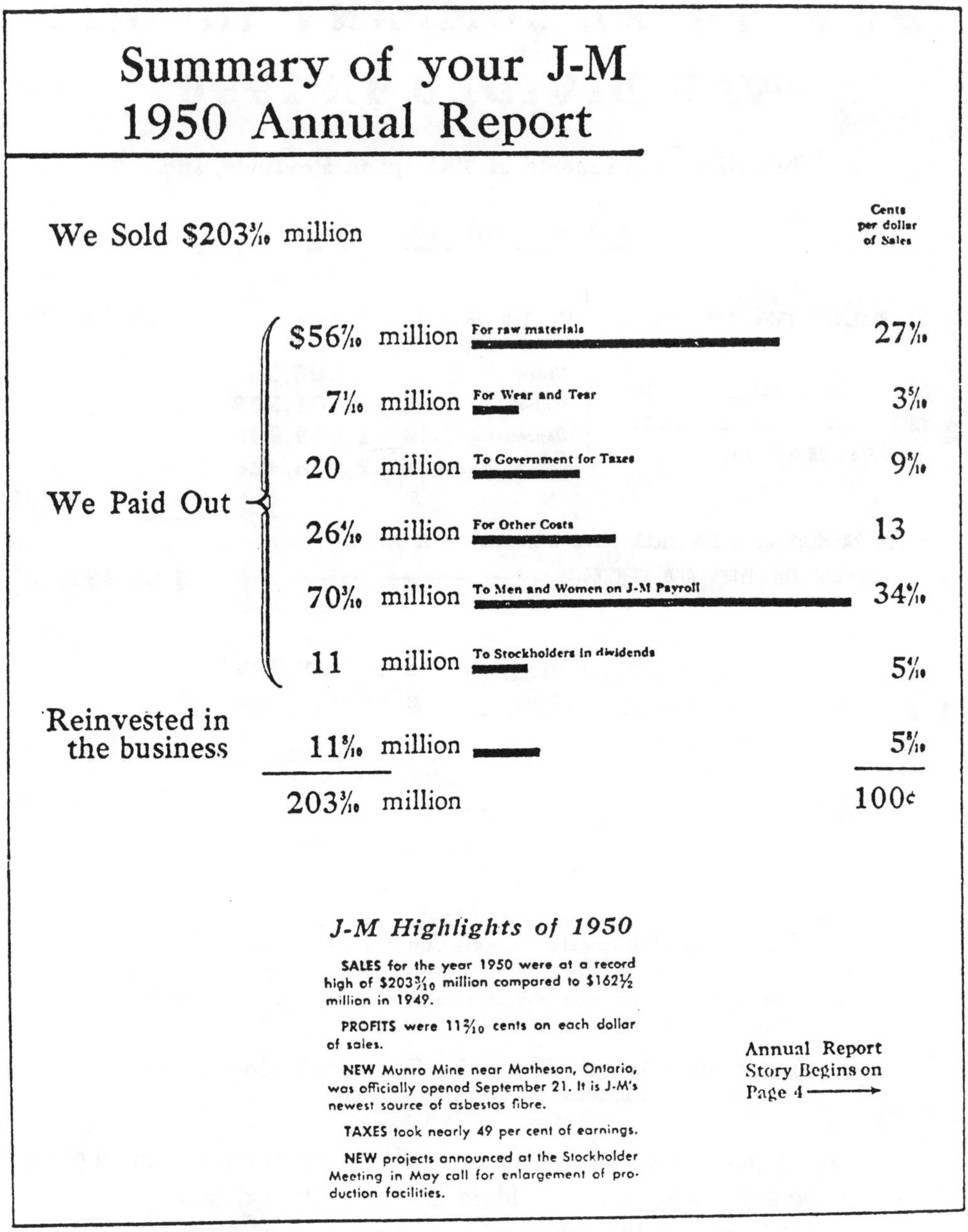

104

FIGURE 148. A Summary of Operations for Employees

The limitations of the "per employee" data should be recognized. Accompanying explanations should attempt to clarify as much as possible. Thus, it is not to be implied that a lower tax expense per employee would result in higher pay. Moreover, the investment per employee should not be construed as the *value* of the company. It may be more or less than this sum. Be that as it may, if it is correctly used, the per employee data can serve a useful purpose in explaining facts to company personnel.

Format of Reports.—Whether or not the employee reads the reports will depend greatly on the form. The same comments made on page 442 as to stockholders' reports are applicable here, and need not be repeated. Simple, frank statements, the effective use of graphs, charts, or illustrations, and employment of color will assist in telling the business story. Moreover, the report should have a certain dignity. Also, it may be found desirable to mail it to the employee's home.

Other Available Media.—Several other channels, in addition to the annual report, are available for getting information to the employee, be it financial or otherwise. These means, with brief comments, are outlined as follows:

1. *House organ.* This means, which may be addressed to customers as well as employees, is often used as a device to present the salient parts of the annual report or periodic financial information. It is a means of building esprit de corps, and presenting timely subjects in 105
the employee's language.
2. *Letters or leaflets (direct mail).* Such means usually generate interest at home, and can be effective in that area.
3. *Bulletin boards.* This is a useful means for getting a brief message to all employees.
4. *Payroll inserts.* Generally this method should be used only for items directly affecting an employee's pay.
5. *Advertisements.* This medium reaches the employees and the public at the same time.
6. *Handbook.* This method is useful primarily to acquaint new employees with company policies, etc.
7. *Personal contact.* This means is one of the best, and the employee's supervisor should be an important cog. Other means of personal contact include employee mass meetings or civic group meetings where facts can be presented.
8. *Films.* This means has been developed more recently as a means of getting visual and auditory contact with employees.

Dangers in Reporting to Employees.—There are some honest objections to furnishing certain types of information to employees. It is not simply a matter of deciding to "share information with our employees" because it will promote better understanding. Quite obviously, there will be times when some data cannot be furnished as it would be inimical to the company's—and the employee's—best interests. Under these circumstances the employee must be told frankly why the request cannot be granted. Fundamentally, the test is whether or not the information would be useful in promoting an understanding of the business. It should be clearly recognized that the dissemination of some information will lead to requests for even more. The company must be prepared to cope wisely with the situation.

Reports to the General Public

The Objective.—Unfortunately there is a great public misconception regarding American business. A large number of people think that business makes unwarranted profits; that corporations are owned by a few wealthy individuals; that large companies are not to be trusted; that business is responsible for rising prices on the one hand and depressions on the other; and that business always profiteers out of any war or defense effort. To answer those who spread such misinformation, it is not enough to reply with broad unsupported generalities. The public needs
106 to know the *facts* about business, since it is they who ultimately will determine the kind of economic order that will predominate. The basic objective is to convey to the general public facts about business in a way it will comprehend. The individual business wants to create a "good impression" concerning itself, and business generally needs to explain the advantages and gains of the free enterprise system to the community at large.

The Controller's Part.—Although the problem may be attacked from several avenues, the fact remains that accounting information must play a major role. It is largely from a misunderstanding by the public of the financial statements, or misunderstanding by those who "tell" the public, that many of the misconceptions have arisen. Clear, simple, and understandable financial statements are among the best tools available to correct these distortions and half-truths.

Since the proper interpretation of the financial operations is a main support in the solution of the problem, a certain responsibility must fall on the accountant—and that means the controller. Of course, he will require the active help and support of those who are experts in persuasion—the public relations director, the advertising manager, etc. However, as the chief problem is the proper presentation and interpretation of accounting data, he must assume a major responsibility. Whether or not the public continues to believe the distortions of those who for selfish reasons do not provide all the facts, whether, indeed, private enterprise will be strengthened, and the public will realize the tangible benefits of this system, depends in no small part on the accounting profession. The presentation of complete, unbiased, and clearly interpreted financial information can contribute much to the confidence of the general public in the American system.

Weaknesses in Present-Day Reports.—With reference particularly to the financial statements and annual reports, there are certain definite weaknesses which have prevented business from getting its story understood by the public. Though some of these were reviewed in the preceding sections, they may be summarized as follows:

1. *Common everyday words are used in a special technical sense.* The most commonly misunderstood term, perhaps, is "surplus," which to the ordinary citizen means excess. Another such term is "reserve." While the word has several connotations to an accountant, to the layman it is something set aside for future use. Such terms as these must be eliminated when presenting information to the public if there is to be a clear understanding.

2. *The form and designation of financial statements are misleading.* "Balance sheets" with the assets on the left and liabilities and net worth on the right appear to be more for the convenience of the bookkeeper than
anything else. To the layman, the question is raised that if assets are 107
equal to the liabilities, how can a company prosper. Again, the many types of "profit" in a statement of income and expense are confusing. Moreover, how can a statement be one of profit and loss?—it is either one or the other. Here, too, accounting tradition must give way to more realistic terms.

3. *Inadequate information is given.* In many instances only partial information is given. For example, sales data may be withheld; yet such figures can be used to good advantage in demonstrating to the public the relationship between sales volume and operating profit. Perhaps nothing breeds distrust as much as half-truths, or a feeling that information is being withheld. Facts should be supplied that will solve a problem but will not give vital information to competition, or otherwise injure the company.

4. *Presentations aid misinterpretation.* Some attempts to lead to misinterpretation are deliberate and fall into the propaganda classification, but in many instances the misunderstanding results from a poor presentation. Examples of what may be described as poor judgment in report presentation include: (*a*) a comment on return on investment, calculated on total capital invested under circumstances when stockholder equity might have been more appropriate; (*b*) an attempt at conveying the impression that the employees received most of the sales dollar when this is not borne out by the facts; (*c*) emphasis on the high level of taxes, with the implication that this condition prevented higher wages, when such may not be the case.

Presenting Figure-Facts to the Public.—Generally, the same principles discussed in previous chapters are applicable in presenting financial information to the general public. The report should contain all the pertinent facts on the subject, presented in an understandable manner. The mass of information should be ignored and the really vital aspects covered. Moreover, in many cases it will be advisable to give figures for several years. Then, too, the use of clear, simple language, color, photography, and charts can be effective.

It is desirable that the subject matter be directed to the audience. Items of particular interest or concern to the public should be emphasized. Some suggested topics, which may be a part of an annual report or of data released at the same or other times, include:

1. The place of free, private enterprise in our economy
2. Unsound legislation
3. Unsound governmental policy
4. Taxation
108 5. Interrelationship of industries; of labor, agriculture, and industry
6. Cooperation between government and industry
7. The relationship of the industry to the community
8. The extent of research
9. The creation of new markets
10. Financial data of many sorts:
    a) Relationship of sales volume and profits
    b) Profit as a percentage of net sales
    c) Reasons for increased profit
    d) Comparison of profits with other periods
    e) The cost of management
    f) The distribution of corporate ownership
    g) Reasons for price increases
    h) Distribution of the sales dollar
11. Relationship with labor
12. The outlook

It is to be observed that the consumer, employee, and stockholder also will have an interest in many of these subjects.

Form of Statements for the Public.—A question arises as to the necessity of preparing any special form of financial statements for the public. As has been previously mentioned, the public as well as the stockholders and employees do not understand the conventional statements. However, the simplified forms are as well suited to the needs of the public as to the owners or employees. No special construction is considered necessary. An illustration of a graphic form of statement which the Aluminum Company of America published in newspapers of the various communities in which their plants are located, as well as in certain financial papers, is shown in Figure 149.

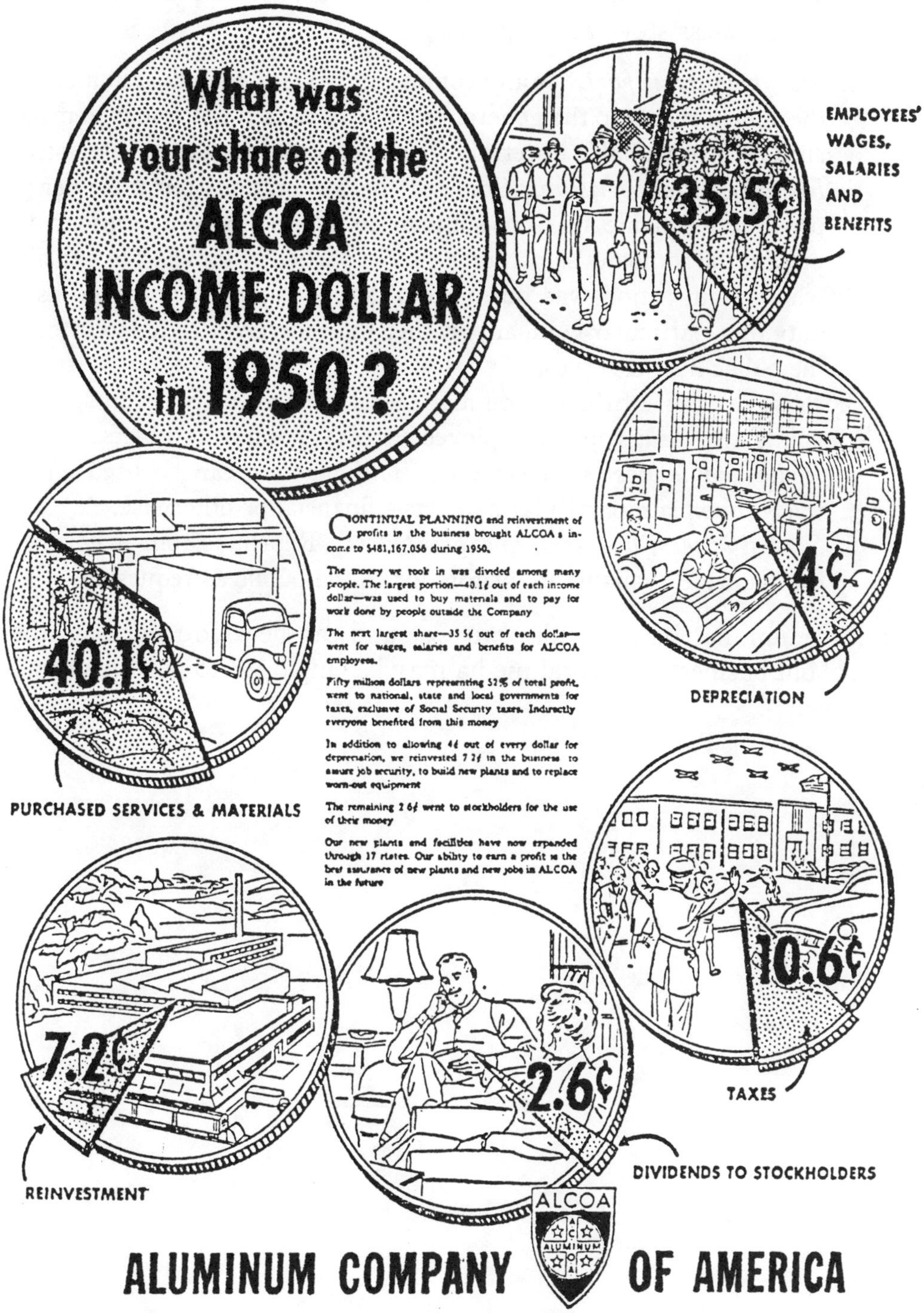

109

FIGURE 149. A Graphic Advertisement Reporting on the Annual Operating Results

Methods of Reporting to the Public.—Several media are available to convey the business story to the public:

1. *Stockholders' report.* Many companies make a wide distribution of the annual report to the general public. A related practice is to make such reports available to certain special groups that may be interested.
2. *Institutional advertising.* Some of the corporations purchase newspaper or magazine space to summarize the results of operations, to present the company's position on some particular topic, or to explain why certain action was taken. Perhaps it might be regarded as a duty of a particular company, rather than merely a right, to inform the public how it serves.
3. *Press releases.* Information may be released to the press on specific points, such as earnings, employee benefits, and new products.
4. *Radio and television broadcasts.* This medium can be used effectively to explain particular subjects—financial or otherwise.
5. *Special letters, booklets, and pamphlets.* Reprints from magazines can be made available to visitors, or to the public as requested.

Each medium has its particular purpose and can be used to present the facts about business. Several media may be employed to get the proper coverage.

REPORTING PRACTICES: CASE STUDIES AND SURVEYS

This collection of readings provides an insight into actual reporting practices across a forty year period. The first paper by B.C. Heacock (1940), President of Caterpillar Tractor Company, provides a first hand account of Caterpillar's approach to communicating financial information to its employees. It focuses upon an experiment with a radio broadcast following the issue of an annual report mailed to both stockholders and employees.

Hartwell's (1941) paper provides a comprehensive overview of U.S. corporate involvement in reporting to employees at the beginning of the 1940s. Thirty five companies are listed and their reports ranked by quality of disclosure (according to ten standards set by the author). Particular issues are discussed by reference to actual corporate reporting examples.

Derry's (1948) conference paper is the original and considerably more detailed version of his 1949 paper reprinted in the previous section. It is included in this section for his extensive discussion of actual U.S. corporate reporting examples that did not appear in the 1949 abridged version.

John Myers (1956), Associate Professor of Accounting at Northwestern University, presents a comprehensive snapshot of reporting to employee practices in the 1950s, based on his review of about sixty of these reports. His analysis concentrates upon presentation of the distribution of the sales dollar, statistical data, qualitative data, and tone of the report.

Two papers offer a view of reporting in the 1970s. Parker (1977) reports on a survey of Australian companies and reviews their reporting methods and report content. Holmes (1977) examines a number of U.K. company reports, detailing their content and presentation approaches. Both writers (one being this editor) declared financial reporting to employees to be a "new phenomenon." This ignorance of the practice's long history was not uncharacteristic of the majority of commentators in the 1970s. Almost prophetically, Holmes stated that "if one places a date on it, and says that it all began in the last five or six years, someone will undoubtedly write to *The Times*, suggesting that he heard the cuckoo long before that."

Making the Annual Report Speak

By B. C. HEACOCK, *President, Caterpillar Tractor Co., Peoria, Ill.*

Bolivar Studios, Inc.
B. C. HEACOCK

Caterpillar Tractor, among the first companies to make an annual report to employees, has continually sought new ways to make these reports more intelligible. Their latest experiment—in the words of President Heacock, "a satisfactory one"—was to use the local radio station to supplement the printed report. The author explains how the program was planned and carried out, and discusses some of the reactions that came from the radio audience.

THE PRACTICE of making an annual report to employees as well as to stockholders is one which has now become so common as to make it difficult to believe that only within the past two or three years has the practice been widely adopted.

The first annual report of our company to be distributed to employees as well as stockholders was that covering the year 1937, released early in February 1938. We were then among the pioneers in the adoption of this practice.

There arose at that time a question which, in the intervening two years, has appeared each year: "Should one report be prepared and issued to stockholders and employees alike, or should there be a separate report for each group?" When preparing to issue our report for the year 1937, there was not enough corporate experience with respect to employee reports to guide our course. Since that time the majority seems to favor the issuance of two separate reports. Our choice for the 1937 report, and for our 1938 and 1939 reports, was the issuance of a single publication.

Favoring the issuance of separate reports is the thought that for effectively telling the story of a year's operations to all employees, the report should be reduced to the simplest possible terms, liberally employing graphic presentations and perhaps omitting the formal balance sheet and profit and loss statement.

We have, however, been reluctant to expose ourselves to the accusation that we had one story to tell to one group of readers and a different story to give another. If this thought did not occur to employees at first, the chances were that it would come up sooner or later.

In trying to produce a report that would be interesting and wholly understandable to employees, it has not, in our opinion, been necessary to "talk down" to them in terms of the first-grade primer. Undoubtedly we are in a more fortunate position in this respect than are many industrial concerns, in that we have 100 percent literacy among our employees — all English speaking, and a large percentage high-school graduates.

In preparing an annual report, therefore, that will be understandable to employees, we have—though admittedly making a long step from the reports of former years—in no degree lessened its value for distribution to stockholders. As a matter of fact, I am sure we have greatly increased that value. Perhaps the old-style reports were wholly intelligible only to bankers, investment houses, and statisticians. The large army of thousands of stockholders is made up of ordinary folks who saved a little money to invest, and who welcome the simpler language and more graphic showing of facts and figures that have characterized conventional reports.

Planned Radio Program

The thought has persisted in our minds that we might find, and would like to find, additional ways to answer more of the many questions occurring among employees concerning the way a manufacturing establishment operates. To expand the report, it seemed to us, would be inadvisable. Our purpose of getting it read might be defeated by its formidable size. This year it occurred to us that radio might ideally solve the problem.

All circumstances made the proposal appear feasible. Our plant is located in a city of 125,000 population. Our pay roll of more than 10,000 people represents about half of the industrial employment of the community. The local radio station, operated on most progressive lines, has a large local listening audience.

We reserved a half hour's radio time, 7:30 to 8:00 p.m., for the Monday following the Saturday on which our annual report was mailed to stockholders and to the homes of all employees. A notice on all bulletin boards informed employees of the 113
broadcast, and asked that they have their copies of the report before them during the radio discussion. An advertisement on the radio page of the local newspapers apologized to the general listening public for using the facilities of the radio station for a talk directed to employees, at the same time welcoming as listeners any others who might care to tune in.

The report having borne my signature as president, it fell to my lot to deliver the radio talk. Page by page it was discussed—some sentences read—some portions amplified—some graphs and charts further explained. Even though nothing had been added to what was in printed form, definite gain would have resulted, for the report was thus brought to the attention of some employees who might otherwise have laid it aside unread. And if it is true, as the psychologists tell us, that some people are ear-minded rather than eye-minded, the spoken word conveyed thoughts that, in print, would not have registered so well to all.

The talk opened with a colloquy between the radio announcer and me, during which we spoke of the difficulty experienced by most people in understanding figures presented in a conventional annual report.

We then began with the first page of the booklet which, by the way, is called "Annual Report to Stockholders and Employees of the Caterpillar Tractor Co." Attention was called to the growth of our company since 1909 and of its gradual development from that time to this. Woven into the discussion were remarks relating to the hard work that has been done in improving our products and to the good fortune that attends us in America because we do have opportunities and incentives to make progress.

Next, reference was made to the officers and directors of the company and to their great responsibility in contributing to the successful operation of our business.

I stressed the importance of sales. "If the customers don't ask us to make something for them—that is, if they don't buy from us—then there simply isn't any work to be done. So hereafter, when you hear that sales have gone up or sales have gone down, just translate it into employment and be
114 glad of the fact that big sales mean more employment and better opportunities for free citizens to earn an honest living."

Aim to Level Employment

In speaking of the effect of fluctuations in business, I told how we try to avoid the effect of those changes, in so far as we are able, by leveling out employment to keep as many as possible employed steadily throughout the year. This was followed by the thought that an employer does not lay off men thoughtlessly and heartlessly when business drops off, as it is not the fault of the employer—it means that customers have made fewer purchases of the things that the factory produces.

It was explained that management does not sit complacently waiting for customers during periods of dull business. On the contrary, our engineering department tries to improve designs, the purchasing department tries to buy materials wisely, the factory works at building a good product, the advertising department tells people about our product, and the sales department busies itself diligently in directing the activities of thousands of men who are out in the field selling our merchandise.

At this point a detailed outline of our sales organization was given. I explained how our distributors in the United States and Canada serve their territories, how each one employs salesmen and a staff of office people, parts men, shop men, and service men.

In our report are a number of charts showing profits, dividends, sales, costs, wages, and taxes. These were explained, and attention was called to the fact that federal taxes alone for 1939 were one and two-thirds million dollars.

The next step moved to stockholders and the dividends we pay them. It was brought out that of nearly 17,000 stockholders, only 224 hold more than 1,000 shares apiece.

These 17,000 owners of the Caterpillar business were described as "common, ordinary folks, located in every State of the United States and its territories and possessions, and in 16 foreign countries. They are people who have saved their money, deprived themselves of some things it would be nice to have spent their money for in former years—so they would have something in the future. Half of them are women, and these women hold nearly one third of the total amount of stock. Many are widows whose husbands have left them some money or insurance to take care of the family after the breadwinner is gone. . . .

"I don't think there is anyone who would argue that these people who have invested their money to make an enterprise such as ours possible, and in the hope that they would get a reasonable return on their investments—I

(Continued on page 6)

Making the Annual Report Speak

(Continued from page 4)

don't think there is anyone who wouldn't agree that they are entitled to a fair return."

Following the information on stockholders and dividends, financing was discussed. "Just as you have the problem of handling your pay check and taking care of your family expenses, the company has the problem of paying its bills and its debts and meeting all of its obligations. Now and then we have been able to put aside a little so that when bad years have come along, we could still carry on operations on a moderate scale."

Explains Depreciation

In referring to costs, the item of depreciation was introduced. "I think it will startle you to learn that for each working day there has to be charged off for wear and tear—or depreciation, as it is called—a sum of about $10,000."

Speaking of the tremendous sums spent in our community, it was brought out that our 1939 pay roll was nearly $19,000,000, most of which was spent locally, in addition to local expenditures by the company for materials, light, heat, power, and transportation. It was emphasized that when costs go up and profits go down, we cannot raise prices, because then the customers would buy less, we would make less, and there would be less employment.

Our experiment with a radio talk is felt to have been a satisfactory one. Comments of employees, in so far as they came to notice, were generally favorable. A gratifyingly large number of others than employees were included in the listening audience—business people, lawyers, doctors, teachers, preachers, farmers. One farmer reported keen interest among several of his neighbors, and spoke of their amazement to learn of the numerous details in the operation of a large manufacturing concern, and of some of the problems that daily confront management.

It is our present thought that a radio talk may well be used regularly in the future to supplement the printed report.

TELLING THE EMPLOYEES

By DICKSON HARTWELL

The annual report as a means of building employee goodwill is discussed by the author, who states that it is an obligation of business management to tell its employees what big business is all about. The essentials of a good report are described and the present reports of major corporations analyzed. Mr. Hartwell is a partner in the firm of Hartwell, Jobson and Kibbee, New York and Chicago public relations counsel.

BIG BUSINESS management has almost completely neglected an opportunity for building understanding and goodwill in two huge and vitally important groups.

The failure of management to educate the first of these—the stockholders—has already been analyzed by the writer in a previous article, "Telling the Stockholders," published in the March 1940 issue of the QUARTERLY. In that article it was pointed out that less than ten per cent of our great corporations issued annual reports that could, in any sense, be considered adequate for the purpose of winning the goodwill and understanding of a major proportion of their stockholders.

Management's failure through annual reports to reduce costly ignorance, and its attendant problems, among the second group—the employees—is probably more serious.

Big Business and Labor

During recent years, the most continuously vexing problem big business has had to face is Labor—Labor with a capital "L." It has been more perplexing than taxation or government regulation. The development of the labor union has not of itself adversely affected our major corporations. But as a means of spreading the belief that the interests of management, capital's representative, are different from those of labor, the union has been a source of increasingly grave concern to management.

It is the responsibility of management, and of no one else, to correct the erroneous impressions now held by millions of working Americans. Stated simply, the crux of the problem is to build up an understanding on the part of all employees as to the exact function and purposes of a big business corporation. Employees should be told—and in words they can grasp without effort—just what happens to the money a business takes in, and why. The story must be told over and over again until it sinks in and becomes as routine as $2 \times 2 = 4$. Management must teach those simple, basic rules, which seem so complicated when stated by the copy book theorists, but which are the "Economic Constitution" under which any sound business must be operated.

Explaining the complications of corporate procedure to labor may appear to be a large order. The question

is not how big the job is, but how important. No group of business men, who in a comparatively short period could conceive, design, perfect, manufacture and create a demand, where none existed, for over 50,000,000 automobiles, 10,000,000 mechanical refrigerators, and 60,000,000 radios, would shirk tackling a job just because it's big. What has been holding them back seems to be a fear of rocking the boat. All management really needs to do is to wake up to the fact that the boat is rocking only because something *hasn't* been
116 done to stop it.

Educating the Employee

There are numerous opportunities for tackling the problem but there is space in this article briefly to discuss only one of them: the annual report. Such reports, when sent to stockholders, have been regarded as of primary value in the important job of stockholder education. Coupled with sound employee policies, there is no reason why similar reports specially prepared cannot serve equally well in building understanding and goodwill among jobholders.

An investigation[1] of several hundred major corporations throughout the country reveals that this elementary approach to the problem of employee education has been almost wholly overlooked or ignored. Despite the fact that the need is as large and as obvious as the national debt, only a small fraction of our major business enterprises today issue such reports to their workers.

But this small fraction for the most part approach the problem with intelligence. The average employee report is much more informative than the average stockholder report. Apparently, where management is sufficiently enlightened to make a special effort to educate its employees, a real effort is made to tell their employees what they want, or ought to want, to know.

The requisites for a good employee report are not easy to determine. The standards which hold for a stockholder report do not, except in a general way, pertain to a report for employees. In the first place, unlike the stockholder, the average employee is not usually eager for information. It is a mistake to assume that he is. Secondly, he may resent and resist (and possibly sometimes with encouragement from union leaders) any effort to win his goodwill, which he may construe as an attempt to divert his crusade for the "rights" of labor. Thirdly, there is apt to be a very wide variance in intellectual capacity within an employee group, much greater than in a stockholder group. Skilled, semiskilled and unskilled labor frequently make up a major proportion of the workers of a company that also may employ a large number of high school and college trained men and women.

But a principal hurdle in the preparation of an employee report is

[1] Of 205 companies replying to a questionnaire sent 525 major corporations, 150 said they issued no employee report, 35 issued a special employee report, 8 reported in their house organs, and 12 said their stockholder reports were sent also to employees. A large majority of those not replying may be presumed not to issue employee reports.

that it sometimes calls for a new kind of courage on the part of management. Men who calmly launch a new product and risk the loss of millions of dollars, frequently shrink from any step that may upset the *status quo* in their labor relations. They move with such caution that they seem not to move at all, and sometimes they don't. Men who are bold enough to tell the whole United States Government to go jump in the lake are white rabbits when it comes to labor policy. But there is no danger and a lot of potential benefit in a carefully developed annual report. This is as good a time as any to start one.

Pointers for a Good Report

In preparing an employee report, it is essential to keep in mind the fundamental but often forgotten principle that *both* management and labor are employees. The best report probably is one which fully describes and explains the results of the sum of a year's efforts on the part of both of them to do the best job they know how. In all but the most exceptional instances, in addition to telling what happened during the year, such a report would certainly meet the following conditions:

1. It would be written in the simplest possible language.

2. It would contain a non-technical financial statement with figures in round numbers.

3. It would record any outstanding achievements, such as in production, sales, or safety.

4. It would be illustrated.

5. It would carry a clear explanation of the purpose of the company and how it benefits the community or the nation.

6. It would describe the relationship of employee to management and stockholder, and explain how a prospering company benefits all.

7. It would explain how and why dividends are paid.

8. It would record changes in policies, developments in pension or other employee welfare plans.

9. It would contain an honest appraisal of the outlook for the future of the company, especially as regards 117
employment.

10. It would be well designed and well printed—something the employee would take home and save.

Within these general standards there is room for infinite variation and adaptation to individual requirements. A report can be treated in any way from a quiz contest to a series of believe-it-or-not cartoons. The important thing is to have a complete report that will be interesting and understood.

On the basis of the above standards, how do reports being issued today compare? Those recently studied might be fairly rated as follows:

CLASS A

Consolidated Edison Company of New York
General Motors Corporation
International Harvester Company
Johns-Manville Corporation
New York, New Haven and Hartford Railroad Company
Standard Oil Company (N.J.)
Swift & Company

CLASS B

Alabama Power Company
Bethlehem Steel Corporation
Boston Consolidated Gas Company
Eastern Air Lines
Great Northern Railway Company
Illinois Central System
National Steel Corporation
New Jersey Bell Telephone Company
New York Telephone Company
The Pullman Company
Thermoid Company

CLASS C

118 American Airlines, Inc.
The Borden Company
Bridgeport Brass Company
Caterpillar Tractor Company
Cleveland Railway Company
Cluett, Peabody and Company
Fifth Avenue Coach Company
General Electric Company
Goodyear Tire and Rubber Company
Kansas City Public Service Company
Monsanto Chemical Company
Nevada-California Electric Corporation
Pittsburgh Coal Company
Remington Rand, Inc.
United Air Lines Transport Corporation
Westinghouse Electric and Manufacturing Company
Yale and Towne Manufacturing Company

Except for the "A" group, which is uniformly excellent, there is some variation in the reports within the groups. In Class B, for example, the Pullman Company, Bethlehem Steel and Great Northern reports are outstanding even if they do not completely meet the standards of Class A. If there had been a "D" rating, several reports in the "C" class—Pittsburgh Coal, Kansas City Public Service, Fifth Avenue Coach, and Cleveland Railways—should doubtless have been included in it.

In the "D" classification, however, are listed only those companies which did not issue any report to their employees. Since it includes the overwhelming majority of the companies queried, the list obviously is too long to be included here. However, the following are outstanding examples:

Aluminum Company of America
Anheuser-Busch, Inc.
Barnsdall Oil Company
Boeing Aircraft Company
Edward G. Budd Manufacturing Company
Celanese Corporation of America
Chesapeake and Ohio Railroad
Chrysler Corporation
Consolidated Oil Corporation
Continental Baking Company
Continental Can Company
Detroit Edison Company
Douglas Aircraft Company
Ford Motor Company
Gimbel Brothers
International Telephone and Telegraph Company
Kennecott Copper Corporation
Libbey-Owens-Ford Glass Company
Los Angeles and Salt Lake Railway
R. H. Macy and Company
National Dairy Products Corporation
National Distillers Corporation
Northern Pacific Railway

Owens-Illinois Glass Company
Packard Motor Car Company
Paramount Pictures, Inc.
Procter and Gamble Company
Public Service Corporation of N.J.
Radio-Keith-Orpheum Corporation
United Aircraft Corporation
United Gas Corporation
Union Pacific Railroad Company
United States Rubber Company
Universal Pictures Company
Virginia Electric and Power Company
Ward Baking Company
White Motor Company
Wilson Brothers
Timken Roller Bearing Company

The fact that a company issues an "A" or a "C" report is not of itself an indication of whether it has good or bad employee relations. It certainly would be possible to have good employee relations and issue a "C" report, or even none at all. On the other hand, it would be possible to have unsatisfactory relations and issue an "A" report. In fact, if relations were unsatisfactory, an "A" report would seem to be essential.

Other Methods of Reporting

In addition to the special reports to employees rated above, there are two other methods of reporting which have been followed. One of these is to send each employee a copy of the regular report to stockholders. While this might be a successful method in theory, in practice only one of such reports studied would be considered satisfactory for employee consumption. This is the report of the General Foods Corporation which is so straightforward and simple, with an attractive and interesting format, that it is a model for any company to study.

Other reports of this type, among them United States Steel, Radio Corporation of America, Boston and Maine Railroad and Stewart-Warner Corporation, would not attract the average employee. Among the Class C reports mentioned above, there are several which are addressed to both "stockholders and employees." But none of them qualifies for an "A" rating as an employee report. 119

Combining stockholders and employee reports into one is on the whole unsound. The stockholder report probably needs more dignity than is necessary for an employee report; in the latter it is possible and may often be desirable to be "folksy" in the approach, strengthening the feeling of unity and company spirit among employees. It is also possible in a separate employee report to devote adequate attention to individual achievement, both as a recognition of past work and as a spur to future endeavor.

In another category are reports included in house organs. An employee magazine would seem to be an excellent place to print an annual report and several companies successfully devote a special issue of their publication to this purpose. However, where the report is run merely as a feature, the results are not usually satisfactory. Those studied in this analysis included:

Socony-Vacuum Oil Company	Very good report, fairly well developed, expressed in clear, understandable English, and well illustrated.
American Rolling Mill Company	Covered in weekly reports of operations in mimeographed bulletin—hardly adequate in view of "A" standards listed above.
Associated Telephone Company	Simple, straightforward and brief, but probably satisfactory for small company.
Brooklyn Union Gas Company	Terse statement with good illustration of finances; inadequate detail.
120 Niagara Hudson Power Company	One-page highlighted summary; entirely inadequate.
Republic Steel Corporation	Simply expressed, hard-hitting language, but requiring amplification.
Southern Pacific Company	Reprint of stockholders report unsatisfactory for employees.
Western Electric Company	Reprint of stockholders report unsatisfactory for employees.

A number of corporations state that they "encourage" their employees to ask for stockholder reports. "Encouraging" an employee to secure and to read a stockholder report is like "encouraging" a customer to purchase. It simply will not do the job. A report has to be made so exciting and so interesting that an employee will want to read it, just as a consumption product must be made so attractive that the customer will want to buy.

It is noteworthy that a number of companies not issuing a printed report do make verbal reports at employees' meetings. Obviously, this type of reporting is better than none at all and, properly handled, especially in conjunction with a printed statement, might be highly effective. But the verbal story does not reach the employee's wife or family and their goodwill not infrequently is as important as his own. Moreover, a printed report is a permanent record. It lasts longer than an employee's memory.

Business Explains Itself

It is important for all employees to be familiar with established company policies, particularly those which directly affect them. While the annual report would seem to be the logical place to state and reiterate these policies, the danger of becoming repetitious must be avoided. Those who had been continuously employed for several years would probably find such recurrent reports boring and obviously only for the benefit of new job-holders.

This repetition could be avoided by the publication of a booklet entitled "Meet the XYZ Corporation." This booklet would serve as an introduction of the employee to the company, and would describe its policies, practices, pension and betterment plans, methods of reward for merit, and in general present the newcomer with a complete picture of his working conditions. Such a booklet could be made to fill one of the most valuable functions of the annual report at a time when an employee is most impressionable—the first day he joins the company.

Southern California Edison

Some individual reports contain excellent examples of how somewhat difficult questions can be clearly and forcefully explained. For example, here is how the Southern California Edison Company explains interest and dividend payments:

"In order to obtain the working tools—equipment of all kinds—which present employees use in providing electric service, the Company had to buy an average per employee, of $80,000 of this equipment. Now the Company could conceivably have rented this equipment from those who provided it. If the Company had rented it, there would be due to the owners a monthly, quarterly or annual rental for its use. But the Company did not rent the equipment. Instead, it hired or borrowed money from bondholders and stockholders and agreed to pay a certain rental (interest and dividends) for the use of this borrowed money."

Johns-Manville

Johns-Manville attacks the same problem in the form of a question which it answers fully and frankly in a manner to inspire confidence:

"Do Our Common Stockholders
Get Too Much Profit? 121

"Answer: Let's look at the record. Then *you* decide whether or not *you* think it's too much. During the last twelve years our Common Stockholders have averaged $2.02 per share each year in dividends. Mind you, this is an average per year. In one year they got as high as $4.75, but in 1932, 1933 and 1934 they got nothing, and in one other year only 50 cents.

"Now, to get a simple picture of what these 'profits' have amounted to, let us suppose that you have bought and own one share of stock. If you had been saving $1.00 per week out of your pay check to purchase this one share, it would require nearly a year and a half to accumulate enough to buy it from some other stockholder at the price at which it was recently selling on the New York Stock Exchange. On this share, the average dividend of $2.02 per share for the past twelve years would have amounted to only 3 per cent. Do you think this return would be too high a rate of interest for the money you had saved?"

Alabama Power

Another ticklish question to discuss with employees is the problem of government regulation. The Alabama Power Company, recognizing itself as a monopoly, faces its responsibility squarely and conscientiously:

"In purchasing from grocery stores, clothing, hardware, and all other mercantile enterprises, the public usually has a choice of more than one from whom to buy, but in the case of the utility (with certain exceptions discussed later), it usually has no choice,—it can secure the service from only one source. It is for this reason that our business is so closely regulated. It is for this reason that all of us,—the stockholders, the directors, the officers, the department heads and every employee, individually and collectively—must constantly bear in mind our obligation to the public, and fulfill them faithfully and well. Ours is a business affected with a public interest; we must have a vital sympathy with our customers and be prepared to give good service and be ready with advice and suggestions to help them get the most from the service they are buying.

"So—we have a very definite obligation, not only to the Company, but to the public, to be uniformly courteous, to avoid being arbitrary, and to satisfy our customers."

That sort of language is in sharp contrast to the confusing ambiguity found in one employee report:

"Since the depreciation reserve accumulated on the basis of previous estimated lives of the properties is in excess of the reserve balance required on the basis of the new estimated useful lives, adjustments have been made in the depreciation reserve account and the earned surplus account to reflect therein the amounts which would have accumulated if the new bases of depreciation had been applied from the dates the properties were first acquired."

Standard Oil of N.J.

The Standard Oil Company (N.J.) explains a surplus of almost 26 million dollars in terms which the man in the street could not fail to understand:

"Let us compare our situation with that of a young married couple. As the years go on they are able to purchase a refrigerator, a radio, a car and perhaps a few shares of stock. Let us assume all these possessions are worth $5,000. But there are still some installments to be paid on the car, there are doctor bills and other amounts to be paid, totaling, say, $1,000. The difference is $4,000 and that is their surplus.

"Does that mean that if the husband loses his job they have $4,000 on which to live? Not at all. Only a small part of that may be cash. To turn the rest into cash they would have to sell their car, radio, refrigerator—many of the things that contribute to their way of living."

General Foods

From the report of General Foods comes a quotation which has a political slant. Few employees could read the following in a national election year and feel that management was anything but absolutely fair on the subject of politics:

"The Management hopes each employee will register and will vote at all elections. It's our precious American privilege. But we do not want any employee, supervisor, or executive to use his company connections to influence, directly or indirectly, the vote of any other employee. Such actions would be undemocratic and properly resented.

"Any company employee or official naturally has the right of any citizen to air his personal views. But the company, as such, takes no political stand."

An Intangible Asset

With such excellent examples to serve as guides, it is obvious that the complexities of any corporation are subject to treatment which will make them understandable to an employee. There is no doubt that understanding is the first step in building goodwill.

The Supreme Court of the United States once declared that goodwill is "the disposition of a customer to return to the place where he has been well served." This is all right as far as it goes, but today goodwill means much more. It is also the disposition of a customer to trade for the first time with a company where he *expects* to be well served. Further, it is the disposition of a person to think favorably of an enterprise even though he may never do business nor come in contact with it.

But there is at least one more
highly important angle of goodwill— 123
one which it is a primary job of management to cultivate. A business or industry that really enjoys goodwill has the kind of a reputation that makes a man say, "Gosh, I'd like to work for that company; they're swell." A corporation which has that kind of goodwill doesn't need to be concerned with the A.F. of L., the C.I.O., or N.L.R.B. About all it needs to worry about is possible overtime charges on keeping its halo adjusted. That sort of thing can run into money, but it's worth it.

PRESENTING THE FACTS ON COMPANY OPERATIONS TO THE EMPLOYEES

By Stephen Arthur Derry
Consulting Management Engineer, Louisville, Kentucky

Company operation reports, like companies, have changed with the times. Perhaps the greatest change is the simplification of the reports for use by labor. In preparing reports for employees, some companies make the mistake of thinking that anything in very simple terms will do.

Today, labor analyzes company reports more keenly than the investors. Unions have high paid analysts on their staffs, whose jobs are to
124 analyze company operating reports for their members.

Because of this and other factors, management must consider very carefully the labor reaction in any report it issues to its employees, stockholders or to the public.

In all my dealings with labor and management, I have found that in almost every instance the source of the differences in opinions was traceable to a report that the company had issued to either its stockholders, employees, or the public.

The conventional dry-as-dust figures in financial statements are as complex to the average employee as the text of a doctor's prescription would be to most of you. The conventional form and terminology of financial reports are as misinterpreted by the average employee as the form and terminology of a brief prepared by an attorney would be misinterpreted by some of you. This experience has led me to but one conclusion; that is, company reports no longer can be considered as an esoteric matter. This fact is very clearly demonstrated when one peruses company reports.

First Conventional Report

The first conventional annual report appears to have been issued in 1858 by the Borden Company. In 1942 (84 years later), the format was humanized. The report talked chattily about Elsie, Borden's philosophical cow. Much was mentioned about taxes and vitamin research. However, the attitude of most companies, in the days of the first Borden report, is clearly demonstrated in a statement issued by the New York Stock Exchange in 1866 which in part reads as follows: "The New York Stock Exchange made no reports, and published no statements, and has not done anything of the kind for the last five years . . . " But 29 years later, in 1895, the New York Stock Exchange endorsed the practice of making annual reports, and in 1900 requested companies applying for listings to publish annual reports.

During the eighties, the Interstate Commerce Commission made it compulsory for the railroads to publish annual reports. These reports were complete and highly detailed, but were, in many instances, set up like timetables and were not only difficult to understand but very hard to read.

The reports seemed to be merely reprints of large portions of the data periodically sent to the I.C.C. by harassed secretaries. The compilation of a variety of information about the railroad business seemed to follow no logical sequence.

Some railroads like the C. & O. have modernized their reports, using
maps, pictures, and lyrical prose to describe their operations. However, 125
as late as 1942, the Union Pacific report contained such uninteresting information as: "The company constructed two riveted truss spans replacing lattice truss and spans and remodeled abutments and pier in one bridge and constructed steel approach span on concrete abutments and steel bent replacing stone abutments. . . . "

First Modern Report

The U. S. Steel report to stockholders issued in 1902 appears to be the first modern report. This report, prepared by Judge Elbert H. Gary, contained 64 pages, plus a large map. Forty pages were devoted to very detailed financial information, and 24 pages were filled with photographs showing views of representative properties owned by the Steel Company. The report revealed operating facts that heretofore no company dared to reveal. The facts were so profusely illustrated that the directors were practically scandalized. In 1939, U. S. Steel reverted to Judge Gary's presentation, amplifying simplicity. The 1942 report very informally told the story U. S. Steel played in the war; it also explained the expansion program and relations with labor. U. S. Steel's 1947 report covers 36 subject headings, including such subjects as more and better facilities, distribution of steel, labor-management relations, community relations, peace and production, operating and financial facts from 1902 to 1947, inclusive.

The April, 1948 issue of the employees' magazine, *Steel News*, very vividly portrays the company operations under such headings as "Your Score in 1947." The theme of this editorial truly rings a bell with the employees, because it makes the employee feel that his job with U. S. Steel is no different than if he were in business for himself. The editor tabulates the company's financial transactions in such a way as to cause the employee to feel that he is the proprietor of his own shop. For example, considering the average U. S. Steel employee as being in business for himself, the average weekly financial transaction would be as follows:

TAKEN IN FROM SALES TO CUSTOMERS		$145.10
PAID OUT FOR:		
Materials necessary for operation	$57.55	
Wear of machinery and tools	6.00	
Machinery replacement cost	1.80	
Taxes on plant	9.31	
Use of stockholders' money	4.84	
More and better facilities	3.84	
Social security taxes and pension	2.12	

126 Deducting total paid out ($85.46) from total taken in, netted him a sum of $59.64 for his time and efforts. This money was his for groceries, clothes, recreation for himself and family.

The magazine also published a personal letter written by Mr. B. F. Fairless, President of U. S. Steel. This letter portrayed the 1947 operations facts in vivid language. The facts were presented convincingly and in such style to make the employee feel that the making of steel was his business. He told the employees that the plant, in 1947, operated 96.7 per cent of capacity. The plant produced 28.6 million tons of steel ingots and castings.

The company received more than $2 billion for its products and the profit was $127.1 million, or 6 cents per dollar sales.

He told the employees what happened to this profit. He pointed out that $903.6 million or 42.6 per cent of all money received from sales was paid for wages, salaries, social security taxes and pensions. He explained raw material costs which amounted to $841.9 million or 39.6 per cent of the total receipts. He pointed out that the employment and raw material purchases totaled $1,745.5 million, or 82.2 per cent of the total received from customers.

Then he showed what happened to the 17.8 cents left out of each dollar received from customers. He elaborated on the wear and exhaustion costs of each sales dollar. He listed the fact that $136.2 million or 6.4 cents of each dollar of sales was paid for taxes. To approximately 228,000 stockholders, the sum of $70.9 million or 3.3 cents on each sales dollar was paid. The remaining $56.2 million or 2.7 cents out of each sales dollar was used to reinvest into the business of keeping you in business.

Special Reports to Employees

The greatest change in preparing reports came out in 1937. Johns-Manville was one of the first companies to issue a special annual report to employees and has continued this practice every year since. The report was printed in large type, conversationally written, and profusely illustrated. Among the outstanding features of this report was a reproduction of a "Bill-of-Material" form to portray the purchase of raw material. Another was the explanation of the meaning of a balance sheet, which, in effect, explained that a balance sheet was merely a statement of what the company owned, owed, and of what the company was worth. It also explains that the balance sheet had nothing to do with the company sales or income, or with how the money was received each year and divided among employees in wages, and among stockholders in dividends.

The theme of the explanation was that a balance sheet was the same 127
as if you took two sheets of paper and on one you listed the cash you have, the value of your home, car, radio, furniture, clothes, and the five dollars your neighbor owes you. Then on the other sheet, list what you owe the grocer, the milkman, the iceman, the amount you owe for the mortgage on your home, and what you owe the finance company on your car.

Then you subtract what you owe from what you own. The result is what you are worth and what your company calls surplus. This may represent property or cash, or both. This figure you place on the second sheet. Then the first sheet, "What you own," and the second sheet, "What you owe and what you are worth," will balance exactly.

An editorial, "Cloth Woven from Rock," was used in introducing the 1947 report. A sample of cloth made from rock was attached to the page.

The 1937 report had such a profound effect on Johns-Manville officials that, in 1938, the same idea was used for the stockholders' report, and they have been doing it ever since. The 1947 annual stockholders' report contained only 23 pages, but very effectively presented.

Special Techniques

General Foods, in 1940, introduced a new technique by presenting its corporate and operating facts in dialogue at a mythical annual stockholders' meeting. The Board Chairman represented the position of the company, then the various officials answered such questions as: "Please give us more details about our sales!" "What are GF's employee policies?" "Tell us about the inventory position." "I'd like to know what independent auditors do for General Foods?" "If there is a member of the firm of auditors present, would he tell us just what procedures they use?" and "On the Balance Sheet, what is meant by 'loans to employees'?"

The Individualized Method

The old simile, "dry as an annual report" passes into oblivion when one reads the 1942 annual report of R. G. le Tourneau Incorporated, Peoria, Illinois. The President of this corporation must be a very religious individual. He begins the report with a quotation from the Bible (Joshua 10:19), "And stay ye not, BUT pursue after your enemies, and smite the hindmost of them; suffer them not to enter into their cities; for the LORD your God hath delivered them into your hand." On the very next page he writes, "I love to build machinery. I love to design it, but I am constantly aware of the fact that it takes skilled men to build this powerful machinery. It takes skilled men to assemble it properly. It takes skilled men to test it thoroughly, and operate it efficiently; and I would like to add that just as the machine needs a man to direct and control it, so man,
128 who is God's mechanical Masterpiece, needs God to direct and control him."

Report with Views on Government

The 1942 report issued by the Diamond Match Company is filled with 100 large fully printed pages, covering the entire field of company lore from taxes, economics, and the future of California to Congress, democracy, and the abundance of blister rust in Diamond's extensive timberland.

Some companies even include their views on government matters. For example, Monsanto Chemical Company's 1942 report frowned on the S.E.C.'s rulings holding that the corporation reports are proxy soliciting material, and if incorrect might subject officials to severe penalty. To this charge Monsanto bravely continued to publish information in its house organ and quarterly reports.

Report with Dollar-per-Man-Hour Breakdown

Monsanto Chemical Company's 1945 annual report introduced a new technique in breaking the income dollar down to "dollar per man hour." The facts were grouped under three headings, namely:

a. "What we took in"
b. "What we paid out"
c. "This left for employees, management, government and stockholders"

Each item, under each heading, was broken down to portray a picture such as this:

Item		*Dollar Per Man Hour*	
TOTAL TAKEN IN		$3.92	
Received from customers	$3.84		
Fees on government contracts	.05		
Other income from investments	.03		
TOTAL PAID OUT		$2.11	
Raw materials	$1.81		
New equipment, etc.	.30		
TOTAL LEFT FOR DISTRIBUTION		$1.81	
Wages and Salaries	$1.02		
Taxes	.58		
Owners of Company for use of money	.15		
TOTAL DISTRIBUTED		$1.75	
BALANCE LEFT			$0.06

This amount was retained in the business for use, such as payment of 129
the plant and buildings, larger inventories, and for payment of wages and salaries in difficult times.

COMIC-STRIP-ART METHOD OF REPORTING FACTS

Joy Manufacturing Company, Pittsburgh, Pennsylvania, introduced a new idea in its 1947 annual report to employees. On the cover page, the cartoonist shows the company coming through the office door labeled "Business Doctor." The opening statement is, "Here I am for my annual check-up, Doc. How do I look?" The report contains 15 pages with one or two cartoons on each page. The cartoon with comic-strip atmosphere and friendly conversational tone portrays the humorous vein of the report, while the printed portions tell the facts. Each item of the usual conventional financial statement is effectively and conclusively stated. Each cartoon tells what happened to the income and what is left. The last page shows the "Doc" bidding the company farewell until next year.

CREATING EMPLOYEE INTEREST IN READING THE ANNUAL REPORT

The Mengel Company, Louisville, Kentucky, presents an interesting story on furnishing facts as to company operations to its employees.

The company, founded in 1877, published its first statement to its employees in 1939. The statement, a one-page leaflet entitled, "Looking Ahead," in addition to announcing a change in top management, stressed customer relations, supplier relations, organization, employee relations, wages, recognition for long service, and a resume of the company's financial obligations to its stockholders and employees. The first annual report was entitled, "Review of 1939 Operations for Employees." This report was in leaflet form containing an explanatory balance sheet, and a statement of operations.

With the 1944 report, management enclosed a card with a few questions thereon, asking the employees and stockholders to express their views and thoughts about the report. Top management was shocked to learn that less than 2 per cent of the employees responded to the survey. The president of the company, who entered the service of the company at the age of 17 as an office boy and 28 years later (1939) was elevated to the top position, was so disappointed that he issued a special statement to the employees. The statement was printed in a leaflet entitled, "Mengel's Pledge to You." The theme of the leaflet was a statement of principles in employee relations, again stressing wages, rates of pay, machine, mechanical process, credit union and retirement plan.

130 As a result of the employee survey, the 1945 annual report was modernized. This report was made "hard to get." The only way a worker could get a copy of the 1945 report was by asking for it, either in person or in writing. The company was again shocked to learn that employees made little or no attempt to get copies of the report. Other innovations were included in the 1946 report, and management decided to stand at the gate and hand out the reports to workers as they left the plant. The result was still disappointing. The 1947 report was greatly improved with more new ideas and filled with unusual charts, graphs, photographs, and detailed information on company operations. One of the features of this report was the breakdown on "Per Dollar Income." The breakdown showed the distribution in this order:

Distribution:		*Per Income Dollar*
Wages and Salary		39¢
Factory employees	$10,621,100	
Salesmen and Supervisors	2,401,300	
Officers and Directors	227,400	
Benefits	709,000	
Total	$13,958,000	
Raw Materials		48¢
Supplies and Services	$17,109,000	
Depreciation		3¢
Depletion	$ 975,000	
Taxes		4¢
Federal, State and Local	$ 1,489,300	
Dividends		2¢
Stockholders for use of their money	$ 778,800	
Remained in the Business		4¢
Improvement and emergency uses	$ 1,517,400	

Management decided to mail the 1947 annual report. The result was the best the company had obtained in creating employee interest in the annual report of the company operations.

Reports Emphasizing Product and Plant Facilities

The B. F. Avery & Sons Company, Louisville, Kentucky, founded in 1825, put out its first modern annual report in 1944. Its theme was the farmer and his implements. The report was well received by the farmer, because the content was pictorially displayed in such a fashion that the farmer felt proud to have a copy of the report. This report revealed for the first time to many inhabitants of Louisville and Kentucky that Avery manufactured modern power-driven farm machinery. It was through this report that the public knew, for the first time, that Avery
could no longer be considered as a small manufacturer of horse-drawn 131
farm equipment.

The 1945 and 1946 Avery reports followed the same theme as 1944, with more emphasis on Avery's products and problems. The theme of the 1947 report stressed new manufacturing facilities and new products. The pages, including the cover, were well balanced with photographs of Avery's tractors, plows, harrows, planters, cultivators, rotary hoes, and several other farm implements in action. Each of these photographs were action pictures demonstrating the practical application of Avery farm equipment. The three middle pages conveyed the financial story. Presentation was conservative but very forcefully portrayed.

I have elaborated on this report because the text was designed to appeal to the farmer. It so happens that many of Avery's employees owned small farms. Thereby, through this appeal the company got across to its employees the importance and uses of the product they help to make.

Reaction to Operation Reports

The officials of the Allegheny Ludlum Steel Corporation, Pittsburgh, Pennsylvania, invited its readers to comment on the company's annual report and company policies. The adverse comments were shocking to company officials. Some of them were: "The United States Government, as big as it is, needs only one Vice-President, how come you have so many." "Be brief and to the point." "Tell the amount earned per common share." "Is it better than the previous year? If not, why? and what can be or is being done about it?" "Just include a little letter or a note, as a father would to a son or daughter, then we would feel that we really belonged." "This survey, to me, seems stupid." "The management should know what its stockholders should know." "I am not a scoffer," said another, "but I think 75 per cent of the subject matter in the average annual report is a waste of time and energy." "It is easy in bad times to omit the stock dividends for the year, but there is never anything said about a cut in the president's salary if he doesn't operate the company at a profit," one said.

These criticisms are worthy of further analysis: The comment "too many Vice-Presidents" reflects a common type of distrust that is a result of misunderstanding. Actually, the company had only one executive vice-president, and only four other vice-presidents. The vice-presidents compare with the secretaries of the President's cabinet. Each vice-president was charged with heading a specific set of activities.

Over 3,000 readers responded to the questionnaire. Of these, 98
132 per cent said that they read the annual report; 53 per cent said that they do not keep the report for future reference; 61 per cent said that they were not satisfied with the report in its present form; 31 per cent claimed that the report was "somewhat interesting"; 10 per cent attested that the report was clear; and 20 per cent claimed that the report was either too general, too technical, too formal, too dull or too vague.

The questionnaire asked the readers to express their opinions on the company's weekly radio program, "Steel Horizons." More than 65 per cent reported that they had never heard the program.

Information That Appeals to Employees

In most instances, the daily job represents the worker's LIFE CENTER. The worker has HOPES, FEARS, AND PRIDE. When a worker reads a report these emotions are uppermost in his mind. He looks for his part in the manufacturing process. He is interested in knowing the company's progress and stability. He is interested in only those financial figures which reveal to him the relation of his own job and his own prospects. He likes to read about his company in the local newspaper. He likes to hear his company mentioned over the radio. He wants to know how the profit is spent. He is interested in knowing the use, importance and value of the product he helped to make. He is desirous of knowing who owns the company for which he works. He is interested in knowing the history of the company and what prospects the company has in the future. He wants to know if the stockholders live in the community, or several thousand miles away from the plant. He wants to know who they are—bankers, investors, women, radio stars, etc. He would like to know if the stock is available to him. I could list a dozen more subjects that interest the worker, such as comparative wage rates for his job with other companies in the community, what benefits the worker receives that are offered by other companies, etc.

When a worker reads management's report on company operations and fails to formulate his own answers to these items I have indicated, it is only natural to get the unfavorable reactions that some companies have experienced.

Presenting Operation Facts to Employees

In presenting operation facts to employees, the universal prerequisites for all companies may be grouped as follows:

a. Establish a sound personnel philosophy
b. Initiate and support progressive labor policies
c. Execute at all times a genuine desire to deal justly with all employees.

When these policies have been inaugurated by the company, then management of the company is ready to formulate a program which will promote better employee-employer relations, and dispel public misunderstandings about the company.

The basic principle of this program should be employee education. The subjects covered in this educational program should be:

1. Financial
   a. The importance of stockholders
   b. Why reserves are needed
   c. Facts on taxes
   d. Why a profit must be maintained
   e. What is break-even point?
   f. Why break-even point is important
   g. Effect of wages on stability of company
   h. Effect of other matters on financial standing of company
2. Operation
   a. The reasons why controlling expenses are important
   b. The effect wages and raw material costs have on profits
   c. The need for maintaining high productivity per worker
   d. The role that inventories have on the cost of the products
   e. The importance of product wastes and rejects
   f. How volume in manufacturing affects prices, wages and wastes
3. Public Relations
   a. The importance of holding custom's good will and general public patronage
   b. Community interest and activity and its effect on employees
4. Human Relations
   a. The importance of harmony with fellow workers
   b. Its effect on the employee himself, management, production, fellow workers, customers, quality and quantity of product

5. Economics
   a. Wage trends in other competitive industries
   b. Importance of advertising and relation of company operations to the economy in the field the company is operating
   c. The importance of balanced economy from within as well as from without

Putting Employee Education Program into Effect

Perhaps the best way to make this type of program effective would be to start training top management. Employees at this level may fully understand all principles of the company operations, but may not be familiar with the details, and, in some instances, do not know how to present operating facts to employees in a manner interesting to the workers.

Getting Operating Facts Across to Employees

134

In getting operating facts across to employees, the following is suggested:

First: Information must originate at the top. This information could be disseminated by memoranda at regular intervals. The information should cover over-all company operations, product data, sales, and other current facts involving the company as a whole.

This information then could be used as a guide by those charged with the responsibility of releasing correct information to the public and employees.

Second: Information must be obtained from without, pertaining to trends in products, prices, and public opinion. Also, information must be obtained from within the company on attitudes and opinions of the supervisors and workers. This gives the employee a feeling that he is a part of management.

Once the desires of top management are known and the feeling and thinking of the workers are analyzed, the company's Director of Industrial and Public Relations is ready to start the third step in getting facts across to employees. This step is the actual conveyance of the information directly to the employees.

Ways and Means of Disseminating Company Information to Employees

The usual channels in conveying information to employees may be grouped as follows:

1. *House Organ*—This medium should discuss the worker and his problems in HIS LANGUAGE. The information released through the house organ must be consistent in its character, always personal, always with employee flavor, and,

by all means, newsy and spontaneous. The theme of the house organ at all times should build a feeling of belonging.

2. *Letters or Memoranda*—When matters come up that involve legal implications which affect both company and employees, the letter or memorandum is probably the best medium to use. The communications should be directed to the employee's home and under no circumstances distributed at the plant. In this way, the employee's family is brought into the discussion and usually the employee's family has a stake in the matter, thereby making it desirable to consider the matter in the atmosphere of the home, instead of the surroundings of the work area.

3. *Leaflets*—The primary use of this means of communication is to get messages across to customers and consumers. The theme of these leaflets should be a discussion of the company's viewpoint of some misundertood or misinterpreted facts about the company, or its product, perhaps some popular subject matter of interest to all workers in the community. Many utility companies insert leaflets with their monthly bills to consumers, and some manufacturing companies give leaflets to their salesmen. 135

4. *Annual Reports.*—This medium has been adequately discussed at the beginning of my talk this afternoon, but, in passing, I might mention that annual reports should be addressed to both stockholders and employees. By doing this it helps to make the employee feel that he is given the same information as is given to the stockholders, and the feeling of being excluded from guarded facts is dispelled. I would also like to mention that it is a mistake for companies to depend wholly on annual reports to get operating facts to employees. The annual report should serve as a summary of actually what took place.

5. *Publicity*—It is a good idea to let the employees in on new products before releasing the information to the press. Nothing makes an employee more distrustful toward his employer than to pick up a trade journal or a newspaper and read about a new product his company has released for sale, or developed of which he knew nothing. Publicity should be given to all worthy achievements of employees. It makes the employee feel that he is appreciated. It strikes deeply into his emotion of pride.

6. *Advertisement*—Perhaps this medium could be best explained by referring to the advertising philosophies used by utility and insurance companies. The next time you read a current magazine such as *Time* or its equivalent, look at these advertisements and note the story they tell about their employees.

7. *Payroll Inserts*—This medium should be limited to those facts pertaining to the employee's pay or conditions affecting his pay. The dissemination of unrelated information in the pay envelope is a gross psychological error. Some companies have made the mistake of inserting such information as, "The president did not receive the $100,000 salary as take home pay reported in the newspaper, because he had to give $60,000 of it for taxes."

8. *Biographies of Brass Hats*—Explaining to the employee how top management personnel was elevated to "Mahogany Row" goes a long way in bringing about a closer feeling from the worker toward top management personnel. A thumbnail sketch of one or more of the top personnel intrigues the worker and removes that mythical idea of some workers that top management personnel are inhuman.

9. *Handbook*—This medium is primarily used for acquainting a new employee with his duties and responsibilities to himself, the company and his fellow workers. Also, the handbook serves as an excellent medium for old employees to keep the general operating policies before them for reference and guide.

10. *Personal Contact*—This medium brings about understanding and feeling in such a way that both the employer and employee benefit. The direct contact with the worker from all levels, up and down, brings about an *esprit de corps* that cannot be accomplished in any other way. The personal contact is one of the best ways to control the oldest communication system known to man—"The Grapevine." Nobody likes a whispering campaign. When the personal contact medium is allowed to drop into the background, the grapevine method of passing information can do more harm than written words can create. The personal contact up and down is very important, not only in the plant or while at work, but at all times.

11. *Film*—This medium combines all the means of communication dis-
136 cussed in my message to you this afternoon. Perhaps the best example of this medium is the sound film produced by the International Harvester Company. The title of this film is "Profits Means Progress for Everyone," which you will see in a few minutes. In reviewing this film, I ask you to observe how this company combined in one medium practically all the things I have discussed with you, plus a lot of things I left out. Notice how the word *progress* is woven with such important words as *customers*, *jobs*, *wages*, *prices*, *production*, *inflation*, *sales*, *stockholders*, *companies*, *food*, *transportation*, *investments*, *plants*, *competition*, *profit*, and *the future*.

Closing Remarks

Before closing, I want to call your attention to the display of annual reports issued by such companies as I have already mentioned, and some that I have not mentioned. On the table to my right, there are complimentary copies of annual reports from several companies, which you may pick up before you leave this afternoon. I want to call your attention to the large chart with all the silver glued to it. This chart was used by management within the last few weeks, as a means to discuss wage-increase demands made by the Union. Also, I ask you to observe the very large portfolio used by one company to fight inflation.

Gentlemen, what I have given you this afternoon is merely a scratch of the surface of what has been done and what can be done in presenting company operating facts to employees.

Thank you, gentlemen. It has been a real pleasure to be with you this afternoon and I only wish it were my privilege to become better acquainted with each and every one of you.

The sound film, which will now be shown, will continue about 26 minutes.

Annual Reports to Employees

By John H. Myers, C.P.A.

This article is a comprehensive analysis of some sixty of the several hundred corporate annual financial reports to employees the author has had occasion to review. It discusses the methods of presentation and choices of what data to present to employees. The companies range from large to small, and all reports referred to were used for general interest rather than in any attempt to make a statistical determination of what is usual.

Annual reports to employees differ markedly from company to company. In about half of the companies studied they also differ from year to year. As to financial information given, they range from being almost a reprint of the report to stockholders, as in the case of American Can Company, to giving no financial information at all. An example of this latter is Esso Standard Oil Company which has not even stockholders to report to in the usual sense of a stockholders' report, since it is wholly owned by Standard Oil Co. (N. J.). The reports range in tone all the way from a report of the people, by the people, and for the people (Allstate Insurance Company) to those where the management just talks to the employees in a patronizing air or to those where the management talks without seeming to make an attempt to communicate anything. One company, to which I wrote for a copy of its report, had given up the attempt to tell its employees about the company and replied that "the sad experience is that most employees are really not interested in the company for which they work."

Distribution of the Sales Dollar

Most of the companies give a distribution of their sales dollar even if no other financial information is given.
Of course, there are cases where this 137
is merely an extra column on a formal income statement; but far more interesting are the efforts by some companies to put in a down-to-earth presentation designed to get the point across. Several companies illustrated a dollar bill divided into various parts; many others used a silver dollar which was divided into segments like the traditional pie chart. Less effective were the illustrations of piles of change of various denominations. For example, if forty-seven cents of each dollar went for materials, there would be a picture of a quarter, two dimes and two pennies. Effectiveness seemed to be lost because the concept of proportionate size was lost. The reader had to read the numbers or count his change instead of just looking.

Sometimes there may be a considerable propaganda element to the presentation, in the desire to show the employees what a large share of the "pot" they really are getting. The Daystrom Company's illustration was most effective from this point of view. For the sales during the year there was a picture of a fellow carrying a sack of one hundred marbles. In the next picture all one hundred were in a circle on the ground and a man, representing all suppliers, was taking a

John H. Myers, Ph.D., C.P.A. (Illinois), is associate professor of accounting at Northwestern University and also serves as a consultant to business. He formerly was engaged in public practice with Arthur Andersen & Co. and with Robert P. Schermerhorn, and also taught at the University of Buffalo.

Dr. Myers has published many articles in financial and accounting journals.

shot at them and knocking out fifty-two of the marbles. The following picture showed an employee knocking out forty of the remaining forty-eight; he really made a killing. Others in turn took their shots at the remaining marbles until, in the end, the owner came along and picked up the one remaining marble.

A couple of companies illustrated the income statement in total, instead of in percentages to net sales, as in the cases previously mentioned. Lion Oil Company made an interesting presentation. The report was about the size of an unfolded pocket checkbook. The first page was a deposit slip for the amount of the total net sales. Each succeeding page was a check to one group of recipients: suppliers, employees, government, owners, etc. Opposite each check was a small stub with the balance brought down and next to the stub was a fairly complete discussion of the item.

Marquette Cement Manufacturing Company also used the check book idea, but supplemented the presentation with a pile of one hundred pennies. First this was divided into two parts: "for costs ahead of us" and "balance left to us." Each of these parts was in turn divided into three parts. The first was split among materials and services, taxes, wear and tear. The second was split among employees, investors, and used in the business. Kimberly-Clark Corporation's pictorial device was a crane taking logs away from a pile of pulpwood. Several other companies similarly had their pictures tied in with their operations.

Other Statistical Data

Only a few companies made any attempt to give the employees balance-sheet information. Some of these, of course, were like American Can, which gives the employees regular statements. Other companies have gone to elaborate means to make the statements self-explanatory. Kimberly-Clark's simplified balance sheet apparently has all the items appearing on the one to stockholders, but also has from two to five lines of explanation under the traditional balance-sheet wording. The Garrett Corporation, in its one report to employees, gave a standard-form balance sheet with lines to explanations out at the side. Radio Corporation of America merely listed the assets with descriptive titles under the heading "What We Own." Similar treatment was given to "What We Owe" and "Owners' Investment." A typical description was "Unpaid bills and accruals to be paid within one year."

In addition to typical income-statement and balance-sheet data, a number of companies show employment statistics. Most common is the showing of payroll plus fringe benefits. A number of companies have set forth comparisons to show the employees how well-off they are. Revere Copper and Brass, Incorporated, presents a graph and a brief discussion of seven different items. Four relate to Revere only—average earning per employee, total payroll, average wages per hour, and average weekly wages and hours. Then there follows a graph of Revere weekly wages and of the cost of living index. The next graph shows three lines: Revere hourly wages, hourly wages in durable goods manufacturing, and in all manufacturing. The last graph shows weekly wages for the same three groups. Marquette Cement does somewhat the same thing with comparisons. One especially interesting one shows productivity per hour (up slightly) and productivity per dollar of pay and benefits (down considerably).

Two companies, Bethlehem Steel Corporation and Esso Standard Oil, have given a considerable amount of extra statistical information. Bethlehem, in a single two-page table, gives data since 1905 on nineteen different items—the same table as in the stockholders' report. Esso's data cover only five years and only a few topics, such as costs of crude oil purchased and an example of the effect of price variation upon the company.

Non-numerical Topics

In addition to the statistical reports, a number of the companies have covered further ground. This might be classified into two types: about the company and about the people. At the two extremes might be placed the 1952 reports of Bethlehem Steel and Allstate Insurance Company. Bethlehem has separate articles on capacity, facility improvements, mining property improvements, taconite, shipyards, etc. Allstate has mostly reviews of what its people have said and done. There are sections on sports, anniversaries, manpower needs, employee education, and others. Only about one-third of the report was devoted to operating data. However, in 1953 the company switched to giving more company data. R.C.A. gives articles on its research, manufacturing, broadcasting, communications, and newly-promoted executives among others. Esso discusses marketing trends, product development, merchandising, refining operations, and "people events."

Tone

The tone of the reports varies widely. Some assume the employees should be addressed on the same plane as the stockholders. Others would seem to reject this viewpoint. American Can's report to "the organization" is essentially the stockholders' report with the jacket and salutation changed. At the opposite extreme, another company set up its report in comic-book style a number of years ago. It apparently realized its error, for subsequent reports have been quite different.

Some of the reports are written as if the employee reader is genuinely interested. Others just report. Many experts on communication today tell us that we should put the human side foremost. Throughout the R.C.A. report a person is prominent in every picture. Marquette Cement has appropriate cartoons on people in the margins, pointing up the significant parts of the story. American Can's report, being as erudite as it is, has no pictures except in the customary "rogue's gallery" of executives.

Evaluation

An evaluation of annual reports to stockholders is not difficult if one confines himself to matters of accounting reporting. Standards are rather well defined, and there seems to be a direction in which these standards are moving. The text part of those stockholders' reports varies widely, but in most cases is somewhat related to the financial statements. However, with employees' reports there is no standard
against which to judge except effectiveness. How can an outsider judge if it was effective? What message was the report supposed to convey effectively? The real answer is that there is no uniformly understood objective as to what employees' reports are to achieve, what the employees want to know, or how to get the message across to them. Some companies apparently try to use the reports as propaganda devices to "butter up" the employees by showing them how well-off they are. Others try to arouse their sense of pride by telling them about the wonders of their company. Some, like the example of Marquette Cement, try to stimulate employees to greater efforts by showing them that wages have gone up faster than productivity. Still others try to make it a report of how their fellow employees are doing.

Some of the annual reports to employees are incorporated in the regular company magazine. Most are separate publications. It would seem that if the magazine is effective, this would be a place to put the report to get it read. Almost all companies offer the employees the regular report to stockholders if they wish it, and tell them how to get it.

(Continued on page 122)

140

Annual Reports to Employees

(Continued from page 102)

In elaborateness the reports range from a two-page folder to Esso's thirty-two page, many-color booklet. There are as many variations in reports as there are in budgets and report directors. This situation will probably continue as long as there seems to be no responsibility to present financial data to employees in accordance with some of the "generally accepted standards" applicable to reports to stockholders.

Financial Reporting to Corporate Employees

A Growing Practice in Australia

by L. D. Parker, B.Ec.(Adel.), B.Phil.(Dundee), A.C.A.,
Lecturer in the Department of Accounting and Finance, Monash University

"He that will not apply new remedies must expect new evils; for time is the greatest innovator."
Francis Bacon, 1561-1626

The communication of information concerning corporate financial performance by presentations specifically designed for employees is a relatively new and growing phenomenon in Australia. Until now it has taken the form of individual company experiments and has gone unrecognised by Australian accountants, both professional and academic. This paper will outline the forms which this reporting technique can take, its potential and its problems, and its present significance for Australian business and the accounting profession.

The Trend Explained

While accountants have for some time been debating the identity of the users of the annual financial report to company shareholders, a considerable number of companies, both in Australia and elsewhere, have seen fit to establish procedures for providing separate financial reports specifically designed for their employees. The attempts in this area have varied considerably in style and quality but cannot be dismissed by the accounting profession as being simply a temporary occurrence. Experiments have been commenced by some large and long-established companies and in some cases have now been continuing for three or more years. Furthermore, there is ample evidence to suggest that the number of companies adopting this practice is on the increase.

What has caused this new trend? While no survey data are yet available in answer to this question, a range of possible reasons do present themselves. Most generally this would appear to be a manifestation of companies' recognition of growing pressures in society for greater democracy in many areas of human endeavour. This is not to suggest that the provision of financial reports especially designed for employees is seen as a way of either forestalling or foreshadowing schemes of worker participation which remains a quite separate issue. The move is also linked to the growing corporate awareness of its social responsibility, both to the community at large and to the workforce which it employs. To the accountants who suspect these rationales to be rather too trite it must be admitted that these are probably not the only reasons for companies embarking upon this type of reporting and indeed it is likely that companies make the decision for a combination of reasons. Nevertheless, many companies are aware of the implications of the changing nature of social and political thought in society and government and are often keen to be seen as anticipating and responding to these new ideas in order not to be considered inflexible or resistant to moves which could benefit the workforce. As a somewhat more negative response, some companies may choose to adopt this new reporting system simply to be in advance of legislation which they fear may force it upon them anyway. It must also be remembered that once it becomes known that a few companies have adopted this reporting system, others may follow in order to "keep up with the Joneses".

Of course, there are more specific causes of this upsurge in reporting to employees. It may be undertaken as a further exercise in corporate "image building". This could extend even further to include blatant propaganda of top management ideals and most certainly reports do exist which exhibit hints of that. Company management may also see this report as one way of going some distance towards meeting union requests for greater dissemination of corporate financial performance information and in fact it may serve as an educational device in assisting union representatives to gain an improved understanding of a company's financial position. On the other hand it might simply be used as an attempt to sidestep union requests for further financial information.

Whether that ploy would be successful must be the subject of some doubt.

The provision of corporate financial information to employees may also be seen as a way of improving the company's formal internal communication network by adding, as it were, another link in the chain and formally providing information which previously may only have circulated inaccurately via the informal communications network (the grapevine) or which may not have circulated at all. A further advantage of this report might well be that if it contains good news, this may stimulate morale among company personnel while bad news is best transmitted to them via this internal system before they learn of it in the national press.

The New Dimension

The uninitiated may wonder what it is that differentiates a financial report to employees from that already issued to company shareholders. An example is not provided in this paper because of the variety of report contents and presentation formats which have thus far emerged, but a brief outline of some approaches can be given. Most commonly, financial information is communicated via articles in the house journal, special lift-outs in the company newspaper or as a completely self-contained publication in newspaper or booklet form. The key contents are a simplified balance sheet and profit and loss statement often accompanied by a funds statement. To date these have mostly been produced in graphical and diagrammatic form. Other components have included statements from the chairman to employees, graphical explanations of the effect of inflation upon profits and liquidity, reports on branch or division activities, details of categories of shareholders, aggregate statistics on employee types, trend graphs of sales, profits, wages and shareholder dividends, health and safety records, etc. The aim behind all this is to present corporate financial performance information to employees in the context of information about a broad spectrum of company activities both financial and non-financial. Ideally this type of report should go some way towards assisting the employee to relate his or her work and position in the company to the results of its activities as a whole. That is admittedly a tall order.

One aspect of reporting to employees which could be an issue for discussion in itself is the virtually unanimous adoption of simplified financial accounts by companies experimenting in the area. The prime mover behind this practice has undoubtedly been the belief that the balance sheet and profit and loss statement as presented to the shareholders have become too complex for the average lay employee's understanding and the belief that the presentation of excessive detail is likely to discourage employees from reading the accounts at all. For this reason also, pie diagrams and bar charts have also been utilised in profit and loss and balance sheet presentations. The growing practice among some companies presenting this type of report has been to issue it to the shareholders as well. Given the recent publication of surveys demonstrating the low readership of financial statements by shareholders (and even lower comprehension),[1] it may be interesting to learn whether greater shareholder readership is achieved through distributing the report to employees.

Australian Developments

In September 1976 a limited survey of major Australian companies was carried out to determine whether the distribution of financial information to employees had assumed any importance in the Australian business and industrial community. The findings outlined in Tables 1 to 4 suggest that the practice has gained a sizeable foothold in a relatively short space of time and that it shows signs of growing quite quickly. The survey does not pretend to have uncovered all of the companies in Australia who reported financial information to their employees in 1976 but it did detect a significant group who have adopted the practice. Table 1 identified 25 major Australian companies (27 per cent of those surveyed)[2] who were in

Table I

Major* Australian Companies Reporting Their Financial Performance to Employees for 1976

Company	Reporting Methods
Ampol Petroleum Ltd.	Special year end report to be issued to employees.
Ampol Petroleum (Victoria) Pty. Ltd.	Simplified accounts in annual report to shareholders and commentary in staff newspaper.
Ansett Transport Industries Ltd.	Commentary on annual accounts in staff journal and matters relating to staff in report to shareholders.
Arnott's Biscuits Pty. Ltd.	Special year end report to be issued to employees.
Australian National Industries Ltd.	Extracts of interim and final report announcements in staff journal and yearly address by chairman.
Australian Paper Manufacturers Ltd.	Audio-visual programme.
The Broken Hill Proprietary Company Ltd.	Special annual report issued to employees (printed in three languages).
The Commercial Bank of Australia Ltd.	Supplementary information re annual report to shareholders in staff newspaper.
The Commercial Banking Company of Sydney Ltd.	Special year end report issued to employees.
The Commonwealth Industrial Gases Ltd.	Short seminars for employees.

Concrete Industries (Monier) Ltd.	Special year end report issued to employees.
Conzinc Riotinto of Australia Ltd.	Special year end report to be issued to employees.
John Fairfax Ltd.	Special year end report to be issued to employees.
Grace Bros. Holdings Ltd.	Special year end report to be issued to employees.
Humes Ltd.	Special year end report issued to employees.
I.C.I. Australia Ltd.	Articles in staff newspaper.
James Hardie Asbestos Ltd.	Special year end report issued to employees.
M.I.M. Holdings Ltd.	1. Financial information included in quarterly publication *MIMAG*, fortnightly *Isa News*, monthly group newssheet *MIM News*. 2. Quarterly summary financial progress reports issued to employees on day of release to stock exchanges. 3. Videotaped interviews with chairman and newsreels on company activities distributed to Mt. Isa and Townsville television and radio stations (also shown to Brisbane-based employees). 4. Edited versions of chairman's address to annual shareholders' meeting by landline to radio stations. 5. Company now developing more graphic presentation of its financial position for employees. 6. Company developing "lower key" internal use of videotaped information to employees.
The Myer Emporium Ltd.	Special year end report issued to employees.
Repco Ltd.	Special year end report to be issued to employees.
T.N.T. Australia Ltd.	Special year end report to be issued to employees.
Tooheys Ltd.	Special year end report issued to employees (in several languages).
Woolworths Ltd.	Special year end report issued to employees.

* This survey covered 92 of the "100 Biggest Companies", based on market capitalisation, *The National Times*, September 13-18, 1976, p. 71. 74 companies responded to circular letters sent on September 27, 1976.

Table 2

Companies* Presently Considering Production of a Special Year End Financial Report to Employees

Australia and New Zealand Banking Group Limited
Burns Philp and Company Ltd.
The Commonwealth Industrial Gases Ltd.
G. J. Coles and Coy. Ltd.
CSR Ltd.
David Jones Ltd.
Union Carbide Australia Ltd.

* These are drawn from the 74 respondents to the survey outlined in Table 1.

the process of reporting to employees on results in the 1976 year.

It can also be seen from the contents of the table that reporting methods are quite varied and range from verbal to video-tape to house journal to independent booklet. Some respondents had even duplicated report contents in several languages.

Table 2 identifies a further group of companies who claimed to be presently considering the introduction of financial reports for employees while Table 3 shows by way of example some companies who although not providing a report specifically for employees had adopted the practice of providing them with a copy of the report to shareholders. On aggregating the results of Tables 1 to 3, it is evident that of major Australian companies as defined in Table 1, 39 per cent of the 92 surveyed were paying serious consideration to the provision of financial performance information to their employees by one means or another.

In the course of this research, further companies outside the Table 1 survey list were found to be reporting financial information to employees and these are detailed in Table 4. Overall, these results must cause the Australian accounting profession to consider seriously the needs of this newly established and rapidly growing financial information user group. The continuance of some companies' efforts in this area for three or more years thus far should also discourage any view that this is but a temporary phenomenon. Accountants whose companies are considering the introduction of such a report for the first time have plenty of examples at their disposal in Australia from which to take some guidance. In addition to these practical considerations, however, early attention by the accounting profession to the problems of accurate simplification of accounts and clarity of presentation to lay readers will facilitate the more effective development of a report which thus far seems to have developed without its participation (or realisation?). Once again if accountants are to retain a place in the communication of financial information within the company they must become involved in the production of employee reports.

Table 3

Examples* of Companies Issuing The Annual Report to Shareholders to Their Employees

Lend Lease Corporation Ltd.
North Broken Hill Ltd.
Thiess Holdings Ltd.
Woodside-Burmah Oil N.L.

* These are drawn from the 74 respondents to the survey outlined in Table 1.

Australian Examples

Some brief descriptions of Australian company experiments in the preparation of special year end reports to employees may be of interest here. Woolworths' 1976 "First Annual Report for Staff" included ten-year bar charts of sales, net profits, the effect of inflation on profit and the number of cents profit in each sales dollar, a photograph of a "sales dollar" split into its expenditure components, a photograph of an "income tax dollar" split into government expenditure categories and statements concerning closures, future developments and various personnel programmes. The report also includes a considerable number of photographs of personnel, work locations, etc. B.H.P.'s "B.H.P. '76 Year in Review" includes a report of statements made by the managing director, profit and loss statement categorised in industry sections, a "plumbing diagram" of sales and major expenses and distributions, a discussion of the effects of inflation upon the steel industry, a discussion of employee turnover and wages and reports on major steel projects, safety statistics, research programmes, migrant employee English classes, oil, gas and mineral activities and results of subsidiaries. The report is printed in three languages.

The Commercial Banking Company of Sydney Limited's "Annual Report to the staff 1976" includes a message from the managing director, discussions of savings and trading bank activities, international and corporate divisions, bankcard and automated systems, statements of future plans, a report on staff facilities and opportunities and pie diagrams of income by division and total expenditures and distributions. "Humes Talk", October 1976, includes statements on the company's position in the present economic climate, a report on overseas development, discussions of research and development, the need for profits, committee arrangements for improving employees' conditions of work, etc., details of internal and external Hume publications for improvement of communication, tables of 1975/76 income and expenditure, employees in Australia and overseas (1968, 1972, 1976) and distribution of group profits, and bar charts of percentage increases in factor prices 1974/76. Also included in the Hume report is a diagram of the preliminary layout of a new factory, reports on divisional activities, environmental policies and personnel policy.

Concrete Industries (Monier) Ltd. issue a basic report from the managing director and an additional sheet of State highlights to each branch. The report covers capital expenditure, industrial activity, personnel training, safety, superannuation, research and future plans and includes charts of usage of each sales dollar, profit on each sales dollar 1971/76, wages/dividends/retained profits 1971/76 and balance sheet (simplified). Tooheys report, "Here's to 'Ee", special edition November 1976, "Our Financial Year: A Special Report to Employees", includes a message from the chief executive, an excessively complex diagrammatic profit and loss/funds statement, bar charts of wages/dividends/retained profit 1972/76, highlights in three languages, balance sheet and location of operations. The Federal Capital Press of Australia Pty. Ltd's "A Report for Employees 1976" included a manager's report, a diagram of produc-

Table 4

Examples of Other Companies Operating in Australia Reporting Their Financial Performance to Employees for 1976

Company	Reporting Methods
The Federal Capital Press of Australia Pty. Ltd. (The Canberra Times—wholly owned subsidiary of John Fairfax Ltd.)	Special year end report issued to employees.
Kemtron Ltd.	Special year end one-page report issued to employees.
Lloyds Holdings Ltd.	Special year end report issued to employees.
Mauri Brothers and Thomson Ltd.	Booklet produced for staff at end of 1975/76 financial year.
U.E.B. Industries Ltd.	Special year end report issued to employees.
Vickers Australia Ltd.	Special mid-year and year end reports to employees.
William Adams and Co. Ltd.	Special year end financial report to employees in house journal.

tion cost distribution, a chart of running cost increases since 1971, a diagrammatic balance sheet, a pie diagram of distribution of the dollar income, charts of circulation and advertising volume 1965/76 and an editorial statement.

Mauri Brothers and Thomson Limited's "Food for thought . . . A Review for Staff: The Company in 1976" contains a message from the managing director, a profit and loss statement presentation, accounts of company history, products, diagram of division structure, group manager and division reports, work locations, etc. Vickers Australia Ltd.'s "Annual Review 1975" was published in English, Greek and Italian. It contained a chairman's message, a managing director's review of company activities and large tables and diagrams covering consolidated profit and loss, expenditure of the sales dollar, comparisons of increases in wages, consumer price index and dividends over five years and reports on safety and age of machine tools.

These examples have been provided in this paper for several reasons. They demonstrate the significant development of this type of reporting in Australia and the considerable importance which companies have attached to it. It becomes clear from observing these reports that much effort has often been expended in their production. Also noticeable is the variety of presentation formats and content which can be found even among such a limited range of examples as cited here. Some of these attempts are not without their faults and problems and it is in these matters that accountants can find questions demanding their earnest consideration. The most efficient use of diagrammatic representations of the balance sheet and profit and loss account without the introduction of distortions is one matter urgently requiring attention. How can accounts be accurately simplified in order to attract and retain lay readership? What are the effects of a patronising chairman's address? How can the tendency towards pro management propaganda be avoided in the report? In what form will the report be most likely to be read?—as a separate publication, as a broadsheet, or in the house journal? These are but a few of the problem areas raised by this new development. What cannot be ignored by the accounting profession in Australia is the evidence of this report's firm entrenchment in corporate communication systems.

The U.K. Parallel

The Australian business and industrial community is not alone in experiencing this development of employee reporting systems. The U.K., for instance, is witnessing a similar process. Companies there which have been producing such reports include G.K.N., Brockhouse Group, B.O.C., John Menzies, Avon Rubber Co., Hargreaves Group, Imperial Group, Marks and Spencer, Tozer Kemsley and Millbourn, Wiggins Teape, Turner and Newall, United Biscuits, D.R.G., Plessey, Scottish and Newcastle Breweries Ltd., etc. Indeed, 1976 has witnessed the announcement of an award to be given by Reed Executive (an employment agency) and *Accountancy Age* for the best produced employee report, and this has aroused a considerable response from British companies. The style and content of the U.K. company reports is quite similar to those produced by Australian companies, although in the U.K. reports possibly more emphasis has been placed upon the distinction between the struggle for adequate profitability and adequate liquidity. Furthermore, it is interesting to note that The Corporate Report,[3] sponsored in the main by The Institute of Chartered Accountants in England and Wales, gave explicit recognition to the need for this report.

Immediate Prospects

What are the implications of this trend for accountants in Australia? The reporting of corporate financial performance to employees appears to have become irreversibly established in Australia and seems likely to grow in significance as a generally accepted form of corporate reporting. It involves a range of possibly contentious issues which accountants are best fitted to investigate, so that the immediate attention of the accounting profession is required if this development is to achieve maximum potential. Accountants who may become involved in the preparation of these reports have little excuse for avoiding the task since the information required for production of such a report is readily available in existing company information systems and since numerous examples of other company's attempts are already available.

The accountant's major role in the production of this report must lie in his technical expertise. He should be best suited for the task of constructing representations of financial accounts which will attract lay readers, retain their attention and provide easy comprehension. That in itself will prove to be no easy task. Indeed this exercise represents the manifestation of a question which has concerned accountants for many years—the identity of the users of financial reports. At first sight it appears that the emergence of this special report represents the judgement of certain sectors of the business community that the annual report to shareholders is not the all inclusive document suitable for all financial information users as accountants have traditionally claimed it to be. In this way the profession now finds itself involved in the exercise of preparing financial reports for specific user categories. Those accountants who refuse to agree to the introduction of this report may well find that it will be produced without their participation.

In the end result accountants must look to their responsibilities in the development of this report since they have always been committed to serving financial information user needs. The findings in this paper provide strong evidence for the view that Australian company management and employees are becoming firmly convinced of the need for and benefits of a financial report to employees. It is now up to accountants to meet that demand.

Footnotes

(1) T. A. Lee and D. P. Tweedie, "Accounting Information: An Investigation of Private Shareholders' Understanding", *Accounting and Business Research*, Winter, 1975, pp. 3-17.
(2) The number, 25, includes two further companies, in the 92 surveyed, which are linked to one of the companies identified in Table 1.
(3) "The Corporate Report: A Discussion Paper", to the Accounting Standards Steering Committee, July, 1975, pp. 21-22.

Cover story

How UK companies report

Some organisations have reported their progress to employees for years, whereas others look on it as a new venture. It can be said that publishing an employee report can have many pitfalls as there are very few guidelines available, so many companies follow their own path. GEOFFREY HOLMES, editor of ACCOUNTANCY, examines a number of employee reports to find out
146 *how companies are faring in this new field*

Many British companies now report as a matter of routine to their employees. This is a comparatively new phenomenon. If one places a date on it, and says that it all began in the last five or six years, someone will undoubtedly write to *The Times*, suggesting that he heard the cuckoo long before that. Nevertheless, it *is* a comparatively new idea, and one which is growing in popularity and importance.

There are no rules. No statute says that a company must report quarterly, half-yearly or annually to its employees; and there is certainly no relevant accounting Standard in this country or, to the best of my knowledge, anywhere else. But that is perhaps to be expected since employee reports are not entirely a financial accounting matter.

ACCOUNTANCY recently wrote to all the companies in the *Financial Times* 30 Index, asking whether they prepared employee reports and, if so, to provide a copy of their latest.

ICI does not produce an employee report, as such, but covers group financial affairs in its divisional newspapers. (Though as the article on p 60 shows, ICI have developed their own method of communication.) United Drapery and John Brown do not currently produce employee reports, although the matter is under consideration at John Brown. The remaining 27 companies in the FT 30 Index provide ACCOUNTANCY's main sample; but in order to find out what other, and possibly smaller, companies were doing, we asked a number of major printing groups specialising in the production of annual accounts to let us have samples of employee reports which they had produced for their customers. These provide a subsidiary sample.

When it comes to size, there is some standardisation. Most employee reports approximate to the international sizes A3, A4, or A5. This magazine is A4; A5 represents half this page size; and A3 double this page size; in each case, we are normally talking about a document which is deeper than it is wide.

Two companies use non-standard sizes: Vickers, with a 'landscape' report, 3¾in x 7¼in; and Beechams, with a much bigger report, 12⅞in x 9¾in. The only company in the sample to use an A5 report was London Brick. Among the rest, A3 (tabloid newspaper format) was marginally more popular than A4.

When it comes to colour, there is wide variation. No company in the sample used a report for employees which was simply in black and white. Indeed, comparatively few used only a single spot colour.

A number of companies used two spot colours (in addition to black, of course): Vickers, magenta and green; Metropolitan, red and green; and Spillers, red and blue.

Four colour reports

When it comes to using four colours, one has to distinguish between companies which use black and three additional spot-colours, and those which use the four-colour ('full-colour') process to include colour photographs. Courtaulds, for instance, used three spot-colours: green, blue, and orange; and BP in 1976 used blue, yellow and magenta. Probably, the most common form of printing was the four-colour process (used by seven of the main sample).

Quality varied enormously, from the sort of printing one associates with an evening newspaper to that of high quality published shareholder accounts. The Beecham Review, which is used in part to transmit information to employees about the annual accounts, is a first class piece of four-colour printing; as is the Dunlop report to UK employees.

Eight companies had an eight page employee report. Four chose four pages (including BP in 1977 when it used four pages of A3 against twelve pages of A4 in 1976). The shortest reports to employees were those of Distillers (two pages) and Hawker-Siddeley, two pages out of sixteen pages of general news. The longest was that of Dunlop with twenty seven pages of A4, equalled in terms of pages by Vickers, but with much smaller pages.

Most companies include a picture of their chairman, and his annual message to the employees. Occasionally (as with P & O), the message comes from the managing director rather than the chairman. Courtaulds and Marks & Spencer were two companies which last year did not have such a message at all.

Sophistication varies widely

The level of sophistication expected of employees varies quite widely. Allied Breweries, for instance, seemed to assume that employees were capable of concentrating only on one page at a time. Their twelve page 'Money Report 1976' consisted of single page mini-articles, each on a separate theme; the chairman on 'The Road to Prosperity'; 'The Lager Boom'; 'Allied People'; and so on, but this basic simplicity is deceptive. The 'Report' manages quietly to get across a number of important messages.

Grand Metropolitan in their 1976 report treated the same sort of basic theme in a completely different way, using four Thelwell cartoons to illustrate the 'Grand Metropolitan Trials', by showing Thelwell's familiar horsewoman clearing the various obstacles which Grand Metropolitan had surmounted fence by fence over the four year period.

At the relatively unsophisticated end of the market was the special edition of St Michael News devoted to the 1976-77 accounts. Because Marks & Spencer received the Queen's Award for export achievement, there was a short piece about exports. Again, there were short articles (even shorter than those of Allied) on such themes as: 'How much did we sell? . . . 'Where does all the money go?' . . . 'What do we do with the £107m profit'?

But the main part of the report is devoted to concepts which are far nearer to the young lady on the shop counter. There is a little piece on 'what happens to each £1 put in the till?'

Imperial Group produces what is essentially a very simple 'Report to Employees' but it is one which is much nearer to conventional shareholder accounts. It has clearly been very carefully designed. As a piece of printing, it makes very excellent use of typography; but it has not the immediate impact to the man in the street, such as that of the Boots' 'Company Report to Staff 77'. (Larger in format than the report of Allied, this report concentrates on getting

their employees

the basic facts across. Boots is among relatively few of the companies in the basic sample of thirty which did not restrict its view of life to the comments of the chairman Mr D. E. M. Appleby BSc(Lond) BSc(Nottm) FCA. He confines himself to three paragraphs, thus allowing seven other directors to give comments on their particular aspects of the business.

Boots is one of the few companies that devotes a sizeable part of its report to trade unions. It shows as part of this centre spread the various unions which are to be found, and the number of staff covered by each. Considerable attention is given to the way which the staff council and committee work.

Both Lucas and Dunlop produce employee reports which are much closer to the normal reports to shareholders. Dunlop, in its report to UK employees 1976, included a spread three pages wide, ie with a third page folding outwards, in which the historic accounts were compared with the inflation adjusted accounts. The bottom right hand of the three pages is devoted to cash flow.

Well-thought out report

The result is a well-thought out, and well-explained account of what happened during 1976; but one which it would probably take a qualified accountant ten minutes or more to absorb.

By way of a sample: having reached the stage where 'profits after tax' have been ascertained, Dunlop explain the next line like this: "But there is still another deduction to come. Some of the businesses which Dunlop operates and controls don't belong entirely to Dunlop. Malaysian Banks, for example, own part of the business in Malaya, Pirelli have a share in quite a lot of our operations, Dunlop France has French shareholders, and so on. Before we arrive at the attributable profit the share of the profits which belongs to these 'minority shareholders' has to be deducted — line 9.'

The explanation goes on: '10. The final attributable profit — line 10 — really belongs to the shareholders of the company, who you will remember provided the funds on line 4. But these profits are not paid out in full.'

The net result is that the Dunlop 'Report to UK Employees' leaves one with the feeling that well to the fore in its design was an accountant or accountants.

When it comes to Lucas, the

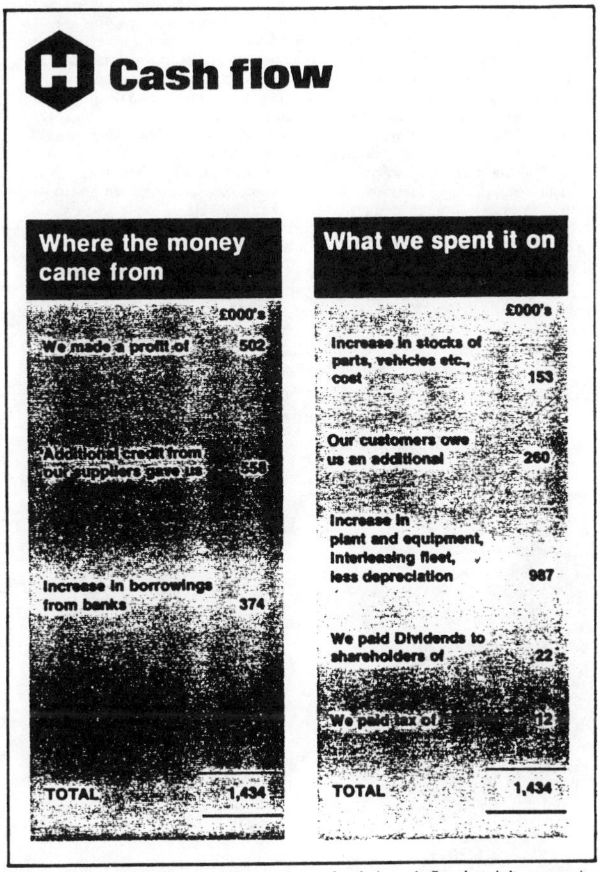

Hanger Investments Group of companies make their cash flow breakdown concise and easy to read.

'Chairman's Review for Employees' again looks rather like part of a set of accounts for shareholders. Indeed, the 'statement by the chairman' is the very same statement that he made to shareholders.

Not a lot has been written about reporting to employees. One firm which has done some work on it is Turquands Barton Mayhew & Co. They produced last year an instructive booklet entitled 'Employee Reporting' which is available from them at: Lynton House, 7 Tavistock Square, London WC1H 9LS; Price £1. They see two reasons for communicating information to employees:

1. 'To inform the employee as part of a general communicative and consultative philosophy, of the corporate environment in which he or she works.
2. 'To put over a particular message eg the need for profit or the effects of inflation.'

As they put it, there is much to be said for combining these two reasons or objectives in the production of an employee report. Indeed, 'To inform the employee of the corporate environment without using the opportunity of

◀ *Mice help Reckitt & Colman say where the money goes*

drawing a conclusion and putting over a message seems a waste. The traditional report to shareholders has not perhaps needed this element to a marked degree because it has generally been assumed that investors or their advisers have the necessary knowledge to draw their own conclusions from the information presented. In very many cases, employees will not have that knowledge available to them and the "message" is in reality a form of education designed to remedy this.'

The booklet sees explanations of the result as a feature of many chairmen's statements to shareholders but believes that: 'A statement to employees generally needs to start from a lower base of assumed understanding on the part of the reader and to marry explanation of the results to a more fundamental education message.'

Turquands Barton Mayhew warned of these pitfalls:

- The temptation to show taxation as taking more than half the profits by omitting a balance sheet which would indicate that most of the taxation was deferred.
- The comparison over a period of years of dividends with wages. The different nature of the shareholder and employee roles makes such a comparison invalid, they believe.
- The comparison of profit earned with capital expenditure without showing a complete picture which a source and application of funds would have given.

148

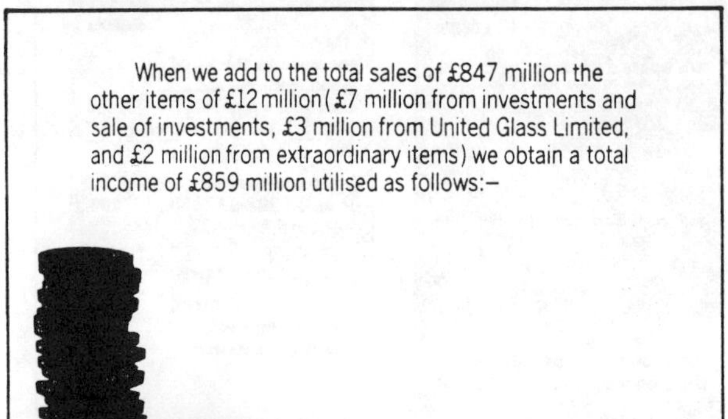

The Distillers Company choose a pile of pennies.

Of the companies in the main sample, only P & O gave what accountants might recognise as a source and application of funds statement; and even that was in a very simple form. One or two other companies did try to show somewhat the same thing diagramatically (among them Turner & Newall). Others, such as GKN, started with total income, and showed in a diagram how this was spent; how much went in cost of materials and services, wages, pensions etc, taxation paid, depreciation and so on.

Normally, the figures that were given were figures for the company or group as a whole; though often, the same sort of segmental information is given about the various products as is given in published reports for shareholders. But, as Turquands Barton Mayhew point out in their booklet: 'It is quite clear that shop-floor employees want to know about the performance of their own particular unit, be it factory, department or company. The performance of the whole group is of much less, even minimal, interest to them.'

This is a barrier of communication which remains to be broken. Work is being done on segmental reporting for investors, and it is likely that this will have an effect upon employee reporting.

Many companies are trying deliberately to foster a group spirit, so they see plant reporting as the very opposite of what they wish to achieve. In any case, the people most likely to be responsible for the production of employee reports are not, in a sense, typical employees.

Most of the companies in the survey were clearly striving to increase employee interest in their accounts, and indeed in their overall success. Nearly all of them gladly provide employees with copies of the annual report and accounts to shareholders, if only they will ask. A number, include a coupon to be filled in and forwarded through the internal mailing system, to make this all the easier.

Perhaps the most inter-active of the employee reports was that by BOC, which provided a two-sided coupon 9" by 3" inviting employees to say: 'I want to know more about . . .'; and containing ample space for questions on the content

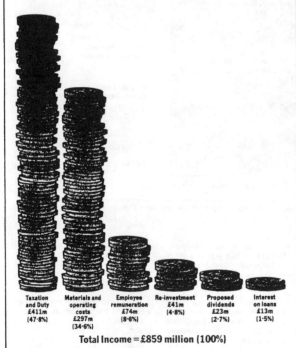

Employees vary so much more than do shareholders, and in their case, the duty of effective communication 'is probably the harder of the two tasks'

of the various pages of the report.

Among the reports received from other sources, we noticed a most effective 'How the money was spent' diagram in the report of Holt Lloyd (motorists will remember the name of Holts, and will certainly know some of their products like Turtle Wax and Molyslip). This diagram takes the form of an aerosol, the body of which shows income from sales etc, and the fan-like spray from which shows how each 100p of sales were spent.

The various Dexion companies all present their reports in basically the same form, and we were provided with those for the group as a whole, in English, French and German; and those of the French companies Feralco S.A. and Readirack S.A., in French; and those of Dexion GmbH, in German.

The Solicitors' Law Stationery Society (well-known under their trade name Oyez) produce a most effective set of tables: 'Where did the sales and profits come from?' . . . 'Where did the profits go to?' . . . 'Cash: where it came from and how we used it' . . . all using various forms of a basic theme depicting the sort of books a lawyer might have in his library. They are one company which does produce a source and application of funds statement which an accountant would recognise as such.

Hogg Robinson, the broking, shipping, forwarding and travel agency people produce a smallish landscape 'Review of our operations for our staff'; which is extremely well designed and makes very effective use of a limited range of colour.

Lesney, the toy people, as rather might be expected, depict their progress in the shape of model cars, and boxes which could remotely contain such cars.

Not many of the property companies seem to produce employee reports. An exception is Slough Estates Ltd which produces a six page folder, not unlike the opening pages of a set of reports and accounts; but which takes the opportunity to explain the position of the company in relation to the Social Security Pensions Act 1975.

Braham Millar publish what they call an 'Informal Annual Report 1977'. They explain that the report given to shareholders has to meet strict legal and other requirements and, consequently has to be written in formal language. 'This simplified version has been prepared so as to make the group's general performance easier to understand. It has been circulated to all personnel as well as shareholders.' This report represents a sort of half-way house. It is simpler than most annual reports and accounts. It has a short chairman's review; a column of 'results in brief' and a full page trading results summary, which is basically a short form profit and loss account. The last page is devoted to a simple man's guide to the balance sheet, which is shown in layman language, in both figures and in the form of two pie diagrams.

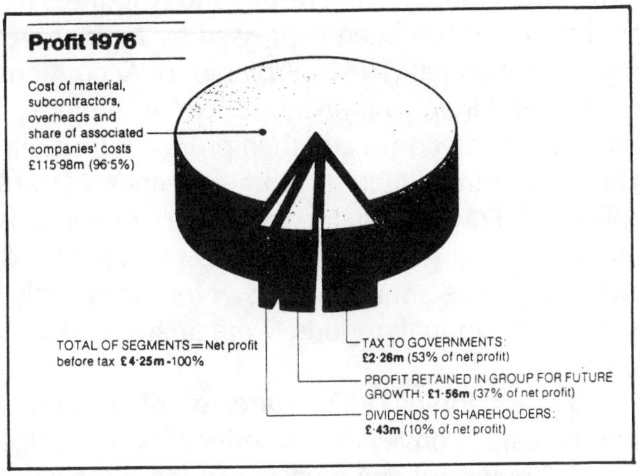

John Mowlem & Company show clearly how the profit cake is divided

We have already looked at one report which has a considerable element of humour in it, being illustrated by a well-known cartoonist. Reckitt & Colman Ltd include a rather amusing table: 'Where the money goes', in which a number of mice appear to amuse themselves with a slab of cheese. It is not quite clear what the mice are doing — they appear to be using it as a means of transport; sticking it in a safe; and breaking bits off its end; and examining it at short range under a microscope — but it is quite an amusing little diagram.

Right at the other end of the spectrum is the RHP 'A review for all employees'. This is quite uncompromising. It looks just like an annual report to shareholders. It is well presented, and beautifully illustrated with pictures of products, and information about where they are made, and where they go. There is comparatively little accounting information in the document; though there is considerable emphasis on the idea that productivity brings prosperity.

Perhaps the most interesting companies are those with their backs, to an extent, against the wall. UBM, for instance, has had four years of declining profits. It includes a quarter page devoted to 'The decline in profits' asking: 'Why was this year worse than last year?' They also go to some pains to explain *why* their net cash inflow from operations was £0.8m less than the profit before tax of £2.7m. It is this sort of thing which does tend to make accounts difficult to understand so far as the layman is concerned.

Wimpey take a very extreme view. They employ full four-colour process thoroughly to show a picture of their chairman, Mr R. B. Smith, and devote the entire document to a message from him to employees, and the text of his statement to shareholders. There are no accounts, no diagrams, and no simplified explanations.

Two points stand out: .

1. Although employee reports are an admirable attempt to make the understanding of financial information easier, some companies do manage to appear patronising.
2. Employee reports require just as much professional care and attention as the annual report and accounts, if not more.

As Oyez Press say in a small booklet which they have prepared entitled 'Company financial information for employees': 'Employees vary much more than shareholders, [so] effective communication in their case is probably the harder of the two tasks.' ■

149

ASSESSING EMPLOYEE INTEREST

Concern about employee interest in and responses to reports especially prepared for them has been expressed by a range of writers across the years. George Bennett (1941), Professor of Accounting at Syracuse University, in an address to the Controllers' Institute, spells out employee interest in three categories and then proceeds to evaluate report content for its ability to attract interest. Daniel Hennessy (1948), President of the Controllership Foundation Inc., summarizes responses of a series of corporate publics (including employees) to a survey of their dissatisfactions with corporate annual reports. Not surprisingly, the survey found that traditional annual reports were inappropriate for an employee audience.

Charles Libby (1952), Director of Training for Johnson and Johnson, Chicago, conveys his experience with the financial information needs and demands of employees. He focuses his discussion on profits and growth, and goes on to outline a set of principles for the preparation of financial reports for employees. Later in the 1950s, Schoen and Lux (1957) released the results of a survey of 164 managerial, professional, and white-collar workers in a midwestern plant of a large U.S. manufacturing company. The results detail readership of annual report and report sections, effective communication of information items, and a comparison between stockholder and non-stockholder knowledge and comprehension of annual report information content.

A British perspective of the employee interest issue is provided by David Flint (1958), (later to become Professor of Accountancy at the University of Glasgow), in an address to the Glasgow Management Studies Conference at St. Andrews. His paper considers report content and method from the perspective of employee interest in the business as a whole and draws on a survey of reporting objectives and practice conducted by the British Institute of Management. Finally a more recent British perspective is contained in Hussey and Craig's (1979) report of a major U.K. survey exploring the attitudes of British employees to employee reports. Results include readership levels, interest levels, understanding, reasons for report production, rated importance of information, content, and presentation.

These papers stand in contrast to the majority of papers published on reporting to employees. Rather than focusing upon the story that management wishes to tell, they focus attention upon employee concerns and information needs and suggest that satisifaction of those needs is the litmus test for effective communication.

Corporate Financial Report Content of Interest to Employees

By George E. Bennett, C.P.A.

THE author is a member of The New York State Society of Certified Public Accountants and of the American Institute of Accountants and is Professor of Accounting at Syracuse University.

This address was made to the Syracuse Control of the Controllers' Institute. In it the author points out the desirability of presenting to corporate employees, in readily com-
150 prehensible form, some of the financial and statistical facts of the enterprise. Though the address was made to corporation Controllers, some of the ideas presented may be used by independent certified public accountants.

* * *

When conditions are propitious, I enjoy being different. Hence, there are times when I enjoy making a speech or reading a paper which I consider unusual. I have that idea in mind tonight.

Undoubtedly, there have been occasions when some of you have let your minds wander a little "out of control" and have thought, to some extent, along the lines I shall follow this evening. Others among you have not thought about the matter at all. Some, will agree, in part, with my central theme; others will say that I am just a "wacky" college professor.

Tonight I intend to talk about the desirability of the furnishing, by the management group of employees, to the operating group of employees, of some useful information about the corporate enterprise which is the employer of both groups and to the service of which both groups of employees are devoting jointly, all their working hours.

At the outset, I admit the existence of three conditions which, if not expressly recognized my me, will cause some of you to say that I have overlooked them completely. The first is that you are employees, not employers; hence, even if you admitted a desire to do something constructive along the lines which I shall suggest, some would find it impossible. The second is that in certain instances companies which have done a great deal for their employees have had painful experiences. The third is that what some of you would call the three outstanding things an employee has in mind regarding his job do not seem to include the basic idea of the points mentioned later.

Those three things are as follows:

1. An employee is interested in getting all he can out of his job. You cannot blame him for that.

2. An employee is interested in holding his job. This is natural.

3. An employee is interested in being able to present his grievances to some one in authority and in having such person listen to them.

The scope of my remarks requires precise definition. I intend, this evening, to offer some suggestions about making available to the employees of the usual manufacturing plant some of the information that could, and often should, be contained in the financial reports issued by the enterprise that owns and operates that manufacturing plant. Too often, as we all know, manage-

---

Presented before a meeting of the Syracuse Control of the Controllers' Institute of America, April 16, 1941.

ment officials restrict those reports to the irreducible minimum of financial statements, expressed in the conventional jargon of accountants, accompanied by only the short report (certificate, so-called) of the independent auditor.

From the viewpoint of those employees of the corporation who may be thought of as its operating force, those statements and that short report are not informative. At best, they will have only some slight meaning to a few members of that group, and no meaning to most of the others. Usually that group of employees never has a chance to see the reports.

In my opinion no report can be called a good report unless the information conveyed thereby is presented in such manner as to interest its readers and to stimulate them to effective action. It is hardly necessary to say that most published reports fall short of that ideal.

Recently I had occasion to review and criticize the published reports of three large-sized business enterprises. Two of them contained practically nothing of interest. It is not unfair to state that, for most persons, they were basically unintelligible. The statements and explanatory notes were so condensed and summarized (with dissimilar elements combined) that, for practical purposes, they were useless. In each report the auditor's short report (certificate) described in similar terms the adequacy of the scope of the examination and expressed the opinion that the statements presented fairly the financial position of the company. The corporate reports contained nothing about the specific conditions of the business enterprises. Yet the two types of business were wholly dissimilar.

The third report, however, was one that was worth, at least, moderate commendation. Some of the ideas therein offered are mentioned later in this paper; some have been mentioned in talks and papers it has been my pleasure to deliver previously upon the topic which interests me this evening.

I submit that those responsible for the first two reports mentioned may be considered as being in a rut. And I submit, also, that those responsible for emitting reports which do not interest and stimulate persons to effective action are in the same rut. Further, I submit that the auditors are not the persons to blame. You in this group who have a point of view which will not permit your outside auditors to suggest improvements in your corporate reporting are equally guilty of being in a rut. Remember, a rut is a rut nevertheless even though lined with soft silk and with petals from fragrant field and garden flowers.

If accounting data are to be used, they must be placed in convenient reach of, and in understandable and interesting form for, those whose interest and confidence are basically essential in making things hum. One does not catch flies with vinegar.

Describing still further the limitations of my remarks, I propose to make no mention here of how report material may be made intelligently available to department heads and to foremen. Reams of printed matter have been written concerning reports directed specifically to them.

On the other hand, I ask you to focus your attention, for the moment, on only some of the means whereby report raw material may be offered in usable form to those who labor on a lower level than that on which managers and foremen work. Even though many workmen have a high degree of intelligence and an ability to comprehend figures, the rank and file should not be considered as being thus equipped.

Many will insist that employees should not enter at all into the picture of net profit activity except to function at top speed with minds empty of everything except what is necessary to make the mechanical motions required to produce and move product. Many believe that they should be subject only to adverse and profane criticism when net profit slumps—slumpage cause to be disregarded. And many in high places say that never should they be given a word of sincere and honest commendation. I submit that this is all wrong. In our work we tend to lose sight of the need to educate and revitalize the men who, because of notions in error and almost without warning, may foment trouble and disorder.

It is revolutionary—hence taboo—to suggest that employers and men in industrial high places need an elementary education, at least, in the economics of labor relations. Seriously: if the rank and file of employees of a business establishment know what actually is going on: where they stand in relation to their fellows and to the profit outcome both individually and collectively; and know that they are not being exploited; order and production activity of high attainment unquestionably will result, even though the end is not always a perfect one.

It seems axiomatic that a candid-camera knowledge of day by day conditions and a wide if not intimate acquaintance with the working men in a plant are basically essential. How many of us can say without equivocation that we have extended ourselves to the point where such knowledge and acquaintance are ours? How many of us have refused to run the chance of soiling the cuffs of our trousers with oily sawdust or metal shavings to acquire such knowledge?

Some reports actually fall away slightly from the straight and narrow way of conventional presentation so that they contain a small (at times weird) collection of statistical tables, curves and graphs. But these are apt to be an unrelated collection, the result of ideas picked up, hit or miss, on the outside. Thus, they represent planning with little or no regard to the specific case and to its currents of underlying conditions (perhaps the term "planning" has been poorly chosen). But even assuming that some of them have a modicum of value, few persons would suggest—and then only in a whisper—that they be copied, even partially, and be tacked on the bulletin boards for all to examine who may desire to do so.

However, such material usually fails to promote what was intended; often, an intended use other than as a space-filler is doubtful. Generally, they are constructed with no thought of appealing to a "man-in-the-street" intelligence. The praise of a swivel-chair critic seems more to be desired than simple manifestations of pleasure and delight from the man with soiled coveralls and dirty hands.

I fear that these suggestions, as here presented, may make me appear in a false light. I am not a Socialist, a Bolshevist, a Fascist, and certainly am no Hitlerite. But since I have had association at numerous times with he whom the politicians speak of as "my friend the working man," I believe I have a fair idea of his point of view. Such being the case, I have more than a mild interest, and more than a theoretical one, in the ideas broached in this paper.

I have attempted to project myself into the position of one of those human automatons who, if given the opportunity to see such portions of reports as involve and concern him — assuming such reports contain these features—would make a definite effort to understand them and, who—assuming an understanding thereof—would appreciate the importance of the part played by him and his fellows in the operation of the plant and hence in the national economic structure. Just what would be of interest to such a person?

Employee confidence can be secured only through cooperation and that confidence is promoted by showing truthfully and in a simple manner what is being accomplished—and the cost thereof. However, that confidence is not promoted to any considerable degree by pointing out that management salaries are ¼ of 1% of sales, or by showing that they are 7 cents per unit of production. The truth may have been told, but the method of telling it is almost useless.

A "pie chart" may be read intelligently in certain circumstances. I saw one the other day—part of the report issued by a large business—which was a beautiful piece of color blending. Yet, except to the figure-trained mentality, I am certain it missed the bull's-eye by a considerable margin; in fact, I think that it missed not only the center but the complete target. Each highly colored segment was labelled with a percentage figure.

Although I am informed that the teaching of arithmetic usually stops in the seventh grade, I know that college seniors experience difficulties with many of its elements; and percentage is a troublesome portion of the subject. Hence, may I raise the query: Is it simpler to understand that 8.7% of each sales dollar was spent for administration, or that a trifle less than 9 cents from each dollar received from sales was so spent?

May not an employee gain a feeling of a certain amount of personal importance, with a resulting pride for his job, if he is shown approximately how many dollars of investment in fixed property elements (buildings, machinery and equipment) are in use in order to carve the niche in the scheme of things in which he has selected to function? How about showing what it costs to make a trained operative of a particular class?

May there not be some value in pointing out in a simple fashion to what extent each dollar of wages could be increased were it possible to eliminate the greater portion of theft and destruction of working materials and tools? And could it not be shown in terms of consumable necessities—or even of the luxuries nowadays considered, by most persons, as necessities—just what is lost per employee classifications or groups when a plant has to shut down for a time? 153

Why is it not a good idea under certain conditions to show graphically in a simple manner where each employee in the business, or in a certain portion of it, stands in relation to others—just how far down or how far up in the picture he is located? And in some such fashion why not show each employee what must be accomplished in order to move upward and onward?

What harm can it do to a business to show how the volume of each salesman's unit sales compares with that of the other salesmen?

In one particular instance one salesman was doing something like $90.000.00 turnover per year at a salary of $50.00 per week plus expenses, while another was doing only $6,000.00 per year on a salary of $25.00 per week plus expenses. Naturally, the ratio of expenditure against return in these two cases was wholly different and led to certain unpleasant employee reactions.

And in the same strain, from another case I found that one section of the plant was costing $5.00 per week per head for supervision, whereas another section was costing only $0.50 per head—yet both were doing the same work at practically the same rates of return.

How often do we show by means of some simple picture how much is being paid out in taxes of various kinds per dollar of sales, or per dollar of payroll? And again, by the same token, how often have we attempted to show the effect of fixed expense on holding down the wage level?

Per dollar of investment, would it ever be prudent, in some plants, to show the yearly amount of executive salaries and indicate how much of the net profit (such salaries excluded) is consumed by them when the deduction is made? Again, how many cents per dollar of sales do executive salaries consume as compared with the working payroll? Further, what part of the total payroll do such salaries comprise?

I have said nothing (except as above) on offering information which may show how bad an executive actually is—as to what loss was caused by poor foresight, and what amount thus was lost to each employee in wages in order that a desired profit minimum might be maintained. For example, what expenditures are being incurred in several directions without any direct result? Charges made to various accounts may, on the surface, appear to be reasonable whereas analysed returns versus analyzed expenditures may show expenditures far in excess of results achieved.

The annual report of one nationwide corporation contains a sheet on what has been done for the employees. It is offered as a statement of management, not part of anything under certificate of audit of the Certified Public Accounting firm. And this is proper; but the matter is one for both parties to confer upon.

The size of the concern will influence the type of information to be offered. The large company has facilities for preparing that material; the smaller one has not facilities to do very much. Nevertheless, generally speaking, both types can and should do more than is being done—particularly in relation to the three outstanding things an employee has in mind regarding his job, as mentioned in the early portion of this paper. The outside accountant should prove of great value in this connection.

What is offered today, especially by the larger company, relates to employee relationship — employee welfare, accident prevention, wage trend, and employment trend. I raise the point of going further than this—of going into operating figures to prove that what is being done is all that reasonably can be expected; for example, the relation of employees to the profit and loss result of the enterprise and even to some of the items displayed in its balance sheet—along the lines above suggested.

Beyond a shadow of a doubt there is value in disclosing many so called intimate details of management—as cost of advertising, cost of management, cost of other indirect factors, etc. But in this connection, it is only fair to mention a certain precaution. When everything is moving smoothly toward a profit end, and things are being done, the situation is much different than when a loss appears certain. In relation to the latter situation employees are apt to misunderstand, and to forget past good times. Then it may seem most pertinent to offer information based upon a fair number of years' experience rather than upon the bad year only. Again, care must be taken to weigh the evidence where large profits are made compared with investment so that misconceptions will not enter the minds of employees. Further, it may be desirable to offer figures which represent the experience of all concerns within a given field. And a business with a high labor factor should not be treated in the same manner as one with a low labor factor.

Some will say that—in the face of the Wagner Act; the attitude of the present Federal Administration; and the reaction of the Securities and Exchange Commission (which apparently favors stereotyped audit reports); to attempt anything is useless. Nevertheless, some concerns are doing things and they have had success. A solution must come when the right type of analysis has been made. If a profit-sharing scheme, for example, underlies the success of a particular venture in this field, well and good. If some other basic method furnishes the approach, also, well and good. The solution may not be easy in a particular case, but it does exist, in my opinion.

The above ideas seem sufficient to indicate the trend of my thoughts on this topic. Should any of you permit your minds to wander back over past experiences—personal and otherwise—I am certain that you could add to the collection of suggestions above offered. If not prejudiced, your intelligence will cause you to agree with me that much can be done with figures to promote better relations between employee and employer. We need better financial reports, or reports supplementary thereto, and also a wide dissemination throughout our manufacturing plants of simplified summaries compiled therefrom which actually tell a story, or emphasize an event, couched in language at the level of the "man in the street."

155

Survey Reveals Financial Information People Want To Know about a Corporation

by Daniel J. Hennessy, President,
Controllership Foundation, Inc.

156 **• Why are the different publics dissatisfied with corporate financial reports? What can corporations and their independent certified public accountants do about it? This article summarizes the findings of a survey recently conducted for the Controllership Foundation by Elmo Roper, research consultant, to determine the answers to these questions.**

CERTIFIED public accountants share with the directors of a company the responsibility to present an up-to-date, effective, simple, and accurate picture of the company's position and progress. While assisting in efforts to simplify accounting terms, they have resisted attempts to "dilute" accounting terminology. Similarly, they have not allowed any substitution for accuracy and reliability. The findings of "What People Want To Know About Your Company" bear directly on that problem.

This new study by the Controllership Foundation indicates that there is little relation between inability to read financial statements and the present public distrust of business. Critics who hold accounting to blame because few understand accounting terms, could as logically expect doctors to be distrusted because few patients can decipher prescriptions!

Specifically, the Foundation study sought answers to these four questions:

How can the modern corporation best tell the public what it wants to know about the corporation's activities?

Who constitutes the public who wants to know?

What do these people want to know?

How, and in what form can the information best be brought to them?

Since the "public" as it exists for any corporation is really a collection of many publics, the study was broken into five subdivisions, one for each of the different groups whose interest in corporate information was to be investigated:

1. Average stockholders.
2. Employees in office and plant.
3. Large investors.
4. National and local labor union officials.
5. Financial analysts and bankers.

Carefully pretested opinion polls with fixed questionnaires were used to reach the first two groups.

Groups 3, 4, and 5, where detailed and considered opinions were to be expected, were given a chance to express them in "depth interviews." The phrase, "depth interview," used learnedly by market researchers and public opinion pollsters, is the rather simple device of "letting them talk." The trained interviewer commonly has in his mind—or in his pocket—a set of questions by which he guides the discussion, and probes for the truth. After the interview is completed, the interviewer writes up a near-verbatim account of it from memory and rough notes.

Average Stockholders

The average stockholder has little interest in corporate financial data. He really has only two questions on his mind: He is naturally anxious to get dividends, so he wants to know what the chances are that "his company" will remain strong enough to safeguard his capital and make enough profit to pay the same or a larger return on the money he has invested. To him these seem simple questions which could be answered simply.

The Report recommends: "For at least half of the stockholders, and possibly 75 per cent of them, it might be more effective public relations technique to send them annually or semi-annually a one-page letter. . . . It would have to be accompanied by a condensed income and surplus statement, and balance-sheet, in order to comply with stock exchange regulations."

This letter would contain answers to the questions vitally interesting to these stockholders, and would include an invitation to write for more information or for the complete financial report.

Employees in Office and Plant

There is a great deal of ignorance and lack of interest among employees about the companies for which they work. Their primary concern is job security. Thirty-seven per cent of the "white collar" workers and 52 per cent of the other workers were uncertain whether 1947 was or was not a year of increasing profits for their companies. Twenty-three per cent of the "white collar" group and 40 per cent of the factory workers were uncertain whether the volume of business had increased in 1947. When asked if they would like to have more information about their companies, more than half of the employees said that they knew enough already.

The Report recommends: "At present the annual report is not a particularly good channel through which to reach many company employees. . . . This is the more true because the employee appetite for information about his company is apparently, at present, a limited one, and one that needs palatable food if it is to be stimulated. There seems no reason to believe that this stimulation cannot occur, however, if the public relations experts really concentrate on the task of providing the kind of news in the kind of package in which employees would be interested.

"The company president, himself, would appear to be a possibly neglected resource in this instance. A quarter of the employees in the study have never seen, heard, or talked to this seemingly mythical figure, and *their* opinion of his 'smartness' is consistently lower than the estimates made by people who have seen him. 157
The results of the study indicate that even hearing him make a speech raises the president in his employee's estimation, and this in turn probably improves company morale. If companies want to create a team spirit within the organization they might well persuade the president to act like a captain instead of a far-off brain truster. If he speaks to his teammates both face-to-face, and frequently also through the carefully written word, he might do much to arouse their interest in, and loyalty to the company."

Large Investors

Most large investors understand the language of accountancy, and are avid consumers of information about the companies in which they have investments. As one investor interviewed expresses it:

> "I want to emphasize that, as far as I'm concerned, it's the figures in a company report that interest me—not the gossip about what may happen in the future."

A list of the items desired by these investors covers practically everything a corporation does. Following are a few points which this group would like to have covered in company annual reports:

1. Description of management personnel—who runs the company.

Daniel J. Hennessy, president and chairman of the board of the Controllership Foundation, Inc., was the second national president of the Controllers Institute of America. He is executive vice-president and a director of the Jamaica Water Supply Company, New York; past president of the Technical Valuation Society; and a former lecturer on the economics of public utility rates, finance, and accounting at the University of Pittsburgh.

---

2. Reconciliation of the surplus and reserve accounts.
3. Consolidated income statements and balance-sheets going back ten years.
4. The company's plans to get more business during the coming year.

158 5. Appraisal of the competitive situation in the company's field of activity.

6. Quarterly reports.
7. Any hidden reserves the company has.
8. The amount of money spent in research, etc.

The Report recommends: "Several respondents made the practical suggestion that two reports are needed, one full of detail but unembellished, for those who really want financial data, the other brief —much more a narration than a statistical manual, and written in a style that will be attractive to stockholders with small holdings. As we have seen, a plan such as this would please the sophisticated group, many of whom rely on SEC reports and stock services, also. For many of them, the present annual report falls between two stools—it is neither good reading matter nor good source material."

Labor Union Leaders National and Local

Some of the research directors of the unions are as able to discuss technicalities of balance-sheets and depreciation reserves as any certified public accountant or financial analyst; others are not so well informed. Opinions expressed about annual reports range all the way from requests for a detailed breakdown of inventories to complaints of the report's general incomprehensibility.

Of course the union officials judge corporation reporting from a special viewpoint. They are engaged in the constant or intermittent game of bargaining. Consequently, they are most interested in facts useful to them in deciding when to ask for a wage increase for their members. They want to be able to support their claim that the company is in position to pay. Although very few accusations were made by labor leaders that annual reports contain willful distortions, many claims were made that corporations attempt to conceal certain pertinent figures. To quote from an interview with a labor leader:

> "When management is making money, they are apt to be secretive for fear we will ask for a decent raise for the workers. When I say secretive, I mean that attempts will be made to cover up the earnings of the company, nothing fraudulent, you understand, but they lay down a smoke screen that is rather difficult to pierce."

Another labor union official suggested:

> "Of course the most important figures of all are the gross and net profit figures. There must, however, be a breakdown of these profits with more detailed information so that it is possible for us to analyze the method by which these profits were determined."

The Report recommends: "The same unembellished, detailed report recommended for large stockholders and professional analysts would, with minor modifications, please labor union officials."

Local labor union officials and shop stewards have no more interest in company financial data than average stockholders, or employees in office and plant. They are primarily interested in having more information on matters that bear on job security.

Following are three quotations from three different interviews taken from the Report:

> "The one thing which every company ought to let its men know about is their security. By that, I mean that the com-

pany should give men some sort of idea of what will be their yearly pay."

"I guess the thing that interests me most about the company is whether or not there is enough work to keep all the men on the job."

"They should add what the outlook for the future is, as well as they can judge, and the sales outlook."

Financial Analysts and Bankers

These experts want all the information that the large investors want, and more. Following is a list of a few of the principal points that they would like to see covered:

1. Comparative income statement and balance-sheet figures for two to ten years back.
2. More information on total labor costs, wage rates, wage raises granted, negotiations with the unions.
3. Better and more informative figures on depreciation reserves and inventories, other reserves, and explanation of methods used in calculating these items.
4. Total income broken down by source from which derived and use to which put.
5. Quarterly or monthly figures supplementing annual reports.
6. More information which will facilitate an approval of management.

But for this group the annual report tells the company's story from . point of view, and this story checked as a routine matter by re. to other sources of information. No an. report issued for stockholders in general i. likely to satisfy the needs of these men.

"What People Want To Know about Your Company" contains many positive recommendations other than those briefly outlined in this article. For instance, the Report suggests that part of the large sums of money now being spent on company annual reports might well be directed into different channels to overcome the misunderstanding and suspicion which almost half the people of the United States have for the facts and figures of business accounting.

[NOTE: "What People Want To Know about Your Company" is the third in a series of surveys by the Controllership Foundation. The first study, "The Public's Acceptance of the Facts and Figures of Business Accounting," (April, 1947), revealed that almost half the people in the United States distrust business reporting. The second, "Whose Corporations Are They?" (October, 1947), disclosed that almost one-third of the people believe that "a handful of men like the duPonts, Fords, etc., own most of the corporations in America." The present study answers the question: "How shall we report the facts of business so that they will be accepted and understood?"]

…REST IN THE FINANCIAL REPORT

A Forward-Looking Statement of the Uses Employees Make of Accounting Information ●

Effective communication of the results of corporate operations is one of the prime requisites for harmonious employee relations. Today, more than ever before, the employee is keenly interested in the financial story of his
160 firm. He wants to know not only what, but also how and why. Accountants and accounting data are uniquely qualified to tell the story to the employee and to provide the necessary analysis and interpretation. That they have not fully succeeded in discharging this responsibility is evidenced by the lack of faith displayed by many readers of financial statements. However, there is reason to believe that this unfortunate situation can be improved if we will attempt to find out what employees want and how the financial statements can make the desired information available and understandable.

Are Employees Interested?

The first important question management should examine is whether or not its employees are really interested in the information presented in the annual financial report. If the information is made available, will employees use it?

Absence of any real display of enthusiasm by employees in the past may have given us cause to wonder about this question. However, discussions with individual employees and employee committees have revealed that there is genuine interest among employees in the financial report. This interest may have been stifled somewhat by an "apparent reluctance" on our part to make the report generally available in the past, but it is still there.

Interest in Company Profits

Whatever other interests they may have in the annual financial report, there is a common desire among all employee readers to find out how much the company earned. The reasons for this vary depending on the nature of the group. Some employees are interested out of sheer curiosity, to see if their company really does make all the profit that companies in general are said to make. Others look to the income figure as a means of supporting their opinion that the company realizes large profits which it ought to share with the employees. Still others, with a more discerning point of view, are interested in the amount of income as a wedge in bargaining for wages or benefits.

When employees are asked what they want to learn from the annual financial report, their first three questions usually are, in this order:

1. What per cent of profit did the company make on its investment?
2. What per cent of profit did the company make on its dollar sales?
3. How much of the profit was reinvested in the business?

The first two questions are not surprising in view of the foregoing general observations. However, the third one is very interesting because of its implications. It is significant and encour-

---

J. Charles Libby *is Director of Training for the Chicago plant of Johnson & Johnson.*

aging that the question deals with reinvestment of earnings and not dividend payments to owners. On the surface there seems to be no resentment of the payment of dividends to owners. But there is a sincere feeling of concern about the adequacy of the provisions for perpetuating and expanding firm operations. This indicates a further use employees would like to be able to make of the financial report, to determine whether enough of the profits are being put back into the business to provide for better working conditions, new equipment, and up-to-date plants. Often we are prone to attribute to employees a shortsighted attitude on profits. Our experience indicates, however, that the long view is very much in the employee's mind as he evaluates accounting data in the annual financial report.

Interest in What Becomes of Profits

In addition to their interest in the amount then, employees want to know how the profits have been used. In a supervisory training program in 1949-1950 (when net income was at a high level), we made very effective use of a comparison of the balance sheets for the years 1948 and 1949 to show specifically where the income of 1949 had been invested. This approach made a lot of sense to supervisors; it not only justified the level of income but also brought the use of profits much closer to them. Requests for inventory reductions and careful capital investment, particularly in new machines and equipment, since they were closest to that kind of expenditure, took on added significance.

In an employee training program developed at about the same time, to tell the story of "The Job We Did in 1949" to wage people, we impressed employees by discussing the profits of the year 1949 in terms of their application to funding for past service on the employee retirement plan and to the construction and equipping of new shipping facilities.

There were further indications of employee interest in the accounting information in the financial statement. They readily accepted the concept of depreciation as a legitimate expense. Furthermore, they were impressed by the fact that the current replacement costs of machines and buildings were considerably higher than their historical costs which governed the annual amortizations for income tax purposes.

Indications of Growth in the Financial Report

A further use employees make of accounting information in the financial statement is to determine whether or not the company is growing. It has been our experience that intelligent employees, with capable management, identify themselves and their interests with the company's to a considerable extent. They take confidence from being an employee of a successful enterprise. Consequently, they look for evidence of progress and success in the financial statement. Theirs may not be the long-range viewpoint of the stockholder, but their interests go much beyond the size of this week's paycheck.

As companies become more diversified and decentralize their operations, the growth of the local operation becomes an inadequate indication of company growth. It may even present a distorted view of the direction. As new operations start, it may be necessary temporarily to divert production volume to them from present plants until the new sales area's potential can be developed. This may create in the present plant the impression that the company is reducing production, unless in some way the over-all picture can be portrayed through presentation of accounting data.

Demand for Complete Reporting

Fundamentally the majority of employees have confidence in management. They are not suspicious of the financial report and the information in it. Not all wage employees are able, of course, to interpret and analyze the financial data that is made available to them. They might draw erroneous conclusions from the facts, and misunderstandings might result. However, even under these circumstances we have learned that it is an unwise policy to suppress information. Doing so merely creates suspicion among the employees of our motives.

Employees ask for more supplementary information in addition to the financial report itself. This additional information should be whatever is necessary to make it possible for them to understand fully the financial re-
162 port. They specifically object, however, to the distribution of a "simplified" statement without making the complete annual report available at the same time.

Principles Governing Preparation of Financial Reports

Based on our experience, we have developed a set of principles which we believe should serve as a guide in the preparation of future financial reports with the employees' interests in mind.

1. Supplementary information should be carefully presented in the kind of language employees can understand. Graphs, pie charts, and other visual means of presenting the information should be used. Among the particular items of supplementary data that should be covered are the following:
   (a) *A preliminary survey* of the highlights of the year's financial data. This can be made more meaningful if the previous year's figures are also shown for comparative purposes. It should show the principle figures that are necessary to give, at a glance, a picture of the year's operation.
   (b) *A graphic presentation* of sales and net income showing the growth of the company.
   (c) *The stockholders' equity* shown graphically. This must be accompanied by a complete explanation of the terms used, e.g., capital stock, capital surplus, retained earnings, etc.
   (d) *Working capital* shown graphically. This should show clearly the increase in working capital as the volume of business increases. To be meaningful to employees, the analysis will have to be supplemented by a description of what makes up working capital.
   (e) *Source and use of funds* should be included in the supplementary data. This is a convenient way of showing the changes in allocation of capital in the corporation.
   (f) *Piecharts* or other graphic means of showing how the sales dollar was spent are excellent for showing pictorially what is sometimes less clear in figures alone.
2. The balance sheet should clearly set out the assets, liabilities, and stockholders' investment. The form used by some firms (see International Harvester's Statement of Financial Condition, October 31, 1950 and 1949) wherein "total net assets" is arrived at by deducting current liabilities from current assets and then adding property and other fixed assets makes a clearer picture. This form shows clearly what the stockholders have invested and how the management has used these funds. It is difficult when presenting the more conventional balance sheet form to justify to employees that the stockholders' investment should appear as a liability. The newer form of statement overcomes this difficulty nicely.
3. Notes, both to the balance sheet and the income statement, should

be stated clearly and in sufficient detail to tell the story fully. Of particular interest to employees is the company's depreciation policy. Also, any asset valuation allowances, estimated liability accounts, and surplus appropriations should be clearly indicated and fully explained in the notes.

4. It is of utmost importance that there be a high degree of consistency in the basic form of the financial report. Terminology too should be consistent. This will allow the employee to become familiar with a form and with terms used to describe the company's financial situation. He will thus develop a feeling of confidence in his ability to understand the report.

5. Employees respect a management that make a sincere effort to explain the company's financial report to them. However, not all employees respond visibly to such presentations; consequently some managements have become discouraged and have given up in despair. We are convinced that some means of communicating the information can be devised by an alert management. Perhaps a visual presentation employing an aid such as the flannel board, Visualcast, flip chart, or overhead projector would be effective. Supervisors who know something about accounting could serve as discussion leaders for their respective groups. This would increase the supervisor's stature in his department as well as take advantage of his acceptance by his fellow workers to make the information and explanation more readily acceptable to them.

Conclusion

To summarize, employees are keenly interested in the financial reports of their corporations. They are interested in the profit figure, both as to its amount and its disposition. They look for indications of growth as described by accounting data in the financial report. They want the statement to tell all the facts fully and clearly in a consistent manner from year to year.

When the annual report looked like something straight out of the financial columns, it was not surprising that employees stayed away from it in droves. But those colorful jobs the company puts out nowadays are something else again. Or are they?

The Annual Report:
164 How Much Do Employees Care?

STERLING H. SCHOEN and MAURICE P. LUX

THOUGH A NUMBER of companies distribute their annual report to employees, management in most cases would probably be hard put to say whether the employees actually read it, still less how much of it they understand. Even the most readable financial reports, some people maintain, are likely to be of minor interest to employees.

Some light is thrown on this question by the results of a survey made by the authors among 164 managerial, professional, and white-collar workers in a midwestern plant of a large national manufacturing company. Although the sample is relatively small, the findings as well as the method employed may be of interest to other companies who want to find out how their annual report is received.

The composition of the sample is shown in Table I.

The survey was conducted one month after the company had mailed the annual report to each employee's home. Approximately half the questionnaires were administered in group meetings where they were filled out and returned immediately. The remainder were distributed individually, to be completed and returned through intra-plant mail. All replies were anonymous.

TABLE 1

Composition of the Sample

Plant superintendents	11	
Second-level supervisors	18	
Foremen	38	
Total Managerial		67
Maintenance engineers	20	
Process & product engineers*	36	
Total Professional		56
Laboratory technicians	20	
Clerical (female)	21	
Total White Collar		41
Total		164

Employee Interest in the Annual Report

MANY COMPANIES go to considerable trouble and expense to "dress up" their annual report for distribution to employees. Do these efforts pay off in increased readership and understanding? The reader survey reported here, carried out in one plant of a nationally known company, found:

- Though the annual report was eminently "readable," many employees, including management personnel, had not read it.
- Among those employees who had read it, many either did not remember or did not understand much of what they read.
- Employees who were stockholders were noticeably better informed about the company's affairs than those who were not.

If management wants employees to know and understand the company's financial position, it must supplement the annual report with other informational media, the study concludes. 165

Since the company had not conducted any meetings to discuss the report or given employees any advance notice of the survey, the respondents had no opportunity to prepare their answers. The company lent its support to the study, however, and everyone participated enthusiastically in completing the questionnaire.

This particular company's annual report is very attractive in design and layout and eminently readable. The cover is colorful; there are many pictures of company products and production facilities; technical data are simplified by means of graphs and charts; and the president's letter is an informative discussion of company plans and problems. In short, it is the type of annual report that might well be expected to arouse considerable interest among employees.

Reader Interest

The actual extent of reader interest in the report is shown in Table 2. In reply to the question, *Have you read the annual report,* about 80 per cent of the superintendents, supervisors, maintenance engineers, process and project engineers, and laboratory technicians answered *Yes.* However, as the table shows, only about 50 per cent of the foremen and clerical employees had read it.

The respondents were also asked whether other members of their

TABLE 2

Employee Readership

	Yes	No
Superintendents	9	2
Supervisors	13	5
Foremen	20	18
Maintenance engineers	16	4
Process & project engineers	29	7
Laboratory technicians	17	3
Clerical	11	10

TABLE 3

Breakdown of Readership by Sections Read

	Summary	Financial Statements	Text Material	Pictures	Skimmed *(Not read thoroughly)*
Superintendents	9	8	7	7	2
Supervisors	13	12	8	8	8
Foremen	16	13	8	12	20
Maintenance engineers	13	12	7	11	9
Process & project engineers	19	15	14	18	22
Laboratory technicians	7	7	3	5	13
Clerical	3	3	2	4	10

166

households had read the report. In 39 of the 164 households to which the annual report was sent, it was read by someone other than the respondent. However, 25 per cent of the respondents did not answer this question.

Answers to the third question, *What portions of the annual report do you read,* are shown in Table 3. From these responses it is evident that the summary is the most popular part of the report and the text material the most often avoided. With the exception of the superintendents, most groups admitted that they had not read the financial report thoroughly—an admission that was confirmed by responses to subsequent sections of the questionnaire.

A good index to reader interest, it was felt, would be the extent to which supervisory personnel discussed the annual report with their subordinates. But only about one foreman in 20 discussed the report with his people, as compared with two-fifths of the second-level supervisors and three-fourths of the superintendents.

How Much Information Gets Across?

A number of items on the questionnaire were designed to find out how much of the information presented in the report actually gets across to employees.

While, on the whole, a majority of the respondents knew whether company sales were larger in 1956 than in 1955 (Table 4), most of the correct answers to this question came from the professional groups. Only 47 per cent of the foremen, and less

TABLE 4

Information on Change in Company Sales

	C*	*Inc***	*N.A.****
Superintendents	8	0	3
Supervisors	14	1	3
Foremen	18	0	20
Maintenance engineers	18	0	2
Process & project engineers	29	1	6
Laboratory technicians	13	1	6
Clerical	6	0	15

*Correct.

**Incorrect.

***No answer. Since those invited to participate in the study did so readily, it is assumed that failure to answer this and subsequent questions meant that the respondents did not know the correct answer.

TABLE 5

Information on Company's Sales for 1956

	Accuracy of Information				No Answer
	Within 1%	*1-5%*	*5-10%*	*10% and over*	
Superintendents	5	2	0	1	3
Supervisors	3	4	2	2	7
Foremen	5	1	2	4	26
Maintenance engineers	5	3	2	3	7
Process & project engineers	4	2	2	11	17
Laboratory technicians	0	0	1	5	14
Clerical	3	0	0	2	16

than one-third of the clerical group (female), knew whether or not last year's sales were better.

Employees were even less informed, it was found, about the company's actual sales figure for the previous year. As Table 5 indicates, while five of the 11 superintendents knew last year's sales within 1 per cent, only five (13 per cent) of the 38 foremen had any such accurate knowledge.

Asked whether net income was larger in 1956 than in 1955, only four of the 11 superintendents gave the correct answer, and only four of the 38 foremen. Apparently the process engineers and the second-level supervisors were best informed on this score.

Again, only five of the superintendents knew the actual income figure for the previous year (Table 6). The maintenance engineers were the only group in which as many as 30 per cent knew the correct figure.

Most employees also did not know whether the company's expansion was greater in 1956 than in 1955. Less than 50 per cent of the respondents in every category gave the right answer to this question. The foremen made the poorest showing, with only one in five replying correctly.

TABLE 6

Information on Company's Net Income for 1956

	Accuracy of Information				No Answer
	Within 1%	*1-5%*	*5-10%*	*10% and over*	
Superintendents	5	0	0	1	5
Supervisors	5	1	2	2	8
Foremen	4	3	0	1	30
Maintenance engineers	6	1	2	3	8
Process & project engineers	5	2	1	7	21
Laboratory technicians	0	0	1	5	14
Clerical	2	1	0	2	16

TABLE 7

Information on Taxes Paid by Company

	Accuracy of Information				No Answer
	Within 1%	*1-5%*	*5-10%*	*10% and over*	
Superintendents	2	0	2	2	5
Supervisors	1	1	2	2	9
Foremen	0	2	2	6	18
Laboratory technicians	1	2	1	6	10
Maintenance engineers	0	0	3	10	23
Process & project engineers	0	0	0	3	17
Clerical	1	1	0	2	17

168

Surprisingly enough, the foremen were also poorly informed about the company's products. Less than half were able to state what group of products constituted the company's largest market. The professional groups made the best showing on this question, with approximately 80 per cent of the engineers knowing the correct answer. Least knowledgeable on this score was the clerical group.

Though the company gives wide publicity to safety by means of bulletin boards, meetings, company magazines, and other media, only 16 foremen knew the comparative safety records for the years 1956 and 1955. As for the amount of taxes paid by the company in 1956 only five of the 164 respondents had any accurate idea (Table 7).

A final question on company finances concerned the distribution of the 1956 sales dollar among materials and supplies, wages and salaries, taxes, depreciation and interest, and net income. As may be seen from Table 8, the number of persons identifying these items correctly was also quite small.

Each person participating in the survey was asked to indicate whether or not he owned stock in the company. It was found that 38 of the

TABLE 8

Information on Distribution of Sales Dollar

	Number Correctly Identifying Each Item*				
	Materials & Supplies	*Wages & Salaries*	*Taxes*	*Depreciation & Interest*	*Net Income*
Superintendents	8	8	8	1	1
Supervisors	13	10	10	2	3
Foremen	12	9	12	1	1
Maintenance engineers	16	14	13	4	8
Process & project engineers	24	13	13	9	11
Laboratory technicians	6	5	8	1	1
Clerical	6	6	5	3	4

*The sales dollar was represented by a pie chart divided into five sections, each section labeled with a figure in cents indicating the actual outlay for that item. Respondents were asked to identify the items represented.

TABLE 9

Stockholders and Non-Stockholders Having Correct Information on Annual Report

Item	Stockholders		Non-Stockholders	
	No.	Per Cent	No.	Per Cent
Sales figure	11	29	14	17
Net income	11	29	16	12
Increase in income	23	61	41	33
Company products	30	80	60	50

164 respondents owned stock. None of the laboratory technicians owned any, and only one of the clerical employees.

Stockholders vs. Non-Stockholders

Analysis of the findings shows that stockholders knew more about the annual report than did non-stockholders (Table 9). As might be expected, the stockholders were better acquainted with the company's financial position. Only a third of the non-stockholders, for example, knew whether the company's income had increased over the previous year, whereas 61 per cent of the stockholders were accurately informed on this point. Fifty-two per cent of the stockholders knew the dividends per share paid by the company in 1956, as compared with only 5 per cent of the non-stockholders. The stockholders were also better informed about the company's safety record, its expansion plans, and the distribution of the sales dollar.

Though it might be argued that some of the questions in this survey dealt with facts and figures that many people might have difficulty in recollecting after a month's time lag, on the whole the findings indicate considerable indifference on the part of these particular employees to the company's efforts to "keep them informed." On the basis of this one small sample, it would be rash to conclude, however, that this attitude is typical of this company's employees generally, still less of U.S. industry as a whole. Rather, the study suggests that "readability" is no guarantee that an employee communication will actually be read, and that the annual report needs to be supplemented by other media if the facts it endeavors to convey to employees are to strike home.

Employees' Interest in the Business: Financial and Other Information

An Address *

By DAVID FLINT, T.D., M.A., B.L., C.A.
Lecturer in Industrial Accountancy, University of Glasgow

THIS paper is not intended to be a complete and comprehensive examination of the subject. It is in many respects incomplete. I should not like you to think that I believe that you could adequately deal with the problem by applying yourself only to the aspects of it to which I refer. What I propose to do is to endeavour to direct your attention to at least
170 some of the principal considerations affecting this subject which in my opinion are worth your examining further. At this hour on a Saturday evening it is perhaps ambitious to hope to do more than merely delay for a short time your succumbing to an understandable inclination for repose. This inclination for repose is not altogether an unsuitable note on which to introduce this topic because there is no doubt that to many the right way to approach this subject is to let it rest.

Stated very simply the question is: should an employee be told any more than what he must know to do his job and how much money is in his pay packet?—this you must tell him. If so,

> *what* should he be told about;
> *how much* should he be told about it; and
> *how* should he be told?

Alternatively,

> *what* should he be able to get information about;
> *how much* information should he get; and
> *how* should the information reach him?

There is a good deal of attention paid nowadays to the employee's relationship with, and attitude to, the firm in which he is employed, by means of various forms of employee participation, joint consultation procedures and co-partnership arrangements—in the wider sense of co-partnership as a belief in the common purpose and common interest of

* Delivered to the University of Glasgow Management Studies Conference at St Andrews on March 22, 1958. Professor Robert Browning, M.A., LL.B., C.A., was in the Chair.

those engaged in business. It is not part of the purpose of this paper, however, to discuss or evaluate different personnel policies, and particularly the various measures that are taken with a view to stimulating or encouraging or promoting an attitude of co-operation on the part of employees.

I accept it for a fact that there does exist a significant volume of opinion which believes for one reason or another that there should be a sharing of information with employees. The amount and type of information will certainly vary, and whereas the large majority of firms will circulate some form of general information about the business it was estimated by an investigating committee of the British Institute of Management that the number of companies in this country giving *financial* information to employees is less than 20 per cent; and the number who do so in a way which can be termed fully is estimated by the Editors of
BUSINESS at only 6 per cent. 171

In a paper on this subject sponsored by the British Productivity Council it is suggested that there are three main purposes in the issue of information to employees:—

(1) to explain certain decisions and actions, so that prejudices and doubts will not result in a lack of co-operation or a non-acceptance of changes in, say, methods of work;
(2) to inform on matters affecting the company, the influence on the national economy, sales, exports, and so on; and
(3) to show ways of doing the job, procedure, use of safety devices.

It is also clear from the statements and actions of individual managements that the real purposes of informing employees may often be political or social and the facts are presented with that end in view. It is, I think, important to give some thought to this question of objectives because the objective will have an effect on the nature of the facts made available, the way they are presented and ultimately on the results achieved. I quote from a paper by Professor Wight Bakke of Yale University on this subject:—

> " I shall concern myself with only one aspect of the communication problem, but the one which seems to be the most important. Do the communications have any effect? Is anybody listening? Do those who listen react as you want them to react? A communication, however well constructed and delivered, is a waste of the time, energy and money of the communicator if it falls on deaf ears or if no response occurs. I assume that you intend your messages to have some effect. You aren't talking to hear yourself talk. Although

> I must confess that I have listened to, and read, some messages from management to their workers which remind me of a sentence in that delightful little parody on England's history, 1066 AND ALL THAT; 'This preface is written to glorify the authors, not to inform the readers.'
>
> " What do you have in mind when you share information about the business with employees? At a very minimum you want them to receive and believe that information. Perhaps your purposes go beyond that. You want them to act more intelligently on their jobs or in negotiations with you. You want them to understand you, and the compulsions you work under, better. You hope they might co-operate more energetically and effectively with management. Perhaps you desire that they should show more interest in, and loyalty to, the firm, even identify their own interests more thoroughly
> 172 with those of the firm. But in any case, *you take action in order to get action.*"

Professor Wight Bakke then goes on to suggest six tests that should be applied, and to some at least of these I will refer later. What I wish to draw attention to is the fact that there is no point in applying yourself to what you're going to present and how you're going to present it if you haven't established an effective channel of communication.

The investigating committee of the British Institute of Management report as their opinion that " the motive in giving financial information to employees plays a large part in determining how successful is the policy " and also report that " it is the opinion of many writers, particularly in the U.S.A., that if information is given in order to press home a particular point, to show what a small proportion of profits go to the shareholders, for example, or to justify the economic system in some way, then the information is less likely to be accepted as accurate and unbiased." This committee also suggest that basically every employee, by reason of his employment, has a moral title to information concerning the progress of his company.

In the survey carried out by the British Institute of Management, of the firms participating 80 per cent of the replies as to objectives were classifiable as follows:—

Identification of interest with employer .	39 per cent (63 firms)
To help understanding of company and economic affairs	21 per cent (34 firms)
To stop rumours and remove misconception	20 per cent (33 firms)

It is interesting to consider the attitude of the trade unions on this question and we have some evidence of this in the memorandum of the T.U.C. to the British Institute of Management on the narrower subject of " disclosure of financial information to employees ". After dealing with the desire and need of trade unions for financial information for the purpose of well informed negotiation the memorandum goes on to say " consideration should be given both by the union and by the management as to the most appropriate manner in which information concerning the progress of the undertaking can also be made available to individual employees: on this point there is evidence suggesting that an effective way is to let employees know that an appropriate statement is available on request. It should not be assumed that a statement satisfactory for this purpose can be made merely by cutting down the detail of the formal balance sheet and profit and loss account and associated documents; rather should it be designed to give a fair picture, consistent with the 173
economic, social and psychological interests of the employees concerned " and further " it should be stressed that the formal provision of documentary financial information is inadequate unless associated with a readiness—and preferably a wish—to discuss it ".

It is interesting to note that the terms of the T.U.C. memorandum leave the initiative to the employee to request an appropriate statement which is to be available, and to open discussion which is to be gladly joined. Any firm pursuing a policy of providing such information is most likely to take steps to achieve the largest possible circulation and to stimulate interest and understanding among as many as possible of those who would not make the effort on their own.

Before becoming too involved in the particular field of financial information I think it would be worthwhile to enumerate as many as possible of the subjects on which firms do take steps to provide information :—

(1) the firm's aims, policy, history, relations with the community, connections and background;

(2) work of the firm, its products, its methods, raw materials used (imported or home-produced), the major processes;

(3) position of the firm in the industry, development of the industry, including skills, inventiveness and the application of research and future plans;

(4) places to which the firm's products go, their uses, details of exports, the state of the order book;

(5) place of the firm and the industry in the national economy, the importance of higher productivity;

(6) promotion policy, training schemes, selection methods, educational facilities;
(7) structure of the firm, lines of authority, the location and activities of departments and/or sections;
(8) objects and functions of joint consultative bodies, names and departments of representatives, minutes of meetings;
(9) suggestion schemes and procedures, the type of suggestion required, successful suggestions, details of awards given;
(10) social and welfare facilities, canteens, first aid and medical service, sporting news and events, personal items, marriages, births, retirements, hobbies;
(11) output figures, production targets, team competition, waste prevention, safety, hygiene, new ideas, the objects of work study, how incentive schemes or bonus systems operate;
174 (12) financial position, explanation of the balance sheet, profit and loss account, " where the money goes ".

A good deal of this may be done by means of induction courses and employees' handbooks. This is particularly so in the case of those subjects of a general nature, for example: the firm's aims; the firm's work and products; welfare facilities, etc.

But many managements may well ask is it really worth the cost of doing it? How many employees are really interested? How many employees are capable of understanding it? Here you are faced with the basic problem of whether, as part of the social responsibility of firms, part of their obligation to the community as a whole, they should make an effort, a considerable effort in many cases no doubt, to create an attitude among their employees that the place of work is something more than merely a place to make a living, that it is somewhere which is a decent and worthwhile place to live—for a large part of their waking time is spent there—and that the firm is doing something it is worthwhile being associated with.

Once you accept the obligation to share information with employees it is a continuing process and we should consider what means should be adopted for this purpose. On examination we find among the firms who practise this such channels in use as:—

(1) passing on information by word of mouth; or by
(2) special talks, lectures and films;
(3) disseminating information through Works Councils and similar committees; or by
(4) notice board announcements, posters or news-sheets;

(5) charts and diagrams; or
(6) works magazines and house journals.

Each of these channels has its own particular advantages: each has its own particular shortcomings. The channel which may be appropriate for one type of information may be quite unsuitable for another. Exchange of information by word of mouth can only be satisfactory where the subject matter is entirely within the understanding of all persons involved. Otherwise it will not only be unsatisfactory but dangerous; not only will you fail to inform and to improve understanding, but you will give scope for distortion and misconception. Much of the effort devoted to methods of sharing information with employees is directed to undoing the harm which may be done by inaccurate and unreliable communications based on rumour and the " grapevine ". Notice board announcements, news-sheets, magazine articles, however well conceived 175
and presented so as to give an objective view with the right emphasis on what is important, will fail if few people take the trouble to read them. The whole personnel policy and the attitude to human relations in the firm must be such as to create and stimulate an appetite for information of this kind.

The T.U.C. say in their submission to the British Institute of Management " Work people are not only concerned with pay packets. Most of their active life is spent at work. Other satisfactions are involved than merely pay packets. In such circumstances only frustrations and perhaps cynicism can result from secrecy and restriction, however traditional it may be in the industry or firm concerned." I believe that many managements accept this point of view that employees do have a wider and deeper interest which can be roused and held by the right kind of approach from management. And the question of the right kind of approach brings me back to one of the points made by Professor Wight Bakke—one of the tests he suggests to find out if it is probable that the information management share with employees will be considered, accepted and lead to a productive response. He states it as follows: " Do the recipients of communications also initiate communications? "

The paper sponsored by the British Productivity Council also recognises this point by stating that " any exchange of ideas either through formal joint consultative machinery or by discussion on the floor of the shop must imply the giving and receiving of information ", and " Information for workers should cover the free exchange of ideas between *all* members of the organisation. It is a three way process—downwards from management through the chain of responsibility to the shop floor, upwards from the shop floor to management, and sideways from manager to manager, foreman to foreman and operative to operative ", and " Ideas flow constantly between individuals in any organisation which, in the aggregate, if they are not based on rumour and speculation, may amount to a valuable contribution towards greater efficiency and better human relationships."

I think that you must all find from experience how very true this is. If you wish someone to accept your authority in some subject on which you may reasonably consider yourself to be better informed you must be prepared to listen to his views on matters of common interest on which he has a fuller knowledge than you. And there is no doubt that there are many matters at the workroom or factory floor level on which employees not only think it probable, but do in fact know, that they are better informed than management. It is important, not only for the efficiency
176 of the business but also for the creation of conditions in which employees will take an interest in what management have to say, that the flow of information from employees should be encouraged. There may be a lot of chaff with a few grains of wheat but it is important that it should all go through the mill. J. Spedan Lewis, founder of the John Lewis Partnership, author of " Partnership for All " and " Fairer Shares ", a practical pioneer of co-partnership, places great emphasis on the right and the need for employees to express themselves.

It can be seen that the relationship between the parties sharing information is important to the acceptance of and interest in the information shared. And this brings me to a further test which Professor Wight Bakke proposes which I believe is important. He states it as follows: " Do the senders trust and respect the recipients? Can the recipients trust and respect the senders? Is there mutual trust? "

This is not something which just happens nor is it a state of affairs which can be created overnight. It is the atmosphere in the firm because of what goes on all the time in innumerable different ways in all the aspects of the firm's business: it is the result of the dominating policy and outlook of the firm towards its employees; its personnel policy; its philosophy of human relations. This situation of mutual trust is inevitably bound up with what has been said about the objectives of the firm in sharing information with employees, or the motives of management in initiating this sharing. If the management wish to share information because they genuinely wish the employees to have a fuller understanding of what concerns and affects the business and wish the employees to understand the full and proper significance of the information they receive, and if they direct themselves conscientiously to this end in the conviction that the information properly understood will produce the desired result then they may achieve success. But there is no doubt that if the information which is shared is specially selected and presented with a particular purpose in view, especially a social or political purpose, any success at all will be short-lived as the good faith of the management will become suspect. This may in turn disturb the whole series of management-employee relationships for all purposes throughout the firm. It can be seen then that the sharing of information is only one factor in a general policy for employees and that without some trust and goodwill at the start it will be useless to expect to achieve much in this way. If management and employees are at arms' length, any supplementary information of the kind with which we are concerned, however well intentioned, however honestly designed, will be immediately suspect and disregarded or perhaps, worse, misrepresented.

Two further points should receive some attention before we leave this 177
general review. Referring back to the listing of the subjects on which information may be provided we should examine whether any harm could be done to the business by giving that information. There is no doubt that this is an obstacle for many managements. Competitors will certainly have an interest in certain types of information such as sales composition and total turnover; processes and methods of production; markets and order books; and new products and research. Different firms will have different problems and there is no doubt that there will be difficulty in many cases to know where the dividing line between secrecy and disclosure should be made. Smaller firms who are not required to publish and file accounts may hesitate about making financial disclosures. It is important however that the problem should be kept in perspective and that managements should be honest with themselves. It would be easy for managements to leap or to clutch at this as a reason, when it may be no more than an excuse, for avoiding the problem altogether.

The second general point to which I wish to draw your attention concerns the ability or capacity of employees to understand the information. This is a matter which does require a lot of thought. The degree of capacity will vary depending on the nature of the information and this will accordingly affect the means which are adopted of disseminating the information. General news and facts about conditions of work and similar matters will generally require no interpretation. Details of output figures, production targets, waste prevention and matters affecting actual operations with which employees are familiar may be suitably dealt with through Works Councils or by short meetings comprising a talk and discussion, whereas topics touching on economics and finance will generally have to be introduced gradually, disclosure and interpretation of facts and figures keeping pace with a general extension of knowledge and understanding. It would be quite unrealistic to expect the sudden introduction of data of this kind to be met with a response other than that of bewilderment. This is perhaps particularly the case with regard to financial information, with which I propose to deal in rather more detail. What I have to submit to you is largely factual and I have drawn to a large extent on the Report of the special investigating committee of the British Institute of Management for much of what I have to say, although the comment on it is my own.

This particular branch of information is presently arousing a certain amount of general interest from the viewpoint that disclosure, explanation and interpretation of more information might affect the employees' attitude to work, to greater effort, to greater interest and to greater
178 understanding of the essential and complementary part that capital (with a small " c ") has to play in production. Much of the interest is political; but at least some of it is genuinely concerned only with improving industrial efficiency. What you have to decide for yourself is whether every employee has, by reason of his employment alone, a moral title to financial information about the firm for which he works. And this apart, you have to decide whether disclosure of financial information will advance the progress of employee's identification of interest with employer, help understanding of the firm and economic affairs, stop rumours and misconceptions, and improve production.

There is throughout the community a lack of understanding of the function of capital and the function of profit; there is at *all* levels in most firms no matter what size (except among those officers directly concerned) a lack of understanding of how much capital is needed, what it is used for, where it comes from, why it has to be paid for. Resentment and objection to profits being used for any purpose other than improvement of working conditions and remuneration in the industry or the firm may well be a barrier to greater effort, to increases in productivity, to greater efficiency. Sharing the fruits of effort is not attractive if the reasons or need for sharing are obscure. If this is the problem how can it be solved? As indicated earlier quite a small proportion—between 6 per cent and 20 per cent—of British firms are tackling it, at least by disclosure of information, and of these the objectives and measure of success must vary. In this connection it is financial information of a general nature which I have in mind and not detailed cost information or operating statements relating to the employees' work and used for control or other purposes, although it is sometimes surprising how little of that detailed day to day information is distributed down the line, even as far as foremen and supervisors. There may well be room here for some improvement in communications, if a greater sense of cost consciousness is to be developed.

The nature of the general financial information made available to employees varies greatly. In a sample examined by the British Institute of Management, of 89 firms giving information of any kind—

	46	gave	the balance sheet	(52 per cent)
and	57	,,	the profit and loss account;	(64 ,, ,,)
	38	gave	sales turnover,	(43 ,, ,,)
	30	,,	labour costs,	(33 ,, ,,)
	18	,,	analysis of unit selling price,	(20 ,, ,,)
and	25	,,	product cost;	(28 ,, ,,)
	62	,,	a forecast of future trading position,	(70 ,, ,,) 179
	44	,,	economic information about the industry in general,	(49 ,, ,,)
but only	18	ran	instruction courses to help employees understand the information.	(20 ,, ,,)

It is interesting to observe that although many firms may claim to give financial information to employees not all of them make it available to all employees. The range of employees included varies greatly—in some cases only senior executives being so favoured. The reaction of employees to information received is particularly interesting in this connection. From case studies conducted by the British Institute of Management it appeared that employees were most interested in development plans and prospects and trade expectations generally. It would, I think, be dangerous to deduce too much from this, as the natural inclination of most employees would be to concern themselves first with the prospects of security of employment on which their whole life and standard of living depend. The longer term effect, particularly on morale, of the more specialised information should not be under-rated, however. Each successive year, as understanding grows, the value of the information may increase. The process is bound to be a slow and gradual one—especially when traditional suspicions and antipathies have to be overcome.

If we consider the means of communication which are available we find that not all are suitable for passing on financial information. Special talks, lectures and films are in many ways very suitable for this purpose. But except in the smallest firms only a limited number of people can attend—to be worthwhile the number at any meeting should not be too large—and in the early years at least these may be looked on as management " stunts " and so suspect. The speaker should be really first class, and the firm's accountant is not necessarily the ideal choice, particularly for an address to foremen and wage employees.

Works Councils may be used as the channel of distribution but the danger in this case is twofold. The representatives may fail to pass on what they have learned or from inadequate understanding may pass on a wrong or misleading version: the management are not in direct contact with the employees. But the dangers of by-passing the Works Council will be familiar to you.

Notice board announcements, posters or news-sheets are hardly suitable for this purpose unless with a very limited objective of perhaps one special point only.

Works Magazines or House Journals have considerable advantages
180 particularly for presenting special articles on particular aspects of financial affairs. As you know, the Magazine or Journal is often posted direct to the employee's home in preference to being handed out in the works, the view being taken that, particularly in the case of male employees, wives and mothers are more interested to read of the firm and they can be expected in due course to exert an influence on the men. In addition, a leisurely reading of a magazine may commend itself to many more readily than attendance at a lecture. An interesting sidelight on the practice of publishing financial information in the House Journal is furnished by the John Lewis Partnership where it is recounted that:—

> " Some members of the John Lewis Partnership were pleased to hear from one of the most eminent of its Buyers that, when she had lately spoken sorrowfully to her small son of the unsatisfactory nature of the latest report from his school, he had expressed his consciousness that the report was not all it should have been and added sympathetically: ' And, Mummy, your figures in the Gazette have not been very good lately, have they ? ' "

The use of charts, graphs and diagrams has considerable attractions as a means of presenting apparently simple information which is by no means simple of understanding. As you know this practice is being widely adopted for the purpose of supplementing financial accounts to shareholders. But there are considerable dangers in the use of graphical presentation at any time. The choice of type of graphic, or of scale, or of the information selected or rejected, even with the best intentions, can materially alter the significance of the information presented and at the worst the graphics may lend themselves to actual manipulation either at the instance of the designer or of the would-be interpreter. Retention of an objective view is rendered more difficult except for the simplest of data. But perhaps the most serious reservation stems from one of the findings of the investigating committee of the British Institute of Management. Although those of us who understand the facts being presented readily accept that a simple presentation by diagram or graph will convey the right idea or impression to the uninitiated this committee found that employees were generally puzzled by presentations of this type. Many people evidently didn't understand what a sales £ was.

There are two additional channels of communication which I suggest to you are worthy of consideration. The first is to invite representatives of the employees to engage an independent person skilled in accounts (not the auditor), selected by them and approved by the management, to discuss certain aspects of the firm's financial affairs at a meeting, or 181
meetings, of employees with a view to interpreting and explaining them. If necessary a management nominee could attend to present the firm's point of view where there was, as there almost always is, room for a difference of opinion. There are of course dangers in such a procedure, but I believe it is worth considering. The second is to provide facilities for comment by the public press on financial matters concerning the firm and to welcome such comment. Employees will without doubt in many cases accept as more reliable the same facts reported by the daily press when, presented by the management, these facts would be disregarded or questioned. In both of these cases, of course, management require to be very confident of themselves and their actions to court the criticism which might be forthcoming.

Whatever channel of communication is used the management will require to consider whether the statutory accounts as issued to shareholders should be made available to employees or whether a special version should be prepared. As a general proposition it seems desirable that if a special version is prepared the statutory accounts should also be available on request. And in connection with the distribution of financial information to employees the position of shareholders has also to be kept in mind. Firstly, it seems desirable that any special version of accounts distributed to employees should also be despatched to shareholders. Secondly, it is suggested that general financial information should not be disclosed to employees at an earlier date than it is communicated to shareholders. Thirdly, it requires to be considered what is to be the position of the shareholders in cases where supplementary information such as turnover, costs, etc. which is not normally disclosed to shareholders is communicated to employees. Have shareholders not got a legitimate complaint if they are in a less favoured position?

But perhaps the most difficult problem for management, even in the most favourable climate for acceptance, is how to educate employees to an understanding of what the information is about. It is as well to be clear that there is a need for instruction at all levels, executives and managers as well as foremen and wage employees. It is sometimes too readily assumed that only the second category are concerned. But it must be appreciated that whatever formal arrangements may be made to disseminate information these will be supplemented by informal discussion. It is essential therefore that those who are accustomed to be regarded with some authority should be able to talk with some competence to junior employees who turn to them for guidance and clarification. This is quite apart from their need for knowledge and under-
182 standing for the more efficient execution of their own duties.

As indicated at the outset this paper has been by no means an exhaustive treatment of the subject; I have not raised all the issues or problems; I have offered very little in the way of proposals or solutions. I hope however that what I have done is to give you a general review, with sufficient detail to stimulate your further interest, of what I believe will be for the future an important and absorbing study.

Employee Reports—What Employees Think

by R Hussey and R J Craig

The interim results of a major UK research survey carried out within companies to explore the impact on individual employees of employee reports.

A survey, was conducted in 1977 and 1978 by the Industrial Relations Unit at St Edmund Hall, Oxford, in conjunction with Touche Ross & Co (UK), to analyse the attitudes of UK employees to employee reports. In the absence of any major Australian research survey on this matter, an analysis of such attitudes may be helpful to those Australian companies currently producing employee reports, or contemplating doing so.

Five companies took part in the UK survey and a random sample of employees at eight locations within the companies were sent questionnaires. This article analyses the results obtained in 298 completed questionnaires and 74 face to face interviews with employees.

Extent of Employee Readership, Interest and Understandability

Tables 1, 2 and 3 show the results of questions aimed at determining whether employees read employee reports, whether they find them interesting and whether they consider the financial information in the reports difficult to understand.

That 21 percent of all respondents found the financial information quite difficult, very difficult to understand suggests that this may be the main reason for 23 percent expressing little or no interest and 24 percent only glancing at or not reading the employee report. Some other variables which may have influenced readership were detected. The type of report itself was found to be important, as also was the relationship between management and employees.

Nevertheless, the fact that 76 percent of all respondents claimed to have read all or most of the reports is encouraging. As one might expect, the readership was highest within the managerial group. The difference between the manual and white collar groups, as far as readership is concerned, was not significant. The response of the latter two groups was particularly encouraging.

Although some of the respondents only glanced at the employee report, subsequent face to face interviews revealed that they would not necessarily advocate the cessation of the publication. Indeed, the principle of the company being seen to be willing to give information was regarded more highly, in some quarters, than the actual information itself.

As far as understanding of financial information is concerned all employee reports should be produced with the intention that the recipient should find it intelligible. A large company may well be confronted with a wide range of employee ability and must decide whether to attempt

R Hussey MSc, ACCA, is Research Associate Industrial Relations Research Unit, Oxford, UK. R J Craig MCom, AASA (Snr) is Lecturer at The University of Newcastle.

TABLE 1
Readership of the Report

	Manual %	White Collar %	Managerial %	Total %
Read the entire report thoroughly	26	33	68	37
Read most of the report	46	40	26	39
Glanced at the report	28	26	6	23
Did not read the report	—	1	—	1

TABLE 2
Interest in the Report

	Manual %	White Collar %	Managerial %	Total %
Very interesting	19	20	26	21
Quite interesting	60	53	60	56
Of little interest	19	25	14	22
A waste of time	2	2	—	1

TABLE 3
Understanding of Financial Information

	Manual %	White Collar %	Managerial %	Total %
Very easy to understand	11	24	76	29
Quite easy to understand	68	51	21	50
Quite difficult to understand	19	20	3	17
Very difficult to understand	2	5	—	4

TABLE 4
Why Company has Produced Employee Report

Reason	%
Trade unions have asked for it	2
There is a legal obligation	9
Employees have been asking for it	12
Prevent higher wage claims	2
Part of company personnel policy	29
To encourage people to work	1
Involve employees more in the company	34
To get employees to accept management viewpoint	7
Don't know/other	4

TABLE 6
Additional Information

	%
Future plans and policies	25
Financial	23
Organisational details	13
Sales/order books	12
Pay and conditions	9
Production/scrap/quality	7
Personnel	7
None/don't know	4

TABLE 5
Amount of Information

	Manual	White Collar	Managerial	Total
	%	%	%	%
Very important	25	7	21	14
Quite important	32	31	27	30
Of little importance	36	46	46	44
No importance	7	16	6	12

to cater for everyone or concentrate on writing for the majority. One solution is to keep the employee report simple but to publicise the fact that shareholder reports are available for any employee who requires more detailed information. The study indicated that the "take up" rate has so far been low and that a company need not be deterred from this practice on the grounds of cost.

Perceptions of Company Motives for Employee Report Preparation

Another of the questions put to employees sought reasons why they thought their company had given them an employee report. The results are shown in Table 4.

It is interesting that over one in five employees believe the report has been issued because there is a legal obligation or because trade unions and employees have demanded it. In contrast, in all meetings with companies participating in the study, management claimed that it took the initiative in producing employee reports, sometimes in an atmosphere of employee apathy. Thirty-four percent of the employees believed that the report was produced to involve them more in the company. It is extremely difficult to measure satisfactorily whether this was achieved.

One question which did look at an aspect of involvement asked the employee how important the information contained in the employee report was in relation to his/her own job. The results are shown in Table 5. One outstanding feature of this table is the response of the manual group, some 25 percent identifying the information as being very important.

During interviews, employees expressed the difficulty they have in identifying the relationship of their job with the overall results of the company or group. Consequently, they would like to see financial information about their own workplace to bridge this gap. There may of course be difficulties of "commercial confidentiality" and even of the practicalities of an accounting system which inhibit the giving of detailed workplace information. If these problems could be overcome, such information would assist in clarifying the relationship of the work an employee does with the information in the employee report.

Companies tend to provide information which is historic, wide-based and financial. During the course of 74 interviews, employees were asked to indicate the matters on which they would like to receive additional information from companies. The results are shown in Table 6.

The employee report may not be a suitable vehicle for providing some of the information although the table does reflect some material which can be incorporated into a report.

Future plans and policies are rarely given in employee reports and there are obvious difficulties surrounding the uncertainty of planning and the possible damage to morale if confident predictions are not met. This is also the area in which managers envisage the greatest difficulties with commercial confidentiality. The extent to which this information can be included in an employee report is doubtful. Some companies do cover part of this information by giving fairly detailed plans on future investment in plant and machinery.

The category "Financial" relates closely to the respondent's own workplace or factory and not to group results. It was often mentioned in terms of "what we make on 'X' product" and "How we did last month in relation to other departments". This information would appear to be similar to that included in the monthly management accounts.

"Organisation details" produced some interesting insights and needs further explanation. A number of the respondents made the point that they did not know the structure of the company, location of other factories and, in some cases, the names and faces of their own senior managers. To illustrate how this arises and also to enlarge upon the question of involvement, consider the following case.

A middle-aged woman clerk in a factory, on her first day of employment with the company, had been shown into a small office and her task of processing invoices explained. She had then carried out this job for the next five years with very little contact with anyone else except for the clerks who brought and took away her work.

One day, without explanation, she

received upon her desk an employee report stating that the company had made a profit of $X million. There were a large number of colourful bar charts showing where the money came from and where it went. When interviewed, she pointed out that in five years no one had ever shown her over the factory, she was even uncertain as to the products of the company, she had never seen and would not recognise the factory general manager and, finally, $X million was beyond any experience she had of money.

It is not suggested that this case is typical. However, the desire for organisational details shown in Table 6 suggests that some employees are not being given quite simple and routine information. It would be easy to include organisational details in employee reports and, by careful planning of how to produce and distribute the report, opportunities can be made to ensure employees are included more effectively in the communication network of a company.

Content and Presentation

The following observations are based on discussions with a large number of companies and from the interviews held with other researchers, practitioners, management representatives from 25 companies and from interviews with 74 employees. Employees interviewed were given a sample of employee reports, a sample which excluded an employee report of the type produced by their own company. The following classification basis was used:

- Light shareholder: A4 size, 2-4 pages; concentrates on financial results; sparing use of diagrams; very few photographs.
- Heavy shareholder: very similar to shareholders' report and accounts in appearance; wide range of information; conservative written style.
- Light Newspaper: 2-4 pages; often part of or enclosed in normal company newspaper; limited information, mostly of a financial nature. There are two sub-divisions: mainly consists of diagrams—usually bar charts; mostly narrative with a few photographs.
- Heavy Newspaper: six pages and over; use of large bar charts, sometimes one to a page; some photographs; more financial information than in light newspaper type and sometimes information on personnel.
- Cartoon: glossy and well produced; use of cartoons, eg trains, matchstick men, barrels of beer; factual content varies but emphasis is on presenting information as simply as possible.

- Throw-aways: these can be regarded as economy issues and may be a single sheet of paper. Can be sub-divided into: financial statements used to give the bare essentials of the financial results; rallying cries containing exhortations and general forecasts, ranging from "Let's pull together" and "We're holding her steady" to "The end is nigh" often clearly depending upon the mood of the chairman. Some figures, isolated and therefore not very meaningful, may appear in the text.

Some employee reports do not fit easily into any one of the above classifications and are a mixture of two or more types. However, the lack of rigour in the classification does not detract from the research conclusions. Future studies may require a more strict classification, both on contents and presentation, to ensure interview findings are accurately interpreted.

Employees were asked to comment upon each of the various types of employee reports they were given and were asked to select the report they would be most likely to read. The results are shown in Table 7.

The following comments which explain the preferences revealed in Table 7 also give some clues as to desirable contents and presentation.

Heavy Shareholder. A large number of interviewees were obviously impressed by the large amount of information given. Some of the respondents said they would only read those parts of the report which interested them and considered the layout assisted this, as different types of information were grouped separately eg financial, personnel. Comments were also made approving the conservative style of narrative as being the most fitting for important information.

As an employee group, the managers interviewed greatly preferred this type of report. To some extent, this was due to the report being seen as a reflection of the company image. A well-produced, lengthy report was regarded as enhancing the reputation of the company, and consequently of the managers, as considerate employers. However, the exclusion of the managerial group would not, on this quite small sample, greatly alter either the conclusions drawn or the reasons given for this preference.

There were very few outright critics of this report, and the unfavourable comments were usually expressed in terms of "I find it dull".

Cartoons. Once again, there was little difference between the number of white collar and manual employees who preferred this type of report. The advocates said, quite simply, that it was the one they would be most likely to read and understand. Many said that they disliked financial statements and this method made them more acceptable.

However, of all the reports, the cartoon type also provoked the greatest hostility from some individuals, who labelled it as "patronising" and "an insult".

Light Newspaper—Narrative Style. The appeal of this type of report was the use of narrative and the interest of photographs. Many of the respondents said they were "turned off" by figures and preferred

TABLE 7
Report Most Likely to be Read

	%
Heavy shareholder	38
Cartoon	30
Light newspaper—narrative	11
Simple shareholder	5
Heavy Newspaper	5
Light Newspaper—diagrams	2
	—
Sub Total	91
Unable to select preference	7
Unlikely to read any	2

a report which was more attuned to their accustomed daily reading matter.

Simple Shareholder. This found favour with a few employees who only wished to know the basic financial facts and wanted them simply presented.

Heavy Newspaper. With this type of report, the employees found the size overwhelming. Quite often they would contain bar charts covering one page and would use very large print. Employees found this presentation difficult to comprehend and expressed disappointment at the amount of information they could glean from such an apparently weighty publication. (One interviewee said "I suppose they think if they write it big enough, we should be able to understand it".)

Light Newspaper—Diagrammatic. This appeared to have the disadvantages of both the heavy newspaper and the light shareholder. The employees who selected this made the point that they would read all of it. Maybe they were the most realistic about the time they would spend on reading an employee report.

A brief note upon the method of research is appropriate. The examples of the reports were varied so that interviewees were not selecting one specific company report but a representative of the classification. They were specifically asked which report they would be most likely to read and not which one they most liked. Some respondents did select reports which they considered to be the "best produced" but this often differed from their "most likely to read" choice. The classifications are, of course, broad and many reports are a mixture of the above types.

The following suggestions concerning the presentation and content of employee reports, which arose from interviews with employees, should be considered by those companies wishing to improve their employee reporting:

Method of Presentation

Firstly, employees do like some narrative content and photographs. The use of large bar charts covering a page may be less valuable than is sometimes thought. Smaller bar charts used for varying presentation and breaking up lengthy paragraphs seem to be more acceptable. Cartoon presentations, although having many advocates, also received the greatest number of criticisms. The restricted use of cartoons to illustrate a point in an accompanying text is better received.

Variety of Content

As far as contents are concerned, it appears a wide range is preferable even if it does mean that each reader is selective and ignores a certain amount. There is value in the company being "seen to be open", although companies will be aware of the cost involved and the danger of information overload. (Table 6 gave a list of information that employees wish to receive in addition to what they currently receive.)

Workplace Information

Perhaps the most important point to make on contents is the desire of employees to receive information about their own workplace. Companies not able or wishing to produce employee reports for each individual factory may wish to consider the following alternatives which some companies are using:

- Giving company-wide information on financial results in the Employee Report but breaking down information on personnel on a factory basis;
- Including individual reports by factory general managers on their own position;
- Producing a one page insert for each factory, highlighting the main features; and
- Allowing local management to give a verbal presentation, comparing and interpreting the factory results with those of the company.

Political Statement or Propaganda

Employees react unfavourably to any suggestion of company propaganda contained in the employee report. The giver of information needs to be aware that the possible recipient may well have a different political viewpoint. The employee report may not be the best, or most appropriate, medium for making subjective claims. It appears preferable to keep the employee reports as objective as possible and to leave wider discussions for a more suitable occasion.

Interpretation and Accuracy

In a desire to simplify the information, some companies allow apparent inaccuracies or misleading interpretations to appear. It is a very difficult problem to reduce a mass of financial information into a simple statement, without risking criticism for misleading people. A verbal presentation to employees, allowing questions to be asked, is one precaution that can be taken to reduce this risk.

Consistency

Some companies have said that, where changes have been made in the employee report from one year to the next, these have been quickly identified by employees. If additional information is given, the report is accepted but, if there are omissions, employees make their own interpretations as to the motives of the company. The study suggested that employees believe information given by management is normally true but suspect that only part of the story is given. Consistency in content and presentation helps to reduce cynicism.

Distribution

Table 8 shows the results of a question in which employees were asked how often reports should be issued.

There is some indication, as one would expect, that employees' requests for more information in quantity and regularity are greatest in those companies where the employee report is on the light side. The requests may also be influenced by the employees' perception of what is available and these perceptions in part will be formed by other communication policies of the company.

Some companies give surprisingly little attention to the distribution of their employee report and expend little effort in ensuring that the employee receives the employee report.

TABLE 8
Frequency of Issue

	Manual	White Collar	Managerial	Total
	%	%	%	%
More often	66	55	47	56
Same as present (annual)	34	42	53	42
Less often	—	1	—	1
None	—	2	—	1

In one company visited, the employee report had been placed on the corner of workbenches for people to take as they left in the evening. Unfortunately, no one told the employees and there was great confusion as to whether the report was intended for them.

That is an extreme example and most companies do try to ensure that the distribution of the report receives the care that such an important document warrants. A number of companies have tried to make the distribution of the report an opportunity for fostering two-way communication. This is usually through the form of mass meetings or a succession of small meetings throughout the organisational hierarchy, where managers comment upon the report and answer questions. Some companies claim great success in improving the understanding of employees at all levels of the financial position of the company and promoting an atmosphere where discussions can take place on issues which, if ignored, could be expected to produce conflicts. Other companies have said that such meetings have resulted in nothing but apathy with no questions being asked.

Comparing these experiences, there would appear to be a number of factors which increase the possibility of the success of these meetings. Firstly, most reports have a high financial content and, while being able to understand simple figures, many employees, including managers, do not have the knowledge to discuss these statements. The meetings should therefore include on the agenda some items where anyone can make a contribution (for example, shortage of storage space or production problems), and management should attempt to relate these factors to the financial information.

Secondly, the most successful companies usually distribute the report a few days prior to the meeting and not at the commencement of the meeting. This allows employees to prepare questions and this is further assisted if prior written questions are encouraged.

Finally, the group accountant or a senior executive is often called upon to make the presentation at such meetings. The danger in this arrangement is the "status distance" between him and his audience. He is a professional relaying facts with which he is demonstrably at ease and they are laymen who in the employment relationship, are possibly in a very subordinate position to him. This can easily inhibit questions. A far more effective method is to allow a local manager to make the presentation. He can comment upon the figures in the light of the immediate workplace situation and respond to an audience with whom, hopefully, he is in daily contact. Of course this presupposes that the local manager has himself been adequately briefed and is equipped with an appropriate degree of expertise in the financial and other data he is presenting.

Conclusions

The art of employee reporting is in its infancy. Whereas the practices and methods of reporting to shareholders have been formulated over a period of 100 years or more and partly enshrined in legislation, no such historical background or legal convention support employee reporting. The absence of legislation and accounting conventions has resulted in the presentation of diverse types of employee reports.

This article has examined the attitude of employees to the wide range of employee reports which companies produce. The extent of readership, interest and understandability of employee reports was encouraging. As perhaps one would have expected, managers were found to be far more likely to have read the entire report thoroughly and to have found it very interesting and very easy to understand, than either manual or white collar employees. The types of employee report found most likely to be read were the "heavy shareholder" and "cartoon" types. (Although cartoon presentations received the most criticisms — mainly on the grounds that they were patronising.)

So far as the presentation and content of an employee report is concerned, the following suggestions, which come from the survey of employee attitudes, should be noted. There was a strong demand by employees for the disclosure of additional and disaggregated information in employee reports. Employees were keen for the disclosure of information concerning their own workplace, rather than to merely receive information for the company as a whole. They were particularly anxious to receive information on future plans and policies; the financial performance of individual products, departments or plants; and organisational details concerning such things as the structure of the company and the names and faces of their own senior managers. Employees were found to like some narrative content and photographs in employee reports. A wide, rather than narrow range of contents was preferred by employees.

The questioning of employees suggested that employee reports should avoid political statements or propaganda; be supported by verbal discussion sessions in order to reduce the risk of misinterpretation; and should be consistent in their content and presentation in order to reduce employee cynicism. Companies should also give far greater attention to the distribution of employee reports.

187

The study revealed an apparent tendency for employee reports to be a monologue. Advantages would appear to lie in developing disclosure into a two-way communication process, a dialogue. Furthermore, the role of the employee report in the employment relationship needs to be more closely determined. There is a danger at the moment of viewing it as a panacea, a cure-all for companies' ills.

Conclusn

It is impossible to predict the future of employee reporting but it is now quite widely established, and further development may be anticipated. One may be a certain standardisation in presentation and content, as our knowledge of the information required and the most effective way to transmit is improved. Another development may be the recognition by companies that employee reporting involves an entire communication process and does not merely involve report writing.

The final results of the research survey, whose interim results have been summarised in this article will be published in June 1979. The response rate to the questionnaire has been 58 percent and the replies of 1983 employees have been collated and analysed. In addition, over 350 face-to-face interviews have been conducted. The results of the completed survey should contribute further knowledge of the issue we have raised in this article.

REPORTING IN AN INDUSTRIAL RELATIONS CONTEXT

This final group of papers considers the provision of financial information to employees in the context of labor-management relations, wage bargaining, and union decision-making. The paper by Brubaker et al. (1949) is the product of a symposium at which the authors each gave an address. Each represented a particular arm of U.S. labor unions and conveyed an impression of how labor leaders of that time viewed financial statements used in labor negotiations. Dale's (1950) paper also examines the way in which accounting information has been used in labor negotiations and offers approaches to deciding what information to provide at the bargaining table. He argues for the importance of the potential accounting contribution to industrial relations.

Two further papers provide a viewpoint from the 1970s. Climo (1976) bases his discussion on the attention paid to this subject by the British accounting profession in its document *The Corporate Report*, but calls for the profession to go much further in research and practice. Accordingly he examines possible accountants' roles and information provision. Cooper and Essex (1977) argue that policies or recommendations in this area of reporting can only be effectively developed through a framework of employee decision-making models. They develop alternative models and present evidence from a case study.

What Kind of Information Do Labor Unions Want in Financial Statements?

A Symposium by Otis Brubaker, Lane Kirkland, William Gomberg, Nat Weinberg, Solomon Barkin, and others

188

• Labor has become a major user of financial information. Many labor men hold that wider use of significant financial information is the road to intelligent wage negotiation. But management and labor do not now agree on what information labor is entitled to have.

It seems apparent that financial information—which is the substance of accounting—is here to stay as a labor bargaining tool. So that accountants can be informed of the attitude and desires of labor leaders on this question, we have excerpted here with the authors' permission certain expressions from public statements and private correspondence of recognized labor leaders. By printing these observations this JOURNAL neither endorses nor opposes any of these statements; its sole purpose here is to report; to tell readers what these labor leaders have to say about financial statements now used in labor negotiations.

Avoid the "Take-It-or-Leave-It" Attitude, says Otis Brubaker, director, research department, United Steel Workers (CIO), in an address before the Michigan Accounting Conference, October 22, 1948

We must have the full facts before us in our bargaining if we are to eliminate the arbitrary "take-it-or-leave-it" approach once so characteristic of much of the bargaining on both sides of the table.

We have a right to know, and we must be furnished, the answers to such questions as:

1. Is industry generally and are particular industries and companies earning a fair return on invested capital?
2. How does a particular company stack up financially with the rest of the industry?
3. Are the total production costs of a particular company competitive?
4. Can the company afford to pay a wage increase?
5. Can it absorb the cost of a wage increase out of profits or from increased output measured either in terms of increases in productivity or in total production?
6. If the company cannot at the moment absorb a wage increase, is there reason to believe that such condition is a temporary one, that new methods, new machinery, new management, or some other change can reasonably be expected to correct?
7. Can or should a company raise

prices in order to escape absorbing a wage increase?

8. Is the productivity of a particular company or industry increasing?

9. How important are wage costs in a particular company's complete cost picture and how have these relationships changed over the years?

10. How does a particular company's financial picture compare with previous years?

11. How do real wage costs, in contrast with absolute wage rates, compare with other costs for a particular company and how do these costs compare with those common to the industry?

There is scarcely a company with which we deal that makes available enough information that we can measure with even approximate accuracy the actual effects of our bargaining. . . .

Even in the area more normally conceived as the accountant's realm, the record is little better. . . . Let us look for a moment at the income or profit-and-loss statement. Its stated purpose is to show the results of operations during a particular fiscal period. This means that it should reflect the ups and downs of the company's finances, both in relation to the similar movements in the business cycle and to the particular company's operating condition. Its purpose certainly is not to "hide" part of the current profit in preparation for a possible operating loss five years hence—yet many companies have chosen to even out their reported profits over a period of years through the use of many and various accounting devices. A few of these with which you are familiar include: (1) the setting up of exorbitant inventory reserves for possible inventory losses; (2) institution of Lifo during periods of rising prices; (3) the setting aside of grossly inflated reserves for income and excess-profits taxes during the war; (4) establishment of large general contingency reserves unrelated to any specified or expected contingency; (5) the reserving of moneys for postwar rehabilitation costs in amounts out of all relation to expected or probable costs; (6) use of inflated depreciation reserves in financial reports which are not in accordance with the depreciation expense reported to the Bureau of Internal Revenue.

All of these accounting devices above listed have a useful place, if properly employed. All have been grievously abused in the last few years by many, if not most, of the major corporations in the United States. As a result, we in the unions and the public generally have come to distrust most of the figures published by the companies.

We think that it is not too much to ask that companies should show in their financial reports such pertinent details as the cost of direct labor, the amount of the salaries paid, a meaningful breakdown of administrative, general, and selling costs, separate listing of income taxes and other taxes with appropriate detail in case of extraordinary adjustments. So, likewise, should be shown the additional detail necessary to permit the calculation of unit costs and productivity, hourly earnings, and the effects of price or wage changes.

A Union's Advice to Its Negotiators Suggests the Thinking Underlying Use of Financial Information. Some excerpts from a research report by the Research and Information Service of the American Federation of Labor

All terms and conditions established by collective bargaining are limited by the employer's ability to pay. That capacity is the controlling fact in all the firm's contracts including its union agreements. The union executive needs this basic information as a guide to all proposals.

An understanding of a company's financial statement is of real assistance to union negotiators in the event the company raises any question of its "ability to pay" requested wage increases. How else can a union counter this type of argument except by analyzing the company's financial statement to find out whether the company claim is true? In addition, the company's financial statements, by giving information concerning profits, inventory and purchasing policy, and financial interest in other corporations, will reflect the company's position in any labor dispute. . . .

It is important to remember that these statements are generally compiled by technically trained accountants, following what are supposed to be "standard accounting practices." The hitch to this is, however, that "accounting practices" are not generally standardized; different accountants use different methods and call the same sum of money by different names. The resulting confusion naturally does not make it any easier for a newcomer to understand these financial statements. . . .

It is not enough simply to know the
190 meaning of the terms included in these financial statements. It is necessary to know how to interpret these statements to find information needed in negotiations. . . .

The most important question union negotiators want a financial statement to answer is "How much money is this company making and how does this compare with its competitors? . . . "

For union purposes, the rate of return on *net worth* is a far more reliable and accurate indicator of profits than the rate of return on *sales*. . . .

Preparation of Financial Information Should Be Influenced by Labor's Needs. Some quotations from Lane Kirkland's address before an accounting conference at the University of Georgia. He is a member of the research staff, AF of L

The representatives of owners and investors work at close quarters with accountants in the ordinary course of their affairs, while it is only rarely that the representatives of employees find themselves in a position to command the ear of any considerable portion of the accounting profession. It is natural therefore that accounting procedures should have been adapted primarily to the needs of management without much concern for their informational value to employees. While we do not believe that the one aim is necessarily incompatible with the other, we are continually experiencing difficulty in getting certain useful information that could easily have been made available through the medium of financial reports if considerations of their potential use as an instrument in bargaining negotiations had been given greater regard in the course of their evolution.

There are, consequently, some modifications that we feel would be desirable if financial statements are to be of maximum use in contract negotiations, and I would like to point out some of them. However, there is little point in considering these modifications unless management generally can be persuaded to take a step that, in many companies, would be more of an innovation than any change in the statement itself—and that is the adoption of the policy of making these financial statements available to their workers' representatives in the first place. Many companies with which we have contracts—and it is significant that they are generally the ones with whom our relations have been most notably harmonious and mutually beneficial—do make a practice of furnishing us with adequate information of this sort when the occasion requires it—but unfortunately, this is not yet a universal practice in industry. I therefore think it would be well worth-while to devote some time to an elaboration of our position on that score.

Recently, in reports to the Federation from our organizers in the field, 82 companies were cited which were considered to be outstanding for good labor relations. Of these companies, 27, or about one-third, made a regular practice of supplying the union with financial reports, so that employees were able to obtain full information concerning the financial results of the joint efforts of management and labor, and they were thereby enabled to act and plan realistically and constructively.

On the other hand, the difficulty of obtaining current and reliable economic information on many of the companies whose workers we represent presents a serious obstacle that must be overcome before negotiations can be conducted on a rational basis and in good faith.

While we avail ourselves of most of the sources of information that are available to the general public—including investor's services such as Moody's and Standard and Poor's, the various commercial and financial chronicles, SEC reports, and other government agencies—all of these sources have serious limitations as far as our needs are concerned, and they cover only a small proportion of the many individual companies with which we have contracts. They are useful only in the case of companies that are listed on the large stock exchanges and which submit returns to the SEC and frequently their data are not sufficiently current to suit our needs. . . .

They fail us in the case of smaller corporations, unincorporated enterprises, and corporations whose ownership and control are closely held. They do not break down the particular operations of a corporation into its industrial components. In these days of horizontally and vertically integrated and mixed corporate structures, it becomes increasingly difficult to get adequate data on the results of operations of particular subentities or plants of a parent company.

We feel that there has been altogether too much said about "patterns" and "rounds" of wage increases. We do not think that there is any place for pat formulas and arbitrary assumptions in our negotiations with individual firms. The soundest approach is the pragmatic approach, gauged to the requirements of the particular company and union involved. No company is the "average" company, and the components of every general trend are mixed in some degree. What one company could very easily afford to do might very well place another in the same industry in serious financial straits, and while we do not aim to protect inefficiency at the expense of decent labor standards, this fact cannot be disregarded in wage negotiations.

There would seem to be no logical reason why we should be obliged to go to great and tortuous lengths in searching for the facts necessary for us to take a realistic and rational position in our negotiations with an employer who is himself sitting on that information all the while. . . .

In deciding what to ask for prior to a bargaining session our representatives do not look upon company earnings as a vein of gold ready to be staked out by whoever is able to bring the most pressure to bear. They realize that there are commitments attached to those earnings and that they must be made to serve many purposes. They do need to know what those earnings are, however, and what the financial position of the company is, in order to estimate what the effects of a given wage increase would be, and what could be considered reasonable and well within the power of the company to grant. . . .

It is hardly possible to make reasonable demands, except by coincidence, without the facts that make possible a determination of what would be reasonable.

Yet many representatives of management are reluctant to reveal their company's earnings position, on the grounds that profits are a highly abstract, almost occult, matter that only management can understand. They say that to give this information to the union would only stir up a furor and give rise to exorbitant demands. While freely acknowledging that there are many complexities and intangibles connected with earnings figures, we submit that demands made in complete ignorance of the true picture are much more likely to be unrealistic than demands made after a study of figures which both parties can accept. . . .

We of course recognize that even with all the basic facts available to both parties, there might still be room for a considerable difference of opinion in the interpretation of these facts. That can hardly be avoided, but there is no reason why it should constitute a barrier to ultimate peaceful agreement, if both parties negotiate in good faith. If each is persuaded of the other's sincerity and coöperativeness, differences of opinion can be resolved over the bargaining table, by compromise and a willingness to give due respect to rational arguments. If essential fundamental facts which both parties are willing to use as a basis for discussion are lacking, wage negotiations will all too often settle down into a simple test of relative strength and endurance, regardless of the actual merits of the case.

We do not, however, consider that this valuable informational service has been adequately rendered in such cases as that of one group of companies with which, for bargaining purposes, we deal through a trade association. Their association has made a practice of furnishing one of our affiliated unions with elaborate statements in certain years in which they took a terrific financial beating, but, somehow, during good years, it can never be induced into providing these facts and figures.

It should of course be unnecessary to
192 point out also that if the reports furnished us are to be suitable for negotiations in good faith, the actual facts should be stated as precisely as it is possible for them to be determined, and should be as free as possible of protective coloration by management. . . .

A few companies have adopted the practice of regularly distributing financial statements to workers in their plants. This may or may not be a constructive and worth-while practice depending always upon the motive behind it and how it is done. The line of demarcation between education and propaganda is often very difficult to draw. It is one of those things that if you do it, it is education, but if someone on the other side of the fence does it, it is propaganda. If the material takes the form of statements so highly condensed as to be virtually meaningless, and completely submerged in a mass of highly-slanted verbal embellishments, and is not supplemented by a willingness on the part of the company to furnish union representatives with information that is sufficiently detailed to be of use for bargaining purposes, it is not likely to promote goodwill.

We do not think, however, that detail should be sacrificed to simplicity. Much time and effort have been devoted to condensing, simplifying, and making more entertaining reading of financial reports, in order that they might be put to use as an advertising or public relations gadget. If as much effort were devoted to the end of providing additional information in those reports for those who have frequent occasion to use them, the interests of the public would be much better served.

In a general sense, we are interested in the same facts regarding the operations of a business as are stockholders and others, with a few more breakdowns needed to give more detail on certain items more closely related to the worker's part in the business. For instance, we need a breakdown of the item "cost of goods sold" in the income statement, which is not usually given. Such a breakdown should show direct labor costs, material and other costs. A further breakdown of "labor costs" is necessary to separate the compensation of wage earners from that of the supervisory force.

Compensation of wage earners will then be available for comparison with other items in the report, such as total net income from sales, and profits before and after taxes. This would also enable us to determine fairly accurately what the total cost to the company of a proposed wage increase would be. It would also then be possible to estimate the productivity of labor in terms of value created in the particular industry per dollar expended for labor—an estimate fully as important as productivity in terms of volume, as a determining factor as regards wages.

Dividend payments, total compensation of management, and income transferred to surplus are also important items in giving workers' representatives a balanced view of the distribution of the company's income.

In the balance-sheet, we are naturally interested in finding out the working capital position of the company, and the net worth, in order to estimate the rate of return on investment. These facts can, of course, be readily determined from most reports as they are now prepared.

The presentation of explanatory data on the company's various reserves, and their purpose, would help clear up any possible misunderstanding that might arise on that account—as would an explanatory statement regarding the procedure followed in inventory valuation.

Information which can be obtained from financial reports is not the only type of data that union representatives need, in order to eliminate guesswork in contract negotiations. Actual rates being paid for various classifications of work, variations of rates within job classifications, actual annual earnings, and the cost of such items as paid sick leave, and overtime work, would be extremely useful in both developing a spirit of mutual confidence and in ascertaining where particular adjustments are needed.

Why Labor Objects to Present Method of Handling Reserves, Inventory Pricing, Depreciation in Financial Statements. Some extracts from an address presented to several accounting organizations in 1948 by William Gomberg, director, management engineering department, ILGWU

Some months ago the research director of District 50 of the United Mine Workers of America published a rather vitriolic article taking the accounting profession to task for using financial statements to conceal and mislead rather than to disclose and enlighten. He said: "The relevant facts in a labor-management dispute are not shown in corporate financial statements. They are concealed and distorted there."

By way of reply an editorial [in THE JOURNAL OF ACCOUNTANCY] states:

> "Published financial statements of corporations are designed primarily for the information of stockholders. . . . Financial statements prepared for varying purposes may be prepared in different ways. If labor unions define the information they want and *can establish the right to obtain such information* from corporations, there will be no difficulty in preparing statements that will fulfill this purpose."

I shall leave it to your consciences whether or not we are entitled to the facts; that is, all the facts, not the subtle interpretive summaries which are the operating statements. . . . I proceed on the assumption that you agree with me that the affairs of private corporations whose operations determine our basic welfare are public business. . . .

Let us examine some of these accounting conventions and see to what extent basic economic doctrines influence individual accounts.

Let us take the subject of inventories. As any practicing accountant knows, there are a number of ways of listing inventory valuations. During the war, when prices could be expected to increase consistently, the most favored method of treating the inventory account was Lifo. The argument for its use could hardly be that it mini- 193
mized risk since there was no chance of prices falling during the war, but of course it did lead to an immediate deflation of the operating profit and so served as a tax reduction measure. Now that the war is over and inflation continues its dizzy upward spiral, we note a movement for the provision of inventory reserves. Lifo is no longer good enough. Some attempt to standardize inventory practices was made in Accounting Research Bulletin No. 29. . . . Now, Accounting Research Bulletin No. 13 made it one of the maxims of accounting that it is not permissible to create reserves for the purpose of equalizing reported income. Yet recently a movement has appeared to create reserves to safeguard a firm against collapse of its inventory values because it assumes that they are overpriced in the present inflationary period. . . .

Even more interesting than these ingenious public profit reducers is the device of taking depreciation twice. I am referring to those companies which have bought back wartime assets. Some took accelerated depreciation during the war and are now redepreciating the same asset. . . . Let me illustrate what I mean. A war asset cost $1,000,000. Its normal depreciation rate is ten years but for tax purposes the company had been allowed five years, and had held it for four years. The company had fully depreciated the asset and brought it back on the books as follows:

Original cost..........	$1,000,000
Normal depreciation— 40%..............	400,000
Non-deduction tax.....	288,000
38% of $600,000.......	$ 312,000

Thus $312,000 gets depreciated all over again.

Others . . . brought the asset on the books at cost less normal depreciation after having taken advantage of accelerated depreciation. Still others . . . brought the asset on the books at "fair value" and depreciation started all over again. . . .

This whole question of depreciation is a fascinating one. Let us assume that a
194 building is built for $1,000,000 and is capitalized at that value. I am a negotiator for the Building Service Employees Union and settle a wage after collective bargaining in which one of the factors has been the normal depreciation rate of the building. The building is then sold after ten years of depreciation at a $500,000 profit over the original cost. I am called in to negotiate, presented with the new capital figure of $1,500,000 and the same depreciation period. What is my answer supposed to be to the employer who claims he can't afford a wage increase or rent reduction?

Another element in the financial statement that has been a favorite target of the labor movement is the various purposeless contingency reserves that had attained such popularity during the war.

SEC Accounting Series Release No. 42 specifies that the purpose of reserves must be listed. The importance that these reserves had attained during the war can be illustrated by the observation that in the steel industry alone they rose from $103 million at the start of 1940 to $395 million at the start of 1945, an increase of 283 per cent. What is most interesting about the use of these reserves is that they reversed an old abuse that used to characterize financial statements. In the old days, when they were prepared primarily for creditors, "non-recurring items" of cost and expense would be charged to surplus and credits of a similar nature were made to income. Now that financial statements have become collective bargaining tools we find the very reverse of this process. In the first place, contingency postwar reserves were set up out of current income and then charged back at later periods directly to surplus. Thus the reserve never appears as an income item but later shows up in surplus. Not only does it reduce the income item, but artificially deflates the percentage earned on net worth by inflating the capital denominator and deflating the current income numerator. . . .

Thus you can readily see from the nature of the accounts that I have listed why we in the labor movement look upon financial statements not as facts but as implicit interpretations of fact.

A good part of the resentment with which business accountants are greeted in trade union circles is that many are attempting to impose their ideas upon union negotiators in very much the same way that they attempted somewhat earlier to force acceptance of their interpretation of data by the business community. . . .

Quite frankly, I feel that even more important than the operating statement in collective bargaining negotiations is the break-even chart accompanied by detailed scheduled breakdown of the basis for the fixed costs. . . . We want to see this basic document to determine how the organization arrives at wage and price policies. All of us agree that a financial operating statement is not a complete picture of the firm's prospects or past functioning. The break-even chart at least shows us something of the firm's methods of economic thinking. . . .

Industry's Failure To Open Books to Labor Amounts to Criminal Assault upon the Welfare of Our Whole Society, Nat Weinberg, director of UAW-CIO research and engineering department, told the Third Annual Public Affairs Conference at Yale Law School, December 10, 1948

Had the great corporations been forced to open their books [in 1945–46] and to grant whatever wage increases their own data showed to be possible within the limits of the then prevailing prices—and had they been forced thereafter to hold those prices—we would not be faced today with the inflationary madness that causes us to fear for the future stability of our economy.

We thought it significant then that [they] refused to submit for public inspection the data requested by the Union. The course of profits since then has left no doubt as to the reasons for the corporations' reticence. . . .

How high should wages go? We have answered this question by saying we want to see a proper balance established among wages, prices, and profits. By this we mean that wages should be high enough to balance consumption against our potential output of consumer goods leaving enough economic resources for maintenance, modernization, and expansion of our productive equipment at a reasonable and socially desirable rate that can be sustained year in and year out.

This last element, a rate of investment that can be sustained, is of extreme importance. . . .

We also concur with the statement made by Senator Flanders last spring when he told the University of Michigan Alumni that ". . . decisions of important groups of labor and industry as to wages, prices, and profits are no longer private matters. They are public matters and must be determined with the public interest as a major element in the decision." Unlike the Senator, however, we believe it is high time to give all elements of the public, through democratically chosen representatives, a direct voice in making those decisions.

If we recognize that the public interest in wage-price-profit decisions . . . conflicts with the interests of those who now make them, it is not enough merely to admonish the private business groups which control our economic life. We do not rely solely on admonition to prevent burglary or mayhem which, after all, are crimes affecting only individuals. All the less reason for us to do no more than stand on the sidelines and deplore while industry perpetrates acts which, in a very real sense, are criminal assaults upon the welfare of our whole society.

We must seek ways to implement our demand for social responsibility in industry. I would like to suggest again, as our union has suggested before, that we make a beginning by requiring our large corporations to make publicly available certain basic information about their price and production policies. . . .

[There were and are many cases] where a corporation had fixed its prices to break even at something less than 30 per cent of capacity. In our view, the public is entitled to know these facts. The citizens of this nation are entitled to know such facts not only about the past but about the present as well.

Are our giant corporations once again preparing to make profits at the bottom of a depression while they provide only one-fourth as much employment, in terms of man-hours, as they did at the crest of the boom? If so, American citizens must act now to prevent a repetition of the 1932 disaster.

It is obvious that big business has no inclination to provide us with this information of its own free will, crucial though the data are to the general welfare.

The Importance of Cost Finding Information to Labor. Some Excerpts from a statement by Solomon Barkin, research director, Textile Workers of America

First, and most significant, is the suggestion that the basic facts must be available to all for inspection. The growing availability of financial reports is indicative of the recognition of this responsibility. It must be extended. Business is private; but the business conduct affects all. The facts of business must therefore be available.

Second, the procedures, instructions, item groupings, and even forms for presentation of reports should, insofar as is possible, be uniform. Exact and precise uniformity is difficult but it is preferred. Certainly there should be a minimum requirement as to uniformity so as to insure comparability. Each industry might similarly set forth an additional list of uniform items which would become the minimum. The work of the trade associations in this connection is most promising. Current diversity of practice is both suspicious and confounding. It is a prerequisite to an intelligent informed reader group. Complex and incomprehensible statements are useless to the readers.

Third, income statements should disclose a detailed outline of income and costs to arrive at net income. In the operating section of an income report, a full statement should be provided of the income and expenditures of the principal sector of the enterprise excluding incidental ventures, and the cost of borrowed money. One of the main problems in the
196 presentation and understanding of income statements for wage and pricing problems is the fact that the sales figure is not fully co-extensive with the actual expenditures and costs during a fiscal year. The present fiscal report should be supplemented by a cost report which compares expenditures with volume of production for the same period. The discrepancy between a fiscal financial statement and a cost report has been particularly marked during recent years while inventories were being built or unloaded. The present submission serves fiscal purposes, but is inadequate for other purposes. The fiscal report must therefore be supplemented with a cost report.

A fully intelligible accounting must offer the analyst a breakdown of expenditures in considerable detail. One special item to which too little attention has been devoted relates to labor expenditures. Much has still to be done to provide more uniform understandings on the meaning of this term so that discussion is not beset by confusion. We would propose to include in this term: (1) payments for hours worked including overtime and shift premiums and non-productive bonuses in addition to the basic pay; (2) payments for time not worked such as paid holidays, vacations, sick leave, rest and meal periods, travel time, reporting time, free services such as meals, clothing, transportation and; (3) the net cost of insurance and pension, both voluntary and legally required and medical and dental services exclusive of first aid. The labor expenditures should be listed separately for the different categories of workers together with man-hours worked and number of employees.

In this analysis of the annual cost statement, all expenditures should be carefully itemized in significant categories. This distinction between the fiscal and cost accounting reports will give all groups a significant insight into cost structures and pricing policies. Many new assumptions and practices will have to be devised for this type of analysis, but it is vital for clear understanding. One specific advantage is that it will more quickly disclose income windfalls and permit their more careful handling.

We propose that the data also disclose the output in physical units of finished products and work in process during a period. These reports should also note the rate of operations compared to total capacity.

Fourth, the intercorporate relations between officers and directors of a company and other business enterprises must be made known. These may have restricted circulation. It is impossible to comprehend most business statements without full information on this fact. Intercorporate relations affect both sales and purchases and other specific policies of a company. In too many cases individual businesses are only vehicles for artificial costing and the siphoning off of income and the allocation of costs in order to benefit specific ownership or management personnel or to arrange for the diminution of the tax load. The profusion of corporate organizations developed by a single business interest and the juggling of accounts among them of course has inspired many inquiries and much suspicion. During the last few years many officers of businesses have capitalized upon their positions for additional personal income through rebates, concessions, or premiums. Many a member of a board of directors has held on to the job to assure business for his major financial interest. The disclosure of the business relations of the heads of business would improve the opportunities for better understanding of the fiscal and cost reports.

Fifth, all deductions and charges against income for special conditions should be itemized and described. Such charges as reserves for contingencies, revaluation of inventories, losses on foreign investments, taxes, self-insurance, and so forth, should be made against surplus. These items should be labeled so that the statement might be readily understood.

Interest charges should be itemized as to cause and recipient. They are frequently returns to the company's principals and truly represent corporate income.

The present policy of reporting corporate officer salaries and bonuses should be extended. The full report should list pension rights, stock options, life insurance, expense allowances, etc. This information is vital in the case of smaller companies because these incomes truly represent a major portion of the corporation's profits and in large companies because of the tendency to reward management through special rights and allowances, personal expenses rather than through higher salaries. The growing importance of management as against the investor makes careful study and segregation of this account particularly important. The inequities which are developing between the rewards for this group of "employees" as against the bulk of the production and lower salaried workers produces considerable tension.

All items of income and cost which are derived from affiliated organizations and other activities must be identified separately.

Charges to the repairs and maintenance accounts must be clearly identified since many of them are truly capital expenditures. Indicative of the importance of this item is the fact that the United States Department of Commerce reports that "capital expenditures charged to current accounts" amounted to well over $2 billion in 1948. Many charges are now made to current cost which might be legitimately accounted in this manner for tax purposes but which require review for collective bargaining negotiations. In this field are research, experimental, and developmental expenses. Donations and charitable contributions constitute a substantial load carried by business enterprise. Labor has frequently inquired whether this item is an appropriate charge in the accounting for collective bargaining.

We ask for a careful enumeration of bond discounts and finance charges, gains and losses on investments, bad debts, extraordinary income and charges, etc.

All charges and credits which are made directly to surplus accounts should be identified so that the trade union can evaluate the significance of the reported net income.

Finally, we propose that the company's pricing policies and practices be clearly set forth. . . . Prices are no longer blindly fixed by impersonal forces of the market. . . . They are . . . affected by the seller. . . .

In setting forth the costing methods and pricing policies, it would be important for these companies to present their direct variable costs, their assumed level of operations for distributing their overhead costs, break-even points, and the margins they add thereto in determining the final price. This is the normal pricing method in American industry. Reports on this practice would be most instructive in revealing the financial and production policy and course of the individual company.

Those suggestions for the types of financial cost and pricing information outline our views on the needs of the day. With these data more intelligent pricing and production policies will be possible. Labor relations could be truly founded on a secure basis of fact. We are now confronted by the absence of much basic data in many areas. Business has held these data tightly and reluctantly offered bits for public consideration. The great need of the day is for further light. The fate of our entire economy is at stake. American business can do its part by agreeing to offer the factual information derived from its experience in such a manner as to enlighten our government, our people and their own employees and customers. Greater rationality will then be possible in industrial relations and in pricing and production policy discussions.

The Accountant's Part in Labor-Management Relations

by Ernest Dale
Graduate School of Business
Columbia University

Financial information is now recognized as a part of labor-management negotiations;
198 **the question is what shall be told, and how. This author examines the manner in which accounting information has been used in recent labor talks, and projects from this experience some ideas on how to decide what kind of accounting information is necessary, desirable, or reasonable at the bargaining table. He discusses ability to pay, some misconceptions arising out of failure to understand accounting, and makes recommendations as to how accountants can help in the settling of labor disputes.**

THE ACCOUNTANT emerged as a major figure in the wage controversies of the recent steel strike. The briefs and arguments of unions and managements were crammed with accounting data, interpretation, and controversy. Both sides used the best accounting talent at their command in the preparation of the briefs and in the testimony before the Presidential Fact-Finding Board. Both have been using increasingly accounting arguments in presenting their case and whatever one's attitude toward this development it may be helpful to be acquainted with the facts and their implications. Accountants' services will probably be more frequently called upon in the future in connection with the following three major aspects of labor-management relations: (1) preparation for negotiations, (2) actual negotiations, and (3) efforts to obtain public support. In addition, accountants render other services to labor-management relations such as payroll and social security accounting, setting up and administering incentive systems and credit unions, preparation of union financial statements, etc.

1. Preparation for wage negotiations. Companies calculate the effect of wage changes on their financial position—in terms of their cash balance, working capital, the budget, perhaps the break-even point, and probable profits at different wage concessions. Unions may use company financial data to estimate the "ability of the firm to pay." There is, however, an important difference in the procedures: the company usually estimates *future* ability to pay; the union, limited in the available data, tends to figure in terms of *past* ability to pay. For example, prior to the contract between the General Motors Corporation and the United Automobile Workers, CIO, of May 23, 1950, both parties used specialized accounting services and techniques to prepare their case and later to estimate the economic effects of the agreement which itself is partially based on economic criteria.

2. **Actual wage negotiations.** During wage negotiations both employers and unions may use financial data to "prove" inability or ability to pay, respectively,

though it should be noted that accounting data often are not used at all. Employers tend to use the argument when the financial situation is adverse, but tend to hold that it is irrelevant in times of prosperity. And unions usually act just the other way. Since financial circumstances in the past have appeared more often unfavorable than favorable, employers have probably made more use of the ability-to-pay argument than the union. One finds it used in negotiations in printing, coal, motion pictures, railroad, public utility, steel, and automobile industries.

The principle of "ability to pay" is at times applied by arbitrators. While rarely used by itself, wage increases tend to be granted, where ability to pay exists, but are not usually made in accordance with such ability. When inability to pay is claimed, the argument tends to be granted where the whole industry establishes such a claim, but not usually if one company lags behind the rest of the industry.

This last consideration appears to point to an important future application and extension of the use of financial data.[1] The growth of unions is leading to an increasingly widespread application of the "standard rate," i.e., the same rate of pay for large groups of employees. A number of developments appear to be leading to multi-unit or industry-wide bargaining, such as the centralization of control, economic analysis and information in international unions and the headquarters of the CIO and AF of L, the union attempt to eliminate competition among companies over wages, the spread of union authority over broader industrial groups, the growth in the size of companies, the possible development of wage leadership by one or a few concerns in an industry, the seeming "linkage" of wage changes.

The question then arises as to according to *whose* ability to pay the union should fix wages. Some argue it should approximate what the most prosperous firm in the industry or bargaining group could pay,[2] though some unionists say they would rather forego great advances at one plant in order to maintain standards and to avoid elimination of the operation of other members of the bargaining group.

On the other hand, the union does not appear willing to fix the rate according to the capacity of the least efficient firm in the group so that labor subsidizes the "incompetent." The likely result is a compromise in which the wage will be fixed according to the ability to pay of the average or representative firm in the group. The very attempt to find the "average" firm will involve an examination of financial data. And most or all of the firms less able to pay than the average firm are likely to claim inability to pay. This may lead to a discussion of their financial status, possible relief from the standard rate, or union interest in coöperation to aid the company to pay the standard rate.[3] This already is the state of affairs in the men's and women's clothing industries where engineering services may be given to companies whose bankruptcy would seriously upset the life of the communities in which they are

This paper is to some extent based on a forthcoming book on *Sources and Criteria of Wage Determination*, to be published by the American Management Association. In the book are analyzed various economic factors, of which financial information may be one of the elements. The author expresses his grateful thanks to the Minnesota Society of Certified Public Accountants and its officers who gave their encouragement and offered a forum of public discussion to parts of this study in inviting the author to discuss it at the University of Minnesota, Minneapolis, May 12, 1949; to Dr. Carman G. Blough, director of research, American Institute of Accountants; Howard Greenbaum, M.S., CPA, Graduate School of Business, Columbia University; Dr. Ralph C. Jones, Associate Professor of Economics, Yale University; Donald Schapiro, B.A., LI.B., Instructor in Law, Yale University; Robert L. Raimon, M.A. of Cornell University, for reading the manuscript and their suggestions; and to William J. Baade, Jr., associate editor, National Foremen's Institute, Inc., James L. Dohr, M.S., LI.B., Professor of Accounting, Graduate School of Business, Columbia University, as well as to a number of officials in the AF of L and CIO who made available written material on this subject and gave their comments.

[1] I am obliged to Professor Neil W. Chamberlain of the Economics Department, Yale University, for his thinking on this point.

[2] "It is clear that the alleged ability of the 19 steel companies to increase wages is being advanced by the Union as an emotionally appealing argument to win a wage increase in the steel industry, which can then be used as a lever to force all employers, regardless of their profitability, to increase wages." Statement on behalf of Bethlehem Steel Company and Bethlehem Pacific Coast Steel Corporation before the Presidential Steel Board, August 15, 1949, p. 20.

[3] *Labor's Monthly Survey* (AFL), of May–June, 1949, p. 3 counsels: "In the present precarious business situation, wise union policies are of utmost importance in negotiating with your employer. Get the facts on his financial condition and outlook from him if possible . . . your future will be more secure if you help him improve his competitive position." For analysis and examples see Ernest Dale, *Greater Productivity Through Labor-Management Co-operation*, American Management Association, New York, 1949, pp. 65–71, 123–137.

located. These "mature" unions may well set an example for others. Such then are some of the reasons why the use of financial data in collective bargaining negotiations is likely to spread as the practice of multi-unit bargaining spreads.

But it should be noted that the "less-than-average" companies probably will oppose the use of the ability-to-pay argument as well as multi-unit bargaining unless consideration is given to their position. Opposition may also come from small companies who may claim they compete on a different basis from the large ones. Difficulties may arise on the definition of an "industry" from firms making several products and having several unions, from the impact of power and management philosophies. In the light of these considerations, the need for
200
individual treatment was fully and ably argued by many steel companies before the Presidential Steel Industry (Fact-Finding) Board.

3. **Support of one's own side and backing from the public.** Finally, financial data are being used to get support from union members, employees, and the public for a position taken in the bargaining negotiations. Our examination of many union and company documents showed that appeal for public sympathy was the major purpose of financial documentation and analysis. In the increasingly fierce and close battle to enlist vital press and radio support for one's cause, financial data are used. Union members and employees as well as the public are presented with "vulgarized" versions of financial statements. A good illustration is the wage negotiation between the United Automobile Workers, CIO, and the General Motors Corporation in 1945–46. The union used the ability-to-pay argument, present and future profit data, criticism of individual accounting judgments, break-even charts, to get public and membership support for its case. The corporation demonstrated the inadmissibility of the arguments under any circumstances. The union got a certain amount of public support and official statements favoring its position. The GM fact-finding board recommended a wage increase of $19\frac{1}{2}$ cents, or 6 cents above the company's offer, partly on the ground that the company would have a very favorable position.[4] It should be noted that when a company finds it necessary to reduce wages or to refuse a wage increase, the union leaders' position with their membership will be made less difficult and there may be a general gain of employee understanding of the company's position if a demonstration and explanation of "inability to pay" can be given.

Finally, there is a tendency for the size of the bargain to affect increasingly larger units, to cause more serious economic chain reactions with the issues more bitterly fought. Collective bargaining is becoming less private and more public in its impact. Hence there has been increasing governmental intervention in the form of fact-finding boards, some of which, particularly in steel and on the railroads, have taken account of the financial position of the companies involved.

How To Decide What Information To Give

In the quest for financial enlightenment in labor-management relationships certain criteria will help management decide what information is called for.[5] The accountant should analyze the nature of the request for financial data, i.e., whether it appears to be "reasonable," "unreasonable," or a misconception. He should advise management on the propriety and fairness of furnishing these data. He should particularly advise management on the probable inferences which may be drawn from any piece of information furnished. Likewise, he should particularly advise management as to the probable effect of furnishing fragments of information, out of context, in response to specific requests. The dangers of using such fragments are obvious, yet in its efforts to present a fair picture management and its accountants may be accused of failure to coöperate if they decline to furnish isolated bits of information without relation to the whole financial picture.

[4] *Commercial and Financial Chronicle*, January 17, 1946, p. 292.

[5] For source material and bibliography, see end of article.

"Reasonable" requests. The criteria for furnishing financial data are in general related to the "reasonableness" of the requests for information. Among the requests usually considered to be reasonable or "necessary" are those involving information which:

(1) can be obtained anyway in the company's annual report, SEC and proxy statements, investment houses;

(2) aid in advancing the mutual objectives of labor and management or help in reducing or reconciling a difference of objectives;

(3) support the company's desire for an appreciation of its problems or aid labor in the proper exercise of its functions. The interpretation of "reasonable" might be varied with the degree to which "good faith" exists between the two parties, the extent to which actual or potential disagreements arising out of financial information can be settled, and the expense involved in furnishing the data.

(4) Disclosure becomes mandatory when the National Labor Relations Board holds that the information requested of the company was needed by the union (a) "if it was to exercise effectively its legitimate function of representing the employees in contract negotiations and of protecting its proper interest,"[6] or (b) if "(the collection of) that information (by the union individually from each member) must have seemed doubtful and certainly attended with great difficulty and loss of time,"[7] or (c) if "an employer bargaining in good faith would not have withheld the information requested."[8] However, the NLRB has held that "an employer should not be compelled to provide information the furnishing of which would impose an impossible or unreasonable burden";[9] e.g., in case of historical data no longer "relevant" (or available) or if only a small number of employees is involved.[10]

Other examples of information which might be considered reasonable for labor to request, and which accountants could work up and advise management to present might include: Specific wage data—"productive labor," i.e., hours worked and paid for in terms of basic pay, overtime, and shift premiums per hour, week, and year; payments for time not worked for, such as vacations, holidays, rest and meal periods, sick leave, travel time; company contributions, such as pensions and insurance, transportation, meals, clothing. These data might be reported according to the type of work, department, or number of employees. Also labor costs in relation to productivity, labor time contained in various products, 200A
a more detailed and informative account of the "labor narrative" in annual reports (union relationships) might be presented, particular accomplishment by the personnel cited. Reasonable requests for information would also include explanation of accounting and financial terms and their inter-relationships.

The NLRB decided that the employer cannot justify refusal to furnish the union such data as individual merit ratings and increases and wage information relating to it,[11] a list of all employees in the bargaining unit by name, department, and payroll number showing the salary of each employee before and immediately after an across-the-board increase (on July 1, 1948), the present salary of each employee, the performance rating points received in the last rating,[12] list of salaries paid to employees in the unit who are not members of the union,[13] methods used to

---

[6] In re *The B. F. Goodrich Company and United Rubber, Cork, Linoleum and Plastic Workers, Local No. 5* (*CIO*), Case No. 8-CA-209, May 6, 1950, (89 NLRB No. 139).

[7] In re *Aluminum Ore Company and Aluminum Administrative Workers' Union Local No. 20661* (AFL) Case No. C-2026, March 31, 1942 (39 NLRB 1286) enforced in *Aluminum Ore Company v. NLRB* 131 F.(2d)485 (CA 7) in which case the court stated, p. 487: "We do not believe that it was the intent of Congress in the legislation that, in the collective bargaining prescribed, the union, as representative of the employees, should be deprived of the pertinent facts constituting the wage history of its members."

[8] *Aluminum Ore Company, op. cit.*

[9] In re *Yawman & Erbe Manufacturing Company and Office Employees International Union Local No. 34* (AFL). Case No. 3-CA-171, April 28, 1950 (89 NLRB No. 108).

[10] In re *Cincinnati Steel Castings Company and International Union, United Automobile, Aircraft and Agricultural Implement Workers of America, Local No. 647* (*CIO*). Case No. 9-CA-91, October 19, 1949 (86 NLRB No. 83).

[11] In re *General Controls Company and International Association of Machinists, Local Lodge No. 1600*, Case No. 21-CA-256, March 22, 1950 (88 NLRB No. 242).

[12] *The B. F. Goodrich Company, op. cit.*

[13] *Yawman & Erbe Manufacturing Company, op. cit.* Also it should be noted that an NLRB Trial Examiner just recommended that Southern Saddlery Company be required to furnish, in support of its claimed inability to pay, this information: total capitalization, recent dividends, financial statement or statement showing expenditures for "wages, raw materials, salaries of officials, depreciation and overhead," plus other data needed for bargaining. (24, *Labor Relations Reporter*, 319).

calculate individual earnings, pay rates and incentive bonuses, production requirements on government orders.[14]

Union research staffs and union accountants who were interviewed and whose writings were examined included in requests for information they deem reasonable some such items as the following (which should be considered in the light of the above criteria):

1. An explanation of major accounting policies, especially in regard to depreciation, various types of reserves, inventory adjustments, profit calculation.
2. Income and expense accounts "in reasonable detail" covering a period of four or five consecutive years.
3. The relationship between salaries and wages; charges to executive, selling, administrative, and labor expenses.
4. Salaries and bonus payments going to company officers and top managers (these are to some extent available through SEC reports, annual reports, Treasury releases, company and proxy statements regarding the remuneration of directors).
5. Stockholders, a disclosure of which may well show the wide distribution of corporation ownership and is in any case available for inspection.

"Unreasonable" requests. Labor demands for information which may damage the company's competitive position should not be complied with, such as, for example, a breakdown of the "cost of goods sold" into major components, even if merely designed to show the proportion of labor costs to other types of cost, a breakdown of manufacturing accounts showing unit costs of each class of goods manufactured during the years under consideration, and the amount going to labor.

Union requests for information on the income of management may include such detailed requests as the following:

1. A statement of pension rights, life insurance, stock options, expense allowances, etc., of top officials.
2. Rebates, concessions, special privileges by company officers.
3. Relationships of company officials with other concerns.
4. A breakdown of salaries, according to administration, office, production, and selling, and a comparison with the income of factory labor.
5. The spread between the top and bottom salaries and a comparison with the average wage.

Union arguments in favor of such disclosures hold that the management sector in business is becoming increasingly important in comparison to the other parts of the enterprise. Some union men feel that the percentage of total revenue received by higher management should be contrasted with the amount paid to investors, factory labor, and lower-salaried employees. This relationship, they believe, is particularly significant in smaller companies. Here management compensation may serve as a yardstick for union wage demands. Not germane to serious study of the question but as examples of one kind of union thinking, one union local annually varies its wage demand in accordance with the number of weeks which top management spends in Florida; in a printing plant wage demands vary according to the number of hours of work top management puts in daily.

Disclosure of management compensation is objected to on the ground that it is irrelevant, being wholly a management function. There is widespread concern that such information might give a false impression to employees who might not know of the corresponding services rendered to this enterprise by the recipients of salaries. It is feared that disclosure would be the first step toward criticism and later bargaining on managerial compensation, leading to an impairment of corporate efficiency: Thus, in the UAW-GM dispute in 1945 the company said that while the union "declares that occasion might arise where it might be necessary for it to consider whether the company is 'paying the president too much money'—whether the directors 'who

[14] Dixie Manufacturing Company, Inc., and Amalgamated Clothing Workers of America (CIO), Case No. 10-C-1538, September 15, 1948 (79 NLRB No. 87).

aren't doing anything might be getting too much money'—whether 'the engineers ought to be sweeping the shop up instead of designing their products'-to yield to such a demand, would mean the end of free enterprise."[15]

Another type of labor request which may be valuable from an educational point of view, but for which it may be difficult to supply data, concerns the sources of total wage payment; i.e., to what extent are wages paid from accumulated cash, liquidation of current assets (inventories), bank loans, floating of bonds or stocks? Questions are also asked how wage increases are financed—through an increase in prices, spreading of overhead costs over a larger output, greater effort by labor, increased mechanization, better management, "squeez-
202 ing" of other costs, reduced profit margins?

Questions about the source of payments may sometimes be answered by cash receipts and disbursements statements such as those presented by E. M. Voorhees in his statement before the Presidential Steel Board, discussed below. Questions about financing of wage increases may also, to some extent, be answered by comparative income statements.

Misconceptions. One of the most important functions of accountants in labor-management relationships relates to their assistance in clearing up misconceptions. Such errors tend to be particularly frequent in union comments on depreciation, profit calculation and representation, surplus, inventory appraisals, and reserves.[16]

Depreciation of fixed assets: some unions' point of view. A number of union spokesmen feel that the switch of depreciation practices from historical costs or costs of acquisition in times of falling prices to replacement costs in times of rising prices is unnecessary. Their criticism of this procedure is that if prices of fixed assets continue to remain high, increased replacement costs will be paid for by continuing high revenue. If revenue falls, the general price level as well as replacement costs are likely to fall. Why, therefore, should a corporation make now a provision toward something that can be perfectly well provided for at the time of need?

While this criticism reveals a lack of comprehension of depreciation as a *cost* necessarily deducted in determining income, other union critics demand that increased replacement costs be met out of profits. They complain that if replacement costs rise, then additional profits must be retained in the business, it being the function of stockholders to provide capital, not the function of consumers or labor.

Another union criticism is directed against corporation practice of what is described as "having their cake and eating it too." They think there is a contradiction in the effort of corporations to ask for and to introduce high depreciation charges and showing greater profits at the same time. One example cited is that of the U. S. Steel Corporation which is said to have made $2 million more profit in 1948 than in 1947, and simultaneously increased accelerated (not "regular") depreciation from $26 million to $55 million. Commented a union research head: "The

ERNEST DALE is an Assistant Professor of Industrial Relations at the Graduate School of Business, Columbia University, and an Associate Fellow of Jonathan Edwards College, Yale University, where he taught accounting. He holds the degree of M.A. from Cambridge University, England, and M.A. and Ph.D. degrees from Yale University. Mr. Dale worked for three years as a cost accountant and statistician in the paper industry. He is the author of several books on labor management relations and of the monograph *The Preparation of Company Annual Reports.*

[15] Walter Gordon Merritt, "General Motors' Statement Before Fact-Finding Board," Statement presented in Washington, D. C., December 28, 1945.

[16] Owing to a limitation of available space, only some depreciation and surplus misconceptions are discussed in this paper. For a detailed example of a point-by-point refutation of the accounting arguments of labor see Statement of Admiral Ben Moreell, President, Jones & Laughlin Steel Corporation, before the Presidential Steel Board, August, 1949, pp. 16–20; and for a refutation of management see Otis Brubaker, *Statements in Reply to Individual Steel Company Presentations Regarding Economic and Related Arguments, Part II*, August, 1949, pp. 75–80.

more you make, the more you depreciate."

Some unions such as the United Electrical Workers and the Textile Workers Union seem to consider depreciation as an accumulated sum of money which is available for the financing of wage increases. Thus the Textile Workers summarize the total depreciation in the textile industry from 1929–41. Comparing this with the expenditures for new plants, they find an unexpended balance of $108 million. This "fund" is said to have been augmented by wartime depreciation allowances of over $100 million a year which have not yet been offset by like expenditures because of limitations on the production of equipment during the war. Also, the sale of capital assets at "tremendous profits" during the last few years is said to have contributed to "a huge financial backlog" from which to finance new equipment without resort to new income.[17]

Depreciation of fixed assets: management's point of view. In the union criticisms it seems to be overlooked that depreciation is an operating expense which is regularly incurred and not an optional expense. It may be argued that even accelerated depreciation in times of rising replacement costs is inadequate, since it is based on the original cost which may be considerably understated and hopelessly out of date.

The use of replacement cost is defended by management on the ground that corporate profits would be considerably overstated (by one billion dollars in 1947 and again in 1948), if the rising cost of replacing plant and equipment were not taken into account. The cash reserves of many companies have been eliminated and borrowings were required because the necessary replacements of plant had to be made at current high prices.[18] "Corporate understatement in costs of the worth of the tools of production that are consumed in production can mean in the end nothing but hidden and serious erosion of the Nation's tools of production."[19] Specifically, a corporation cannot be sure that its future revenue will be adequate to pay the then prevailing prices of replacement. The desire to show fair profits would seem natural and advantageous to all concerned. In any case, accelerated depreciation would be offset by reduced or no depreciation so that the whole matter would come out all right over the life of the asset and be in addition a valuable counter-cyclical device.

Management's view has been upheld in an important case in which the arbitrator held that "if we are interested in employment and employee incomes, there is no assurance that the available assets accumulated in the past would or should be eaten into in order to maintain employment under currently unprofitable conditions."[20]

Surplus: union comment. The amount contained in the surplus has come under close scrutiny in union comments. "Surplus" like "reserves" are frequently believed to represent a "fund," consisting of cash hoarded up by the company. Some people assume that the company does not know what to do with the surplus, and ask that this "fund" be disbursed as dividends, wages, and taxes, etc.

One union representative who was interviewed pointed out that his company was started with common stock subscriptions of three million dollars. Ten years later "surplus" (the equity of these stockholders) had risen to $75 million. He felt that this increase had been largely contributed by consumers and the company's employees. Should not those parties get a greater share in this equity, he asked?

Others argue that the amount of capital (or surplus) per worker is of no interest to the union when its members have no work, for while the amount of capital in 1932 was the same as in 1929, "capital could not provide jobs"; increasing amounts of capital may displace workers,

[17] *The Nation's Most Prosperous Industry*, Research Department Economic Report, New York, Textile Workers Union of America, January 10, 1948, p. 7.

[18] *Profits*, Report of a Subcommittee of the Joint Committee on the Economic Report on Profits Hearings, U. S. Government Printing Office, Washington, D. C., 1949, p. 48.

[19] Enders M. Voorhees, Profits Hearings, *op. cit.*, p. 54.

[20] Douglass V. Brown, arbitrator in the case of the Textile Workers Union of America, CIO and the Fall River Textile Manufacturers Association, New Bedford Cotton Manufacturers' Association, January 15, 1949, in *Labor Arbitration Reports*, Volume 11, The Bureau of National Affairs, Inc., Washington, D. C., 1949, p. 989.

as in the telephone industry.[21] A part of these difficulties appears to be semantics. Popular usage of such words as "surplus" and "reserves" are different from technical accounting usage. This problem may be overcome in time if the recent recommendations of the American Institute of Accountants to abandon use of these words are made more widely known and followed.

Perhaps also a better understanding of surplus might be reached if accountants were to analyze its sources and uses: (a) Surplus, by source, is really a conglomeration or cross-section of all assets. The composition of earned surplus might be shown in terms of the various assets it represents. Sometimes this might be done by printing the balance-sheet not as total assets on one side equalling total liabilities and
204 capital on the other, but by deducting liabilities from assets and showing that the source of the net assets was money paid in for capital stock, plus retained earnings.

Surplus, by use, may be shown as working capital or as "unappropriated" in order to maintain employment in years of loss. It may be a kind of insurance fund for the protection of the stockholders' capital in the event of declining business and losses.[22]

The Real Opportunity for Accountants

The use of accounting and financial data in labor-management relations is an established fact. It is likely to spread. It raises a number of serious problems, such as the competence of those handling accounting data, the validity of accounting concepts, methods of presenting financial information. Specifically, if accounting is to be more useful in labor-management relations, I suggest that there may need to be improvements in adapting accounting knowledge to the ability to comprehend by those concerned with it. We need more widespread acquaintance in management and labor with basic accounting principles. An increasing number of people will be concerned with accounting data, but will be unable to go through the preparation of a CPA or the equivalent. A basic ability to analyze accounting problems or at least the ability to use the expert accountant's recommendations in policy formation—if this could be developed—would be of inestimable aid.[23]

Even more important are further improvements in the explanation of accounting data. This will require studies of what readers of annual reports want as well as analysis of the type of information which appears to be necessary for an understanding of a company's financial position.[24]

We need further standardization and comparability of accounting data, an even greater emphasis on consistency in accounting policies, and an explanation of accounting judgments designed to reduce many of the present misunderstandings.

Why don't we do more publicizing and explaining of accounting research? The excellent research of the American Institute of Accountants, the American Accounting Association, the Controllership Foundation, the National Association of Cost Accountants, and the pioneer accounting work of other organizations, many universities, and professional individuals might be made more widely known, more widely available, and more easily understandable.

Knowledge of what accounting can do and what it cannot do is essential. This refers to the contributions which accounting can make as well as to the limitations imposed upon it. For instance, an important limitation is that contrary to widespread popular belief accountants are

---

[21] *Economic Outlook*, CIO, May, 1948, pp. 7–8.

[22] But see for a different point of view O. J. Curry, *Utilization of Corporate Profits in Prosperity and Depression*, University of Michigan, Ann Arbor, 1941.

[23] Good examples in this direction are the basic accounting courses at the Columbia and Harvard Graduate Schools of Business, at Yale University, and some other institutions of learning. See also Donald Schapiro and Ralph Wienshienk, *Cases, Materials and Problems on Law and Accounting*, The Foundation Press, Brooklyn, 1949, pp. 1–80, for an excellent summary of double-entry bookkeeping and analysis of financial statements.

[24] An excellent example of what might be done is the 1948 Employee Report of the Marquette Cement Manufacturing Company. This 16-page comic-strip paper entitled "Tom, Dick and Harry—The Marquette Team" illustrates pictorially the income statement in a conversation between a number of employees and a barber-stockholder. The whole report is pitched on a professional, yet interesting level and is accompanied by the actual stockholder report. A poll of the employees revealed a high degree of understanding of the report. For a general analysis of the presentation of accounting data see Ernest Dale, *The Preparation of Company Annual Reports*, American Management Association, New York, 1946.

not at liberty to furnish labor freely with any information it may want. This is a matter for company officials to whom accountants report and it is up to management what information should be given out.

Conclusion: Need for a Factual Approach

A compromise needs to be worked out between management's desire to have labor treat the company's economic problems with understanding—which can usually be done only on the basis of knowledge—and management's fear that such knowledge may be used against itself. Similarly, a compromise needs to be reached between labor's need for data to prepare its case properly and labor's use of the data against the proper interests of the economic unit with which it deals.

In this direction a factual approach in the use of financial data might be developed. Labor and management might meet in a *factual conference* before the actual bargaining negotiations and arrive at an agreement on the facts at issue. This would require the development of criteria, the collection of vital facts and the avoidance of the "double standard."

The factual approach might be aided by the employment of the "*impartial accountant*" (chosen jointly by labor and management) somewhat akin to the impartial umpire. The certified public accountant can play an increasingly important role in labor-management negotiations by aiding the two parties in the collection of data, explaining data, advising and interpreting, informing on accounting practices in comparable situations. If appointed jointly by the two parties, he might act as an intermediary; management might disclose merely to him the financial status of the company and labor might trust his judgment on the firm's ability to pay, where both have agreed on the admissibility of the argument. In this way the dictates of secrecy and competent consideration would both be fulfilled.

Also in the promotion of the factual approach, the use of the *cash statement* may be an important new device in bargaining negotiations. Published financial statements are not easy to understand. However, a summary of cash receipts and cash outgo has an easily grasped resemblance to personal finance. Represented either in terms of the last or the coming year, the cash statement would show total cash receipts (from the sale of goods, interest, and dividends) and cash disbursements (for materials, wages, salaries, rent, taxes, interest, machinery and buildings, dividends). The difference will indicate whether there is cash available for 205
a wage increase. The whole demonstration might be made in terms of one individual employee by dividing total money figures by the total number of employees.

An interesting statement of corporate cash receipts and expenditures was presented to the Presidential Steel (Fact-Finding) Board by Enders M. Voorhees of the U. S. Steel Corporation.[25] (See Exhibit I, somewhat modified by the author for the sake of clarity.)

This statement presents a summary of the cash items from both the income and balance-sheet accounts of U. S. Steel covering three and a half years. The summary of the last column of Exhibit I shows that from 1946 to June 30, 1949, U. S. Steel received in exchange for goods and services sold to customers about $7^1/_3$ billion cash. U. S. Steel paid out $7^1/_2$ billion or $134 million more than it received from its customers and from sales of facilities. This $134 million cash receipts "deficit" was covered to the tune of $118 million by selling government bonds and the rest from a $16 million reduction of cash. The statement shows that all of U. S. Steel's profits since January 1, 1946, have been distributed with an additional disbursement of $134 million so that *past* profits did not exist for diversion to *future* wages.

The union in its reply[26] calls Mr. Voor-

[25] Enders M. Voorhees, *Statement before the Presidential Steel Board*, August 22, 1949, pp. 60-61 and the verification of the cash flows, pp. 64-65. See also Statement by Admiral Ben Moreell, *op. cit.*, pp. 22-23, Table 4, showing funds available from operations and funds spent for plant and equipment and for dividends, 1923-June 30, 1949.

[26] Otis Brubaker, in his *Statements in Reply to Individual Steel Company Presentations Regarding Economic and Related Arguments, Part II*, *op. cit.*, pp. 130-132.

hees' statement "a sober argument . . . (which) deserves an answer." Apart from a criticism that the company did not borrow any money this period, but reduced instead its funded debt, the union argues that for a wage increase merely "a shifting of the balances between a number of factors—prices, wages, profits, and perhaps borrowing" is required; it intimated that the amount of dividends paid to common stockholders alone exceeded the cash deficit shown. On the whole, Mr. Voorhees' cash budget seems to have been illuminating—and undemolished so far.

A more far-reaching method for gauging the effect of wage changes on company financial conditions is the ***break-even chart***. This deserves special attention from accountants, partly because their help is needed to improve this tool, partly because it has been used by some unions to support their claims for wage increases (auto, steel, textiles). The break-

UNITED STATES STEEL CORPORATION

Exhibit I: CASH FLOW--IN AND OUT--JANUARY 1, 1946-JUNE 30, 1949
(In Millions)

206

A Unadjusted Statement of Receipts and Disbursements	Totals	B Adjusting Totals to Cash Basis Explanation	Amount	Adjusted Cash Receipts and Disbursements
Receipts from Customers--The Public	$7,412.3	Add--Proceeds from sales of properties Less--Increase in uncollected receivables	$28.6 74.5	$7,366.3
Disposed of as follows Employment costs U. S. Steel's direct employment	3,174.0	Less-Increase in unpaid employment costs	55.5	3,118.5
Products and services bought Provides employment by suppliers and by their suppliers in turn	2,912.9	Add--Payment of war costs and other items charged reserves Increase in inventories and deferred costs Less--Increase in amounts owed to suppliers	43.7 136.4 52.4	3,040.6
Wear and exhaustion Provides employment by suppliers of new plants and equipment and by their suppliers in turn	405.6	Add--Use of proceeds from sales of properties Other amounts expended Total expenditures for property additions and replacements	28.6 347.4	781.6
Taxes Provides employment by governments and by their suppliers in turn State, local and miscellaneous) Federal income)	469.6	Less--Increase in unpaid taxes	180.6	289.0
Interest Compensation for savings loaned) Dividends) Compensation for savings invested)	257.9	Less--Increase in unpaid dividends Repayment of borrowed money	4.4 16.8	253.5 16.8
Income reinvested	192.3	Less-Used toward increased receivables, inventories and expenditures for property additions and replacements	192.3	---
Total Disbursements	$7,412.3		$ 87.7	$7,500.0

Deficit in cash		$ 133.7
Met from		
Sale of Government Securities	$118.1	
Decrease in cash funds: Balance January 1, 1946 $231.8 Balance June 30, 1949 216.2	15.6	$ 133.7

Exhibit 1:

Cash Flow-In and Out

January 1, 1946–June 30, 1949

BREAK-EVEN CHART SHOWING EFFECT OF WAGE INCREASE

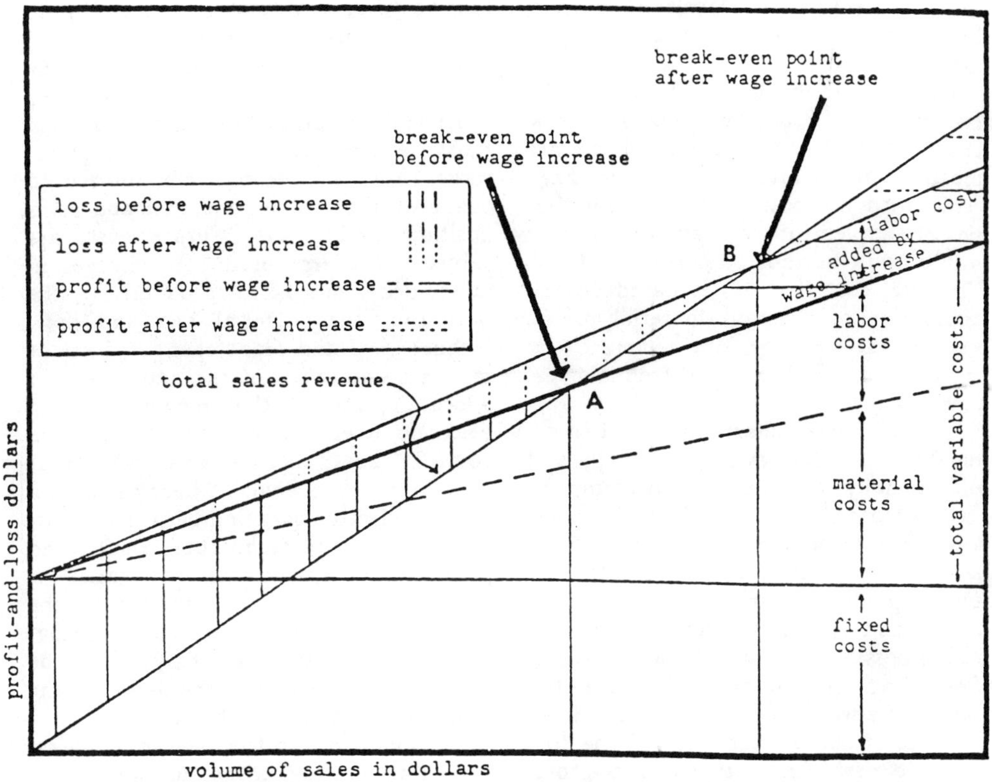

The break-even chart above shows a large number of company income statements, at various levels of sales, and the effect of a wage increase upon them. The inter-relationship of a number of strategic economic factors is shown on this chart more effectively than could be demonstrated by many other methods of presentation and analysis. Also some major implications of economic changes on profitability are immediately apparent, easily understood and remembered. Remedial action is suggested.

In the above chart sales volume in dollars is shown on the horizontal axis, profit and loss on the vertical axis. Total sales volume rises in a straight line from the meeting point of the two axes. Fixed costs are a straight line, variable costs, divided into materials and labor costs, rise with the volume of sales. The meeting point of the total cost line with the total sales revenue is the break-even point (A). The effect of a proposed wage increase is shown by the top diagonal line which represents a percentage of labor costs to be added. The total cost curve is raised consequently and cuts the total sales revenue at a higher point to the right (B). To put this into a formula, if A represents fixed costs, and B are total variable costs (consisting of L or labor costs, and M or material costs), we get:

$$\text{Break-even point} = \frac{A}{1 - B} = \frac{A}{1 - \frac{L + M}{x}}$$

Break-even point after wage increase of 10 per cent $= \dfrac{A}{1 - \frac{1.1\,L + M}{x}}$

The author wishes to express his gratitude to Professor Walter Rautenstrauch of the School of Engineering, Columbia University, and to Robert L. Raimon, for their generous help and discussion of the break-even chart. Professor Rautenstrauch is a pioneer in developing the break-even chart which is fully described in his recently published book *The Economics of Industrial Management* (1949), written jointly with Raymond Villers. Mr. Raimon prepared a lengthy paper on the subject which is to be published at a later date.

even chart shows the profitability of the enterprise at various levels of output, i.e., the areas of profit and loss, roughly as shown in Chart I.

The break-even chart is based on the assumption of constant selling prices, product and distribution mix. Costs are usually divided into variable and fixed costs (with the possible further subdivision of supplementary costs which vary with output, but not proportionately so). The total cost function is based on the assumption of constant material prices, wage rates, size of plant, efficiency of management and labor, and technological changes.

The break-even chart is a useful short-run device for portraying graphically and educationally a whole series of company income statements, as well as the point
208 at which the company makes no profit or loss, i.e., break-even point "A." It may enable prediction and analysis of the future and corrective control. It also makes possible a study of the impact of cost changes on profits; i.e., the initial impact of a wage change might be studied in terms of the upward shift of the cost curve, its new inter-section with the total sales revenue through an upward shift to the left to the new break-even point "B" (i.e., indicating the increase in sales revenue or reduction of other costs required in order to make the same amount of profit). New charts might be drawn to show secondary impacts of the wage change in terms of changing efficiency by labor and/or management, cost composition, and even the plant size. The resulting break-even point can be considered as a kind of "sticking point" below which management will be reluctant to go at any time, and unable to do so for long periods of time.

It should be noted that both the methods of computing the break-even chart and the predictions based on them must be accepted with considerable reserve. Future revenues are subject to changes in total demand, demand composition, and prices. Future costs are subject to alteration due to changes in factor prices and factor productivity, the nature of the material mix and flow, technological and plant changes; account must also be taken of the nature of cost allocation and of the impact of rising prices on inventory costs and depreciation costs. It should also be remembered that once break-even analysis becomes a subject of collective bargaining, then accounting methods and techniques, costing and pricing policies, and the justification of expenditures may be questioned by the union. Nevertheless, it should be recognized that break-even analysis can be made a valuable tool in the quest for the resolution of wage conflicts.

All this points to the need for coöperation of accounting, economics, and statistics to improve the measurement of revenue, the contributions of the different factors of production and the sharing of gains, on the basis of mutually agreed fairness. Some such developments, as suggested might perhaps increase the useful contributions which the accountant is able to make to labor peace and economic progress. The field of industrial relations would benefit particularly from the competence which the accountant could bring to it. END

APPENDIX

Source material for further discussion of accounting in labor-management relations

A. UNION SOURCES AND ATTITUDES

SOLOMON BARKIN, Director of Research, Textile Workers Union of America, "Labor's View of the Financial Statement," Address delivered to the National Association of Cost Accountants' meeting, Albany, New York, February, 1949, mimeographed; extract in THE JOURNAL OF ACCOUNTANCY, May, 1949, pp. 375–377.

OTIS BRUBAKER, Research Director, United Steelworkers of America-CIO, "Labor's Interest in Industry Financial Statements," an address presented before the Michigan Accounting Conference, sponsored by the Michigan Association of Certified Public Accountants and the School of Business Administration of the University of Michigan, October 23, 1948, mimeographed.

R. G. Cranch, former AF of L accountant, *Factors in Wage Determination*, prepared in the Research Department of the AF of L, Washington, D. C., 1939, typewritten.

William Gomberg, Director, Management Engineering, International Ladies' Garment Workers' Union, "A Trade Unionist Looks at Financial Statements," mimeographed address. Reprinted in part in *Labor and Nation*, May-June, 1948, pp. 13–15, 36.

Joseph L. Kirkland, AF of L Accountant, "What Labor Looks for in Corporate Reports," Address to the Second Annual Accounting Institute, The University of Georgia, Athens, Georgia, published in *Georgia Business*, April, 1949, pp. 33–42.

Donald Montgomery, Chief of the Washington Office, UAW-CIO, Statement on Profits for UAW-CIO before the Subcommittee of the Joint Committee on the Economic Report, Washington, D. C., December 17, 1948, mimeographed.

Robert R. Nathan, Oscar Gass and G. Griffith Johnson, *Economic Factors Relating to Wage Negotiations in the Steel Industry for 1947*, United Steelworkers of America, Pittsburgh, Pennsylvania, January 10, 1947.

Walter P. Reuther, President, UAW-CIO, *Purchasing Power for Prosperity*, The Case of the General Motors Workers for Maintaining Take-Home Pay, UAW-CIO, General Motors Department, Detroit, Michigan, October 26, 1945, pp. 55–76.

Elmo Roper, *A Report on What Information People Want About Policies and Financial Conditions of Corporations*, prepared for The Controllership Foundation, Inc., New York, April, 1948, Vol. II, mimeographed, pp. 199–321.

Textile Workers Union of America, "A Guide for Studying Net Income Statements," Research Department, April 10, 1942, mimeographed.

Textile Workers Union of America, *The Nation's Most Prosperous Industry*, Research Department Economic Report, New York, January 10, 1948.

United Electrical, Radio and Machine Workers of America, CIO, *How Corporations Conceal Profits and How to Understand Your Corporation's Financial Report*, New York, 1943.

Nat Weinberg, Director, Research and Engineering Department, UAW-CIO, "A Union Reaction to Corporate Reports," Speech before the Detroit Chapter, Public Relations Society of America, October 27, 1948, mimeographed.

Norman Zolot and John Arcudi, *How to Read Financial Statements*, prepared for the Connecticut Federation of Labor, no date, mimeographed.

Economic Outlook (CIO)

The CIO News

International Association of Machinists, "Tips for the Bargaining Table. How to Read a Financial Statement," *Research Bulletin*, November, 1947, to April, 1948.

American Federationist (AF of L)

American Federation of Labor, "How to Read a Financial Statement," prepared by the Research and Information Service of the AF of L, AFL Research Report, Vol. I, No. 5, May, 209
1948.

Labor's Monthly Survey, "Union Responsibility Based on Information," November, 1948.

American Federation of Labor, *Wage Negotiations*, "Do You Have the Facts?" The Federation, Washington, D. C., no date.

"What Kind of Information Do Labor Unions Want in Financial Statements?" A symposium, The Journal of Accountancy, May, 1949, pp. 368–77.

Robert R. Nathan, *A National Economic Policy for 1949*, Robert R. Nathan Associates, Washington, D. C., 1949.

Robert R. Nathan, *Economic Position of the Steel Industry—1949*, Robert R. Nathan Associates, Washington, D. C., 1949.

A number of the large unions examine several hundred financial statements annually and prepare financial analyses. But there is usually no formal program, but rather a routine service rendered by the international union on request.

United Steelworkers of America

"Fact Sheets Showing the Financial Positions of Individual Companies as Compiled by the Research Department of the United Steelworkers of America," 1949.

"Fact Sheets Showing Most Recent 1949 Data and Comparisons with 1948 Periods," Exhibit 6B to the Steel Industry Board, 1949.

"Statements in Reply to Individual Steel Company Presentations Regarding Economic and Related Arguments, Parts I and II," to the Steel Industry Board, 1949.

"Statement of Philip Murray before the Steel Industry Board," 1949.

B. OTHER SOURCES

ERNEST DALE, *Preparation of Company Annual Reports*, Research Report No. 10, American Management Association, New York, 1946.

R. PARKER EASTWOOD, "The Break-even Chart as a Tool for Managerial Control," American Management Association, *Production Series No. 186*, 1949, and the references quoted therein.

FRED R. FAIRCHILD, *Profits and The Ability to Pay Wages*, The Foundation for Economic Education, Inc., Irvington-on-Hudson, New York, August, 1946.

RALPH C. JONES, "Impact of Inflation on Corporate Reserve Policies," *Financial Management Series No. 93*, American Management Association, 1949, pp. 18–30.

WALTER GORDON MERRITT, "General Motors'
210 Statement Before Fact-Finding Board," Statement presented in Washington, D. C., on December 28, 1945.

NATIONAL ASSOCIATION OF MANUFACTURERS, *Industry's View: "Answer to the CIO's 1948 Wage Case,"* May 6, 1948, mimeographed.

Profits, Report of a Subcommittee of the Joint Committee on the Economic Report on Profits Hearings, U. S. Government Printing Office, Washington, D. C., 1949.

HAROLD H. WEIN, "Wages and Prices—A Case Study," *The Review of Economic Statistics*, 1947, pp. 108–123.

THE JOURNAL OF ACCOUNTANCY (*various articles*)

The Accounting Review (*various articles*)

Also, the following briefs to the Presidential Steel Industry Board of 1949:

Allegheny Ludlum Steel Corporation, H. G. Batcheller, President, August 15, 1949.

American Chain & Cable Company, Inc.

The Babcock and Wilcox Tube Company, Luke E. Sawyer, Executive Vice President, August 17, 1949.

Bethlehem Steel Company and Bethlehem Pacific Coast Steel Corporation, August 15, 1949.

A. M. Byers Company, L. F. Rains, President, August 10, 1949.

Colorado Fuel and Iron Corporation.

Continental Steel Corporation.

Copperweld Steel Company, "Statement of Facts and Supporting Brief on Behalf of Copperweld Steel Company"; "Statement in Rebuttal."

Crucible Steel Company of America, William H. Colvin, Jr., President.

Firth Sterling Steel and Carbide Corporation, August 6, 1949.

Follansbee Steel Corporation, Mark Follansbee, President, "The Case of Follansbee Steel Corporation;" "Statement of Follansbee Steel Corporation in Reply to the Rebuttal Submitted by Mr. Otis Brubaker of the United Steelworkers of America."

Great Lakes Steel Corporation and The Hanna Furnace Corporation, J. J.. Jeffrey, Director of Personnel, August 18, 1949.

Inland Steel Company, Clarence B. Randall, President, August, 1949.

Jones & Laughlin Steel Corporation, Ben Moreell, President.

Lukens Steel Company, Robert W. Wolcott, President, August 15, 1949.

Northwestern Steel and Wire Company, Paul W. Dillon, President, August 30, 1949; Charles A. Farnham, Supt. of Labor Relations, August 18, 1949.

Republic Steel Corporation, W. A. Paton, August 19, 1949; C. M. White, August 19, 1949; H. Tippit, August 19, 1949.

Rotary Electric Steel Company, N. D. Devlin, President, August 11, 1949.

Sharon Steel Corporation.

Superior Steel Corporation, C. I. Collins, President, August 18, 1949.

United States Steel Corporation:

"Productivity in the Steel Producing Subsidiaries of U. S. Steel," R. Conrad Cooper, August 22, 1949.

"Statement Regarding the Emergence of 'Patterns' in the Steel Industry," John A. Stephens, August 30, 1949.

"Statement before the Presidential Steel Board," Enders M. Voorhees, August 22, 1949.

"Statement Regarding Robert R. Nathan's Data in 'Economic Position of the Steel Industry—1949,'" Horace C. Stringfield, August 29, 1949.

"Supplement to Statement Regarding Robert R. Nathan's Data in 'Economic Position of the Steel Industry—1949,'" Horace C. Stringfield, August 31, 1949.

The Youngstown Sheet and Tube Company, Frank Purnell, President, August 19, 1949.

DR. JULES BACKMAN, "Economics of A Fourth Round Wage Increase" (Answer to the Nathan Report), August, 1949.

"Report to the President of the United States on the Labor Dispute in the Basic Steel Industry," by the Steel Industry Board, July 15, 1949 (appointed by the President), Submitted September 10, 1949.

END

The Role of the Accountant in Industrial Relations

by TOM CLIMO, BA (California)
Lecturer in Accounting, University of Kent 211

The author regards *The Corporate Report* as a 'breakthrough' by the profession regarding the provision of information for employees. But in his view the report still has serious shortcomings, and more research is needed.

There is enough legislation around to convince any accountant of the need for him to recognize the importance of the provision of information to employees. Above and beyond the minimum disclosure obligations relating to numbers employed, total wage bill and pension arrangements existing under the Companies Acts 1948 and 1967 and the Finance Act 1970, the Contracts of Employment Act 1963 and the Health and Safety at Work Act 1974 require employers to provide certain information about their work place to present and prospective employees.

Two more recent Acts of Parliament, however, take things further. The Employment Protection Act 1975 places a duty on employers to disclose certain information on redundancy situations and more generally to supply information, lack of which would materially impede the union in collective bargaining and the disclosure of which would be in accordance with good industrial relations. The Industry Act 1975 lays down a number of items on which a Minister may require a manufacturing company to inform recognized independent trade unions.

But even more than these attempts by government to extend the scope of entity reporting, the breakthrough for the accounting profession came with the publication in August 1975 of *The Corporate Report*, a discussion paper prepared by a working party for the Accounting Standards Committee to re-establish the aims of entity reporting. The conventional view this report seeks to replace was expressed by The Institute of Chartered Accountants in England and Wales in 1952 as Recommendation N15. This stated: 'The primary purpose of the annual accounts of a business is to present information to the proprietors, showing how their funds have been utilized and the profits derived from such use'.

Given the conservative nature of this aim, *The Corporate Report* could not have chosen a more contrasting one. Section 3.2 of the report states: 'The fundamental objective of corporate reports is to communicate economic measurements of and information about the resources and performance of the reporting entity useful to those having reasonable rights to such information'.

Not being content to leave the matter here, the report identifies those having a reasonable right to entity information, among which, not surprisingly, are employees. Not content to make this identification, the report even lists the information requirements of employees, and in Appendix 3 gives an example of an employment report the working party would like to see incorporated in current annual accounts.

Six statements

The employment report was only one of six statements considered necessary by the working party in addition to the profit and loss, balance sheet, and source and application of funds statements. The other additional one which concerned employees was the proposed statement of value added, intending to show how the benefits of an entity are shared between employees, providers of capital, the state and reinvestment.

But before we begin an analysis of the value added statement, it may be useful to place the role of the accountant in the context of six areas where information is considered to be of importance for industrial relations. This is done so as to expose accountants to the wider issues of industrial relations, thereby avoiding the popular fallacy of identifying the role of the accountant in industrial relations with the provision of information for wage bargaining.

Accounting information would seem to be useful in the following circumstances:

(1) Reporting on the health and safety of the workplace with an analysis of the relationship (if any) between alternative payment systems and accidents;
(2) Reporting on the effect of productivity bargaining, and the monitoring of profit sharing schemes;
(3) Reporting on planning agreements made between the entity and government commensurate with the aims of the National Enterprise Board and the effect of these agreements on job security;
(4) Reporting on current and alternative distributions of income and the effect these have on the efficient allocation of resources;
(5) Reporting for the needs of worker-controlled enterprises, the so-called industrial democracy set-up;
(6) Reporting for the purposes of negotiating a wage settlement.

There is a problem encountered in each of these circumstances. Information is demanded because a decision needs
212 to be taken. For example, the following six questions can be answered only by having information:

(i) Do we require more safety factors?
(ii) Would measured-day-work be preferable to payment-by-results?
(iii) Will employment numbers remain stable over the next five years?
(iv) What determines the proportion of profit that is paid out as dividends and retained for future growth?
(v) What performance criteria should be set in order to distinguish between environmental change and managerial decision-making?
(vi) Should we settle now at an across-the-board *x* per cent pay increase, or risk the possibility of indeterminable delay by claiming a *y* per cent pay rise?

Union functions

Decisions relating to these matters, however, are not taken directly by the employee group. A representative, who would either be a shop steward or a full-time union official, would be elected whose role would be to make decisions commensurate with the wishes of the group he represents. Therefore, in the provision of useful information, the role of these elected officials must not be ignored. As far as the author can tell, *The Corporate Report* gives no attention to the role of these representatives and as such there is a difficulty in defending their approach against the criticism made at anything the TUC has had to say on information requirements, namely, that it is nothing more than a 'shopping list'. No rigorous attempt is made to co-ordinate decisions which are to be taken with information which is to be provided. Indeed, we have to go back to 1965 and the Donovan Commission for an assessment of the role of shop stewards.

Fortunately, following on from the findings of the Donovan Commission, Messrs David Cooper and Simon Essex, of the University of Manchester, in a forthcoming article have given a very useful summary of the activities of shop stewards, relating their various roles with the decisions to be taken and the types of information such decisions might call for. Table 1 presents their findings.

TABLE I

SUMMARY OF SHOP STEWARDS ROLE, DECISIONS AND INFORMATION NEEDS

Role	*Decisions*	*Information*	
Union duties	Inter-union disputes	Membership of all unions in enterprise	
	Grievances	Grievance procedures in enterprise Grievance records including results	
	Recruitment	Type of member (age, sex) Density of membership in enterprise Current wages and wage structure	
	Subscriptions	Union membership in enterprise Outstanding dues	
Pay bargaining	Amount of claim	Future cash flows of enterprise Current and future performance of enterprise Contribution per employee – current and expected Labour productivity Cost structure of plant	Ability to pay
		Current pay structure – current and expected Value added – current and expected Members' cost of living – current and expected Agreements of similar workers in plant and locality	Minimum acceptable
	Contest claim	Support from other unions Local unemployment levels Demand for product Current stock levels Union density	
Security and satisfaction	Demand extra safety expenditure	Accident and compensation record of enterprise Noise and toxicity levels Safety of new machinery and working methods	
	Management of the enterprise	Liquidity Cash flows Profitability Investment plans Labour and capital ratios Mergers and takeovers proposed	of enterprise in the future
	Contest closures	Job opportunities in locality Age structure	
	Extent of job satisfaction	Extent motivating factors available Absenteeism Changes to work methods and organization planned	

(Source: David Cooper and Simon Essex, 'Accounting Information and Employee Decision Making', submitted to *Accounting, Organizations and Society*.)

The list of information requirements in Table 1 points to four maxims:

(1) Information should be future oriented;
(2) Future information necessitates an indication of the probabilities of various outcomes;
(3) Much information will be non-financial and even non-quantitative;
(4) Much information will relate to the environment of the entity and may not be currently collected by the entity.

It is now interesting to look at the information requirements considered necessary for disclosure to employees by the working party, as we have some kind of standard by which to judge their findings. They say in sections 2.16–2.17 that 'Employees and prospective employees require information in assessing the security and prospects of employment and information for the purpose of collective bargaining. The matters which are likely to be of interest to past, present and prospective employees include the ability of the employer to meet wage demands, management's intentions regarding employment levels, locations, and working conditions, the pay, conditions and terms of employment of various groups of employees and the contribution made by employees in different divisions. In addition, employees are likely to be interested in indications of the position, progress and prospects of the employing enterprise as a whole and about individual establishments and bargaining units'.

Returning to our four maxims, the working party's list seems to concur with each of them. They definitely speak of the prospects of the employing enterprise; they surely would not argue that such prospects must be weighed-up against likely or unlikely counter-prospects; much of the information they list would be non-financial and non-quantitative, and much of it is not at present collected.

But the working party have satisfied the standard with regard to only two of the roles of the shop steward: pay bargaining and security and satisfaction. Union duties are not considered at all. As *The Corporate Report* intended its information to be directed at the employee group in general and not specifically at the shop steward, this may not be as serious as might be thought. Although, once this is said, it would seem that the employees themselves should want to see information under this heading, if, for no other reason, but for monitoring one aspect of the decision-taking of the shop stewards they have elected.

Value added report

More serious than the omission of one important role of the shop steward in their determination of information requirements is the way in which the working party have formulated value added.

It would seem from their disclosed intent to report on entity prospects that value added would relate to the amount of funds considered to be available for payment over some future period. Otherwise, the negotiator will be negotiating a pay settlement under the preposterous assumption that each of the next five years (say) will be like the last one. We would have expected, therefore, to have seen a value added statement that would be based on future estimates of entity performance. After all, the wage is bargained on the prospects of future performance, not the success or otherwise of past performance.

If this is indeed how we would reason, the value added statement proposed in the report is a big disappointment. It is cast unashamedly in historic cost terms: turnover less bought-in materials and services equals value added. This formulation of value added seems to violate at a stroke three of the four maxims which it appeared was conceded in the information requirements for employees listed by the working party.

It may have been thought that the statement of value added was not one which would have an influence on wage bargaining, but such incredible naïveté would be hard to impute to them. It is perhaps more the case that it is one thing to speak of the need for future-oriented information and another explicitly to design a statement of value added which was future-oriented. Even this, however, may be putting the case too strongly. A middle position may be that, knowing how vehemently management would resist making public their expectations, the main purpose of re-drafting the aims of entity reports would be best served by letting the forecasting issue resolve itself elsewhere, eg, in the proposed planning agreements to be made between entity managers and the National Enterprise Board.

Whatever the reasons, it is suggested that value added be included with the other five areas in need of research according to Appendix 6 of *The Corporate Report*, as it is unsatisfactory in the state proposed by the working party.

This article began with a brief résumé of some existing legislation relating to the provision of information to employees. The Employment Protection Act 1975 seemed to be the one with the most potential applicability, if only either or both material impediment and good industrial 213
relations could be defined. The responsibility for their definition fell on the Advisory Conciliation and Arbitration Service (ACAS), and in July of this year they published a draft code of practice, *Disclosure of Information to Trade Unions for Collective Bargaining*, which was to be a guide to both employers and employees. Although space does not permit a full critique, we consider briefly the conclusion of the ACAS document.

Section 5.3 of the ACAS document concludes that 'Trade unions should identify in advance of negotiations, as far as practicable, the information they require for collective bargaining'. The question ACAS fail to consider is whether trade unions know how to determine what information they require. As no research appears to have been made by ACAS as to either the ability of employees' representatives to understand entity financial and productive data, or the existence and appropriateness of decision models for different types of decisions, the degree to which their conclusion provides any guidelines is debatable.

Providing information

The role of the accountant in industrial relations does not shift radically from his role as a provider of entity information useful for decisions to be made concerning the progress of an entity. The entity remains the same, the objectives, decisions and user group become different. The accountant's responsibility is to supply available entity data which is relevant for the types of decisions to be taken for employees.

He has a responsibility to surmount any ideological prejudices and offer assistance in the determination and re-design of entity data collection so that relevant data may be given to the employees' representative in the form of useful information. Not only would it be against the law to do otherwise; it would be an extreme discredit to a profession whose role is to provide useful entity information to those having a reasonable right to this information.

Accounting, Organizations and Society, Vol. 2, No. 3, pp. 201–217. Pergamon Press, 1977. Printed in Great Britain.

ACCOUNTING INFORMATION AND EMPLOYEE DECISION MAKING*

DAVID COOPER

and

SIMON ESSEX

Department of Accounting and Business Finance,
University of Manchester

Abstract

214 This paper argues that policies or recommendations regarding the provision of information for employee decision making can only be fruitfully developed within the framework of models of employee decision making. Descriptive model building, incorporating a model of the decision maker, his objectives, and the environment in which he operates, is essential for the provision of information to help employees improve their welfare. The paper develops alternative models and concludes by presenting, as a guide to future research, some tentative evidence about the decision making of one group of employee representatives in plant level negotiation in the U.K.

The purpose of this paper is to consider the information needs of one potential set of users of accounting information, namely employees. We intend to add to the limited amount of research that has considered the information needs of employees and unions and thereby aid in the development of "external reporting models which satisfy not only the needs of investors and creditors but also employees, represented by their labour unions" (Horwitz & Shabahang, 1971, p. 224). There has been a growing realisation over the last few years that published accounts might be used by different sorts of people, having differing objectives.

We are concerned with information for employees because we believe that organisations should be accountable not only to providers of finance but also (at the very least) to those who work in them (Medawar, 1976). Employees, unlike shareholders, have little opportunity to diversify the risks associated with their relationship with an organisation. Further, we perceive current developments in the U.K. that tend to emphasise the "rights" of employees to information both about the enterprise in which they work and about the corporate sector in general.[1]

In Belgium, the Netherlands, Denmark, Norway and Sweden there exist detailed legal requirements about the provision of information in order to facilitate effective employee participation in decision making. In the United States the case decisions of the National Labour Relations Board which have attempted to clarify the legal obligation to "bargain in good faith" are influential in extending the provision of information to employees. Similarly, the International Labour Organisation in its Recommendation 129 suggests wide-ranging information disclosure to employees: "the information should . . . include all matters of interest to workers relating to the

*We would like to thank John Arnold, Tom Climo, Tony Hope, Mike Sherer, Tony Tinker and the anonymous referees for helpful comments on earlier drafts of this paper. Responsibility for any remaining errors and the opinions expressed, rests, however, with the authors.

[1] Examples of legislation in the U.K. that extend the disclosure requirements of the Companies Acts are the Industrial Relations Act (1971), Health and Safety at Work Act (1974), Employment Protection Act (1975), and the Industry Act (1975). The Bullock Committee Report on Industrial Democracy (1977) extends the notion of accountability.

operation and future prospects of the undertaking and to the present and future situation of the workers" (I.L.O., 1974, section 15). Details of current practice relating to company communication and information provision are summarised by Smith (1975).

If accounting is concerned with the provision of information useful for decision making, then the accounting profession will be required to satisfy the informational needs of employees. Accounting does not develop in isolation from society. Similarly the provision of information for employees will be influenced by the legal and quasi-legal developments in a particular society. Accountants should be concerned with the provision of information to facilitate effective or desirable decisions; decisions that enable the decision makers (individual or organisation) to survive and prosper in its environment. The provision of information to employees is thus a particular example of the provision of useful information for decision making purposes. The "conventional" exhortations about accounting information would therefore seem to be applicable. Information must be decision relevant; the information should influence actions and improve the behaviour and performance of employees and their unions. When data is unintelligible, out-of-date or unassociated with the problem at hand, then it cannot be regarded as valuable information. It is inevitable, therefore, that a consideration of information requirements will involve consideration of the decisions and problems for which the information is intended to be used. Accountants need not only to use models developed by other disciplines, but also need to be able to evaluate and develop these models. Given the lack of well developed and substantial models of employee decision making, decision making as well as information provision will be central concerns of this paper.

In the section that follows we will examine the criteria for choice of information and explain our preference for the decision orientated approach to employee information needs. Thereafter we survey briefly some of the deductive models of employee decision making and the associated information requirements. For our purposes, these models are limited because of their divorce from reality and we thus consider, in the next section, the role of trade unions in society and the information that they would require to fulfil that role. Subsequently we develop an *a priori* decision model of shop stewards and present some tentative evidence as to the decisions made and information used by that particular set of employee representatives. Finally, we summarise our conclusions and indicate possible future research strategies.

DECISION ORIENTATED APPROACH TO EMPLOYEE INFORMATION NEEDS

It is well established that data, if they are to be of value, must be relevant (for example, Marshak, 1959; Felltham, 1968). There are, however, at least two interpretations of the concept of relevance. The "consumer sovereignty" approach to the provision of information is concerned with servicing the desires or wants of the decision maker. It involves asking the consumer, in this case, employees or their representatives, what information he would find useful. The resulting shopping list is compared with the information currently provided and with the information lists provided by other "relevant" bodies. Political bargaining or lobbying results in some consensus about disclosure.

The result of such negotiations is marginal adjustment to the *status quo*. User demands for information will be based on perceptions of the sorts of information systems that are currently available. For example, studies that test the association between decision outputs (e.g. levels of wage) and decision inputs (e.g. accounting data) provide limited guidance about choice of information as they are constrained by the current environment of the decision taker (Horwitz & Shabahang, 1971). For example, a union official may want historic cost based information to help him formulate his claim. His demand is more likely to be based on the perception that historic cost information can be provided than on a belief that such information will be helpful to him in satisfying his need to formulate a claim advantageous to his members.

The second, and preferred, approach to the information choice problem may be called the decision orientated approach (Sterling, 1972). Information should be provided that is required as input to the decision model which enables a decision maker to satisfy his goals and result in an improvement in his welfare. The decision orientated approach suggests that we need to consider the decisions that employees or their *representatives should take* in order to satisfy their *objectives*. The three emphases in the previous sentence are worthy of further consideration.

Employees have tended for social, political and economic reasons to form unions to bargain over the nature of, and rewards for, their work (Webb & Webb, 1920; Wootton, 1955). Unions are a collectivity whose purpose is to promote the welfare of the members of that organisation; a function that can best be achieved by combination and concerted, unified action. Most employees delegate their decision making associated with bargaining to the union organisation. The nature of that organisation inevitably varies considerably between unions and between countries. We might generalise, however, to suggest that national decision making is dealt with by the national union officer and the national union organisation
216 and regional, local and firm agreements involve union branch secretaries. A shop steward tends to be involved in firm and plant agreements as he is "a local union representative who has definite responsibility for the first stage of local negotiations, but is neither a full time officer nor a branch secretary with recognised negotiating rights in that capacity" (Clegg *et al.*, 1961, p. 180). In assessing the information that will be relevant to employee representatives we must therefore specify the particular representatives concerned. Further, the decision orientated approach to the provision of information suggests the need to consider the decisions that the identified representatives should take. The objectives of the decision maker are clearly relevant to this normative approach to decision making.

Since we are concerned with employees, their objectives and the objectives of their representatives it is necessary to consider the congruence between the objectives of employees and those of the union and its officials (including shop stewards). Clearly, an assumption of goal consensus would be a naïve one. Many union officials are concerned with maintaining and enhancing their careers within the labour movement. Nevertheless we consider that union officials are likely to act in the interests of their members. There may be occasions for disagreement about the appropriate means to achieve their members' best interests and some officials may be disproportionately concerned with their own sectional interests. Nevertheless the relationship between an official and his constituents frequently rests on a voting nexus, not a cash one. In situations where there is a longstanding disagreement about objectives, then either the membership leaves the union (and joins an alternative union) or the union officials leave the membership (and are replaced by officials who are more representative of the members' wishes).

The objectives of any individual or organisation involves both intention (as indicated for example, by official statements) and a commitment to satisfy that intention (as evidenced, for example, by an allocation of resources). Accordingly, we must look beyond official statements of objectives to the allocation of resources within unions. Indeed use of the decision orientated approach requires some consideration of what the allocations "should be". Considerations of "should be" necessitates an understanding of the role and functions of unions in our society and in changing that society.

Consider the likely elements of an employee's utility function. We might suggest that economic rewards, job security and job satisfaction represent important elements of employee utility. Without evidence about the outcomes that employees regard as desirable, this list of components of a utility function may only be regarded as tentative. We suggest as an initial hypothesis that union officials therefore aim to achieve either increased pay or job security (including long term tenure of the job and safety) or job satisfaction (which may include satisfactory working conditions, relationships with peers and superiors as well as opportunities for achievement, recognition and self-fulfilment), or some combination of these elements.

However tentative the objective function that we derive, two issues are clear. Firstly employee objectives cannot be "boiled down" to a notion of maximisation of wages. "Labour is more than a commodity because it cannot be isolated from the life of the labourer" (Flanders, 1968). The work situation cannot be isolated from the general life of the employee and thus social relations cannot be ignored in the specification of employee objectives. Unions and their officials have broad organisational, political, and social objectives as well as a concern to improve the economic security and status of their members (for example, see Trade Union Congress, 1966, paragraphs 97-98).

The second point is that the satisfaction of employee objectives may be most profitably pursued in terms of changing the economic, social and political *status quo*. Changes in the balance of power between classes in a society or indeed changes to the organisation of a society might be legitimate union activities. Employee representatives, in order to improve the welfare of their members, may be concerned with wage levels, job security, working conditions, industrial and community health, industrial democracy, national income and the quality of life. These "political" issues are not avoided by refusing to explicitly consider them; such a failure provides tacit approval for the existing role of unions and their officials. Unlike the consumer sovereignty approach to the provision of information, the decision orientated approach focuses on satisfying the needs of the users rather than servicing the users' demands. The approach does require, however, careful consideration of the needs and the objectives of the decision maker.

These objectives cannot be pursued independently of other groups in society: suppliers, customers, providers of finance and creators of the infra-structure for the nation are all relevant. Employee representatives cannot in the long run pursue policies that completely alienate customers or investors or any other group associated with an organisation; the organisation will cease to exist. This interdependence requires that models of employee decision making must take account of bargaining behaviour. The decision orientated approach necessitates the identification of decision models that relate action on behalf of the decision maker to his objectives.

DEDUCTIVE MODELS OF EMPLOYEE DECISION MAKING AND THE ROLE OF INFORMATION THEREIN

Accounting – and industrial relations – have tended to look to economics for decision models relevant to its concerns. Increasingly, however, the limitations of most simple economic models have become apparent in industrial relations – and to a lesser extent in accounting. A model is a representation of the world (or an aspect of it) and many economic models represent the world as being capable of accurate and complete representation. Classical economic analysis is frequently based on a decision model that states that choices (or actions) are made by individuals so as to maximise their subjective expected utility (SEU). Such an analysis involves the identification of all possible sources of action, assigning a value (or utility) to each possible outcome associated with an action and assessing the probability of such outcomes occurring. The action with the highest expected utility is then chosen.

Consider the simple (and inevitably simple minded) example of how a union negotiator might formulate a claim, as summarised in Table 1. The negotiator, in order to determine a pay claim may identify three possible courses of action: to demand a pay rise of £8 per week, a pay rise of £6 per week or a pay rise of £4 per week. These are seen as the only possibilities; a rise of below £4 is totally unacceptable to his members, a rise of above £8 is totally unacceptable to the employer,[2]

TABLE 1. A simple example of a claim decision using the S.E.U. framework

Actions (demand)	Outcomes (agreed)	Associated utility*	Probability	Expectations
£8	£8	10	0.2	2
	£6	8	0.5	4
	£4	5	0.3	1.5
				7.5
£6	£6	9	0.6	5.4
	£4	6	0.4	2.4
				7.8
£4	£4	7	1	7.0

* Measured in units of utility.

[2] These levels may be interpreted as indicating the settlement or bargaining range (Walton & McKersie, 1965; Warr, 1973).

and for ease of calculation there is only one discrete point between these two levels.[3] Associated with each of these courses of action, he may identify possible outcomes – for example the pay claim could be accepted, or reduced to a lower level. To each of these outcomes he could attach a utility. Notice that there need not be a linear relationship between utilities and monetary values and that utility is likely to be higher, for example, when a £6 demand is agreed than when £6 is agreed after £8 had been demanded. Similarly the union official could assess the likelihood of each of these outcomes. On the assumptions made, the official would demand a pay rise of £6 per week, producing an expected utility of 7.8 units.

There are basically two functions for information in this basic S.E.U. model. First a decision maker requires information to construct the model
218 – to identify the outcomes and assess their associated utilities and probabilities. In our example, the union official would value information relating to the possible outcomes and their likelihood of occurrence. This information is likely to include details of the enterprise's ability to pay and the attitudes of his membership.

The second function of information in the S.E.U. model is to provide feedback to the decision maker in order that he may revise his model. In our example, the results of recent decisions could be combined (e.g. using Bayes theorem) with the original model specification in order to produce a more accurate model. More details, and elegant, consideration of the role of information in the S.E.U. model is contained in Demski (1972) and Feltham (1973).

This type of deductive analysis can be made more sophisticated and perhaps more relevant by introducing the bargaining aspect of decision making. Game theory is concerned with decision situations where results are dependent on the inter-actions of two or more "players". Thus far, however, decision theorists have concentrated on analysing situations when the game is concerned to divide, by co-operative means, a fixed sum. The theory of games is largely undeveloped in the area of non-constant sum, non co-operative games (for example, see Coddington, 1968).

Yet employee decision making is not likely to occur in co-operative situations where the bargaining is about the share of the cake. The size of the sum to be distributed will be a decision variable; the size of the cake will be influenced by the bargain struck.

The recognition of a bargaining and inter-active aspect of decision making does, however, introduce a third role for information. In the non-co-operative, non-constant sum case it will often pay a player to publicise his plans. Information may be used as part of the bargaining process in order, for example, to influence other players' perceptions of the payoffs (Schelling, 1960). The threat of a strike is intended to influence the employer's payoff expectations. Information may also be used to reduce the non-co-operative nature of the situation. The announcement of a decline in demand for a product or a cash crisis in a company may encourage co-operative bargaining behaviour.

The relative sophistication of game theory and the formal elegance of the S.E.U. model cannot hide at least four difficulties of this approach.[4] The measurement of utility is crucial to these types of analyses. It seems inappropriate to regard monetary values as adequate surrogates for the political, sociological and psychological dimensions of employees' utilities. Despite the efforts of decision theorists, there is still no operational single measure of utility (see, for example, Hull *et al.*, 1973).

The second difficulty with our normative approach is that the union official is a representative of his members and will be required to satisfy a variety of possibly inconsistent desires. Theories of choice by collectivities have been relatively unfruitful as yet. Morris (1974) and Cohen *et al.* (1972) indicate the diversity of approaches. Somehow, however, the union official will have to synthesise individual desires into a practical bargaining strategy.

The third difficulty which we consider is associated with the time taken to make decisions. The dynamics of the decision making process means that the probabilities of the identified outcomes, the utility associated with each outcome and the range of alternative actions will be constantly changing. Models that recognise the time dimension of the decision making process

---

[3] This is merely a simplifying assumption; the analysis would be unchanged (but far more complex mathematically) if the set of outcomes were continuous.

[4] For a comprehensive survey of these deductive approaches to bargaining theory see Foley & Maunders (1977), especially Chapter 4.

are essential.

Finally, models of decision making based on the maximisation of subjective utility seem to lack predictive ability when complex choices are involved. A great deal of evidence in psychology suggests that due to cognitive limitations, man cannot behave in the way suggested by statistical decision theory (Tversky & Kahnemann, 1974). In particular man is a conservative processor of information, anchoring his decisions on past evidence and adjusting only marginally when new information is presented (Slovic, 1972). Organisations also have limited information processing capacity (Williamson, 1967; Galbraith, 1973).

DESCRIPTIVE MODELS OF EMPLOYEE DECISION MAKING

The deductive models of decision making represent decision makers as sophisticated statisticians and their environment as exceedingly simple, capable of being completely and accurately represented and predicted. Since we are ultimately interested in the provision of information to employees and their representatives we are concerned with practical, real world phenomena. To make useful prescriptions for information provision we are therefore concerned to accurately describe the real world and how decisions are actually taken. We therefore concentrate on a descriptive model of decision making, based on the idea that individuals and organisations are intentionally rational but limited by the complexity of the environment in which they operate (Simon, 1957). This idea of bounded rationality, which derives from experiments to determine how man actually makes decisions, tends to emphasise the difficulties of specifying the attributes in the detail required by the S.E.U. model. Thus a descriptive model tends to concentrate on "a description of the choice process that recognises that alternatives are not given but must be sought; and a description that takes into account the arduous task of determining what consequences will follow on each alternative" (Simon, 1959). Observation of how decisions are actually made suggests that a decision maker will attempt to achieve a satisfactory outcome through the use of simple decision rules, "rules of thumb" that enable a decision maker to cope with the complexity of his environment.

Models of decision making based on bounded rationality involve the following observations. A "problem" requiring solution does not appear from nowhere: the nature of problem recognition needs careful consideration in any theory of decision making (Pounds, 1969). Solutions to a problem are often inherent in the way the problem is identified. A union official's recognition, for example, that the union members need more money, implies the "solution" of obtaining more money. Re-phrasing the problem as one of a declining standard of living opens up the solutions of price controls, tax adjustments and a general enquiry into the causes of the decline (and hence an enquiry into the issue of who benefits from decisions taken in the "national interest").

Search for solutions and identification of the consequences that might result from any solution is normally severely limited. Decision making does not involve a ranking of all alternatives. Alternatives have to be found and generally the first alternative action that seems to be satisfactory will be carried out. The search for a satisfactory alternative will be based on experience of past decision making. Learning is crucial in an environment that is rapidly changing – the past, in such circumstances, is not a good predictor of the future. Adaptive decision models (and information necessary for these models) are required in rapidly changing conditions.

Although generalised models of decision making in organisations have been developed (e.g. Ference, 1970) decision models specific to employees and their representatives do not seem to be well developed. It is not clear whether the environment within which they make decisions is rapidly or slowly changing. To resolve these sorts of problems will require research into decision making by employees and their representatives. There is an urgent need, if accountants are to provide relevant information, to investigate models of bounded rationality in a complex and changing environment than have as their purpose, the improvement of the welfare of workers.

For ease of exposition we may distinguish three levels or inter-connected systems in which union officials are involved in decision making designed to result in outcomes that will affect the welfare of employees. The three systems – national, industrial and plant – are clearly inter-dependent. Their relative importance in a society will depend on historical and institutional features of that society.

In most Western societies, unions negotiate with the government and representatives of other national bodies about national economic and social performance. National economic policy will affect the size of the real national income and the manner in which the national production will be distributed. These policies will inevitably have material consequence for the employees and the unions will need to negotiate in terms of improvements to the welfare of their membership. National social policy will affect the quality of life in the society; the relationship between man and man. Educational, medical welfare and cultural policies will affect the welfare of employees and their families. Union officials, like all the other parties to negotiations on national policies need models of the economy and society that enable them to predict the consequences for the satisfaction of their objectives, of alternative strategies that they may pursue.

220 Full time union representatives are frequently concerned about national agreements. For example in the U.K. negotiations between union officials and those of the particular industry's employer federation will normally be concerned with basic wage rates, bonuses and overtime rates (Parker, 1974). In industries that have one major employer or union, the negotiation will frequently include detailed negotiation about changes in the industry's structure. Again, in such negotiations, union officials require some understanding of the likely effects of their demands. The impact of changes, for example, in technology and in industrial structure need to be considered by local union officials. Such a consideration necessitates the use of a model, explicitly or implicitly.

Unions are involved with plant level negotiations as well as national and industry negotiations. In the U.K., the Donovan Commission (1968) drew widespread attention to the fact that a great deal of industrial relations was conducted at the plant level. Plant managers and shop stewards bargain not only over basic pay but also over health and safety issues and general working conditions (Parker, 1974). Decision making by shop stewards requires a decision model that encompasses safety at work, real opportunities for job satisfaction, evaluations of potential closures and, in general, concern with the overall management of the plant. The conflict with plant managers inherent in these negotiations emphasises the potentially non co-operative nature of union negotiations.

Before accountants can begin to provide relevant information for the negotiations in which union officials are likely to be involved, it is essential that predictive models are developed and communicated to unions. In that way, officials can understand and foresee the possible consequences of their actions. The difficulties of developing such models may be reduced by their recursive nature: Beer's experiences in Chile (1975, especially pp. 423–452) indicate the feasibility of developing models of the economy and the sub-systems which it comprises. The provision of information cannot be determined in isolation from the development and utilisation of models relevant to the decision making of union officials. And, as Wilensky has argued (1967, p. 123) the separation of information provision from its use and interpretation will attract providers of information who are "either crude empiricists or conformists content to 'backstop' the preconceptions of policy makers".

INFORMATION FOR THE DECISION MAKING OF SHOP STEWARDS

In the previous section we have emphasised the need to observe the decision making of employee representatives and to develop decision models appropriate for the objectives and situation of the decision maker. The necessary information can then be provided. Observation in the real world requires, however, an initial idea of what variables are "of interest". This initial idea serves to guide observation.

In this section we indicate how such a set of guidelines was developed for one type of employee representative, the shop steward. The approach outlined here should be regarded as a prior stage rather than an alternative to the decision orientated approach and the development of decision models relevant to employees.

We concentrate on U.K. shop stewards largely because of their increasing power and influence as negotiators in Britain (Donovan, 1968). By selecting shop stewards as the subjects of our study we are concentrating on those employee representatives whose role entails decision making in the context of workplace bargaining and whose power is based on the support of their workmates (Goodman & Whittingham, 1973). A survey of the industrial relations literature[5] suggests three

[5]For example, Goodman & Whittingham (1973); Clegg *et al.* (1961); McCarthy (1972); Parker (1974); Nicholson (1976); Warren (1971).

general functions for the shop steward. From the identification of these functions we may deduce various decisions that the shop steward will make. From these deduced decisions, and the assumption that shop stewards are concerned to improve the welfare of the employees they represent, we derive a model of shop steward decision making. We then identify the type of information inputs specified by the model. Finally, through a survey of shop stewards in the U.K. engineering industry we provide some evidence about the validity of our conclusions.

The role of the shop steward and his information requirements

We shall consider the role of the shop steward in terms of the functions or jobs he is expected or expects to fulfil (Katz & Kahn, 1966). For each of the functions identified, we indicate the decisions likely to be taken and the information required to make these decisions. Table 2 summarises the activities of shop stewards and indicates the type of information such decisions might call for.[6] This table should not be regarded as an all embracing statement of roles, decisions to be made or information required. It attempts to indicate, *a priori*, the items of information that are likely to be of importance to a shop steward. Many of these items will be used for a number of decisions and could be valuable to shop stewards. Yet, other items of information may have little value and act, at best, as confirmatory messages, and at worst, as "noise". In other words, the costs of information production and usage have been ignored in the table.

Traditionally shop stewards have been regarded as union administrators, acting as a communication channel between the union and management. The decisions associated with this role involve inter-union disputes, recruitment drives and methods of handling individual grievances. The information necessary to perform such tasks and make these decisions relates to details of union (and non-union) membership; statistics summarising the membership in terms of numbers, density, category of worker and relative position compared with other unions in a large multi-union plant or firm.

A key area of shop steward activity is pay negotiations. The flexibility of national agreements has enabled an increasing number of topics to be brought within the legitimate scope of workplace bargaining – legitimate, since it was impossible for them to be settled elsewhere. These topics included incentive payments, special payment for dirty or dangerous work, merit allowances and grading for particular skills, job evaluation, overtime, clothing allowances and so on. Thus, areas which had previously been management prerogatives have come within the ambit of joint regulation. In the formulation and negotiation of a pay claim, a steward may have to decide the amount of the claim. This amount will be influenced by the amount that the firm could afford, the minimum that his members would accept, the strength of the workers' case if opposition is met, the appropriateness of incentive payments offered by management, and relative difficulty (or danger, or dirtiness) of different jobs and the bonus which a particular job merits and 221
the time it should take. A steward would also decide on the method of presenting, and extent to which he should press, the claim.

To assist his decisions, the shop steward would require information relating to the organisation's ability to pay the claim and information related to the sum that is minimally acceptable to his constituents. Ability to pay refers to the enterprise's future capacity to pay a certain level of wages and remain viable. Information relating to the future is therefore relevant. For the workplace bargaining that a shop steward is likely to be involved in, the relevant enterprise will be the plant. Information of a disaggregated nature, relating to the cost and revenue structure of the specific plant, will be relevant. Ability to pay may be regarded as the future cash flows of "the enterprise" less those sums necessary to maintain the enterprise's operating capacity. Maunders (1977) provides further discussion of alternative measures of ability to pay. "The enterprise" will be the plant to the extent that the managers of the plant are autonomous to negotiate wages.

The sum that is minimally acceptable to a shop steward's constituents is likely to depend on the employees' expectations regarding their future contribution to the "value added" of the plant, their expectations about rates of general price inflation and their expectations about their position relative to other workers in the locality and in similar plants elsewhere. Value added has

[6] See Essex (1975) for further details of the role of shop stewards.

TABLE 2. Summary of shop stewards role, decision models and information needs

Role	Decisions	Information	
Union duties	Inter-union disputes	Membership of all unions in enterprise	
	Grievances	Grievance procedures in enterprise	
		Grievance records including results	
	Recruitment	Type of member (age, sex)	
		Density of membership in enterprise	
		Current wage and wage structure	
	Subscriptions	Union membership in enterprise	
		Outstanding dues	
Pay bargaining	Amount of claim	Future cash flows of enterprise	Ability to pay
		Current and future performance of enterprise	
		Contribution per employee – current and expected	
		Labour productivity	
		Cost structure of plant	
		Current pay structure – current and expected	Minimum acceptable
		Value added – current and expected	
		Members' cost of living – current and expected	
		Changes in nature of job – current and expected	
		Agreements of similar workers in plant and locality	
	Contest claim	Support from other unions	
		Local unemployment levels	
		Demand for product	
		Current stock levels	
		Union density	
Management of the enterprise	Demand extra safety expenditure	Accident and compensation record of enterprise	
		Noise and toxity levels	
		Safety of new machinery and working methods	
	Economic viability of enterprise	Liquidity	Of enterprise in the future
		Cash Flows	
		Profitability	
		Investment plans	
		Labour and capital ratios	
		Mergers and takeovers proposed	
	Contest closures	Job opportunities in locality	
		Age structure	
	Extent of job satisfaction	Extent 'motivating' factors available	
		Absenteeism	
		Changes to work methods and organisation planned	

not been, and indeed due to the problems of "jointness" may never be, satisfactorily measured. Climo's recent attempt (1976) is based on the assumption that employees wish to maximise their cash resources over time.

In his role of a "manager", the shop steward is concerned about the efficiency of the plant's operation both in an economic and social sense. Both the National Board for Prices and Incomes (1968) and the Government Social Survey (1968) found that shop stewards were increasingly dealing with health, safety, general working conditions, the pace and quality of work, manning, redundancy and recruitment. The shop steward is concerned with decisions about how the organisation should be operated and the possibilities of plant closure or expansion. He is also concerned with the social performance of the organisation: he makes decisions about demands for health and safety expenditure as well as about the opportunities for job satisfaction in the organisation. These types of management decision require information about economic plans (including proposed pricing, output, investment and financing policies) as well as accident, noise, turnover and absenteeism records.

The messages that our *a priori* analysis has for the providers of information may be summarised as follows:

(1) Information should be future orientated. To assess an organisation's ability to pay, for example, the relevant concern in bargaining is the future ability of an organisation to pay a wage demand. To assess economic efficiency, future operating and investment plans of the organisation need to be considered. To assess social efficiency, the safety of machinery to be introduced must be evaluated. Such considerations and evaluations suggest that information should include an indication of the likelihood of various outcomes occurring in the future.

(2) Information should relate to the specific decisions. Thus plant level information is relevant to bargaining. Most published accounting information, however, relates to legal and not economic or social entities. In short, it is not decision orientated. Organisations have been reluctant to disaggregate or "break down" the information relating to the legal entity to information relating to the individual plants.

(3) Information should relate to the environment of the organisation. Information about the level of claim that is regarded as the minimum acceptable requires consideration of wage opportunities outside the specific organisation. Future economic and social plans can only be assessed in the light of the potential of the situation. It is highly probable that such information will not be purely financial: physical and social indicators are likely to be just as relevant to a shop steward's decisions as is financial information.

Having identified as far as possible the information that might be required it seems appropriate to consider briefly the extent to which existing information supplies in the U.K. match up to these needs. Inevitably these supplies change over time and it is likely that current legislative proposals will increase the role of accounting information as a supplier of information.

One source of information is the published accounts. Such accounts were never designed for use by employees and it is therefore not surprising that they have been criticised as being inadequate. For example, Maunders & Foley (1974) have summarised the limitations of accounting reports for employee use. Accounts are frequently six months or more out of date when they are 223
published, they relate to company rather than plant level information and they are primarily records of the past. Maunders and Foley also consider the limitations of accounting measurement conventions. This particular limitation will be reduced by the recommendations of the Inflation Accounting Committee (1975) and subsequent developments in the implementation of their scheme of replacement cost accounting. That Committee's concern with maintaining the operating capacity of the firm will be shared by many employees. Nevertheless, the complexity of accounts, the belief that they are susceptible to manipulation by management, their aggregated nature and their concentration on financial data which are only a part of likely information needs, results in the attitude that accounts are inadequate and hence, infrequently used (see Table 6).

Various large companies in Britain also produce publications, often distributed to employees, which present some manpower statistics (e.g. numbers employed, labour turnover, industrial disputes and wage statistics). An increasing number of companies also produce for their workers simplified versions of their published accounts. Yet, as long as the nature of the information supplied is determined by management and the methods of collections and measurement of the various indices are poorly specified, then it is likely that the documents will be regarded as managerial propaganda.[7]

[7] On inspection these documents are subtly partisan – minimising the contributions paid to shareholders (by ignoring the benefits likely to accrue to shareholders from retained earnings) and emphasising the benefits to employees.

Other sources of information will depend on the specific institutional environment of the employee representative. Union branch meetings and joint Shop Stewards Committees serve as channels for the communication of local information on pay and conditions. The pamphlets produced by the Labour Research Department, the Institute of Workers' Control, Social Audit and Counter-Information Services, provide information obtained from a variety of sources (of varying reliability) about the economic and social performance of specific companies. Finally the Trades Union Research Unit, Ruskin College, Oxford, has produced fully documented pay claims for use in negotiations. For example, the Ford Wage Claim (T.G.W.U. 1971a) and the I.C.I. Claim (T.G.W.U. 1971b) used a variety of sources to substantiate their claims to find out about the
224 companies.

Some evidence about the shop steward's role, decision making and information requirements

The discussion of the role of the shop steward has assumed that there is a progression from the specifications of functions to the specification of associated decisions and then the specification of the decisions' information requirements. We trust the logical validity of our analysis is clear; the progression has been based on the belief that shop stewards wish to improve their constituents' welfare and the decisions they will make will be influenced by that wish. Implicit in the progression has been a model of how the information provided will enable the shop steward to effectively discharge his role. Our analysis can only be empirically validated by confrontation with the real world. It is therefore necessary to subject the analysis to some empirical testing. We will concentrate first on the accuracy of our description of the work of shop stewards, secondly on the information which stewards receive and use at present and thirdly on what further information shop stewards think they would like. Existing empirical work in these areas is sparse and accordingly we have been forced to restrict our analysis to data obtained from three main sources:

(1) The Government Social Survey (1968) of Workplace Industrial Relations.

(2) The same work repeated in 1972 and published two years later (Parker, 1974).

(3) A pilot questionnaire survey covering shop stewards in the engineering industry in the Manchester area (Essex, 1975).

The common features of these studies are an assessment of the factors which stewards regard as most useful in acting in their members' interests and a measure of the key areas of a shop steward's job. The first survey was based on interviews in 1966 with 1200 shop stewards, randomly selected from six unions. That survey's most significant finding for our purpose is reproduced as Table 3.

There was considerable consensus amongst all the parties who were interviewed (that is, stewards, foremen, works managers, and personnel officers) that the most common arguments advanced by stewards in workplace bargaining were

TABLE 3. Justification for claims

	% who mentioned
Abnormal conditions of work	22
Changes in the nature of the job	21
The amount of work done	18
The quality of the labour or skill required for the job	17
Comparisons with other workers in the same place of work	14
Comparisons with other workers in different places of work	13
Job evaluation or unrealistic targets	10
The cost of living	9
The level of profits in the firm	3
Other answers	10
$n = 683$	

From Government Social Survey (1968).

(a) comparisons with other workers in the same or different places of work;
(b) abnormal conditions of work; and
(c) changes in the nature of the job.

Although the survey did not consider the information relevant to a shop steward's job, it would certainly appear that information about conditions and the nature of the job, together with comparative information, would be useful.

The 1972 survey (Parker, 1974) indicates the functions of the shop steward. Table 4 indicates the range of issues of concern to shop stewards and with whom they negotiated (or whether the issue was regulated by collective agreement). It would seem that collective bargaining sets the basic guidelines for shop steward activity. Shop stewards seem to concentrate on what we have previously referred to as the "management of the enterprise" especially its social performance.

The two Government Social Survey studies only indirectly provide relevant information about the role of the shop stewards. Accordingly we surveyed a sample of 230 shop stewards who were members of the Amalgamated Union of Engineering Workers in the Greater Manchester area.[8] The results of this survey must be used very carefully and its conclusions regarded as tentative as the study achieved only a 24.8% response rate and both the sample selected and the questionnaire design are limited. It would be improper to draw any general conclusions from a study concentrating on shop stewards from one industry in one geographical location at one point in time. The possibility that shop stewards in different unions and even the same union in different locations (having varying local traditions) may perform other roles should not be overlooked. We are also unable to determine the representativeness of our own sample of engineering stewards to the population of engineering stewards in Manchester.

A forced choice questionnaire, such as the one used in our survey involves the researcher coding the responses for the respondent. In other words, our image of reality has been imposed on the respondents by the questionnaire. Forced choice answers also tend to "prompt" the respondent, particularly when the respondent is asked about information which he has probably never received.

These limitations suggest that data about the shop steward's role should also be collected by observational methods. Until such data can be compared with our own, it would be unwise to regard our survey as anything other than a highly tentative indication of the roles, decisions made and information requirements of one subset of all shop stewards. It would be erroneous to conclude that the results indicate anything other than public attitudes. The difference between these attitudes and subsequent actual behaviour has also been documented many times (see the collection edited by Thomas, 1971).

TABLE 4. Persons who dealt with bargaining issues*

Issue	% of stewards who settled the issue (1) Frequently	(2) Rarely	% for whom the issue was settled by collective agreement
Basic pay	12	15	59
Bonuses	24	24	49
Other pay†	7	12	21
Health questions	11	21	28
Safety questions	30	30	36
General working conditions	35	31	27
Overtime	30	23	34
Discipline‡	7	32	20
Redundancy questions§	4	17	28

* From Parker (1974).
† This figure is the average of the separate responses for "dirty work", job evaluation, and merit money.
‡ This is the average suspensions, dismissals, and other disciplinary action.
§ This is the average of short time, and redundancy questions.

[8] Copies of the research instrument may be obtained from David Cooper, University of Manchester.

TABLE 5. "How important are these possible areas of negotiation in your job as Shop Steward?"

Area of negotiation \ Degree of importance	Frequency of response				Total score	Mean score
	Very important 4	Fairly important 3	Not very important 2	Not at all important 1		
Basic pay	55	2	2	3	233	3.76
Safety questions	46	15	0	1	230	3.71
Health questions	48	10	3	0	228	3.74
General working conditions	43	18	1	0	228	3.68
Redundancy threats	44	9	5	2	215	3.58
Bonuses	30	23	5	3	202	3.31
Other pay issues	25	23	10	2	191	3.18
Changes in the job	17	26	11	4	172	2.97
Discipline	16	23	14	6	167	2.83
Overtime	5	18	18	19	129	2.15

Sophisticated analysis of the survey results is
226 not appropriate. Instead, we "scored" each response by a simple additive process. For example if basic pay was seen as a "very important" area of negotiation, the response was scored 4 points. If "fairly important" it scored 3 points, if "not very important" 2 points and if "not important at all", the response was given a score of 1. Although this method of scoring implies equal appearing intervals which might not be justified it nevertheless provides an indication of the strength of response. The results of the questionnaire are summarised in Tables 5-8. In these tables we include the total "score" and the mean score, i.e. the total score divided by the number of responses. In most cases the rankings are identical and so we refer to the total scores. We indicate in the text where significant differences in the rankings occur.

Table 5 indicates that there is considerable consensus that the main areas of negotiation for the shop stewards are basic pay and various conditions of work. The results of our survey provide considerable clarification of the issues discussed earlier in relation to the shop steward's role and emphasise the significance of the shop steward in pay bargaining and management of the enterprise.

Table 6 indicates the importance of the union and other shop stewards as sources of information for use in bargaining over pay. One of the problems with accounting information is its lack of disaggregation so it is not surprising that company accounts are not highly ranked, although it is unfortunate that information from plant management was rarely provided. Yet it is difficult to assess the indirect influence of published financial information (i.e. on union sources, press comment, etc.). Note that the potential usefulness of company accounts may be greater than its current use would suggest. Published accounts are rarely in a monopoly position with regard to information about a company yet their relative importance might well change if the data provided

TABLE 6. "How important are these sources of information to use in bargaining over pay?"

Information sources \ Degree of importance	4	3	2	1	Total	Mean
From the Union	31	7	0	0	145	3.82
Other shop stewards	20	18	5	1	145	3.3
Company's accounts	13	19	2	6	119	2.98
Provided by management in the plant	8	15	6	9	98	2.58
Seen in the press	4	7	10	18	75	1.92
No important sources	–	–	–	–	(4)	–

TABLE 7. Factors important in a 1975 pay claim

Justifying factors \ Degree of importance		4	3	2	1	Total	Mean
(a)	Cost of living	57	5	0	0	243	3.92
(b)	Comparisons with others in same workplace	43	10	2	2	208	3.65
(c)	Profit made by the firm	41	9	2	4	199	3.55
(d)	Changes in conditions	30	23	4	1	198	3.42
(e)	Comparisons with workers' elsewhere	30	18	8	4	194	3.23
(f)	Changes in the job	28	19	7	2	185	3.3
(g)	Other workers have just claimed successfully	23	23	7	7	182	3.03
(h)	The firm has an urgent order	24	23	1	9	176	2.89
(i)	Dividend paid to shareholders	29	12	5	11	173	3.04
(j)	Level of sales	25	17	6	8	171	3.05

227

were relevant to users' needs (i.e. if they were, indeed, information).

Table 7 summarises the responses of the shop stewards when they were asked to evaluate possible factors used to justify a pay claim. We might interpret items (a), (b), (d), (e) and (f) as the information the shop steward uses to assess the likely demand of his constituents. Items (c), (g), (h), (i) and (j) might similarly be interpreted as the information used to assess the enterprise's ability to pay. Note that items (i) and (j) are ranked higher when the mean rather than the total score is used.

When the stewards were asked to rank the important justifying factors used for pay claims in 1970, the only significant difference was that the cost of living item ranked ninth, rather than the third rank in 1975. This difference probably reflects the increased rate of inflation at the later date. The lower ranking is in line with the findings of the earlier Government Social Survey (1968). Indeed the two studies agree, by and large, on the relative importance of most factors. The major difference between our results and those of the Government Social Survey (1968) is the importance of the firm's profits in our study. Perhaps during the period between the two surveys shop stewards have come to regard accounting profits as a good predictor of a firm's willingness to pay a wage claim.

The final question represents a departure from earlier empirical work. Stewards were asked to assess the importance of information which they might receive in the future. As can be seen from Table 8, the three items of information which relate to the future (namely expectations about

TABLE 8. Importance of information currently inaccessible

Item \ Degree of importance	4	3	2	1	Total	Mean
Expected lay-offs	48	10	2	1	227	3.72
Output per worker	36	20	5	0	214	3.51
Plans to change production	44	15	2	1	206	3.32
Planned mergers or take-overs	41	7	4	5	198	3.47
Current value of firm's assets	31	14	5	11	187	3.07
Amount spent on research	26	17	13	3	184	3.12
Cost of materials	20	23	13	4	179	2.97
Sales per workers	25	16	7	9	171	3.0
Managers' pay	23	12	12	12	164	2.78

lay-offs, production changes, and take-overs) are all ranked in the top half of the table by total scores and are ranked in the top four by mean scores. Output and profit per worker are the other factors seen as most relevant. The concern of shop stewards for future orientated information is emphasised further since it was found that 28 respondents regarded all three items of future information as "very important" and a further 15 regarded two of the three items as "very important" and the third as "fairly important". Together, these account for the expressed views of 69.5% of those who replied, which is a forceful case for the disclosure. Although indications of what shop stewards want is not necessarily a good indicator of what they need to effectively discharge their role, it seems that a re-orientation of accounting information would be of benefit to
228 these potential users.

The results of our survey appear to be confirmed by previous studies and in large measure correspond with the summary of shop steward decision making and information requirements presented in Table 2. Table 5 suggests that functions of pay bargaining and management of the enterprise (especially working conditions and job security) dominate the negotiating aspects of the shop steward's job. Table 6 indicates the current role of published accounting information. A comparison of Table 7 and Table 8 suggests that the information requested by shop stewards does not fully match their needs as indicated in Table 7. In general, though, our findings do not lead us to substantially modify Table 2. We should emphasise again, however, that Table 2 should be regarded as a guideline in observation of shop stewards' decision behaviour, and is not a substitute for fundamental consideration of the decisions shop stewards do take and should take to improve the welfare of their constituents.

CONCLUSION

In this paper we have developed an approach to the identification of information relevant to employees and their representatives. The notion of relevance requires, we maintain, the identification of users' needs as opposed to his wants. Information relevant to an employee representative or a union official will relate to the decision model that he should be using in an attempt to improve the welfare of workers. We considered the use of a deductive model based on the idea that individuals act so as to maximise their subjective expected utility. Such a model (or class of model) does not possess the realism to form the basis of information prescriptions.

A model of how employee representatives make decisions and how they ought to make decisions in their membership's best interests is a pre-requisite for any recommendation about the provision of information to employees. If our analysis is accepted, then it is essential that accountants become involved in research to identify union and employee decision models. Regrettably many recent approaches (e.g. Tylecote, 1975; Climo, 1976; Halfpenny & Abell, 1977; and Tylecote, 1977) concentrate on economic variables and can thus only be regarded as partial models of employee decision making.

As an interim measure, and not as an alternative to the development of employee decision models and specification of information needs, the idea of providing employee representatives with access to an organisation's financial records has considerable appeal (see Coates & Topham, 1974; Cooper, 1977). Opening the books would temporarily avoid the need to specify decision models for employee representatives. Such a move might also allay the fears of some union officials about the deliberate distortion of information provided by management.

The previous section of this paper has presented some evidence about how one type of employee representative seems to make decisions. By providing an initial specification of the types of decision making the shop steward makes, we have intended to provide some guidance for future research, perhaps based on direct observation.

Finally we wish, on the basis of the empirical research presented above, to make one or two speculations about developments in accounting practice. We have suggested that shop stewards are likely to find disaggregated data about the future performance of the plant more useful than aggregated data. Company information has limited relevance in settling local pay claims. This is most obvious in the case of multi-national companies where "local" pay claims may in fact be national claims. Shop stewards are also likely to find information relating to future events more useful than information relating to past events.

Note however, that this information need not be financial and may not relate to the enterprise under consideration. We have suggested, for example, that information about union density in the plant may be relevant to decisions associated with all three roles of the shop stewards. If accountants are indeed information providers, then there should be little concern with his extension of their traditional function.

The belief that information about the world outside the plant or enterprise will be useful to shop stewards also has implications for the function of the accountant. The provision of information about the local cost of living, job opportunities in the area and agreements made in other plants suggests that the information provider should produce reports relevant for decisions *about* an enterprise rather than reports *on* an enterprise. We thus return to the idea that information for a decision model, rather than either information for a decision maker or information on a particular enterprise, should be provided by accountants.

BIBLIOGRAPHY

Beer, S., *Platform for Change* (New York: Wiley, 1975).

Report of the (Bullock) Committee of Inquiry on *Industrial Democracy*, Cmnd. 6706, (London: HMSO, 1977).

Clegg, H., Killick, A. & Adams, R., *Trade Union Officers* (Oxford: Basil Blackwell, 1961).

Climo, T., Disclosure of Information to Employees' Representatives: A Wage Bargaining Decision Model, unpublished, University of Kent. 1976.

Coates, K & Topham, T., *The New Unionism* (Harmondsworth, Middlesex: Penguin, 1974). 229

Coddington, A., *Theories of the Bargaining Process* (London: Allen & Unwin, 1968).

Cohen, M. D., March, J. G. & Olsen, J. P., A Garbage Can Model of Organizational Choice, *Administrative Science Quarterly* (March, 1972), pp. 1–25.

Cooper, D. J., Information for Trade Unions, in B. V. Carsberg and A. J. B. Hope (eds.), *Current Issues in Accountancy* (Philip Allen, 1977).

Demski, J., *Information Analysis* (New York: Addison-Wesley, 1972).

Royal Commission (Donovan) on *Trade Unions and Employers' Association: 1965–1968 Report*, Cmnd. 3623 (London: HMSO, 1968).

Essex, S. R., *The Use of Accounting Information by Employees*, unpublished M.A.(Econ.) dissertation, University of Manchester, 1975.

Feltham, G., The Value of Information, *Accounting Review* (October 1968), pp. 684–696.

Feltham, G., *Information Analysis* (American Accounting Association, 1973).

Ference, T. P., Organisational Communication Systems and the Decision Process, *Management Science* (1970), pp. 83–96.

Flanders, A., Bargaining Theory: The Classical Model Reconsidered, in B. C. Roberts, ed., *Industrial Relations: Contemporary Issues* (London: Macmillan, 1968).

Foley, B. & Maunders, K., *Accounting Information Disclosure and Collective Bargaining* (London: Macmillan, 1977).

Galbraith, J., *Designing Complex Organisations* (New York: Addison-Wesley, 1973).

Goodman, J. & Whittingham, J., *Shop Stewards* (London: Pan, 1973).

Government Social Survey, *Workplace Industrial Relations* (London: HMSO, 1968).

Halfpenny, P. & Abell, P., Claims and Settlements: An Exploratory Study of Trade Union Bargaining Power, paper presented to British Sociological Association Annual Conference, Sheffield, 1977.

Horwitz, B. & Shabahang, R., Published Corporate Accounting Data and General Wage Increases of the Firm, *Accounting Review* (April, 1971), pp. 243–252.

Hull, J. C., Moore, P. G. & Thomas, H., Utility and its Measurement, *Journal of the Royal Statistical Society*, series A, (1973), pp. 226–247.

Report of the Inflation Accounting Committee, *Inflation Accounting*, Cmnd. 6225, (London: HMSO, 1975).

International Labour Organisation, *Communication between Management and Workers in the Undertaking*, Recommendation 129, I.L.O., 1974.

Katz, D. & Kahn, R., *The Social Psychology of Organisations* (New York: Wiley, 1966).

Marschak, J., Remarks on the Economics of Information, in *Contributions to Scientific Research in Management* (University of California, Los Angeles, 1959), pp. 79–98.

Maunders, K. & Foley, B., How much should we tell Trade Unions?, *Accountancy Age* (February 22, 1974).

Maunders, K., 'Ability to Pay' in Labour Negotiations – Some Observations Based on a Theory of Collective Bargaining, paper presented to Accounting Staff Seminar, University of Manchester, 1977.

McCarthy, W., *The Role of the Shop Stewards in British Industrial Relations*, Royal Commission on Trade Unions and Employers' Associations, Research Paper no. 1, 1972.

Medawar, C., The Social Audit: A Political View, *Accounting, Organizations and Society* (1976), pp. 389–394.

Morris, P., Decision Analysis – Expert Use, *Management Science* (1974), pp. 1233–1242.

National Board for Prices and Incomes, *Payment by Results Systems*, Report no. 65, Cmnd. 3627, (London: HMSO, May 1968).

Nicholson, N., The Role of the Shop Steward: An Empirical Case Study, *Industrial Relations Journal* (1976), pp. 15–27.

Parker, S., *Workplace Industrial Relations, 1972* (London: HMSO, 1974).

Pounds, W. F., The Process of Problem Finding, *Industrial Management Review* (Fall, 1969).

Schelling, T. C., *The Strategy of Conflict* (Harvard, Conn.: Harvard University Press, 1960).

Simon, H. A., *Models of Man* (New York: Wiley, 1957).

Simon, H. A., Theories of Decision Making in Economics and Behavioral Science, *American Economic Review* (June, 1959), pp. 259–283.

Slovic, P., From Shakespeare to Simon, *Oregon Research Institute, Research Monograph*, Vol. 12, No. 42, 1972.

Smith, R., *Keeping Employees Informed* (British Institute of Management, 1975).

Sterling, R. R., Decision Orientated Financial Accounting, *Accounting and Business Research* (Summer, 1972).

Thomas, K., ed., *Attitudes and Behaviour* (Harmondsworth, Middlesex: Penguin, 1971).

Trade Union Congress, *Trade Unionism: Evidence of the T.U.C. to the Royal Commission on Trade Unions and Employers' Associations* (T.U.C., 1966).

Transport and General Workers Union, *The Ford Wage Claim* (T.G.W.U., 1971a).

230 Transport and General Workers Union, *A Positive Employment Programme for I.C.I.* (T.G.W.U., 1971b).

Tversky, A. & Kahnemanm, D., Judgement under Uncertainty: Heuristics and Biases, *Science*, Vol. 185, 1974, pp. 1124–1131.

Tylecote, A. B., Determinants of Changes in the Wage Hierarchy in U.K. Manufacturing Industry 1954–1970: A Test of a New Theory of Wage Determination under Collective Bargaining, *British Journal of Industrial Relations* (1975), pp. 65–77.

Tylecote, A. B., A New Model of the Wage Bargaining Process, unpublished paper, University of Manchester, 1977.

Walton, R. E. & McKersie, R. B., *A Behavioural Theory of Labor Negotiations* (New York: McGraw-Hill, 1965).

Warr, P., *Psychology and Collective Bargaining* (London: Hutchinson, 1973).

Warren, A., The Challenge from Below: An Analysis of the Role of the Shop Steward in Industrial Relations, *Industrial Relations Journal* (1971), pp. 52–60.

Webb, S. & Webb, B., *History of Trade Unionism* (London: Longman, 1920).

Wilensky, H. L., "The Failure of Intelligence: Knowledge and Policy in Government and Industry", Proceedings of the Nineteenth Annual Winter Meeting, Industrial Relations Research Association, 1967, as reprinted in L. W. Porter and K. H. Roberts, eds., *Communication in Organisations* (Harmondsworth, Middlesex: Penguin, 1977), pp. 118–131.

Williamson, O. E., Hierarchical Control and Optimum Firm Size, *Journal of Political Economy* (1967), pp. 123–138.

Wootton, B., *The Social Foundations of Wage Policy* (London: Allen & Unwin, 1955).

Bibliography

BIBLIOGRAPHY

Anderson, W.R., "Should a Company Tell?: Disclosure of Information to Employees", *Accountant*, April 8 1961, pp.403-407.

Anonymous, "Telling Your Story to Your Employees", *Illinois Manufacturer's Costs Association Monthly Bulletin*, February 1939, pp.1-2.

Barloon, M.J., "Financial Reports to Employees", *Harvard Business Review*, Autumn 1941, pp.124-131.

Bennett, G.E., "Corporate Financial Report Content of Interest to Employees", *New York Certified Public Accountant*, October 1941, pp.63-68.

Bennett, L.W., "Annual Report to Employees", *Cost and Management*, October 1939, p.308.

Botsford, H., "How a Plant Publication Helps", *Trained Men*, (USA), April 3 1923, p.6.

Brubaker, O., Kirkland, L., Gomberg, W., Weinberg, N. and Barkin, S., "What Kind of Information Do Labor Unions Want in Financial Statements", *Journal of Accountancy*, May 1949, pp.368-377.

Budd, B.I., "The Use of Company Publications", *American Electric Railway Association Proceedings (1922)*, 1923, pp.156-160.

Burnham, W.C., "A Simplified Income Statement for Employee Use", *National Association of Cost Accountants Bulletin*, Vol 30, No 22, Sec 1, July 15 1949, pp.1325-1335.

Climo, T., "The Role of the Accountant in Industrial Relations", *Accountant*, December 16 1976, pp.701-703.

Cooper, D. and Essex, S., "Accounting Information and Employee Decision Making", *Accounting, Organizations and Society*, Vol 2, No 3, 1977, pp.201-217.

Dale, E., "The Accountant's Part in Labor-Management Relations", *Journal of Accountancy*, July 1950, pp.12-25.

Derry, S.A., "Presenting the Facts on Company Operations to the Employees", *Proceedings of Ohio State University Tenth Annual Institute on Accounting*, May 21 1948, pp.41-53.

Derry, S.A., "How to Communicate Financial Information to Employees and What to Say", *Journal of Accountancy*, April 1949, pp.307-311.

Dyson, J.R., "Audits for Employees: The Right to Know", *Accountant*, March 8 1973, pp.309-310.

Eakin, F., "Business Resorting to Issuance of Special Reports to Employees", *Controller*, July 1938, pp.184-190.

Flint, D., "Employees' Interest in the Business: Financial and Other Information", *The Accountants Magazine*, November 1958, pp.778-790.

Fuller, J.A., "Presentation of Company Information to Shareholders and Employees", *Cost and Management*, September 1948, pp.280-286.

Hartwell, D., "Telling the Employees", *Public Opinion Quarterly*, March 1941, pp.93-101.

Heacock, B.C., "Making the Annual Report Speak", *Executives Service Bulletin*, April 1940, pp.3-4, 6.

Heckert, J.B. and Willson, J.D., "Reports to Employees and to the General Public", in *Controllership*, New York, Ronald Press Co., 1952, pp.445-462.

Hennessy, D.J., "Survey Reveals Financial Information People Want to Know About a Corporation", *Journal of Accountancy*, September 1948, pp.224-227.

Holmes, G., "How UK Companies Report to Their Employees", *Accountancy*, November 1977, pp.64-68.

Hussey, R. and Craig, R.J., "Employee Reports - What Employees Think", *The Chartered Accountant in Australia*, May 1979, pp.39-44.

Irwin, J.W., "Periodical Reports to Employees", *Executives Service Bulletin*, January 1939, pp.7-8.

Lewis, N.R., Parker, L.D. and Sutcliffe, P., "Financial Reporting to Employees: The Pattern of Development 1919 to 1979", *Accounting, Organizations and Society*, Vol 9, No 3/4, 1984, pp.275-289.

Libby, J.C., "Employee Interest in the Financial Report", *Illinois Certified Public Accountant*, September 1952, pp.43-46.

Myers, J.H., "Annual Reports to Employees", *New York Certified Public Accountant*, February 1956, pp.100-102.

Parker, L.D., "Financial Reporting to Employees: A Growing Practice in Australia", *The Chartered Accountant in Australia*, March 1977, pp.5-9.

Schoen, S.H. and Lux, M.P., "The Annual Report: How Much Do Employees Care?", *Personnel*, July-August 1957, pp.40-45.

Wallace, F., "Getting Down to Earth in Explaining Profits to Employees", *Controller*, February 1946, pp.75-77.

Yorston, R.K., "Reporting Financial Information to Employees", *The Australian Accountant*, February 1960, pp.80-88.

Further Reading

SELECTED TEXTS AND MONOGRAPHS

Arthur Young Management Services, *Sharing the Facts: Current Law and Practice on Disclosure of Information*, London 1976, 58p.

British Institute of Management, *Presenting Financial Information to Employees*, London, British Institute of Management, 1957, 110p.

Craig, R. and Hussey, R., *Keeping Employees Informed*, Sydney, Butterworths, 1982, 166p.

Doris, L., *Modern Corporate Reports to Stockholders, Employees and the Public*, New York, Prentice-Hall, 1948, 309p.

Hammill, A.E., *Simplified Financial Statements*, London, Institute of Chartered Accountants in England and Wales, 1979, 106p.

Heron, A.R., *Sharing Information with Employees*, California, Stanford University Press, 1942, 204p.

Hilton, A., *Employee Reports: How to Communicate Financial Information to Employees*, Cambridge, Woodhead-Faulkner, 1978, 113p.

Jones, D.M.C., *Disclosure of Financial Information to Employees*, London, Institute of Personnel Management, 1978, 268p.

Marsh, A. and Hussey, R., *Survey of Employee Reports*, Tolley Publishing Co., Croydon, 1979, 52p.

Metropolitan Life Insurance Company, Policyholders Service Bureau, *Telling Employees About Business Operations: The Company*, New York, Metropolitan Life Insurance Co., 1948, 56p.

Metropolitan Life Insurance Company, Policyholders Service Bureau, *The Annual Report to Employees*, New York, Metropolitan Life Insurance Co., circa 1940, 52p.

Metropolitan Life Insurance Company, Policyholders Service Bureau, *More Information for Employees Regarding Their Company*, New York, Metropolitan Life Insurance Company, circa 1939, 52p.

Mitchell, W., *What People Want to Know About Your Company*, New York, Controllership Foundation Inc., October 1948, 63p.

Moore, R., *Disclosure of Company Information to Trade Unions (UK)*, Adelaide Unit for Industrial Democracy, Department of Labor and Industry, South Australia, 1979, 60p.

Parker, L.D., *The Reporting of Company Financial Results to Employees*, London, The Institute of Chartered Accountants in England and Wales, Research Committee, Occasional Paper No 12, September 1977, 85p.

Research Institute of America, *How to Tell Your Company's Story to Employees - Stockholders - the Public*, New York, Research Institute of America Inc., 1947, 56p.

Roper, E., *Report on What Information People Want About Policies and Financial Conditions of Corporations*, New York, Controllership Foundation Inc., April 1948, 2 Volumes, 149p and 321p.

Sanders, T.H., *Company Annual Reports - to Stockholders, Employees and the Public*, Boston, Massachussets, Harvard University, Graduate School of Business Administration, Division of Research, 1949, 338p.

Selvage, J.P. and Lee, M.M., *Making the Annual Report Speak for Industry*, (compiled for the National Association of Manufacturers of the USA), New York, McGraw-Hill, 1938, 168p.

Taylor, D.W., *Employee Information Sharing*, Canberra, Department of Employment and Industrial Relations, 1982, 108p.

SELECTED ARTICLES AND PAPERS

"Accountant's Responsibility For Disclosure", (Editorial), *Journal of Accountancy*, January 1947, pp.3-5.

"Accounting and the Labor Problem", (Editorial), *Journal of Accountancy*, February 1947, p.91.

"Accounting Information For Labor Unions", (Editorial), *Journal of Accountancy*, August 1947, pp.90-91.

"Allan Wood Tells Employees - Annual Report Information Meetings are Part of the Communication Program", *Iron Age*, April 21 1960, p.110.

American Institute of Accountants, Secretary, "Labor's Interest in Accounting", *Journal of Accountancy*, January 1947, pp.78-80.

American Management Association, *Reporting to Employees and The Public on Profits and Productivity*, New York, American Management Association, 1947, 42p. (Financial Management Series No 88).

Archer, C., "Reporting to Employees", *Office Management and Equipment*, July 1949, pp.27-28, 60.

Baird, D.G., "Utility Dramatizes Its Annual Report", *American Business*, July 1949, pp.14-15, 44-45.

Bee, C., "Saying Goodbye to Bowling Scores", *Canadian Business Management*, November 1979, p.42+.

Bell, D.W., *A Company's Annual Report to its Employees*, London, Industrial Participation Association, 1975, 21p.

"Benefits of Explaining Your Business to Employees", *Nations Business*, July 1975, pp.26-28.

Bennett, K.W., "Don't Hide Co. Profits from Employees", *Iron Age*, June 1975, pp.28-30.

Bensahel, J.G., "Don't Shield Employees from Bad News", *International Management*, September 1975, pp.49-50.

Berylson, K.J., "Accountant's Role in Industrial Relations", *New York Certified Public Accountant*, June 1946, pp.300-306.

Bezanson, A., *The Employee Publication*, Pennsylvania Department of Labor and Industry Proceedings of the Industrial Relations Conference 1921, 1922, pp.179-196.

Biklin, P.F., *The Successful Employee Publication*, New York, McGraw-Hill, 1945, 179p.

Broad, S.J., "Employee Financial Statements", *Trusts and Estates*, January 1947, pp.15-16.

Franklin, W.H., *Reporting to Employees and the Public on Profits and Productivity*, American Management Association, 1947, pp.28-40.

Gibson, C., "Accountants Role in Employee Communications", *Accountancy*, February 1978, pp.118-121.

Gilling, D.M., "Role of Accounting in Modern Society: The Case of Labour Relations", *Accounting Education*, November 1975, pp.27-35.

Gogarty, J.F., "What Employees Expect to be Told", *Management Accounting*, November 1975, pp.359-360.

Goodlad, J., "Disclose Present or Communicate", *Management Accounting*, November 1978, pp.446-447.

Goodlad, J.B., *Disclosure of Financial Information to Employees: A General Survey of the Current Practice of 6 Large UK Organisations*, London, Institute of Cost and Management Accountants, 1976, 45p.

Greer, H.C., "Explaining Profits to Employees", *Journal of Accountancy*, July 1946, pp.76-77.

Hajek, J.C., "Employee Communications - Tell It Like It Is: Tailor-Make Plan Benefit Statements", *Financial Executive*, Vol 43, July 1975, pp.46-49.

Hamilton, S., "Among the Company Accounts", *The Accountants Magazine*, August 1977, pp.354-390.

Harrison, A., "Employee Accounts: A Guide to the Future?", *Accountant*, December 22/29 1979, pp.790-791.

Henderson, M., "House Journals - The Management Idea That Got Away", *Director*, June 1975, p.332.

Hendriksen, D., "Company Reports: Beware of Glossing Over the Facts", *Industrial Management*, February 1976, pp.11-12+.

Hennessy, D.J., "What is Wanted in Company Annual Reports?", *Controller*, June 1948, pp.296-304.

Holmes, S., "Management Discloses", *Accounting*, Vol 86, 1975, pp.90, 92, 94, 96.

Hoover, D.D., "Employee Publications and the Utility Industry", *Public Utilities Fortnightly*, August 3 1961, pp.185-186.

"How to Create a Top Employee Publication", *Industrial Marketing*, September 1962, pp.112-115.

"How to Keep Employees Well Informed", *Personnel Management*, July 1977, pp.13+.

Hussey, R., *Who Reads Employee Reports*, London, Touche-Ross & Co., 1979, 32p.

Hussey, R. and Craig, R.J., "Why Some Companies Do Not Issue Employee Reports", *The Chartered Accountants in Australia*, March 1980, pp.45-49.

"Information for Employees", *Accountant*, May 29 1975, p.690.

"Information for Employees", *Accountant*, October 27 1977, pp.521.

Inglis, J.B., "Reports to Stockholders, Management and Labor", *Journal of Accountancy*, January 1947, pp.16-21.

Institute of Chartered Accountants in England and Wales and the Institute of Personnel Management, *Assisting Employees in the Understanding and Use of Financial Information*, London, 1978.

"Its Good Business to Tell Employees About Profits", *Industry Week*, October 12, 1970, pp.28-33.

Jarchow, C.E., "Interpretation of the Corporation's Financial Position to its Audiences - Trends in Annual Reporting", *Controller*, September 1947, pp.445-449, 462.

Jenkins, C., "A Trade Unionists Viewpoint on Financial Information Requirements", *Management Accounting*, November 1975, p.359.

Jenkinson, M.W., "Workers Interest in Costing (a Factor in Industrial Re-Construction)", *Accountant*, March 8 1919, pp.185-195. (Also *Australian Accountant and Secretary*, July/August 1919, pp.19-23).

Jones, D.M.C., "Designing Accounts to Inform More Effectively", *Management Accounting*, November 1975, p.359.

Jones, S., "Managing Multi-Plant Employee Publications", *Personnel Journal*, November 1961, pp.269-270.

Kaye, L.S., "Even Stiffer Requirements Loom for Communication", *Business Insurance*, December 26, 1977, pp.21-22.

Knowlton, D., "Semantics of Annual Reports", *Accounting Review*, October 1947, pp.360-366.

Knowlton, D., "Financial Statements Need Not be Failures as Public Relations Tools for Management", *Journal of Accountancy*, November 1947, pp.401-407.

Knowlton, D., "Semantics of Annual Reports", *Canadian Chartered Accountant*, February 1948, pp.77-78.

"Labor's Interest in Accounting", (Editorial), *Journal of Accountancy*, October 1946, pp.271-272.

"Labor's Interest in Financial Information", (Editorial), *Journal of Accountancy*, January 1949, pp.5-6.

Lawrence, S.R., "Telling the Financial Story of Employees", *Public Relations Journal*, April 1964, pp.18-20.

McCarthy, J.E., "Realistic Accounts and Statements - For Management - For Labor", (Address before the Third National Accounting Conference), Chicago, Illinois, *Edison Electric Institute Bulletin*, November 15, 1939, pp.535-536.

McNutt, G.C., "Putting the Annual Report Together", *Industrial Marketing*, December 1942, pp.22-23, 132.

Martin, R., "Producing an Employee Report", *Management Accounting*, September 1977, pp.341-344.

Marsh, A. and Hussey, R., *Employees and the Employees Report: A Research Paper*, Oxford, Touche Ross & Co., 1977, 21p.

Maunders, K.T. and Foley, "Accounting Information, Employees and Collective Bargaining", *Journal of Business Finance and Accounting*, Spring 1974, pp.109-127.

Mayall, R.L., "Sensitizing Your Management to the Needs of the Annual Report", *Public Relations Journal*, September 1977, pp.12-14+.

Metropolitan Life Insurance Company, Policyholders Service Bureau, *Telling Employees About Their Company*, New York, Metropolitan Life Insurance Company, circa 1946, 39p.

Miller, J., "Financial Information for Employees", *The Accountant*, May 29 1975, pp.690+.

Miller, M.J., "Employers Duty to Give Economic Data to Unions", *Journal of Accountancy*, January 1956, pp.40-49.

"Miniature Charts Present a Company Economic Position", *Management Record*, December 1958, p.413.

Morley, M.F., "Information for Scottish Wage Negotiators", *C.A. Magazine*, December 1977, pp.23-24.

Mosher, I., "Wages and Profits", *Journal of Accountancy*, January 1947, p.68.

Myers, H., "Good and Bad in Employee Reports", *Rydges*, January 1979, pp.22-24.

National Association of Accountants, "Departures in Communicating Accounting Data to Foremen: A Summary of Practice", (Accounting Practice Report), *NA Bulletin*, Vol 44, No 16, Section 3, January 1963, 24p.

New York Stock Exchange, *Telling Your Corporate Story - To Shareholders, To Employees, To the Financial Community, To the Public*, New York, New York Stock Exchange, April 1963, 28p.

Newcomb, R. and Sammons, M., "Trends in Reporting to Employees", *Advertising Age*, November 24 1948, p.74.

Newcomb, R. and Sammons, M., "Trends in Employee Annual Reports", *Advertising Age*, April 29 1958, p.110.

Newcomb, R. and Sammons, M., "Employees Do Care How Your Business is Doing", *Industrial Marketing*, May 1958, pp.103-104.

Newcomb, R. and Sammons, M., "Annual Report Grows Up at Last", *Industrial Marketing*, November 1958, pp.121-123.

Newcomb, R. and Sammons, M., "How to Talk Costs", *Industrial Marketing*, March 1959, p.96.

Newcomb, R. and Sammons, M., "How to Avoid the Communications Rut", *Industrial Marketing*, May 1959, p.94.

Newcomb, R. and Sammons, M., "Employee Magazines Grow Brave: Grow Up", *Industrial Marketing*, August 1959, pp.119-120.

Newcomb, R. and Sammons, M., "Reports to Employees as Seen by Two Employee Relation Specialists", *Advertising Age*, February 1965, p.92.

Newcomb, R. and Sammons, M., "New Trends Shown in Employee and Stockholder Reports", *Advertising Age*, July 7 1969, p.54.

Newcomb, R. and Sammons, M., "New Company Publications are Headed in Right Direction", *Advertising Age*, October 27 1969, p.98.

Newcomb, R. and Sammons, M., "Communications in Industry: Here are Top Employee Reports", *Advertising Age*, September 18 1972, p.70.

Newcomb, R. and Sammons, M., "Employee Publication Trends: More Stress on Benefits Policy", *Advertising Age*, August 8 1979, p.40.

Norkett, P., "Participant Reporting", *Certified Accountant*, April 1977, pp.115-116, 118-121.

O'Farrell, P.J., "Accounting: A Labor Viewpoint", *University of Tulsa, Accounting Papers of the 19th Annual Conference of Accountants*, 1965, pp.33-42.

O'Meara, J.R., "Helping Employees Understand Economic Realities", *Conference Board Record*, December 1968, pp.44-51.

Parker, L.D., "Accounting Responsibility Towards Corporate Financial Reporting to Employees", *Accounting Education*, November 1977, pp.62-93.

Pillsbury, W.F., "Organized Labor's Views of Corporate Financial Information", *Journal of Accountancy*, June 1958, pp.45-56.

Polking, K., "Employee Publications: Six Ways to Make Them Work for You", *Business Management*, July 1964, pp.43-47.

Pound, G.D. "Some Accounting and Auditing Perspectives of Reporting to Employees", *Australian Accountant*, December 1978, pp.689-692.

Powlison, K., "Explaining Profits to Employees", *National Association of Cost Accountants Year Book*, 1946, pp.188-196.

Powlison, K., "Explaining the Facts to Employees", *Controller*, March 1947, pp.130-134, 164.

"Presenting Financial Facts to Employees", *Management Accounting*, November 1975, pp.359-360.

"Printed Word Lasts", *Personnel Journal*, February 1967, pp.113-114.

"Profit Publicity: Interim Reports and Interpretation to Employees", *Trusts and Estates*, December 1946, pp.567-571.

"Proxy Tells All to Employees", *Factory Management*, December 1958, p.108.

"Public Interest in Profits in Relation to Wages and Prices", (Editorial), *Journal of Accountancy*, November 1947, pp.356-357.

Purdy, D.E., "Some Comments on the Future Approach to Company Reports", *Accountancy*, June 1978, pp.87-88.

Reeves, T.K., *Information Disclosure in Employee Relations*, Bradford, MCB Publications, 1980.

Roberts, E., "Your Company Newspaper Could be a Profit Producer", *Personnel Journal*, December 1962, pp.547-584.

Rosenthal, H.C., "Your Next Annual Report: Modern or Model T", *Printers Ink*, December 17 1956, pp.45-46, 50, 52, 57.

Saberson, R.E., *Employees House Organs*, Boston, Garnshaw Printing Corporation, 1921, 7p.

Sanders, T.H., "Annual Report: Portrait of a Business", *Harvard Business Review*, January 1949, pp.1-12.

Scott, W.D. & Co., "How Employees See Industrial Relations and Communication Issues", *Industrial Relations Prospect Conference*, Melbourne, November 28 1977.

"Send Annual Reports to All Workers Plea", *Accountancy*, December 1976, p.9.

"Shareholders Now Share Their News", *Personnel Management*, February 1978, pp.16-17.

Simon, E., "Benefit Messages Offer Broader Corporate Aids", *Business Insurance*, May 29 1978, pp.42+.

Smith, A.H., "Reporting Financial Data to Management, Stockholders and Employees", *Ohio C.P.A.*, Spring 1960, pp.65-76.

Southgate, M., "Plessey Researches Financial Reporting", *Industrial Marketing*, April 1977, pp.112, 114, 116.

Surface, F.M., "Interpretation of the Corporation's Financial Position to its Audience - Need for Understanding", *Controller*, September 1947, pp.444, 461-462.

Surlin, S.H. and Walker, B., "Employee Evaluation of Handling News of a Corporate Newspaper", *Journalism Quarterly*, Spring 1975.

Swift, M.H., "Clear Writing Means Clear Thinking Means ...", *Harvard Business Review*, January/February 1973, pp.59-62.

Tarzian, J., "What's the Inside Story?", *Editor and Publisher*, April 17 1965, pp.17+.

Taylor, D., Webb, L. and McGinley, L., "Annual Reports to Employees - The Challenge to the Corporate Accountant", *The Chartered Accountant in Australia*, May 1979, pp.33-39.

"Telling Employees", *Financial Executive*, June 1975, p.67.

Thomas, W.E., "One Approach to the Problem of Communicating Accounting Information", *Accounting Review*, July 1951, pp.395-399.

Thompson, S., "Involving a Financial Policy and Strategy Which Includes Considerations of Employees Information Needs", *Management Accounting*, November 1975, p.360.

Tinsley, N., "Employee Communications ... An ICI Approach", *Accountancy*, November 1977, pp.60-62.

Unwin, A., "Communicating Company Information", *Industrial Communication and Training*, 1978, pp.363-369, 416-426, 461-465, 502-509; 1979, pp.24-27, 72-74, 119-122.

Wagel, W.H., "Right to Know", *Personnel*, September 1977, pp.42-44.

Walker, R.G., "Misinformed Employee", *Harvard Business Review*, May 1948, pp.267-281.

Wallace, F., "Profits ... in Payroll Terms: Getting Down to Earth in Explaining Profits to Employees", *Trusts and Estates*, May 1946, pp.466-487.

Walsh, W., "Getting Nearer to Disclosure", *Accountant*, April 12, 1973, pp.503-504.

Webb, L. and Taylor, D., "Employee Reporting: Don't Wait for It", *The Australian Accountant*, January/February 1980, pp.30-34.

Welty, G., "Employees: Who Do They Listen To?", *Railway Age*, March 23 1964.

Werth, P.M., "How to Produce Effective Employee Publications", *Public Relations Journal*, December 1967, pp.21-23.

"What Companies are Saying About Economics", (Articles from Employee Publications), *Management Record*, Vol 24, July/August, pp.23-36; September, pp.30-31; October, pp.14-17; November 1962, pp.24-27; Vol 25, February, pp.24-37; 1963, March, pp.33-36.

Whitlock, A.N., "Explaining the Annual Report: Caterpillar Tractor Puts Questions and Answers in its Employee Magazine", *Journal of Accountancy*, July 1953, pp.84-86.

White, W.R., "More Corporate Reports for Employee Readers", *Public Relations Journal*, February 1970, p.19.

"Why I'm Working on the Railroad: Case History in Business Relations", *Trusts and Estates*, February 1947, pp.158-160.

Wilders, M.G., "The Disclosure of Financial and Related Information", *Journal of General Management*, Autumn 1979, pp.12-22.

Wood, F.E., "Function of the Financial Executive in Industrial Relations", *Cost and Management*, May 1954, pp.171-175.

Accounting Books Published by Garland

NEW BOOKS

■ *Altman, Edward I., *The Prediction of Corporate Bankruptcy: A Discriminant Analysis.*
New York, 1988.

■ Ashton, Robert H., ed. *The Evolution of Accounting Behavior Research: An Overview.*
New York, 1984.

■ Ashton, Robert H., ed. *Some Early Contributions to the Study of Audit Judgement.*
New York, 1984.

■ *Bodenhorn, Diran. *Economic Accounting.*
New York, 1988.

---

* Included in the Garland series Foundations of Accounting
† Included in the Academy of Accounting Historians, Classics Series, Gary John Previt, ed.

■ *Bougen, Philip D. *Accounting and Industrial Relations: Some Historical Evidence on Their Interaction.*
New York, 1988.

■ Brief, Richard P., ed. *Corporate Financial Reporting and Analysis in the Early 1900s.*
New York, 1986.

■ Brief, Richard P., ed. *Depreciation and Capital Maintenance.*
New York, 1984.

■ Brief, Richard P., ed. *Estimating the Economic Rate of Return from Accounting Data.*
New York, 1986.

■ Brief, Richard P., ed. *Four Classics on the Theory of Double-Entry Bookkeeping.*
New York, 1982.

■ Chambers, R. J., and G. W. Dean, eds. *Chambers on Accounting.*
New York, 1986.
Volume I: Accounting, Management and Finance.
Volume II: Accounting Practice and Education.
Volume III: Accounting Theory and Research.
Volume IV: Price Variation Accounting.
Volume V: Continuously Contemporary Accounting.

■ *Clark, John B. (with a new introduction by Donald Dewey). *Capital and Its Earnings.*
New York, 1988.

■ Clarke, F. L. *The Tangled Web of Price Variation Accounting: The Development of Ideas Underlying Professional Prescriptions in Six Countries.*
New York, 1982.

■ Coopers & Lybrand. *The Early History of Coopers & Lybrand.*
New York, 1984.

■ Craswell, Allen. *Audit Qualifications in Australia 1950 to 1979.*
New York, 1986.

■ Dean, G. W., and M. C. Wells, eds. *The Case for Continuously Contemporary Accounting.*
New York, 1984.

■ Dean, G. W. , and M. C. Wells, eds. *Forerunners of Realizable Values Accounting in Financial Reporting.*
New York, 1982.

■ Edey, Harold C. *Accounting Queries.*
New York, 1982.

■ Edwards, J. R., ed. *Legal Regulation of British Company Accounts 1836-1900.*
New York, 1986.

■ Edwards, J. R. ed. *Reporting Fixed Assets in Nineteenth-Century Company Accounts.*
New York, 1986.

■ Edwards, J. R., ed. *Studies of Company Records: 1830-1974.*
New York, 1984.

▪ Fabricant, Solomon. *Studies in Social and Private Accounting.*
New York, 1982.

▪ Gaffikin, Michael, and Michael Aitkin, eds. *The Development of Accounting Theory: Significant Contributors to Accounting Thought in the 20th Century.*
New York, 1982.

▪ Hawawini, Gabriel A., ed. *Bond Duration and Immunization: Early Developments and Recent Contributions.*
New York, 1982.

▪ Hawawini, Gabriel A., and Pierre A. Michel, eds. *European Equity Markets: Risk, Return, and Efficiency.*
New York, 1984.

▪ Hawawini, Gabriel A., and Pierre Michel. *Mandatory Financial Information and Capital Market Equilibrium in Belgium.*
New York, 1986.

▪ Hawkins, David F. *Corporate Financial Disclosure, 1900-1933: A Study of Management Inertia within a Rapidly Changing Environment.*
New York, 1986.

▪ *Hopwood, Anthony G. *Accounting from the Outside: The Collected Papers of Anthony G. Hopwood.*
New York, 1988.

▪ Johnson, H. Thomas. *A New Approach to Management Accounting History.*
New York, 1986.

▪ Kinney, William R., ed. *Fifty Years of Statistical Auditing.*
New York, 1986.

▪ Klemstine, Charles E., and Michael W. Maher. *Management Accounting Research: A Review and Annotated Bibliography.*
New York, 1984.

▪ *Langenderfer, Harold Q., and Grover L. Porter, eds. *Rational Accounting Concepts: The Writings of Willard Graham.*
New York, 1988.

▪ *Lee, T. A., ed. *The Evolution of Audit Thought and Practice.*
New York, 1988.

▪ Lee, T. A., ed. *A Scottish Contribution to Accounting History.*
New York, 1986.

▪ Lee, T. A. *Towards a Theory and Practice of Cash Flow Accounting.*
New York, 1986.

▪ Lee, T. A., ed. *Transactions of the Chartered Accountants Students' Societies of Edinburgh and Glasgow: A Selection of Writings, 1886-1958.*
New York, 1984.

▪ *Loft, Anne. *Understanding Accounting in Its Social and Historical Context: The Case of Cost Accounting in Britain, 1914-1925.*
New York, 1988.

▪ McKinnon, Jill L.. *The Historical Development and Operational Form of Corporate Reporting Regulation in Japan.*
New York, 1986.

▪ *McMickle, Peter L., and Paul H. Jensen, eds. *The Auditor's Guide of 1869: A Review and Computer Enhancement of Recently Discovered Old Microfilm of America's First Book on Auditing by H. J. Mettenheimer.*
New York, 1988.

▪ *McMickle, Peter L., and Paul H. Jensen, eds. *The Birth of American Accountancy: A Bibliographic Analysis of Works on Accounting Published in America through 1820.*
New York, 1988.

▪ *Mepham, M.-J. *Accounting in Eighteenth-Century Scotland.*
New York, 1988.

▪ *Mills, Patti A., trans. *The Legal Literature of Accounting: On Accounts by Diego del Castillo.*
New York, 1988.

▪ *Murphy, George J. *The Evolution of Canadian Corporate Reporting Practices: 1900-1970.*
New York, 1988.

▪ *Mumford, Michael J., ed. *Edward Stamp—Later Papers.*
New York, 1988.

▪ Nobes, Christopher, ed. *The Development of Double Entry: Selected Essays.*
New York, 1984.

- Nobes, Christopher. *Issues in International Accounting.*
  New York, 1986.

- Parker, Lee D. *Developing Control Concepts in the 20th Century.*
  New York, 1986.

- *Parker, Lee D., ed. *Financial Reporting to Employees: From Past to Present.*
  New York, 1988.

- *Parker, Lee D., and O. Finley Graves, eds. *Methodology and Method in History: A Bibliography.*
  New York, 1988.

- Parker, R. H. *Papers on Accounting History.*
  New York, 1984.

- Previts, Gary John, and Alfred R. Roberts, eds. *Federal Securities Law and Accounting 1933-1970: Selected Addresses.*
  New York, 1986.

- *Reid, Jean Margo, ed. *Law and Accounting: Nineteenth-Century American Legal Cases.*
  New York, 1988.

- *Sheldahl, Terry K., ed. *Accounting Literature in the United States before Mitchell and Jones (1796): Contributions by Four English Writers, through American Editions, and Two Pioneer Local Authors.*
  New York, 1988.

■ Sheldahl, Terry K. *Beta Alpha Psi, from Alpha to Omega: Pursuing a Vision of Professional Education for Accountants, 1919-1945.*
New York, 1982.

■ Sheldahl, Terry K. *Beta Alpha Psi, from Omega to Zeta Omega: The Making of a Comprehensive Accounting Fraternity, 1946-1984.*
New York, 1986.

■ *Sheldahl, Terry K., ed. *Education for the Mercantile Countinghouse: Critical and Constructive Essays by Nine British Writers, 1716-1794.*
New York, 1988.

■ Solomons, David. *Collected Papers on Accounting and Accounting Education (in two volumes).*
New York, 1984.

■ Sprague, Charles F. *The General Principles of the Science of Accounts and the Accountancy of Investment.*
New York, 1984.

■ Stamp, Edward. *Edward Stamp—Later Papers.* *See* Michael J. Mumford.

■ Stamp, Edward. *Selected Papers on Accounting, Auditing, and Professional Problems.*
New York, 1984.

■ *Staubus, George J. *Activity Costing for Decisions: Cost Accounting in the Decision Usefulness Framework.*
New York, 1988.

■ Storrar, Colin, ed. *The Accountant's Magazine—An Anthology.*
New York, 1986.

■ Tantral, Panadda. *Accounting Literature in Non-Accounting Journals: An Annotated Bibliography.*
New York, 1984.

■ *Vangermeersch, Richard G. *Alexander Hamilton Church: A Man of Ideas for All Seasons.*
New York, 1988.

■ Vangermeersch, Richard, ed. *The Contributions of Alexander Hamilton Church to Accounting and Management.*
New York, 1986.

■ Vangermeersch, Richard, ed. *Financial Accounting Milestones in the Annual Reports of the United States Steel Corporation—The First Seven Decades.*
New York, 1986.

■ *Walker, Stephen P. *The Society of Accountants in Edinburgh, 1854-1914: A Study of Recruitment to a New Profession.*
New York, 1988.

■ Whitmore, John. *Factory Accounts.*
New York, 1984.

■ *Whittred, Greg. *The Evolution of Consolidated Financial Reporting in Australia: An Evaluation of an Alternative Hypothesis.*
New York, 1988.

■ Yamey, Basil S. *Further Essays on the History of Accounting.*
New York, 1982.

■ Zeff, Stephen A., ed. *The Accounting Postulates and Principles Controversy of the 1960s.*
New York, 1982.

■ Zeff, Stephen A., ed. *Accounting Principles Through the Years: The Views of Professional and Academic Leaders 1938-1954.*
New York, 1982.

■ Zeff, Stephen A., and Maurice Moonitz, eds. *Sourcebook on Accounting Principles and Auditing Procedures: 1917-1953 (in two volumes).*
New York, 1984.

■ *Zeff, Stephen a., ed. *The U. S. Accounting Profession in the 1890s and Early 1900s.*
New York, 1988.

REPRINTED TITLES

■ *American Institute of Accountants. *Accountants Index, 1920* (in two volumes).
New York, 1921 (Garland reprint, 1988).

■ American Institute of Accountants. *Fiftieth Anniversary Celebration.*
Chicago, 1937 (Garland reprint, 1982).

■ American Institute of Accountants. *Library Catalogue.*
New York, 1919 (Garland reprint, 1982).

■ Arthur Andersen Company. *The First Fifty Years 1913-1963.*
Chicago, 1963 (Garland reprint, 1984).

■ Bevis, Herman W. *Corporate Financial Reporting in a Competitive Economy.*
New York, 1965 (Garland reprint, 1986).

■ Bonini,. Charles P., Robert K. Jaedicke, and Harvey M. Wagner, eds. *Management Controls: New Directions in Basic Research.*
New York, 1964 (Garland reprint, 1986).

■ **The Book-Keeper and the American Counting Room.*
New York, 1880-1884 (Garland reprint, 1988).

▪ Bray, F. Sewell. *Four Essays in Accounting Theory.* London, 1953. *Bound with* Institute of Chartered Accountants in England and Wales and the National Institute of Economic and Social Research. *Some Accounting Terms and Concepts.*
Cambridge, 1951 (Garland reprint, 1982).

▪ Brown, R. Gene, and Kenneth S. Johnston. *Paciolo on Accounting.*
New York, 1963 (Garland reprint, 1984).

▪ Carey, John L., and William O. Doherty, eds. *Ethical Standards of the Accounting Profession.*
New York, 1966 (Garland reprint, 1986).

▪ Chambers, R. J. *Accounting in Disarray.*
Melbourne, 1973 (Garland reprint, 1982).

▪ Cooper, Ernest. *Fifty-seven years in an Accountant's Office. See* Sir Russell Kettle.

▪ Couchman, Charles B. *The Balance-Sheet.*
New York, 1924 (Garland reprint, 1982).

▪ Couper, Charles Tennant. *Report of the Trial ... Against the Directors and Manager of the City of Glasgow Bank.*
Edinburgh, 1879 (Garland reprint, 1984).

▪ Cutforth, Arthur E. *Audits.*
London, 1906 (Garland reprint, 1982).

▪ Cutforth, Arthur E. *Methods of Amalgamation.*
London, 1926 (Garland reprint, 1982).

[redacted]

■ Deinzer, Harvey T. *Development of Accounting Thought.*
New York, 1965 (Garland reprint, 1984).

■ De Paula, F.R.M. *The Principles of Auditing.*
London, 1915 (Garland reprint, 1984).

■ Dickerson, R. W. *Accountants and the Law of Negligence.*
Toronto, 1966 (Garland reprint, 1982).

■ Dodson, James. *The Accountant, or, the Method of Bookkeeping Deduced from Clear Principles, and Illustrated by a Variety of Examples.*
London, 1750 (Garland reprint, 1984).

■ Dyer, S. *A Common Sense Method of Double Entry Bookkeeping, on First Principles, as Suggested by De Morgan. Part I, Theoretical.*
London, 1897 (Garland reprint, 1984).

■ *† Edwards, James Don. *History of Public Accounting in the United States.*
East Lansing, 1960 (Garland reprint, 1988).

■ *† Edwards, James Don, and Robert F. Salmonson. *Contributions of Four Accounting Pioneers: Kohler, Littleton, May, Paton.*
East Lancing, 1961 (Garland reprint, 1988).

■ *The Fifth International Congress on Accounting, 1938 [Kongress-Archiv 1938 des V. Internationalen Prüfungs- und Treuhand-Kongresses].*
Berlin, 1938 (Garland reprint, 1986).

[redacted]

■ Finney, A. H. *Consolidated Statements.*
New York, 1922 (Garland reprint, 1982).

■ Fisher, Irving. *The Rate of Interest.*
New York, 1907 (Garland reprint, 1982).

■ Florence, P. Sargant. *Economics of Fatigue and Unrest and the Efficiency of Labour in English and American Industry.*
London, 1923 (Garland reprint, 1984).

■ *Fourth International Congress on Accounting 1933.*
London, 1933 (Garland reprint, 1982).

■ Foye, Arthur B. *Haskins & Sells: Our First Seventy-Five Years.*
New York, 1970 (Garland reprint, 1984).

■ *† Garner, Paul S. *Evolution of Cost Accounting to 1925.*
University, Alabama, 1925 (Garland reprint, 1988).

■ Garnsey, Sir Gilbert. *Holding Companies and Their Published Accounts.* London, 1923. *Bound with* Sir Gilbert Garnsey. *Limitations of a Balance Sheet.*
London, 1928 (Garland reprint, 1982).

■ Garrett, A. A. *The History of the Society of Incorporated Accountants, 1885-1957.*
Oxford, 1961 (Garland reprint, 1984).

■ Gilman, Stephen. *Accounting Concepts of Profit.*
New York, 1939 (Garland reprint, 1982).

▪ Gordon, William. *The Universal Accountant, and Complete Merchant* ... [Volume II].
Edinburgh, 1765 (Garland reprint, 1986).

▪ Green, Wilmer. *History and Survey of Accountancy.*
Brooklyn, 1930 (Garland reprint, 1986).

▪ Hamilton, Robert. *An Introduction to Merchandise, Parts IV and V (Italian Bookkeeping and Practical Bookkeeping).*
Edinburgh, 1788 (Garland reprint, 1982).

▪ Hatton, Edward. *The Merchant's Magazine; or, Tradesman's Treasury.* London, 1695 (Garland reprint, 1982).
Hills, George S. *The Law of Accounting and Financial Statements.*
Boston, 1957 (Garland reprint, 1982).

▪ *A History of Cooper Brothers & Co. 1854 to 1954.*
London, 1954 (Garland reprint, 1986).

▪ Hofstede, Geert. *The Game of Budget Control.*
Assen, 1967 (Garland reprint, 1984).

▪ Howitt, Sir Harold. *The History of the Institute of Chartered Accountants in England and Wales 1880-1965, and of Its Founder Accountancy Bodies 1870-1880.*
London, 1966 (Garland reprint, 1984).

▪ Institute of Chartered Accountants in England and Wales and The National Institute of Social and Economic Research. *Some Accounting Terms and Concepts. See* F. Sewell Bray.

■ Institute of Chartered Accountants of Scotland. *History of the Chartered Accountants of Scotland from the Earliest Times to 1954.*
Edinburgh, 1954 (Garland reprint, 1984).

■ *International Congress on Accounting 1929.*
New York, 1930 (Garland reprint, 1982).

■ Jaedicke, Robert K., Yuji Ijiri, and Oswald Nielsen, eds. *Research in Accounting Measurement.*
American Accounting Association, 1966 (Garland reprint, 1986).

■ Keats, Charles. *Magnificent Masquerade.*
New York, 1964 (Garland reprint, 1982).

■ Kettle, Sir Russell. *Deloitte & Co. 1854-1956.* Oxford, 1958. *Bound with* Ernest Cooper. *Fifty-seven Years in an Accountant's Office.*
London, 1921 (Garland reprint, 1982).

■ Kitchen, J., and R. H. Parker. *Accounting Thought and Education: Six English Pioneers.*
London, 1980 (Garland reprint, 1984).

■ Lacey, Kenneth. *Profit Measurement and Price Changes.*
London, 1952 (Garland reprint, 1982).

■ Lee, Chauncey. *The American Accomptant.*
Lansingburgh, 1797 (Garland reprint, 1982).

■ Lee, T. A., and R. H. Parker. *The Evolution of Corporate Financial Reporting.*
Middlesex, 1979 (Garland reprint, 1984).

■ *† Littleton, A. C.. *Accounting Evolution to 1900.*
New York, 1933 (Garland reprint, 1988).

■ Malcolm, Alexander. *The Treatise of Book-Keeping, or, Merchants Accounts; In the Italian Method of Debtor and Creditor; Wherein the Fundamental Principles of That Curious and Approved Method Are Clearly and Fully Explained and Demonstrated ... To Which Are Added, Instructions for Gentlemen of Land Estates, and Their Stewards or Factors: With Directions Also for Retailers, and Other More Private Persons.*
London, 1731 (Garland reprint, 1986).

■ Meij, J. L., ed. *Depreciation and Replacement Policy.*
Chicago, 1961 (Garland reprint, 1986).

■ Newlove, George Hills. *Consolidated Balance Sheets.*
New York, 1926 (Garland reprint, 1982).

■ North, Roger. *The Gentleman Accomptant; or, An Essay to Unfold the Mystery of Accompts; By Way of Debtor and Creditor, Commonly Called Merchants Accompts, and Applying the Same to the Concerns of the Nobility and Gentry of England.*
London 1714 (Garland reprint, 1986).

■ **Proceedings of the Seventh International Congress of Accountants.* Amsterdam, 1957 (Garland reprint, 1988).

■ Pryce-Jones, Janet E., and R. H. Parker. *Accounting in Scotland: A Historical Bibliography.*
Edinburgh, 1976 (Garland reprint, 1984).

■ *Reynolds, W. B., and F. W. Thornton. *Duties of a Junior Accountant* [three editions].
New York, 1917, 1933, 1953
(Garland reprint, 1988).

■ Robinson, H. W. *A History of Accountants in Ireland.*
Dublin, 1964 (Garland edition, 1984).

■ Robson, T. B. *Consolidated and Other Group Accounts.*
London, 1950 (Garland reprint, 1982).

■ Rorem, C. Rufus. *Accounting Method.*
Chicago, 1928 (Garland reprint, 1982).

■ Saliers, Earl A., ed. *Accountants' Handbook.*
New York, 1923 (Garland reprint, 1986).

■ Samuel, Horace B. *Shareholder's Money.*
London, 1933 (Garland reprint, 1982).

■ *The Securitites and Exchange Commission in the Matter of McKesson & Robbins, Inc. Report on Investigation.*
Washington, D. C., 1940 (Garland reprint, 1982).

■ *The Securities and Exchange Commission in the Matter of McKesson & Robbins, Inc. Testimony of Expert Witnesses.*
Washington, D. C., 1939 (Garland reprint, 1982).

■ Shaplen, Roger. *Kreuger: Genius and Swindler.*
New York, 1960 (Garland reprint, 1986).

■ Singer, H. W. *Standardized Accountancy in Germany. (With a new appendix.)*
Cambridge, 1943 (Garland reprint, 1982).

- *The Sixth International Congress on Accounting.*
  London, 1952 (Garland reprint, 1984).

- Stewart, Jas. C. (with a new introductory note by T. A. Lee). *Pioneers of a Profession: Chartered Accountants to 1879.*
  Edinburgh, 1977 (Garland reprint, 1986).

- Thompson, Wardbaugh. *The Accomptant's Oracle: or, a Key to Science, Being a Compleat Practical System of Book-keeping.*
  York, 1777 (Garland reprint, 1984).

- *Thornton, F. W. *Duties of the Senior Accountant.* New York, 1932. *Bound with.* John C. Martin. *Duties of Junior and Senior Accountants, Supplement of the CPA Handbook.*
  New York, 1953 (Garland reprint, 1988).

- Vatter, William J. *Managerial Accounting.*
  New York, 1950 (Garland reprint, 1986).

- Woolf, Arthur H. *A Short History of Accountants and Accountancy.*
  London, 1912 (Garland reprint, 1986).

- Yamey, B. S., H. C. Edey, and Hugh W. Thomson. *Accounting in England and Scotland: 1543-1800.*
  London, 1963 (Garland reprint, 1982).